JAMES THOMSON (B. V.)

THE COMPLETE POEMS

JAMES THOMSON (B. V.)

THE COMPLETE POEMS

Edited by A. J. Spatz

CHARLES & WONDER
MMXII

Charles & Wonder
PURVEYORS OF FINE LITERATURE
Arlington, VA

James Thomson (B. V.)
The Complete Poems
Edited by A. J. Spatz

First Print Edition

ISBN 978-1-937620-03-5

Published by Charles & Wonder
charlesandwonder.com

CONTENTS

THE CITY OF DREADFUL NIGHT AND OTHER POEMS (1880)

VANE'S STORY AND OTHER POEMS (1881)

A VOICE FROM THE NILE AND OTHER POEMS (1884)

POEMS UNCOLLECTED BY THOMSON
(1852-1882)

EPIGRAMS

UNCOLLECTED TRANSLATIONS

TIMELINE

23 Nov. 1834	Birth of James Thomson in Port Glasgow, Scotland
1836	Birth of Thomson's sister
1839	Sister dies in infancy
1840	Father suffers a stroke at sea on the *Eliza Stewart*
1840-42	Thomson family lives at various addresses on the East side of London
1842-1852	Spends holidays with the family of William Gray (a friend of his parents)
1842	Birth of Thomson's brother John
1842	Enrolls in the Royal Caledonian Asylum (London), a residential school for Scottish orphans; it had formerly been the school of writer Charles Mackay
1843	Mother dies
1850	Enrolls in the Royal Military Asylum (Chelsea, London)
	Thomson's classmate George Duncan also enrolls at Chelsea
5 Aug. 1851	Sent to Ballincollig, Ireland, to complete his training as army schoolmaster
	Befriends Joseph Barnes (garrison master) and his wife Alice
	Meets Charles Bradlaugh and Matilda Weller (two years his junior)
1852	Writes his earliest surviving poem ("The Dawn of Love" in "Four Points in a Life")
16 Jan. 1853	Returns from Ballincollig to Chelsea
19 July 1853	Death of Matilda Weller
late (?) 1853	Death of Thomson's father
7 Aug. 1854	Enlisted in full capacity as army schoolmaster
1854-55	Assigned to South Devon Militia Regiment (Plymouth)
1855-56	Assigned to Rifle Brigade (Aldershot)
1856-60	Assigned to 55th Foot Regiment (Dublin and Curragh Camp)
	Winters with Duncan family until they depart for India (1860)
1856	Befriends John Grant, a younger army schoolmaster and Chelsea alumnus, in Dublin
circa 1856	Befriends James Potterton, a fellow army schoolmaster, with whom he studies German and later corresponds
	Begins to translate Heine
1857	Completes the long poem "The Doom of a City"
July 1858	Publishes first poem ("The Fadeless Bower") in *Tait's Edinburgh Magazine*, under the pseudonym "Crepusculus"

1858-59	Contributes essays to the *London Investigator* (edited by Bradlaugh) on Burns and Emerson, among others; first adopts the pseudonym "Bysshe Vanolis" (soon abbreviated to "B. V.")
4 March 1859	Writes "A Real Vision of Sin"
June 1860	55th Foot Regiment transfers from Dublin to Aldershot
1860	Bradlaugh founds *The National Reformer,* a chief periodical for the Secularist ("Freethinker") movement
1861	55th Foot Regiment transfers from Aldershot to Jersey
	Thomson writes most of the early long poem "Ronald and Helen"
May 1862	55th Foot Regiment transfters from Jersey to Portsmouth
30 Oct. 1862	Thomson receives discharge from army, for being part of a group that refused to state which one of its members swam to a boat in an area where bathing was prohibited
1862-74	Contributes articles and poems to *The National Reformer* under the pen-name "B. V."
late 1862	Moves into Bradlaugh house
circa 1860-63	Loses religious sentiment expressed in early poems; begins periodic binge drinking
1863	Works briefly as Secretary to the Polish Committee, but is dismissed due to "intemperance" and subsequent disappearance at an important moment (according to Bradlaugh's later account)
circa 1864	Befriends Austin Holyoake and W. E. Jaques
1864	Writes "Vane's Story"
	Writes a few articles for the *Daily Telegraph,* but declines offer to supply regular pieces "to order"
1865	Finishes the idyllic poem-suites "Sunday at Hampstead" and "Sunday Up the River"
1866	Bradlaugh founds the National Secular Society and becomes a close associate of Anne Besant (who later moves into Bradlaugh's house; Bradlaugh had been separated from his wife)
Oct. 1866	Thomson moves out of Bradlaugh house to rent lodgings of his own in Pimlico district of London
1867	Writes the poem "Two Lovers"
	Translates Leopardi's *Operette morali* (Moral Tales)
1867-68	Writes the poem "In the Room"
1868	*The National Reformer* prosecuted for blasphemy and sedition by the British Government (acquitted)
1869-72	Resides at 240 Vauxhall Bridge Road in Pimlico
1869	Spends most of the year occupied with "Weddah and Om-el Bonain" and various articles
Oct. 1869	"Sunday Up the River" appears in *Fraser's Magazine,* one of Thomson's few publications outside a Secularist periodical; Bradlaugh declined to publish the poem some years earlier
	Has first photographic portrait taken, after waiting an hour

	during four attempts to photograph another customer's baby (which, he tells friends, caused the grumpy facial expression in his own picture)
4 Nov. 1869	Burns old papers and letters, over the course of five hours
19 Nov. 1869	Thomson has a 2-hour lunch meeting with James Anthony Froude, editor of *Fraser's Magazine*
1870	Drafts most of "The City of Dreadful Night"
Jan.-Feb. 1872	"Weddah and Om-el Bonain" appears in the *National Reformer*
	Thomson corresponds with and befriends W. M. Rossetti. Rossetti later recorded a first impression of him: "He talked extremely well, and without, I think, any symptom of defective education, except that his *h's* were sometimes less aspirated than they should be. Not that he *dropped* his *h's,* and he certainly never inserted them when they ought not to come. There was no trace of the Scotchman in his pronunciation."
April 1872	Thomson travels to the United States for the Champion Gold and Silver Mines Company, for which he had been working as Secretary; he spends a total of 7 months in Colorado
5 Aug. 1872	Thomson sends a story-length letter to W. M. Rossetti, detailing his time in Colorado with many anecdotes
Jan. 1873	Thomson returns to London and takes lodgings at 230 Vauxhall Bridge Road, a few doors down from his previous address
	The mining company covers Thomson's expenses but refuses to pay his salary in full for the Colorado assignment
July 1873	Thomson obtains a post, via Bradlaugh, as special correspondent for the *New York World* in Spain, and is sent to cover the Carlist insurrection, which proves uneventful
early Sept. 1873	Suffers twice from sunstroke, at Alsasua and San Esteban, during which time he works out a portion of "Dreadful Night" (as he later recounted to a friend). His left eye remains injured until November
23 Sept. 1873	Thomson arrives in London, as recalled by the *New York World* after two months abroad; the newspaper withholds his salary of £5/week for his having only sent 3 letters while in Spain, despite Thomson's protests of very little to report
1873	Finishes "Dreadful Night" (final changes made in 1874)
Spring 1874	"The City of Dreadful Night" published in 4 consecutive issues of *The National Reformer* (March 22, April 12, April 26, May 17)
April 1874	Begins correspondence with Bertram Dobell (later his editor and publisher)
10 April 1874	Death of Thomson's friend Austin Holyoake
13 April 1874	Thomson moves to 60 Tachbrook Street, Pimlico
May 1874	Begins correspondence with novelist George Eliot
Sept. 1874	Befriends William Maccall and Charles Watts
1875	Begins correspondence and friendship with poet Philip Bourke Marston
Summer 1875	Parts with Bradlaugh and leaves *The National Reformer*

Sept. 1875	Begins writing articles for *Cope's Tobacco Plant,* signing miscellaneous articles with the pen-name "Sigvat" (which he had used in an essay from the 1860s)
Dec. 1875	Thomson moves to 35 Alfred Street (renamed 7 Huntley Street around June 1877), near the British Museum
Jan. 1876	George Holyoake and G. W. Foote co-found *The Secularist;* Thomson is engaged as a regular contributor
Feb. 1876	Suffers a severe fall, which keeps him indoors for several days
March-April 1876	Publishes "Carlist Reminiscences" in *The Secularist*
Jan. 1877	G. W. Foote founds *The Liberal;* Thomson contributes occasional articles for most of the year, until the two men have a falling out
June 1877	*The Secularist* merges into the *Secular Review,* under G. W. Foote's editorship; Thomson ceases contributing articles
Feb. 1878	Thomson begins writing "The Pilgrimage to Saint Nicotine" after the *Cope's* editor takes interest in his proposal
Sept. 1878	Writes the poem "I Had a Love"
Dec. 1878	*The Plenipotent Key to Cope's Correct Card of the Peerless Pilgrimage to Saint Nicotine of the Holy Herb* (Cope's Tobacco Plant; brochure), with verse by Thomson and picture by John Wallace
1879	Signs of failing health begin to appear; suffers routinely from insomnia ("my old friend") while the frequency and duration of his binge drinking increases
July 1879	Begins correspondence with poet George Meredith
April 1880	*The City of Dreadful Night* (Reeves & Turner); the volume is well received by critics and proves a relative financial success
mid-1880	Karl Marx writes a letter to Thomson congratulating him on the beauty of his Heine translations
29 June 1880	Thomson meets George Meredith in Dorking
Oct. 1880	Thomson's problems with his left eye return
	Bradlaugh elected MP for Northampton
1881	*Vane's Story* (Reeves & Turner); date on title page is 1881, but volume gets printed in Oct. 1880
April 1881	*Essays and Phantasies* (Reeves & Turner)
	Two visits to Leicester with the Wright family, for a total of 8 weeks away from London
early 1881	*Cope's Tobacco Plant* discontinued
Summer 1881	Writes two articles on Robert Browning, one each for the Browning Society (which later appoints him to its committee) and *Gentlemen's Magazine*
1881-82	Makes several visits to Leicester for weeks at a time
Oct. 1881	Thomson stops making entries in his diary
Nov. 1881	Writes "A Voice from the Nile"
Jan. 1882	Writes "The Sleeper"
March 1882	Writes "Insomnia"
Spring 1882	Ends a visit to Leicester in a fit of drunkenness, and returns to

	London in great despondency
	Thomson's landlord bars him from entering his lodgings; he breaks in several times
12 May 1882	Thomson is arrested and under a false name and spends 12 days' imprisonment in a hospital
1 June 1882	Collapses in the rooms of Philip Marston; his friends take him to the University College hospital, while Percy Holyoake (son of the late Austin Holyoake) spends the night looking for him
3 June 1882	Death of Thomson from internal bleeding, age 47
8 June 1882	Thomson buried at Highgate Cemetery beside his friend Austin Holyoake, author of the Secularist Burial Service which was read at the funeral

---

1884	*A Voice from the Nile* (Reeves & Turner); edited by Dobell, with "Early Poems" section; first version of Dobell's "Memoir"
	Satires and Profanities (Progressive Publishing Company); Preface by G. W. Foote
	Shelley published privately by Dobell (190 copies)
1886	William Maccall: *A Nirvana Trilogy: Three essays on the career and literary labours of James Thomson* (Watts & Co.)
1889	*James Thomson: Selections from his contributions to Cope's Tobacco Plant* (Cope's Smoke-Room Booklets, Vol. 3); Introductory Note by Walter Lewin
	Henry Stephens Salt: *The Life of James Thomson ("B. V.")* (Reeves & Turner); First edition (revised in 1914)
1892	*Poems, Essays and Fragments* (A. & H. Bradlaugh; Reeves & Turner); edited with an Introdutcion by John M. Robertson
1895	*Poetical Works,* 2 Vols. (Reeves & Turner; Bertram Dobell); edited by Dobell; revised version of Dobell's "Memoir"
1896	*Biographical and Critical Studies* (Reeves & Turner; Bertram Dobell)
1905	*Essays, dialogues, and thoughts (Operette morali and Pensieri) of Giacomo Leopardi, translated by James Thomson ("B. V.")* (G. Routledge); edited by Bertram Dobell
1910	*Walt Whitman: The Man and the Poet* (Bertram Dobell); Introduction by Dobell
	Bertram Dobell: *The Laureate of Pessimism: A sketch of the life and character of James Thomson ("B. V.")* (Bertram Dobell)
1914	Henry Stephens Salt: *The Life of James Thomson,* Revised edition (Watts & Co.)
1917	J. Edward Meeker: *The Life and Poetry of James Thomson (B. V.)* (Yale University Press)
1963	*Poems and Some Letters of James Thomson* (Southern Illinois University Press); edited by Anne Ridler

INTRODUCTION

James Thomson (1834-1882) was born on November 23 in Port Glasgow, Scotland, the first of three children. His father, first officer of the *Eliza Stewart*, suffered a stroke at sea in 1840, resulting in the family's move to London and the admission of the young James Thomson to the Royal Caledonian Asylum in 1842. After the death of his mother the following year, Thomson distinguished himself as a student, and in 1850 enrolled in the Royal Military Asylum to pursue a career as an army schoolmaster.

Sent to Ballincollig, Ireland, to complete his training in 1851, Thomson met the two important figures in his life: his great love Matilda Weller, who was to die two years later, and the freethinker Charles Bradlaugh, who was to publish much of Thomson's writing in his periodical *The National Reformer* from its founding in 1860 until the two men parted ways in 1875.

Thomson served as schoolmaster in the army from 1854 until his discharge in 1862, and for the remaining two decades of his life he supported himself as a secretary for various companies and, increasingly as the years wore on, as a freelance writer for several periodicals. His first published poems appeared under the pseudonyms "Crespusculus" and "Bysshe Vanolis" (soon abbreviated to "B. V."), the latter of which he used for much of his career, in homage to Shelley and Novalis, and to distinguish himself from the earlier Scottish poet James Thomson (1700-1748).

In 1874 Thomson gained recognition with the publication his most famous poem "The City of Dreadful Night" in four installments of the *National Reformer*. After parting with Bradlaugh, Thomson wrote articles for the trade journal *Cope's Tobacco Plant*, which allowed him to keep free rein in the choice of subjects. His first book of poems was published in 1880, as the joint endeavor of the publishers Reeves & Turner and Thomson's admirer Bertram Dobell, who later became the poet's editor and promoter. The following year a second book of Thomson's poems was published, along with the first collection of his prose, but literary recognition came too late to avert Thomson's lifelong struggles with insomnia and alcohol. Despite a revival in poetic productivity during the last two years of his life, he died in London, exhausted and virtually penniless, at the age of 47.

A BRIEF GUIDE TO THE POEMS

The following commentary is meant to introduce the reader to some of Thomson's strongest work, and to offer an outline of his accomplishments. It is not intended to serve as an exhaustive survey, but more as a guide to getting started. Where appropriate, I have included some historical background and side remarks of that nature; but the underlying belief is that the poems speak best for themselves. If a few minor pieces, which would otherwise escape notice, get the attention they deserve, then a point for Thomson will have been most properly scored.

THE CITY OF DREADFUL NIGHT (1870-1874)

Thomson's magnum opus is his long poem "The City of Dreadful Night." The poem's searing negativity branded Thomson a pessimist, even though his other works are not half so ominous. The reputation, on account of the poem's strength, is nonetheless deserved: "Dreadful Night" is the darkest poem in the language since *Macbeth.*

What most impacted readers in Thomson's day was the poem's fierce language of dissent. If there is such a thing as the ideology of everyday life, then for Victorian England it was an optimistic belief in progress and the value of industry. To appreciate Thomson's power we should imagine him speaking against such an emotionally positive backdrop, where both capitalism and imperialism were in full swing:

> Surely I write not for the hopeful young,
>   Or those who deem their happiness of worth,
> Or such as pasture and grow fat among
>   The shows of life and feel nor doubt nor dearth,
> Or pious spirits with a God above them
> To sanctify and glorify and love them,
>   Or sages who foresee a heaven on earth.

Thomson's beliefs were hardly hostile to mankind, but his stance of opposition makes them appear overwhelmingly negative, and that seems to have been his intention. "Dreadful Night" is a rending of the veil: critics have sometimes dismissed the poem as morbid or merely pessimistic, but reading it straight through shows it to be delibrerately aggressive, a calculated procedure of intellectual violence. Around the middle (XII), Thomson depicts a train of men filing into a cathedral, each stating his purpose there in a quatrain that ends with the password: "I wake from daydreams to this real night." The reformer, the opium-eater, the comedian, the monk, the monarch, the pastor, the drunk—each in turn admits the vanity of his illusion. After preparing the reader with this emptying-out, there comes the sermon from "the dark pulpit" (XIV), which states the moral kernel of the poem:

> I find no hint throughout the Universe
> Of good or ill, of blessing or of curse;
>   I find alone Necessity Supreme;
> With infinite Mystery, abysmal, dark,
> Unlighted ever by the faintest spark
>   For us the flitting shadows of a dream.

This may well have been Thomson's creed, but it is only the poem's creed inside the cathedral. Beyond its confines, "Dreadful Night" is not exactly a poem of "infinite Mystery," because it is simply packed with curses. It pictures a universe whose every hint bodes ill.

The poem features some of Thomson's most powerful "situational imagery" (to coin a term), such as the man who makes the rounds of the city with the empty regularity of a clock (II), the voice chanting of the desert with a hollow and ultimately self-defeating refrain (IV), the un-man crawling the dank forest floor in a futile attempt to return to the womb (XVIII), and the opposing statues of sphinx and angel at the poem's conclusion (XX).

These passages are among the most striking and original of Thomson's creations. Far from being mere sensual scenes, they are moral parables clothed in horror. Like those in Dante or Kafka (or "The Twilight Zone"), these situations seem to be stuck in time, repeating eternally. Their influence on Modernist poems like *The Waste Land* has long been acknowledged; but Thomson was never really a symbolic poet, and he was too early for comparative anthropology and the Theosophical movement, two trends that rather fascinated England at the turn of the century. The deliberate pacing and the moral weight of each episode, building up to a climax of absurdity, cast shadows that reach all the way forward to the literature of Existentialism. Thomson's poem is dark, not occult. Of the many rituals it depicts, every one of them is obsessive, desperate, and meaningless.

The tone, moreover, is very uncommon for its time. Throughout the poem, Thomson adopts a kind of "objective" presentation, reporting events with much more detachment than was the norm in 19th-Century poetry. The possible model for this approach may have been Shelley's "Ozymandias" sonnet, which would fit into "Dreadful Night" perfectly except for its implied daylight.

The sections of "Dreadful Night" alternate between the poet's direct remarks, which use a seven-line stanza, and portrayals of action, which typically open in a six-line stanza but depart into other forms. Nowhere does it seem complex, because it works so successfully. Overall, the poem's AB structure, with its continual flip-flop from commentary to action, may have been a subtle (very subtle) allusion to Dante's *Vita Nuova*, and in any case it stands as a distant echo of that model.

"The City of Dreadful Night" is likely to remain an iconic poem of the late 19th Century. Its title alone is memorable enough to have been borrowed by both Rudyard Kipling and O. Henry for story collections, and its intensity certainly earns it a place beside the best of Browning, Tennyson, and the earlier Romantics.

A REAL VISION OF SIN (1859)

This admittedly minor piece was ostensibly written because Thomson was annoyed at Tennyson's poem "The Vision of Sin," although it is closer in surface form to "The Two Voices." (Generally speaking, Thomson seems to have disdained much of the laureate's work.)

The poem is not ambitious, but like "Dreadful Night" it has an almost physical intensity of conception, and despite only a handful of truly good lines it makes an impression. "A Real Vision of Sin" plays with an aesthetic of extremes: in his portrayal of depravity, Thomson is disgusting almost for the sake of sport. Even to eyes grown accustomed to shock art, the poem is shockingly profane.

On a formal level, Thomson's blunted lines are suited to their purpose. As with his best work, he does not explore different perspectives or sift through subtleties, but commits himself to one point: that sin is a matter not of theology but of brutality. (Tennyson's poem, by comparison, seems more like "The Vision of Bad Manners.")

It may seem strange to mention elegance of technique, but it is nonetheless remarkable to see how cleverly Thomson works in the backstory of the husband and wife, to the extent that the swampy setting of this episode becomes their entire universe. For a piece apparently written in one day, and not even written so much as tossed off in irritation at another poet's being a dilettante in matters of good and evil, "A Real Vision of Sin" does more than it set out to do. One is tempted to draw a connection between the slime here and the semi-human creature amid the "humid leafage" of section XVIII in "Dreadful Night." As elsewhere, the less Thomson drew on the conventions of his own time, and the less he wrote to its tastes, the greater a poet he became.

TWO LOVERS (1867)

It is unfortunate that "Two Lovers" has always stood in the shadow of Thomson's greatest narrative piece, "Weddah and Om-el-Bonain," because it is one of those rare double-barreled poems that actually works.

At first glance, the story is about two star-crossed lovers, one Christian and one Muslim, who are kept apart by their cultures. This is not exactly a new premise: usually the implied point is that the cultures take themselves too seriously and shouldn't interfere with the romantic devotions of young people. The unusual turn here is that the lovers take the cultures very seriously—each other's, anyway. He converts to Christianity on his deathbed in order to join her in the afterlife; while she, soon to die herself, converts to Islam. Neither learns of the other's generous act.

The plot is what we might call a "pathetic tragedy," without meaning anything pejorative by that. The characters are set up to fail; they act; and the conclusion is that they do fail. But Thomson's other barrel takes aim, and announces that the whole idea was misguided:

> Let the great gods, if they indeed exist,
> Fight out their fight themselves; for they are strong:
> How can we puny mortals e'er assist?
> How judge the supra-mortal right and wrong?

As the poem concludes, one realizes that Thomson has set up an echo-chamber of parentheses. In the admirable pacing of the poem, the lovers seem to exist amid the heavy atmosphere of fate. And yet, because they know nothing of each other's act, they die happy. And yet, they have no cause to be happy, and the whole religious stage might well not even exist, and their hope for any afterlife whatsoever might well have been in vain.

Thomson was not usually an ironic poet in this sense, and "Two Lovers" is a stand-out in his work. Its narrative economy is superb, and its refocusing in the final stanzas—telescoping the story, as it were, through a collapsable spyglass, shaft by shaft—achieves an affect which our own age can appreciate perhaps more than Thomson's. The poem remains one of the consummate performances in his entire body of work.

WEDDAH AND OM-EL-BONAIN (1868-1869)

Readers have always enjoyed "Weddah and Om-el-Bonain" a lot, and some have turned around afterward to wonder why. Swinburne, for example, hailed it as a poem of "forthright triumphant power"; and later changed his mind. W. M. Rossetti, who read the poem about a decade before Swinburne did (and who was friends with Thomson), attributed his own first favorable reaction to "a somewhat extravagant and uncritical enthusiasm." Melville, meanwhile, on the other side of the Atlantic, said that the poem "gave me more pleasure than anything of modern poetry that I have seen in a long while. The fable and the verse are alike extremely beautiful. It is exactly the kind of gem which some of Keats' poems are."

In the end, it is Melville's unqualified praise that seems to account for the feeling most readers have about "Weddah," which occupied Thomson almost exclusively in 1869. And indeed the poem would have achieved a more widespread and lasting recognition, except that it is marred in places by Thomson's roundabout delivery, which seems to have set at least one small flaw into nearly every stanza he wrote.

That defect was perhaps congenital to the era: it appears throughout the poetry of the Victorian period. But Thomson lacked the ability to redeem this misfiring with steady, quotable, knockout stanzas. In consequence, "Weddah" leaves many beautiful images in the mind, and yet one can never quite find a stanza to quote. Most resonant of all, perhaps, is the image of Weddah as a warrior, disaffected, severe, unspeaking, chillingly accurate—but where *is* that image? Thomson's effects turn out to be diffuse in their origins. The image is there, it is just spread out across several spots, and the effect is a cumulative one. The poem feels like a masterpiece, but on close inspection it looks almost like apprentice work. If one is not competing with Thomson, one is tempted to discard the close inspection.

As Nietzsche remarked, the meter of poetry throws a veil upon the mind: and in cases like this, one is content to let it be a wedding veil. "Weddah" as a whole succeeds in ways that only a fine poem can, and it invites re-reading if only for pleasure.

INSOMNIA (1882)

"Insomnia" is one of Thomson's most famous poems, which is indeed a strange thing to say about a poet who is virtually unread. For all that, beneath its iconic title lies a strong poem which gives the impression that it could have been written by Edgar Allan Poe.

Poe is perhaps the closest parallel to Thomson: both lived to around the same age (just shy of 50), both suffered from insomnia and alcoholism, both died in the gutter, and both were scarred early in life by the death of a beloved.

In poetic terms, "Insomnia" has much in common with "The Raven," at least in terms of plot and overall atmosphere. But in one sense at least, Thomson's poem is more modern: the poet simply suffers from insomnia, and no explanation is offered. As he lies abed, he is haunted systematically by the various Hours of the night—an idea which Thomson may well have gotten from Leopardi, who personified the Hours in his prose dialogue "Copernicus."

As in "Dreadful Night" and "Two Lovers," Thomson's concept here once again seems to herald the methods of Existential literature. The irony is entirely situational, and the wit of Thomson's invention is brilliant even in this quite gloomy poem. The poet espies the Hour's wings folded beneath its mantle, and asks why it doesn't stop haunting him to fly through the night. The Hour replies:

> "My wings shall open when your eyes shall close
> In real slumber from this waking drear;
> Your wild unrest is my enforced repose;
> Ere I move hence you must not know me here."
> Could not your wings fan slumber through my brain,
> Soothing away its weariness and pain?
> "Your sleep must stir my wings . . . "

A depiction of the poet's tedious suffering follows, with several other images adapted from Leopardi (notably from the "Canto notturno"), until he at last quits his bed and wanders the streets at dawn. The poem is an unflinching portrayal, and quite rightly seems a bit longer than it ought to be.

Unlike his other dark poems, there is humor here, albeit of a very subtle self-mockery. Grief would merit one raven; but for pointless insomnia of the Thomson variety, the haunters have to work in shifts.

THE SLEEPER (1882)

Thomson's gifts did not include the talent for drama. He could construct and report a plot, but he was not an adept storyteller; he could invent situations, but characters somewhat eluded him; he could be urgently, powerfully lyrical, but he could not fashion compelling dialogue. "The Sleeper" is a poem that avoids all his weaknesses and plays to all his strengths.

No other poem in Thomson's corpus has quite the delicacy of "The Sleeper," and no other poem seems to suggest so much while describing so little. It is a model of its kind.

The plot is uneventful: a woman dozes off in a chair. But how much seems to happen! One senses the poet's envy of her cat-nap as much as his attraction to her, and a palpable sense of care seems to hover about the portrait. Her minute actions while drifting into sleep suggest a blithe sexual fantasy, paced and controlled so admirably by the poet that one simply sees the woman. At the very climax, he rescues the poem from voyeurism:

> I feel an awe to read this dream
> So clearly written in her smile;
> A pleasant not a passionate theme,
> A little love, a little guile;
> I fear lest she should speak revealing
> The secret of some maiden feeling
> I have no right to hear the while.

Thomson's reserve here is an inextricable part of his moral nature, and as in "Two Lovers," it marks a shift in focus away from the subject and toward more general considerations. Such a move is not uncommon in poetry; it is even typical in some regards; but it is the poetry version of the moral at the end of a fable. That Thomson so often ended his poems with this maneuver tells us what kind of poet and man he was: hardly the "aesthete" the age demanded, but at bottom a moralist.

SUNDAY UP THE RIVER (1865)

Thomson wrote several suites of short lyrical poetry, which might be taken together as his "weekend works." Perhaps the most affecting of these is "Sunday Up the River."

It has been said, quite incorrectly, that Thomson rewrote "The Doom of a City" when he hammered out the shorter but more massive "Dreadful Night." It would be much more defensible to say that "Doom," finished when the poet was only 23 years old, laid up a great stock of ideas and images which Thomson was destined to mine for other poems. And "Sunday Up the River," with its beautiful rowing scenes, is the poem which owes the most to his earlier effort.

It is hard to pick out the very best from among the twenty short pieces that compose the poem, and probably that is something best left to the taste of the individual reader. But it should be mentioned that there are indeed few poems in English which deliver this kind of purity. (Not the modern "purity" of abstraction one finds claimed for Mallarmé or the English aesthetes, but the innocent purity of folk poetry such as one finds in the songs of Campion and Shakespeare.)

Melville, whose quote stands on the back cover of this edition, set "Sunday Up the River" in contrast to "Dreadful Night," and his perception was insightful. Like perhaps all good poets, Thomson was essentially two or three poets rolled into one complex person. His severe side produced the dark and indeed Gothic masterpieces such as "Dreadful Night" and "Insomnia"—the terror-visions of the urban cosmos. His other side was a country lark, irresponsible because innocent, and innocent because enjoying rest and sunshine. After all, who needs philosophy in the country?

One could search the libraries in vain for another poet who is so convincing about leisure. T. S. Eliot famously remarked that for those with a strong personality, their poetry was "an extinction of personality." Well, so is a vacation; and this poem, refreshingly, is both.

The overwhelming influence on "Sunday Up the River" is Heinrich Heine, whose lyrics Thomson had been translating in the mid-1860s. The ironies of the German poet are absent, but the charm and the cool breeze so characteristic of his work is in full bloom. It is one of the curiosities of poetry as an art that Thomson, so powerful as a poet of dark despair, should be so well suited to translate Heine—and to emulate him so winningly. But such is the art.

It is worth pointing out that Thomson's stance against organized religion, and his alliance with the Freethought movement, is tacitly stated in the poem's title. No churchgoing for this poet: for him, the rowboat and the countryside. And, in passing, a plug for Jameson's Irish Whiskey (VIII):

> I have watered this, though a toothful neat
> Just melts like cream down the throttle:
> But it's grand in the punch, hot, strong, and sweet:
> Not a headache in a bottle.

The final piece (XX) bears a striking resemblance to Baudelaire's famous poem "L'Invitation au Voyage"—which is not the sort of poem that Baudelaire is famous for either. It is possible that Thomson used it as a model (it was published in the 1857 edition of *Les Fleurs du Mal);* yet while there is a real affinity between Thomson and Baudelaire, the surprising thing is that Thomson seems not to have noticed his French counterpart. In any case, this final lyric breaks off at the end with a sudden fantasy—millions of years have passed, and the poet still drifts in the boat with his beloved. This single, superfluous fancy is the most original stroke in the poem* and it is found elsewhere in Thomson's writing, notably in the other and slightly earlier "Sunday" suite.

SUNDAY AT HAMPSTEAD (1863-1865)

"Sunday at Hampstead" is a more social version of "Sunday Up the River," depicting a small group of Londoners enjoying the weekend away from the city—"Too grateful to God for His Sabbath / To shut its hours in a church." It captures the light-hearted mood of several young adults enjoying free time, and smirking at their wealthy employers who must remain in the city while their exploited workers look down upon it from a hilltop:

> *They* drawl and stare and simper,
> So fine and cold and staid,
> Like exquisite waxwork figures
> That must be kept in the shade.

While this sort of snarky humor pervades the poem, there is another element which is possibly more unique to Thomson as a poet of the mid-19th Century. For five sections in the middle of the poem (V-IX), a character referred to as "Lazy" tells the others what life was like during preceding ages, in intervals of 10,000 years.

The number alone is striking for a poem of 1863. A myriad years is twice the Biblical account of the world's existence, and Thomson telescopes this span five times, at each colossal step imagining previous civilizations. For 21st-Century readers this is still imaginative, even if we are somewhat used to it, but in Thomson's day it was still a radically new idea. Darwin's groundbreaking work *On the Origin of Species* had been published only a few years before, in 1859; and while Charles Lyell's revolutionary *Principles of Geology* had made its mark on the public mind when it appeared in 1830, it is hard to find any trace of its impact in a poem before Thomson's. For Thomson to be playing with the timescales of archaeology, in such a casual manner,

* When "Sunday Up the River" was first published in *Fraser's Magazine,* these concluding lines were omitted; in this edition they are marked off by a line of asterisks.

shows a remarkable readiness in him to accept new ideas: doing it in conversation is one thing, but to put it into poetry, a ceremonial artform if ever there was one, requires quite another degree of commitment. One doesn't see other Victorian poets behaving with such familiarity in the company of *aeons.* Thomson, in this pleasant poem of weekend idleness, proves himself in this regard a few great leaps ahead of his time.

A VOICE FROM THE NILE (1881)

The notion that human culture has existed for vast swaths of time, most of which lie beyond the earliest human records, makes its first appearance as a normal, everyday thought in Thomson. In "Sunday at Hampstead," Thomson moved beyond the Judeo-Christian worldview with timescales that dwarf the Bible's "5,000 year" story, which until the booms of geology and paleontology in the middle of the 19th Century was still what most people assumed to be the age of the world. In his late poem "A Voice from the Nile," Thomson revisits the same idea in a more solemn mood.

To speak in the voice of someone else is an old habit among poets. Thomson here adopts the persona of the Nile (an interesting development, when we recall that he had written so many "rowboat passages" in earlier poems). It has been mentioned that he lacked the gift for drama, and the performance is only somewhat convincing. It has also been mentioned that Thomson was not a superior technician of the line, and his blank verse here is merely serviceable.*

But the point is not really to suspend disbelief, or to dazzle with a verbal virtuosity. The point is to throw civilization into perspective, to show it as a variety of scarcely significant details in the vast fabric of nature. And with this agenda, Thomson is indeed convincing.

Again, as in "Sunday at Hampstead," he plays the game of telescoping ages. The great river courses forward from the Temple of Karnak and the early Dynasties to the classical period (of either the later pharaohs or the Greek and Roman conquests); then it coasts through early Christianity and at last slides past Islam:

> Then I flow forward not a thousand years,
> And see again a woman and a babe,
> The woman haloed and the babe divine;
> And everywhere that symbol of the cross
> I knew aforetime in the ancient days,
> The emblem then of life, but now of death.
> Then I flow forward some few hundred years,
> And see again the crescent, now supreme
> On lofty cupolas and minarets
> Whence voices sweet and solemn call to prayer.

It is common to hear students arguing that later religions have recycled earlier ones, especially in their rites and symbology, as if this notion were a piece of news not widely known throughout the world for centuries. But

* It seems that everyone in England could write decent blank verse by the middle of the 19th Century, which perhaps explains why Robert Browning varied its rhythm and texture so wildly in his own dramatic monologues.

one does not often hear the argument made by a famously bountiful river, in a tone of almost weary reflection. Thomson's concept, still fresh in his day, might have been handled more clumsily; but he had been thinking the thought for a long time, and had the proper artistic distance from it. His treatment results in a voice which is scornful, to be sure, but which surprises us by ultimately proving so urbane:

> For thirty generations of my corn
> Outlast a generation of my men,
> And thirty generations of my men
> Outlast a generation of their gods:
> O admirable, pitiable man,
> My child yet alien in my family.

IN THE ROOM (1867-1868)

Thomson's other poem of "impersonation" was very unlike "A Voice from the Nile," and with its sense of variety it resembles his suites of short poems. It is "In the Room," which lets the furniture do the talking.

"In the Room," with its awareness of material objects and their role in the world of commerce, seems like a poem that could have been written in the 1920s. This is especially due to its main point: that a dresser can outlast a person. As the poem proceeds through its round of complaining voices, one gradually learns the room is in a boarding-house: the furniture greatly preferred the prior tenant, a cheerful young woman, to its current occupant, a gloomy journalist who is clearly Thomson's reductive self-portrait.

To give away the end of the poem is no crime, because any reader can see it coming a mile away. What fascinates is not the story, but the sense of anxiety among the articles of furniture. They are not looking forward to being packed up and re-sold for use in other separate rooms. And, like us, they make themselves the measure of all they can understand, as the bed pronounces ("Who spoke in deep and ponderous bass"):

> But we shall have short peace or rest;
> For soon up here will come a rout,
> And nail him in a queer long chest,
> And carry him like luggage out.
> They will be muffled all in black,
> And whisper much, and sigh and weep:
> But he will never more come back,
> And some one else in me must sleep.

Thomson's humor was not the less entertaining for being so grim.

"In the Room" shows Thomson at his best. Rather than narrating a story, which was not his strong suit, he relates a situation, and a particularly modern one. He uses the merry fiction of animate furniture to show how few illusions he had, whether about himself or about life in his era. He turns the stanza to advantage, conjuring up forward momentum in the absence of incident. And he commits himself to a single point—Thomson's best poems always possess a substantial thematic unity. It adds up to a beguiling and memorable poem.

MINOR PIECES:
LOW LIFE—VIRTUE AND VICE
L'ANCIEN RÉGIME—BILL JONES ON PRAYER
ADDRESS ON THE OPENING OF THE NEW HALL

I mention these poems together because they are of comparable merit, although they differ in subject matter and in mode. Together they show Thomson as he probably was in life, an honest man of unusual moral conscience, who identified himself with both the working class and the Freethinkers.

These poems are in no way complex or intimidating to enter: written for a general audience, they are among the poet's most accessible pieces. "Low Life" in particular almost forecasts the dialect poems of Kipling (born in 1865, just like the poem), and the argument of "Virtue and Vice" seems like it came from one of Blake's scrapbooks.

The sarcasm of "L'Ancien Régime" is a bit unusual for Thomson, and in comparison to the other works mentioned here the poem may strike some readers as a touch immature. But it manages to carry out its agenda well enough, and the simpering tone matches the poem's content. Its attack is as much on the king as on the sychophantic society he leads, and the poem forms an interesting foil with the more utopian vision of "The Lord of the Castle of Indolence." Indeed, one suspects that if Thomson had been more ironic (like later poets), he might have placed them next to each other in his first book, instead of separating them with a few other pieces.

"Bill Jones on Prayer" and the "Address" are both espousals of Thomson's moral atheism, which is essentially no more than disbelief in the supernatural. As he puts it in the latter poem, the creed was not so much godlessness as a simple no-nonsense humanism:

> Buddha and Jesus, Zeno, Socrates,
> Mohammed, Paine, Voltaire,—alike from these
> The precious metals we accept with joy;
> But pray, friends, spare us from the proved alloy!

In his 1913 book *The Victorian Age in Literature*, G. K. Chesterton sets aside a few sentences for Thomson, who was clearly not a favorite of his:

> There are many other minor names of major importance; but for one reason or other they do not derive from the schools that had dominated this epoch as such. Thus Thompson, the author of *The City of Dreadful Night*, was a fine poet; but his pessimism combined with a close pugnacity does not follow any of the large but loose lines of the Swinburnian age. But he was a great person—he knew how to be democratic in the dark.*

The big problem with such a fine estimation as this is that it is too short.

* Chesterton's misspelling of Thomson's name was probably a slip of the pen: earlier in the same chapter he had finished a rather long assessment of the Catholic poet Francis Thompson, with whom his sympathies were more consonant.

THE HEINE TRANSLATIONS

It is a pity that Thomson never made an all-out effort to translate the lyrics of Heine. His versions appear effortless, and capture the charm of the German poet so well that one laments he could not get paid to concentrate on the project for a year.

Thomson evidently recognized the merit of his work on Heine, and placed a substantial portion of translations at the end of his first volume. The relative success of *The City of Dreadful Night and Other Poems* in 1880 quickly put a second collection in process, and again Thomson chose to let Heine have the last word, this time with the touching poem "Childhood."

These decisions of placement have been preserved in this volume—or rather, they have been restored, since they were overriden in the 1895 two-volume edition of Thomson's *Poetical Works.* There, Thomson's friend and editor Bertram Dobell dismantled the volumes which Thomson had assembled, and rearranged the poems to suit his preferences. Dobell buried all the poems he considered inferior in the "Early Poems" section of volume II, regardless of whether they were early poems or not, and cut other long poems without justification. The benefit, trifling though it be, was that all the Heine translations could be placed together.

Unfortunately, not even that act of editorial intrusion could put all the Heine verses in one place, because there are several additional pieces of Heine scattered throughout Thomson's other poems. "Vane's Story," for instance, concludes with a Heine translation; earlier, it even includes four quatrains in German. "Weddah" includes a prefatory note containing yet another four quatrains, this time translated, but without rhyme. "Sunday Up the River" (XIV) holds yet another quatrain.

In any event, this edition puts Thomson's versions back in the places he chose for them, and gathers the remainder in the "Uncollected Translations" section at the end of the book. They easily earn their position among his more enjoyable writings, and like his translations from Saint-Amant—collected here for the first time in any edition—they show a side of Thomson which many editors have pushed into the background.

FOUR POINTS IN A LIFE (1852-1858)

This early suite is easily overlooked among Thomson's other poems of the 1850s, which are seldom of high quality. Its tone is unique in his work: all four poems are steady and clear, and they are free of the effusive vagueness that misguides the poet's other apprentice efforts. Shelley may have been a kindred spirit to Thomson, as far as thinking outside the age is concerned; but his poetry had a detrimental influence on Thomson, who was equally out of his element amid nature scenery and serenades, and who was never open to the sort of elemental mysticism and mythologizing that underlies most Romantic art. Thomson's longer pieces of imitation Shelley ("Tasso and Leonora"; "A Happy Poet"; "A Festival of Life"; "Shelley") inhabit a sort of poetical elephants' graveyard.

"Four Points in a Life" is not major poetry, but it certainly is solid poetry. It does read like an imitation of Shelley, but unlike Thomson's other affectations, it is saved from silliness by the grounding element of plain reality. Where Thomson's other early pieces fall into a trance of aimless repetition, these are concise: they do their thing and move on. The combination works, and by yoking Shelley's lyrical generosity to the journalistic virtues of observation and brevity, Thomson sounds like a precursor of the mature Yeats:

> Is this the second childhood's feeble sadness?
> My eyes are dim now and my hair is white;
> Yet never did the sunshine give more gladness,
> Never young spring burst forth in green delight
> More freshly; never was the earth more fair,
> Never more rapture in the common air.

This works as poetry because it gets to the point, speaking inspiredly rather than just inhaling for thirty or forty lines about how inspired it is.

Moreover, it does not read like "thesaurus verse," where a thing is said in terms that keep changing the subject. Throughout these four short lyrics Thomson keeps the subject in focus for the reader, using plain diction and exhibiting a degree of artistic control which he could not always command even in his prime. One suspects that if Tennyson had not already claimed this manner, Thomson might have written more of it himself.

THE PILGRIMAGE TO SAINT NICOTINE

There is a kind of poem which is easy to understand when you look at it, and which begins to sound very complicated when you try to explain it to someone. "The Pilgrimage to Saint Nicotine" is just that type of piece.

When Thomson parted ways with Charles Bradlaugh in 1875, he put *The National Reformer* behind him and found a job writing articles for the trade journal *Cope's Tobacco Plant*, published in Liverpool. After working there for a few years, Thomson and the house cartoonist John Wallace jointly conceived of a special project, to be produced annually as a Christmas special. The first installment was released in 1878 as "The Pilgrimage to Saint Nicotine."

The basic idea had a triple aim: first, to celebrate the virtues of tobacco; second, to satirize the public figures of the day; third, to concoct a parody of Chaucer. The Chaucer parody was itself in two parts, with Thomson's comic verse serving as a sort of caption to Wallace's illustration, which was a riff on the famous Stothard painting "Procession of the Canterbury Pilgrims" (an engraving of which was then very popular).

In itself, the piece is nothing more than a silly pastime for customers of the Cope Brothers, but some of its details shed an interesting light on the era. The picture shows an "Anti" being trampled under the horse of John Ruskin, and drafts of the following year's project treat opponents with similar slapstick offense. This sort of thing had sold newspapers and magazines like *Punch* for many years, and it remains the basis of editorial cartoons; but its use in what is essentially a tobacco advertisement is something perhaps very new. If nothing more, it shows that the print medium was beginning to have very porous boundaries, and that distinctions between entertainment, journalism, and advertisement were not immune to mutual trespass.

The complete text of the 1878 poem appears with Thomson's other works for the first time in this edition. Bertram Dobell, Thomson's friend and posthumous editor, cut much of the first part, and all of the second, from the two-volume *Poetical Works* published in 1895, and for unknown reasons he did not reprint the illustration either, despite expressing a desire to do so. Two APPENDICES in this edition complete the presentation: the first identifies each of the 65 caricatured personages by name (the poem often refers to them elliptically), and the second reprints the prose section from the 1878 pamphlet, from which these identifications derive (Thomson's verse does not cover the upper half of the picture in much detail). It is not known whether Thomson wrote the prose, or even contributed to it; and while this editor's guess is that he played a large part in its writing, that remains a total conjecture.

This edition also presents three fragmentary passages from a sequel entitled "In Pursuit of Diva Nicotina." The text comes from an unpublished manuscript, and shows Thomson taking a more serious approach the second time around—but the work seems to have been left incomplete, and *Cope's Tobacco Plant* was discontinued in 1881.

"I HAD A LOVE"

Among the other manuscript pieces that appear in this volume is the outstanding poem here titled "I Had a Love."

Bertram Dobell relates the poet's wish that the piece remain unpublished; and then dwells on the poem, quoting and summarizing it, for five full pages of his 1895 *Poetical Works*. Anne Ridler examined the manuscript and published the poem in its entirety in her 1963 *Poems and Some Letters of James Thomson*, which unfortunately played favorites even with some of the texts it included (such as "Sunday Up the River"). Now that another fifty years have elapsed, the poem at last joins the full roster of its companions.

Thomson's reasons for suppressing the poem were undoubtedly personal. He had composed a confession, laying his heart bare: it must have seemed a sacrilege to give public eyes access to something so private. His explanation to Bertram Dobell offered up a flimsy excuse:

> Above [lines] merely copy rough pencil draft; too hard and harsh in both conception and execution for attempt at polishing—far more truth than poetry in it. *

Thomson's express wish to suppress the poem evidently came in a later communication. In any case, his critique was either momentary or disingenuous, because the poem as it stands is among his greatest compositions—direct, sincere, moving, and powerful in expression.

"I Had a Love" is Thomson's one real elegy for Matilda Weller, the girl he fell in love with when he was sixteen or so (she was younger), and who died

* Thomson's manuscript note, dated 19 Sept. 1878; quoted by Anne Ridler, *Poems and Some Letters of James Thomson*, p. 274.

in 1853, leaving him deeply distraught before he had reached his twentieth year. All in their circle, including her family, had assumed they would marry when she came of age. And one wonders indeed if Thomson's love poetry, except for this single poem, was a fantasy that she is still alive, or was written for a subsequent romance, or was a use of poetic convention meant to evade the topic entirely.

The only other poem which seems to feature Matilda is "Vane's Story," the lead poem of Thomson's second volume. There, however, she appears as a phantom in a dream, and the poem is more about Vane (a weak stand-in for Thomson) expressing his opinions about various things, while very much indulging in a fantasy of reunion. "I Had a Love," on the other hand, is an unselfish cry of the heart, with no illusions. It is a kind of cold shower for the soul, a wake-up call to look reality in the face.

The poem came at the end of what Thomson often called his "seven songless years"—the period of his life running roughly 1873-1880, during which time he wrote prose almost exclusively. He had largely finished "Dreadful Night" in 1873 after drafting much of it in 1870 (only the final touches came in 1874). Some have speculated that the poem exhausted his powers, but it is probably more true that he was preoccupied with writing that brought him an income. Moreover, a book was expected of him as early as 1874, and the constant preparations and delays no doubt sidetracked him considerably. In 1875 came his split with Charles Bradlaugh and his departure from the *National Reformer,* and once set adrift he undoubtedly had to focus, to his own chagrin, on more practical matters than poetry.

By 1878, Thomson had been writing for *Cope's Tobacco Plant* for about two years, and had settled into a new phase of his life. Plans for "The Pilgrimage to Saint Nicotine" were probably underway by September. And in all likelihood it was at that moment that the change sank in, and he was able to accept that the door had fully closed on the earlier phase of his life. Thomson met Bradlaugh and Matilda Weller at the same time of his life, at Ballincollig, in 1851: the break with Bradlaugh after nearly fifteen years must have cast his reflections back to her as well.

"I Had a Love" is, in short, Thomson's recognition that the past is irrevocable. Or, as he himself had earlier expressed it, in "Dreadful Night" XVIII, speaking about the futile and even grotesque attempt to recover the past:

> For this is law, if law there be in fate:
> What never has been, yet may have its when;
> The thing which has been, never is again.

ABOUT THIS EDITION

This volume falls into two major sections. The first half reproduces Thomson's collected poems in his own ordering of them—as established by the two books *The City of Dreadful Night* and *Vane's Story,* which were published during his life; plus the first half of the posthumous collection *A Voice from the Nile,* which by Dobell's account the poet had arranged himself. The two-volume edition of Thomson's *Poetical Works,* edited by Dobell in 1895, departed from Thomson's ordering, and the present edition affords an opportunity to restore the work of the poet's hand. This being the overriding intent, two of Dobell's other changes have here been reversed: Thomson's dedications for the books published during his life, omitted from the 1895 edition, have been restored; and the selection of "Early Poems," appended by Dobell to the posthumous volume of 1884, has been moved and reorganized under a more appropriate heading.

The second part of this edition gathers all Thomson's verse not collected by the poet himself, under the merely factual heading "Poems Uncollected (1852-1882)." This covers his entire writing career, from his earliest efforts to the end. The chief portion of these poems is arranged chronologically, albeit some guesswork has contrived the placement of undated pieces. Two long poems which Dobell reprinted only in part—the massive early work "The Doom of a City" and the late satirical piece "The Pilgrimage to Saint Nicotine"—are presented here in their entirety.

Also, this edition preserves the poem "By the Sea" (which is presumably Dobell's arrangement of the songs from the long poem "Ronald and Helen") as it appeared in the 1884 "Early Poems" group. Dobell's general ordering of texts, as mentioned above, was not found worth perpetuating; but this piece, being a unique arrangement of lines to which Thomson may have leant his hand, was not found worth discarding.

Additionally, this second part of Thomson's poems includes several pieces which the poet never published, such as the powerful late poem "I Had a Love," which seems to have been his break out of the period he referred to as his "seven songless years." Such unpublished works here follow the text of the 1963 volume edited by Anne Ridler, *Poems and some letters of James Thomson.* A few other fragments of verse have been culled from Thomson's essays, a process started by previous editors but left rather unfinished. These and the poems researched by Ridler have not been specially marked in the text, since the intent of this edition is to present Thomson's work as he left it in this world, and not to detail a documentary history of its various fortunes thereafter.

The fragments of a second and unpublished satirical piece for *Cope's Tobacco Plant,* meant to accompany a caricature painting entitled "In Pursuit of Diva Nicotina," were provided by David Levy of George Mason University from his copies of the original manuscript. Like the "Pilgrimage to Saint Nicotine," this verse was commissioned by a tobacco trade journal to go with a satirical illustration, and represents not just a key phase in Thomson's later years, but an interesting spot in the history of periodicals. The project in general is thought to have been conceived jointly by Thomson and John Wallace (working under the pseudonym George Pipeshank) for *Cope's.* Envisioned at first as an annual collaboration, it was discontinued after the death of the poet.

The conclusion of "Poems Uncollected" comprises two subsections which deserve a brief explanation, since they break the otherwise chronological presentation.

The short poems grouped under the heading "Epigrams" were apparently written in batches by Thomson, and were not printed together when they first appeared in magazines. Thomson does not appear to have corralled them himself, and their grouping may well be the work of Dobell or other early editors; but as long as the poet's role in their grouping remains ambiguous, keeping them together is the only defensible choice.

The final subsection of translations is more or less chronological, but groups the texts under the original authors. More than thirty of the translations and fragments included here have not been collected previously, and were combed from Thomson's essays and reviews. Previous editors, again, began this task but did not see it through; they seem to have let favoritism over certain pieces interfere, or perhaps were driven by a desire to see the poet adhere to a certain image. The present editor has opted to include all extant translations, fragmentary as they may be, so that the reader may better appreciate Thomson's ability as a verse translator, and may also observe the fairly wide range of material he chose to work on—from the giddy revelry of Saint-Amant to the confrontational solemnity of Leopardi to the self-consciously clowning lines of Lessing. Thomson's translation of Novalis' *Hymn to the Night* has not been included here due to its length and its mismatch with the other contents (it is largely prose), and because it deserves to be reprinted with Thomson's version of the *Operette morali* of Leopardi.

As a final note: Thomson's own footnotes to the poems appear as they did in the original printings. My footnotes, which have been kept to a minimum, are set in square brackets.

—A. J. Spatz, 2012.

THE CITY OF DREADFUL NIGHT AND OTHER POEMS (1880)

TO THE MEMORY

OF

THE YOUNGER BROTHER OF DANTE

GIACOMO LEOPARDI

A SPIRIT AS LOFTY

A GENIUS AS INTENSE

WITH A YET MORE TRAGIC DOOM

THE

CITY OF DREADFUL NIGHT

Per me si va nella città dolente.

—Dante

Poi di tanto adoprar, di tanti moti
D'ogni celeste, ogni terrena cosa,
Girando senza posa,
Per tornar sempre là donde son mosse;
Uso alcuno, alcun frutto
Indovinar non so.

* * *

Sola nel mondo eterna, a cui si volve
Ogni creata cosa,
In te, morte, si posa
Nostra ignuda natura;
Lieta no, ma sicura
Dell' antico dolor . . .
Però ch' esser beato
Nega ai mortali e nega a' morti il fato.

—Leopardi

PROEM.

Lo, thus, as prostrate, "In the dust I write
 My heart's deep languor and my soul's sad tears."
Yet why evoke the spectres of black night
 To blot the sunshine of exultant years?
Why disinter dead faith from mouldering hidden?
Why break the seals of mute despair unbidden,
 And wail life's discords into careless ears?

Because a cold rage seizes one at whiles
 To show the bitter old and wrinkled truth
Stripped naked of all vesture that beguiles,
 False dreams, false hopes, false masks and modes of youth;
Because it gives some sense of power and passion
In helpless innocence to try to fashion
 Our woe in living words howe'er uncouth.

Surely I write not for the hopeful young,
  Or those who deem their happiness of worth,
Or such as pasture and grow fat among
  The shows of life and feel nor doubt nor dearth,
Or pious spirits with a God above them
To sanctify and glorify and love them,
  Or sages who foresee a heaven on earth.

For none of these I write, and none of these
  Could read the writing if they deigned to try;
So may they flourish in their due degrees,
  On our sweet earth and in their unplaced sky.
If any cares for the weak words here written,
It must be some one desolate, Fate-smitten,
  Whose faith and hopes are dead, and who would die.

Yes, here and there some weary wanderer
  In that same city of tremendous night,
Will understand the speech and feel a stir
  Of fellowship in all-disastrous fight;
"I suffer mute and lonely, yet another
Uplifts his voice to let me know a brother
  Travels the same wild paths though out of sight."

O sad Fraternity, do I unfold
  Your dolorous mysteries shrouded from of yore?
Nay, be assured; no secret can be told
  To any who divined it not before:
None uninitiate by many a presage
Will comprehend the language of the message,
  Although proclaimed aloud for evermore.

I.

The City is of Night; perchance of Death
  But certainly of Night; for never there
Can come the lucid morning's fragrant breath
  After the dewy dawning's cold grey air:
The moon and stars may shine with scorn or pity;
The sun has never visited that city,
  For it dissolveth in the daylight fair.

Dissolveth like a dream of night away;
  Though present in distempered gloom of thought
And deadly weariness of heart all day.
  But when a dream night after night is brought
Throughout a week, and such weeks few or many
Recur each year for several years, can any
  Discern that dream from real life in aught?

For life is but a dream whose shapes return,
  Some frequently, some seldom, some by night
And some by day, some night and day: we learn,
  The while all change and many vanish quite,
In their recurrence with recurrent changes
A certain seeming order; where this ranges
  We count things real; such is memory's might.

A river girds the city west and south,
  The main north channel of a broad lagoon,
Regurging with the salt tides from the mouth;
  Waste marshes shine and glister to the moon
For leagues, then moorland black, then stony ridges;
Great piers and causeways, many noble bridges,
  Connect the town and islet suburbs strewn.

Upon an easy slope it lies at large
  And scarcely overlaps the long curved crest
Which swells out two leagues from the river marge.
  A trackless wilderness rolls north and west,
Savannahs, savage woods, enormous mountains,
Bleak uplands, black ravines with torrent fountains;
  And eastward rolls the shipless sea's unrest.

The city is not ruinous, although
  Great ruins of an unremembered past,
With others of a few short years ago
  More sad, are found within its precincts vast.
The street-lamps always burn; but scarce a casement
In house or palace front from roof to basement
  Doth glow or gleam athwart the mirk air cast.

The street-lamps burn amid the baleful glooms,
  Amidst the soundless solitudes immense
Of ranged mansions dark and still as tombs.
  The silence which benumbs or strains the sense
Fulfils with awe the soul's despair unweeping:
Myriads of habitants are ever sleeping,
  Or dead, or fled from nameless pestilence!

Yet as in some necropolis you find
  Perchance one mourner to a thousand dead,
So there: worn faces that look deaf and blind
  Like tragic masks of stone. With weary tread,
Each wrapt in his own doom, they wander, wander,
Or sit foredone and desolately ponder
  Through sleepless hours with heavy drooping head.

Mature men chiefly, few in age or youth,
  A woman rarely, now and then a child:
A child! If here the heart turns sick with ruth
  To see a little one from birth defiled,
Or lame or blind, as preordained to languish
Through youthless life, think how it bleeds with anguish
  To meet one erring in that homeless wild.

They often murmur to themselves, they speak
  To one another seldom, for their woe
Broods maddening inwardly and scorns to wreak
  Itself abroad; and if at whiles it grow
To frenzy which must rave, none heeds the clamour,
Unless there waits some victim of like glamour,
  To rave in turn, who lends attentive show.

The City is of Night, but not of Sleep;
  There sweet sleep is not for the weary brain;
The pitiless hours like years and ages creep,
  A night seems termless hell. This dreadful strain
Of thought and consciousness which never ceases,
Or which some moments' stupor but increases,
  This, worse than woe, makes wretches there insane.

They leave all hope behind who enter there:
  One certitude while sane they cannot leave,
One anodyne for torture and despair;
  The certitude of Death, which no reprieve
Can put off long; and which, divinely tender,
But waits the outstretched hand to promptly render
  That draught whose slumber nothing can bereave. *

* Though the Garden of thy Life be wholly waste, the sweet flowers withered, the fruit-trees barren, over its wall hang ever the rich dark clusters of the Vine of Death, within easy reach of thy hand, which may pluck of them when it will.

II.

Because he seemed to walk with an intent
  I followed him; who, shadowlike and frail,
Unswervingly though slowly onward went,
  Regardless, wrapt in thought as in a veil:
Thus step for step with lonely sounding feet
We travelled many a long dim silent street.

At length he paused: a black mass in the gloom,
  A tower that merged into the heavy sky;
Around, the huddled stones of grave and tomb:
  Some old God's-acre now corruption's sty:
He murmured to himself with dull despair,
Here Faith died, poisoned by this charnel air.

Then turning to the right went on once more
  And travelled weary roads without suspense;
And reached at last a low wall's open door,
  Whose villa gleamed beyond the foliage dense:
He gazed, and muttered with a hard despair,
Here Love died, stabbed by its own worshipped pair.

Then turning to the right resumed his march,
  And travelled street and lanes with wondrous strength,
Until on stooping through a narrow arch
  We stood before a squalid house at length:
He gazed, and whispered with a cold despair,
Here Hope died, starved out in its utmost lair.

When he had spoken thus, before he stirred,
  I spoke, perplexed by something in the signs
Of desolation I had seen and heard
  In this drear pilgrimage to ruined shrines:
Where Faith and Love and Hope are dead indeed,
Can Life still live? By what doth it proceed?

As whom his one intense thought overpowers,
  He answered coldly, Take a watch, erase
The signs and figures of the circling hours,
  Detach the hands, remove the dial-face;
The works proceed until run down; although
Bereft of purpose, void of use, still go.

Then turning to the right paced on again,
   And traversed squares and travelled streets whose glooms
Seemed more and more familiar to my ken;
   And reached that sullen temple of the tombs;
And paused to murmur with the old despair,
Hear Faith died, poisoned by this charnel air.

I ceased to follow, for the knot of doubt
   Was severed sharply with a cruel knife:
He circled thus forever tracing out
   The series of the fraction left of Life;
Perpetual recurrence in the scope
Of but three terms, dead Faith, dead Love, dead Hope. *

III.

Although lamps burn along the silent streets,
   Even when moonlight silvers empty squares
The dark holds countless lanes and close retreats;
   But when the night its sphereless mantle wears
The open spaces yawn with gloom abysmal,
The sombre mansions loom immense and dismal,
   The lanes are black as subterranean lairs.

And soon the eye a strange new vision learns:
   The night remains for it as dark and dense,
Yet clearly in this darkness it discerns
   As in the daylight with its natural sense;
Perceives a shade in shadow not obscurely,
Pursues a stir of black in blackness surely,
   Sees spectres also in the gloom intense.

The ear, too, with the silence vast and deep
   Becomes familiar though unreconciled;
Hears breathings as of hidden life asleep,
   And muffled throbs as of pent passions wild,
Far murmurs, speech of pity or derision;
But all more dubious than the things of vision,
   So that it knows not when it is beguiled.

No time abates the first despair and awe,
   But wonder ceases soon; the weirdest thing
Is felt least strange beneath the lawless law
   Where Death-in-Life is the eternal king;
Crushed impotent beneath this reign of terror,
Dazed with mysteries of woe and error,
   The soul is too outworn for wondering.

* Life divided by that persistent three = $^{1.XX}/333$ = .210.

IV.

He stood alone within the spacious square
Declaiming from the central grassy mound,
With head uncovered and with streaming hair,
As if large multitudes were gathered round:
A stalwart shape, the gestures full of might,
The glances burning with unnatural light:—

As I came through the desert thus it was,
As I came through the desert: All was black,
In heaven no single star, on earth no track;
A brooding hush without a stir or note,
The air so thick it clotted in my throat;
And thus for hours; then some enormous things
Swooped past with savage cries and clanking wings:
But I strode on austere;
No hope could have no fear.

As I came through the desert thus it was,
As I came through the desert: Eyes of fire
Glared at me throbbing with a starved desire;
The hoarse and heavy and carnivorous breath
Was hot upon me from deep jaws of death;
Sharp claws, swift talons, fleshless fingers cold
Plucked at me from the bushes, tried to hold:
But I strode on austere;
No hope could have no fear.

As I came through the desert thus it was,
As I came through the desert: Lo you, there,
That hillock burning with a brazen glare;
Those myriad dusky flames with points a-glow
Which writhed and hissed and darted to and fro;
A Sabbath of the Serpents, heaped pell-mell
For Devil's roll-call and some *fête* of Hell:
Yet I strode on austere;
No hope could have no fear.

As I came through the desert thus it was,
As I came through the desert: Meteors ran
And crossed their javelins on the black sky-span;
The zenith opened to a gulf of flame,
The dreadful thunderbolts jarred earth's fixed frame;
The ground all heaved in waves of fire that surged
And weltered round me sole there unsubmerged:
Yet I strode on austere;
No hope could have no fear.

As I came through the desert thus it was,
As I came through the desert: Air once more,
And I was close upon a wild sea-shore;
Enormous cliffs arose on either hand,
The deep tide thundered up a league-broad strand;
White foambelts seethed there, wan spray swept and flew;
The sky broke, moon and stars and clouds and blue:
Yet I strode on austere;
No hope could have no fear.

As I came through the desert thus it was,
As I came through the desert: On the left
The sun arose and crowned a broad crag-cleft;
There stopped and burned out black, except a rim,
A bleeding eyeless socket, red and dim;
Whereon the moon fell suddenly south-west,
And stood above the right-hand cliffs at rest:
Yet I strode on austere;
No hope could have no fear.

As I came through the desert thus it was,
As I came through the desert: From the right
A shape came slowly with a ruddy light;
A woman with a red lamp in her hand,
Bareheaded and barefooted on that strand;
O desolation moving with such grace!
O anguish with such beauty in thy face!
I fell as on my bier,
Hope travailed with such fear.

As I came through the desert thus it was,
As I came through the desert: I was twain,
Two selves distinct that cannot join again;
One stood apart and knew but could not stir,
And watched the other stark in swoon and her;
And she came on, and never turned aside,
Between such sun and moon and roaring tide:
And as she came more near
My soul grew mad with fear.

As I came through the desert thus it was,
As I came through the desert: Hell is mild
And piteous matched with that accursed wild;
A large black sign was on her breast that bowed,
A broad black band ran down her snow-white shroud;
That lamp she held was her own burning heart,
Whose blood-drops trickled step by step apart:
The mystery was clear;
Mad rage had swallowed fear.

As I came through the desert thus it was,
As I came through the desert: By the sea
She knelt and bent above that senseless me;
Those lamp-drops fell upon my white brow there,
She tried to cleanse them with her tears and hair;
She murmured words of pity, love, and woe,
She heeded not the level rushing flow:
And mad with rage and fear,
I stood stonebound so near.

As I came through the desert thus it was,
As I came through the desert: When the tide
Swept up to her there kneeling by my side,
She clasped that corpse-like me, and they were borne
Away, and this vile me was left forlorn;
I know the whole sea cannot quench that heart,
Or cleanse that brow, or wash those two apart:
They love; their doom is drear,
Yet they nor hope nor fear;
But I, what do I here?

V.

How he arrives there none can clearly know;
Athwart the mountains and immense wild tracts,
Or flung a waif upon that vast sea-flow,
Or down the river's boiling cataracts:
To reach it is as dying fever-stricken;
To leave it, slow faint birth intense pangs quicken;
And memory swoons in both the tragic acts.

But being there one feels a citizen;
Escape seems hopeless to the heart forlorn:
Can Death-in-Life be brought to life again?
And yet release does come; there comes a morn
When he awakes from slumbering so sweetly
That all the world is changed for him completely,
And he is verily as if new-born.

He scarcely can believe the blissful change,
He weeps perchance who wept not while accurst;
Never again will he approach the range
Infected by that evil spell now burst:
Poor wretch! who once hath paced that dolent city
Shall pace it often, doomed beyond all pity,
With horror ever deepening from the first.

Though he possess sweet babes and loving wife,
  A home of peace by loyal friendships cheered,
And love them more than death or happy life,
  They shall avail not; he must dree his weird;
Renounce all blessings for that imprecation,
Steal forth and haunt that builded desolation,
  Of woe and terrors and thick darkness reared.

VI.

I sat forlornly by the river-side,
  And watched the bridge-lamps glow like golden stars
Above the blackness of the swelling tide,
  Down which they struck rough gold in ruddier bars;
And heard the heave and plashing of the flow
Against the wall a dozen feet below.

Large elm-trees stood along that river-walk;
  And under one, a few steps from my seat,
I heard strange voices join in stranger talk,
  Although I had not heard approaching feet:
These bodiless voices in my waking dream
Flowed dark words blending with sombre stream:—

And you have after all come back; come back.
I was about to follow on your track.
And you have failed: our spark of hope is black.

That I have failed is proved by my return:
The spark is quenched, nor ever more will burn,
But listen; and the story you shall learn.

I reached the portal common spirits fear,
And read the words above it, dark yet clear,
"Leave hope behind, all ye who enter here:"

And would have passed in, gratified to gain
That positive eternity of pain
Instead of this insufferable inane.

A demon warder clutched me, Not so fast;
First leave your hopes behind!—But years have passed
Since I left all behind me, to the last:

You cannot count for hope, with all your wit,
This bleak despair that drives me to the Pit:
How could I seek to enter void of it?

He snarled, What thing is this which apes a soul,
And would find entrance to our gulf of dole
Without the payment of the settled toll?

Outside the gate he showed an open chest:
Here pay their entrance fees the souls unblest;
Cast in some hope, you enter with the rest.

This is Pandora's box; whose lid shall shut,
And Hell-gate too, when hopes have filled it; but
They are so thin that it will never glut.

I stood a few steps backwards, desolate;
And watched the spirits pass me to their fate,
And fling off hope, and enter at the gate.

When one casts off a load he springs upright,
Squares back his shoulders, breathes with all his might,
And briskly paces forward strong and light:

But these, as if they took some burden, bowed;
The whole frame sank; however strong and proud
Before, they crept in quite infirm and cowed.

And as they passed me, earnestly from each
A morsel of his hope I did beseech,
To pay my entrance; but all mocked my speech.

No one would cede a little of his store,
Though knowing that in instants three or four
He must resign the whole for evermore.

So I returned. Our destiny is fell;
For in this Limbo we must ever dwell,
Shut out alike from heaven and Earth and Hell.

The other sighed back, Yea; but if we grope
With care through all this Limbo's dreary scope,
We yet may pick up some minute lost hope;

And sharing it between us, entrance win,
In spite of fiends so jealous for gross sin:
Let us without delay our search begin.

VII.

Some say that phantoms haunt those shadowy streets,
And mingle freely there with sparse mankind;
And tell of ancient woes and black defeats,
And murmur mysteries in the grave enshrined:
But others think them visions of illusion,
Or even men gone far in self-confusion;
No man there being wholly sane in mind.

And yet a man who raves, however mad,
Who bares his heart and tells of his own fall,
Reserves some inmost secret good or bad:
The phantoms have no reticence at all:
The nudity of flesh will blush though tameless,
The extreme nudity of bone grins shameless,
The unsexed skeleton mocks shroud and pall.

I have seen phantoms there that were as men
And men that were as phantoms flit and roam;
Marked shapes that were not living to my ken,
Caught breathings acrid as with Dead Sea foam:
The City rests for man so weird and awful,
That his intrusion there might seem unlawful,
And phantoms there may have their proper home.

VIII.

While I still lingered on that river-walk,
And watched the tide as black as our black doom,
I heard another couple join in talk,
And saw them to the left hand in the gloom
Seated against an elm bole on the ground,
Their eyes intent upon the stream profound.

"I never knew another man on earth
But had some joy and solace in his life,
Some chance of triumph in the dreadful strife:
My doom has been unmitigated dearth."

"We gaze upon the river, and we note
The various vessels large and small that float,
Ignoring every wrecked and sunken boat."

"And yet I asked no splendid dower, no spoil
Of sway or fame or rank or even wealth;
But homely love with common food and health,
And nightly sleep to balance daily toil."

"This all-too-humble soul would arrogate
Unto itself some signalising hate
From the supreme indifference of Fate!"

"Who is most wretched in this dolorous place?
  I think myself; yet I would rather be
  My miserable self than He, than He
Who formed such creatures to His own disgrace.

"The vilest thing must be less vile than Thou
  From whom it had its being, God and Lord!
  Creator of all woe and sin! abhorred
Malignant and implacable! I vow

"That not for all Thy power furled and unfurled,
  For all the temples to Thy glory built,
  Would I assume the ignominious guilt
Of having made such men in such a world."

"As if a Being, God or Fiend, could reign,
At once so wicked, foolish and insane,
As to produce men when He might refrain!

"The world rolls round for ever like a mill;
It grinds out death and life and good and ill;
It has no purpose, heart or mind or will.

"While air of Space and Time's full river flow
The mill must blindly whirl unresting so:
It may be wearing out, but who can know?

"Man might know one thing were his sight less dim;
That it whirls not to suit his petty whim,
That it is quite indifferent to him.

"Nay, does it treat him harshly as he saith?
It grinds him some slow years of bitter breath,
Then grinds him back into eternal death."

IX.

It is full strange to him who hears and feels,
  When wandering there in some deserted street,
The booming and the jar of ponderous wheels,
  The trampling clash of heavy ironshod feet:
Who in this Venice of the Black Sea rideth?
Who in this city of the stars abideth
  To buy or sell as those in daylight sweet?

The rolling thunder seems to fill the sky
  As it comes on; the horses snort and strain,
The harness jingles, as it passes by;
  The hugeness of an overburthened wain:
A man sits nodding on the shaft or trudges
Three parts asleep beside his fellow-drudges:
  And so it rolls into the night again.

What merchandise? whence, whither, and for whom?
  Perchance it is a Fate-appointed hearse,
Bearing away to some mysterious tomb
  Or Limbo of the scornful universe
The joy, the peace, the life-hope, the abortions
Of all things good which should have been our portions,
  But have been strangled by that City's curse.

X.

The mansion stood apart in its own ground;
  In front thereof a fragrant garden-lawn,
High trees about it, and the whole walled round:
  The massy iron gates were both withdrawn;
And every window of its front shed light,
Portentous in that City of the Night.

But though thus lighted it was deadly still
  As all the countless bulks of solid gloom;
Perchance a congregation to fulfil
  Solemnities of silence in this doom,
Mysterious rites of dolour and despair
Permitting not a breath or chant of prayer?

Broad steps ascended to a terrace broad
  Whereon lay still light from the open door;
The hall was noble, and its aspect awed,
  Hung round with heavy black from dome to floor;
And ample stairways rose to left and right
Whose balustrades were also draped with night.

I paced from room to room, from hall to hall,
  Nor any life throughout the maze discerned;
But each was hung with its funereal pall,
  And held a shrine, around which tapers burned,
With picture or with statue or with bust,
All copied from the same fair form of dust:

A woman very young and very fair;
Beloved by bounteous life and joy and youth,
And loving these sweet lovers, so that care
And age and death seemed not for her in sooth:
Alike as stars, all beautiful and bright,
These shapes lit up that mausoléan night.

At length I heard a murmur as of lips,
And reached an open oratory hung
With heaviest blackness of the whole eclipse;
Beneath the dome a fuming censer swung;
And one lay there upon a low white bed,
With tapers burning at the foot and head:

The Lady of the images, supine,
Deathstill, lifesweet, with folded palms she lay:
And kneeling there as at a sacred shrine
A young man wan and worn who seemed to pray:
A crucifix of dim and ghostly white
Surmounted the large altar left in night:—

The chambers of the mansion of my heart,
In every one whereof thine image dwells,
Are black with grief eternal for thy sake.

The inmost oratory of my soul,
Wherein thou ever dwellest quick or dead,
Is black with grief eternal for thy sake.

I kneel beside thee and I clasp the cross,
With eyes forever fixed upon that face,
So beautiful and dreadful in its calm.

I kneel here patient as thou liest there;
As patient as a statue carved in stone,
Of adoration and eternal grief.

While thou dost not awake I cannot move;
And something tells me thou wilt never wake,
And I alive feel turning into stone.

Most beautiful were Death to end my grief,
Most hateful to destroy the sight of thee,
Dear vision better than all death or life.

But I renounce all choice of life or death,
For either shall be ever at thy side,
And thus in bliss or woe be ever well.—

He murmured thus and thus in monotone,
  Intent upon that uncorrupted face,
Entranced except his moving lips alone:
  I glided with hushed footsteps from the place.
This was the festival that filled with light
That palace in the City of the Night.

XI.

What men are they who haunt these fatal glooms,
  And fill their living mouths with dust of death,
And make their habitations in the tombs,
  And breathe eternal sighs with mortal breath,
And pierce life's pleasant veil of various error
To reach that void of darkness and old terror
  Wherein expire the lamps of hope and faith?

They have much wisdom yet they are not wise,
  They have much goodness yet they do not well,
(The fools we know have their own paradise,
  The wicked also have their proper Hell);
They have much strength but still their doom is stronger,
Much patience but their time endureth longer,
  Much valour but life mocks it with some spell.

They are most rational and yet insane:
  An outward madness not to be controlled;
A perfect reason in the central brain,
  Which has no power, but sitteth wan and cold,
And sees the madness, and foresees as plainly
The ruin in its path, and trieth vainly
  To cheat itself refusing to behold.

And some are great in rank and wealth and power,
  And some renowned for genius and for worth;
And some are poor and mean, who brood and cower
  And shrink from notice, and accept all dearth
Of body, heart and soul, and leave to others
All boons of life: yet these and those are brothers,
  The saddest and the weariest men on earth.

XII.

Our isolated units could be brought
  To act together for some common end?
For one by one, each silent with his thought,
  I marked a long loose line approach and wend
Athwart the great cathedral's cloistered square,
And slowly vanish from the moonlit air.

Then I would follow in among the last:
  And in the porch a shrouded figure stood,
Who challenged each one pausing ere he passed,
  With deep eyes burning through a blank white hood:
Whence come you in the world of life and light
To this our City of Tremendous Night?—

From pleading in a senate of rich lords
For some scant justice to our countless hordes
Who toil half-starved with scarce a human right:
I wake from daydreams to this real night.

From wandering through many a solemn scene
Of opium visions, with a heart serene
And intellect miraculously bright:
I wake from daydreams to this real night.

From making hundreds laugh and roar with glee
By my transcendent feats of mimicry,
And humour wanton as an elvish sprite:
I wake from daydreams to this real night.

From prayer and fasting in a lonely cell,
Which brought an ecstasy ineffable
Of love and adoration and delight:
I wake from daydreams to this real night.

From ruling on a splendid kingly throne
A nation which beneath my rule has grown
Year after year in wealth and arts and might:
I wake from daydreams to this real night.

From preaching to an audience fired with faith
The Lamb who died to save our souls from death,
Whose blood hath washed our scarlet sins wool-white:
I wake from daydreams to this real night.

From drinking fiery poison in a den
Crowded with tawdry girls and squalid men,
Who hoarsely laugh and curse and brawl and fight:
I wake from daydreams to this real night.

From picturing with all beauty and all grace
First Eden and the parents of our race,
A luminous rapture unto all men's sight:
I wake from daydreams to this real night.

From writing a great work with patient plan
To justify the ways of God to man,
And show how ill must fade and perish quite:
I wake from daydreams to this real night.

From desperate fighting with a little band
Against the powerful tyrants of our land,
To free our brethren in their own despite:
I wake from daydreams to this real night.

Thus, challenged by that warder sad and stern,
  Each one responded with his countersign,
Then entered the cathedral; and in turn
  I entered also, having given mine;
But lingered near until I heard no more,
And marked the closing of the massive door.

XIII.

Of all things human which are strange and wild
  This is perchance the wildest and most strange,
And showeth man most utterly beguiled,
  To those who haunt that sunless City's range;
That he bemoans himself for aye, repeating
How Time is deadly swift, how life is fleeting,
  How naught is constant on the earth but change.

The hours are heavy on him and the days;
  The burden of the months he scarce can bear;
And often in his secret soul he prays
  To sleep through barren periods unaware,
Arousing at some longed-for date of pleasure;
Which having passed and yielded him small treasure,
  He would outsleep another term of care.

Yet in his marvellous fancy he must make
Quick wings for Time, and see it fly from us;
This Time which crawleth like a monstrous snake,
Wounded and slow and very venomous;
Which creeps blindwormlike round the earth and ocean,
Distilling poison at each painful motion,
And seems condemned to circle ever thus.

And since he cannot spend and use aright
The little time here given him in trust,
But wasteth it in weary undelight
Of foolish toil and trouble, strife and lust,
He naturally claimeth to inherit
The everlasting Future, that his merit
May have full scope; as surely is most just.

O length of the intolerable hours,
O nights that are as æons of slow pain,
O Time, too ample for our vital powers,
O Life, whose woeful vanities remain
Immutable for all of all our legions
Through all the centuries and in all the regions,
Not of your speed and variance *we* complain.

We do not ask a longer term of strife,
Weakness and weariness and nameless woes;
We do not claim renewed and endless life
When this which is our torment here shall close,
An everlasting conscious inanition!
We yearn for speedy death in full fruition,
Dateless oblivion and divine repose.

XIV.

Large glooms were gathered in the mighty fane,
With tinted moongleams slanting here and there;
And all was hush: no swelling organ-strain,
No chant, no voice or murmuring of prayer;
No priests came forth, no tinkling censers fumed,
And the high altar space was unillumed.

Around the pillars and against the walls
Leaned men and shadows; others seemed to brood
Bent or recumbent in secluded stalls.
Perchance they were not a great multitude
Save in that city of so lonely streets
Where one may count up every face he meets.

All patiently awaited the event
  Without a stir or sound, as if no less
Self-occupied, doomstricken while attent.
  And then we heard a voice of solemn stress
From the dark pulpit, and our gaze there met
Two eyes which burned as never eyes burned yet:

Two steadfast and intolerable eyes
  Burning beneath a broad and rugged brow;
The head behind it of enormous size.
  And as black fir-groves in a large wind bow,
Our rooted congregation, gloom-arrayed,
By that great sad voice deep and full were swayed:—

O melancholy Brothers, dark, dark, dark!
O battling in black floods without an ark!
  O spectral wanderers of unholy Night!
My soul hath bled for you these sunless years,
With bitter blood-drops running down like tears:
  Oh dark, dark, dark, withdrawn from joy and light!

My heart is sick with anguish for your bale;
Your woe hath been my anguish; yea, I quail
  And perish in your perishing unblest.
And I have searched the highths and depths, the scope
Of all our universe, with desperate hope
  To find some solace for your wild unrest.

And now at last authentic word I bring,
Witnessed by every dead and living thing;
  Good tidings of great joy for you, for all:
There is no God; no Fiend with names divine
Made us and tortures us; if we must pine,
  It is to satiate no Being's gall.

It was the dark delusion of a dream,
That living Person conscious and supreme,
  Whom we must curse for cursing us with life;
Whom we must curse because the life he gave
Could not be buried in the quiet grave,
  Could not be killed by poison or the knife.

This little life is all we must endure,
The grave's most holy peace is ever sure,
  We fall asleep and never wake again;
Nothing is of us but the mouldering flesh,
Whose elements dissolve and merge afresh
  In earth, air, water, plants, and other men.

We finish thus; and all our wretched race
Shall finish with its cycle, and give place
  To other beings with their own time-doom:
Infinite æons ere our kind began;
Infinite æons after the last man
  Has joined the mammoth in earth's tomb and womb.

We bow down to the universal laws,
Which never had for man a special clause
  Of cruelty or kindness, love or hate:
If toads and vultures are obscene to sight,
If tigers burn with beauty and with might,
  Is it by favour or by wrath of Fate?

All substance lives and struggles evermore
Through countless shapes continually at war,
  By countless interactions interknit:
If one is born a certain day on earth,
All times and forces tended to that birth,
  Not all the world could change or hinder it.

I find no hint throughout the Universe
Of good or ill, of blessing or of curse;
  I find alone Necessity Supreme;
With infinite Mystery, abysmal, dark,
Unlighted ever by the faintest spark
  For us the flitting shadows of a dream.

O Brothers of sad lives! they are so brief;
A few short years must bring us all relief:
  Can we not bear these years of laboring breath?
But if you would not this poor life fulfil,
Lo, you are free to end it when you will,
  Without the fear of waking after death.—

The organ-like vibrations of his voice
  Thrilled through the vaulted aisles and died away;
The yearning of the tones which bade rejoice
  Was sad and tender as a requiem lay:
Our shadowy congregation rested still
As brooding on that "End it when you will."

XV.

Wherever men are gathered, all the air
  Is charged with human feeling, human thought;
Each shout and cry and laugh, each curse and prayer,
  Are into its vibrations surely wrought;
Unspoken passion, wordless meditation,
Are breathed into it with our respiration;
  It is with our life fraught and overfraught.

So that no man there breathes earth's simple breath,
  As if alone on mountains or wide seas;
But nourishes warm life or hastens death
  With joys and sorrows, health and foul disease,
Wisdom and folly, good and evil labours,
Incessant of his multitudinous neighbors;
  He in his turn affecting all of these.

That City's atmosphere is dark and dense,
  Although not many exiles wander there,
With many a potent evil influence,
  Each adding poison to the poisoned air;
Infections of unutterable sadness,
Infections of incalculable madness,
  Infections of incurable despair.

XVI.

Our shadowy congregation rested still,
  As musing on that message we had heard
And brooding on that "End it when you will;"
  Perchance awaiting yet some other word;
When keen as lightning through a muffled sky
Sprang forth a shrill and lamentable cry:—

The man speaks sooth, alas! the man speaks sooth:
  We have no personal life beyond the grave;
There is no God; Fate knows nor wrath nor ruth:
  Can I find here the comfort which I crave?

In all eternity I had one chance,
  One few years' term of gracious human life:
The splendours of the intellect's advance,
  The sweetness of the home with babes and wife;

The social pleasures with their genial wit:
  The fascination of the worlds of art,

The glories of the worlds of nature, lit
  By large imagination's glowing heart;

The rapture of mere being, full of health;
  The careless childhood and the ardent youth,
The strenuous manhood winning various wealth,
  The reverend age serene with life's long truth:

All the sublime prerogatives of Man;
  The storied memories of the times of old,
The patient tracking of the world's great plan
  Through sequences and changes myriadfold.

This chance was never offered me before;
  For me this infinite Past is blank and dumb:
This chance recurreth never, nevermore;
  Blank, blank for me the infinite To-come.

And this sole chance was frustrate from my birth,
  A mockery, a delusion; and my breath
Of noble human life upon this earth
  So racks me that I sigh for senseless death.

My wine of life is poison mixed with gall,
  My noonday passes in a nightmare dream,
I worse than lose the years which are my all:
  What can console me for the loss supreme?

Speak not of comfort where no comfort is,
  Speak not at all: can words make foul things fair?
Our life's a cheat, our death a black abyss:
  Hush and be mute envisaging despair.—

This vehement voice came from the northern aisle
  Rapid and shrill to its abrupt harsh close;
And none gave answer for a certain while,
  For words must shrink from these most wordless woes;
At last the pulpit speaker simply said,
With humid eyes and thoughtful drooping head:—

My Brother, my poor Brothers, it is thus;
This life itself holds nothing good for us,
  But ends soon and nevermore can be;
And we knew nothing of it ere our birth,
And shall know nothing when consigned to earth:
  I ponder these thoughts and they comfort me.

XVII.

How the moon triumphs through the endless nights!
How the stars throb and glitter as they wheel
Their thick processions of supernal lights
Around the blue vault obdurate as steel!
And men regard with passionate awe and yearning
The mighty marching and the golden burning,
And think the heavens respond to what they feel.

Boats gliding like dark shadows of a dream
Are glorified from vision as they pass
The quivering moonbridge on the deep black stream;
Cold windows kindle their dead glooms of glass
To restless crystals; cornice dome and column
Emerge from chaos in the splendour solemn;
Like faery lakes gleam lawns of dewy grass.

With such a living light these dead eyes shine,
These eyes of sightless heaven, that as we gaze
We read a pity, tremulous, divine,
Or cold majestic scorn in their pure rays:
Fond man! they are not haughty, are not tender;
There is no heart or mind in all their splendour,
They thread mere puppets all their marvellous maze.

If we could near them with the flight unflown,
We should but find them worlds as sad as this,
Or suns all self-consuming like our own
Enringed by planet worlds as much amiss:
They wax and wane through fusion and confusion;
The spheres eternal are a grand illusion,
The empyréan is a void abyss.

XVIII.

I wandered in a suburb of the north,
And reached a spot whence three close lanes led down,
Beneath thick trees and hedgerows winding forth
Like deep brook channels, deep and dark and lown:
The air above was wan with misty light,
The dull grey south showed one vague blur of white.

I took the left-hand path and slowly trod
Its earthen footpath, brushing as I went
The humid leafage; and my feet were shod
With heavy languor, and my frame downbent,

With infinite sleepless weariness outworn,
So many nights I thus had paced forlorn.

After a hundred steps I grew aware
  Of something crawling in the lane below;
It seemed a wounded creature prostrate there
  That sobbed with pangs in making progress slow,
The hind limbs stretched to push, the fore limbs then
To drag; for it would die in its own den.

But coming level with it I discerned
  That it had been a man; for at my tread
It stopped in its sore travail and half-turned,
  Leaning upon its right, and raised its head,
And with the left hand twitched back as in ire
Long grey unreverend locks befouled with mire.

A haggard filthy face with bloodshot eyes,
  An infamy for manhood to behold.
He gasped all trembling, What, you want my prize?
  You leave, to rob me, wine and lust and gold
And all that men go mad upon, since you
Have traced my sacred secret of the clue?

You think that I am weak and must submit
  Yet I but scratch you with this poisoned blade,
And you are dead as if I clove with it
  That false fierce greedy heart. Betrayed! betrayed!
I fling this phial if you seek to pass,
And you are forthwith shrivelled up like grass.

And then with sudden change, Take thought! take thought!
  Have pity on me! it is mine alone.
If you could find, it would avail you naught;
  Seek elsewhere on the pathway of your own:
For who of mortal or immortal race
The lifetrack of another can retrace?

Did you but know my agony and toil!
  Two lanes diverge up yonder from this lane;
My thin blood marks the long length of their soil;
  Such clue I left, who sought my clue in vain:
My hands and knees are worn both flesh and bone;
I cannot move but with continual moan.

But I am in the very way at last
  To find the long-lost broken golden thread
Which unites my present with my past,

If you but go your own way. And I said,
I will retire as soon as you have told
Whereunto leadeth this lost thread of gold.

And so you know it not! he hissed with scorn;
I feared you, imbecile! It leads me back
From this accursed night without a morn,
And through the deserts which have else no track,
And through vast wastes of horror-haunted time,
To Eden innocence in Eden's clime:

And I become a nursling soft and pure,
An infant cradled on its mother's knee,
Without a past, love-cherished and secure;
Which if it saw this loathsome present Me,
Would plunge its face into the pillowing breast,
And scream abhorrence hard to lull to rest.

He turned to grope; and I retiring brushed
Thin shreds of gossamer from off my face,
And mused, His life would grow, the germ uncrushed;
He should to antenatal night retrace,
And hide his elements in that large womb
Beyond the reach of man-evolving Doom.

And even thus, what weary way were planned,
To seek oblivion through the far-off gate
Of birth, when that of death is close at hand!
For this is law, if law there be in Fate:
What never has been, yet may have its when;
The thing which has been, never is again.

XIX.

The mighty river flowing dark and deep,
With ebb and flood from the remote sea-tides
Vague-sounding through the City's sleepless sleep,
Is named the River of the Suicides;
For night by night some lorn wretch overweary,
And shuddering from the future yet more dreary,
Within its cold secure oblivion hides.

One plunges from a bridge's parapet,
As if by some blind and sudden frenzy hurled;
Another wades in slow with purpose set
Until the waters are above him furled;
Another in a boat with dreamlike motion

Glides drifting down into the desert ocean,
  To starve or sink from out the desert world.

They perish from their suffering surely thus,
  For none beholding them attempts to save,
The while each thinks how soon, solicitous,
  He may seek refuge in the self-same wave;
Some hour when tired of ever-vain endurance
Impatience will forerun the sweet assurance
  Of perfect peace eventual in the grave.

When this poor tragic-farce has palled us long,
  Why actors and spectators do we stay?—
To fill our so-short roles out right or wrong;
  To see what shifts are yet in the dull play
For our illusion; to refrain from grieving
Dear foolish friends by our untimely leaving:
  But those asleep at home, how blest are they!

Yet it is but for one night after all:
  What matters one brief night of dreary pain?
When after it the weary eyelids fall
  Upon the weary eyes and wasted brain;
And all sad scenes and thoughts and feelings vanish
In that sweet sleep no power can ever banish,
  That one best sleep which never wakes again.

XX.

I sat me weary on a pillar's base,
  And leaned against the shaft; for broad moonlight
O'erflowed the peacefulness of cloistered space,
  A shore of shadow slanting from the right:
The great cathedral's western front stood there,
A wave-worn rock in that calm sea of air.

Before it, opposite my place of rest,
  Two figures faced each other, large, austere;
A couchant sphinx in shadow to the breast,
  An angel standing in the moonlight clear;
So mighty by magnificence of form,
They were not dwarfed beneath that mass enorm.

Upon the cross-hilt of the naked sword
  The angel's hands, as prompt to smite, were held;
His vigilant intense regard was poured
  Upon the creature placidly unquelled,

Whose front was set at level gaze which took
No heed of aught, a solemn trance-like look.

And as I pondered these opposèd shapes
  My eyelids sank in stupor, that dull swoon
Which drugs and with a leaden mantle drapes
  The outworn to worse weariness. But soon
A sharp and clashing noise the stillness broke,
And from the evil lethargy I woke.

The angel's wings had fallen, stone on stone,
  And lay there shattered; hence the sudden sound:
A warrior leaning on his sword alone
  Now watched the sphinx with that regard profound;
The sphinx unchanged looked forthright, as aware
Of nothing in the vast abyss of air.

Again I sank in that repose unsweet,
  Again a clashing noise my slumber rent;
The warrior's sword lay broken at his feet:
  An unarmed man with raised hands impotent
Now stood before the sphinx, which ever kept
Such mien as if with open eyes it slept.

My eyelids sank in spite of wonder grown;
  A louder crash upstartled me in dread:
The man had fallen forward, stone on stone,
  And lay there shattered, with his trunkless head
Between the monster's large quiescent paws,
Beneath its grand front changeless as life's laws.

The moon had circled westward full and bright,
  And made the temple-front a mystic dream,
And bathed the whole enclosure with its light,
  The sworded angel's wrecks, the sphinx supreme:
I pondered long that cold majestic face
Whose vision seemed of infinite void space.

XXI.

Anear the centre of that northern crest
  Stands out a level upland bleak and bare,
From which the city east and south and west
  Sinks gently in long waves; and thronèd there
An Image sits, stupendous, superhuman,
The bronze colossus of a winged Woman,
  Upon a graded granite base foursquare.

Low-seated she leans forward massively,
With cheek on clenched left hand, the forearm's might
Erect, its elbow on her rounded knee;
Across a clasped book in her lap the right
Upholds a pair of compasses; she gazes
With full set eyes, but wandering in thick mazes
Of sombre thought beholds no outward sight.

Words cannot picture her; but all men know
That solemn sketch the pure sad artist wrought
Three centuries and threescore years ago,
With phantasies of his peculiar thought:
The instruments of carpentry and science
Scattered about her feet, in strange alliance
With the keen wolf-hound sleeping undistraught;

Scales, hour-glass, bell, and magic-square above;
The grave and solid infant perched beside,
With open winglets that might bear a dove,
Intent upon its tablets, heavy-eyed;
Her folded wings as of a mighty eagle,
But all too impotent to lift the regal
Robustness of her earth-born strength and pride;

And with those wings, and that light wreath which seems
To mock her grand head and the knotted frown
Of forehead charged with baleful thoughts and dreams,
The household bunch of keys, the housewife's gown
Voluminous, indented, and yet rigid
As if a shell of burnished metal frigid,
The feet thick-shod to tread all weakness down;

The comet hanging o'er the waste dark seas,
The massy rainbow curved in front of it
Beyond the village with the masts and trees;
The snaky imp, dog-headed, from the Pit,
Bearing upon its batlike leathern pinions
Her name unfolded in the sun's dominions,
The "MELENCOLIA" that transcends all wit.

Thus has the artist copied her, and thus
Surrounded to expound her form sublime,
Her fate heroic and calamitous;
Fronting the dreadful mysteries of Time,
Unvanquished in defeat and desolation,
Undaunted in the hopeless conflagration
Of the day setting on her baffled prime.

Baffled and beaten back she works on still,
  Weary and sick of soul she works the more,
Sustained by her indomitable will:
  The hands shall fashion and the brain shall pore,
And all her sorrow shall be turned to labour,
Till Death the friend-foe piercing with his sabre
  That mighty heart of hearts ends bitter war.

But as if blacker night could dawn on night,
  With tenfold gloom on moonless night unstarred,
A sense more tragic than defeat and blight,
  More desperate than strife with hope debarred,
More fatal than the adamantine Never
Encompassing her passionate endeavour,
  Dawns glooming in her tenebrous regard:

To sense that every struggle brings defeat
  Because Fate holds no prize to crown success;
That all the oracles are dumb or cheat
  Because they have no secret to express;
That none can pierce the vast black veil uncertain
Because there is no light beyond the curtain;
  That all is vanity and nothingness.

Titanic from her high throne in the north,
  That City's sombre Patroness and Queen,
In bronze sublimity she gazes forth
  Over her Capital of teen and threne,
Over the river with its isles and bridges,
The marsh and moorland, to the stern rock-bridges,
  Confronting them with a coeval mien.

The moving moon and stars from east to west
  Circle before her in the sea of air;
Shadows and gleams glide round her solemn rest.
  Her subjects often gaze up to her there:
The strong to drink new strength of iron endurance,
The weak new terrors; all, renewed assurance
  And confirmation of the old despair.

1870-1874.

TO OUR LADIES OF DEATH *

Tired with all these, for restful death I cry.
—SHAKESPEARE: *Sonnet* 66.

Weary of erring in this desert Life,
Weary of hoping hopes for ever vain,
Weary of struggling in all-sterile strife,
Weary of thought which maketh nothing plain,
I close my eyes and calm my panting breath,
And pray to Thee, O ever-quiet Death!
To come and soothe away my bitter pain.

The strong shall strive,—may they be victors crowned;
The wise still seek,—may they at length find Truth;
The young still hope,—may purest love be found
To make their age more glorious than their youth.
For me; my brain is weak, my heart is cold,
My hope and faith long dead; my life but bold
In jest and laugh to parry hateful ruth.

Over me pass the days and months and years
Like squadrons and battalions of the foe
Trampling with thoughtless thrusts and alien jeers
Over a wounded soldier lying low:
He grips his teeth, or flings them words of scorn
To mar their triumph: but the while, outworn,
Inwardly craves for death to end his woe.

Thus I, in secret, call, O Death! to Thee,
Thou Youngest of the solemn Sisterhood,
Thou Gentlest of the mighty Sisters Three
Whom I have known so well since first endued
By Love and Grief with vision to discern
What spiritual life doth throb and burn
Through all our world, with evil powers and good.

The Three whom I have known so long, so well,
By intimate communion, face to face,
In every mood, of Earth, of Heaven, of Hell,
In every season and in every place,
That joy of Life has ceased to visit me,
As one estranged by powerful witchery,
Infatuate in a Siren's weird embrace.

* The Three Ladies suggested by the sublime sisterhood of Our Ladies of Sorrow, in the "Suspiria de Profundis" of De Quincey.

First Thou, O priestess, prophetess, and queen,
  Our Lady of Beatitudes, first Thou:
Of mighty stature, of seraphic mien,
  Upon the tablet of whose broad white brow
Unvanquishable Truth is written clear,
The secret of the mystery of our sphere,
  The regnant word of the Eternal Now.

Thou standest garmented in purest white;
  But from thy shoulders wings of power half-spread
Invest thy form with such miraculous light
  As dawn may clothe the earth with: and, instead
Of any jewel-kindled golden crown,
The glory of thy long hair flowing down
  Is dazzling noonday sunshine round thy head.

Upon a sword thy left hand resteth calm,
  A naked sword, two-edged and long and straight;
A branch of olive with a branch of palm
  Thy right hand proffereth to hostile Fate.
The shining plumes that clothe thy feet are bound
By knotted strings, as if to tread the ground
  With weary steps when thou wouldst soar elate.

Twin heavens uplifted to the heavens, thine eyes
  Are solemn with unutterable thought
And love and aspiration; yet there lies
  Within their light eternal sadness, wrought
By hope deferred and baffled tenderness:
Of all the souls whom thou dost love and bless,
  How few revere and love thee as they ought!

Thou leadest heroes from their warfare here
  To nobler fields where grander crowns are won;
Thou leadest sages from this twilight sphere
  To cloudless heavens and an unsetting sun;
Thou leadest saints into that purer air
Whose breath is spiritual life and prayer:
  Yet, lo! they seek thee not, but fear and shun!

Thou takest to thy most maternal breast
  Young children from the desert of this earth,
Ere sin hath stained their souls, or grief opprest,
  And bearest them unto an heavenly birth,
To be the Vestals of God's Fane above:
And yet their kindred moan against thy love,
  With wild and selfish moans in bitter dearth.

Most holy Spirit, first Self-conqueror;
  Thou Victress over Time and Destiny
And Evil, in the all-deciding war
  So fierce, so long, so dreadful!—Would that me
Thou hadst upgathered in my life's pure morn!
Unworthy then, less worthy now, forlorn,
  I dare not, Gracious Mother, call on Thee.

Next Thou, O sibyl, sorceress and queen,
  Our Lady of Annihilation, Thou!
Of mighty stature, of demoniac mien;
  Upon whose swarthy face and livid brow
Are graven deeply anguish, malice, scorn,
Strength ravaged by unrest, resolve forlorn
  Of any hope, dazed pride that will not bow.

Thy form is clothed with wings of iron gloom;
  But round about thee, like a chain, is rolled,
Cramping the sway of every mighty plume,
  A stark constringent serpent fold on fold:
Of its two heads, one sting is in thy brain,
The other in thy heart; their venom-pain
  Like fire distilling through thee uncontrolled.

A rod of serpents wieldeth thy right hand;
  Thy left a cup of raging fire, whose light
Burns lurid on thyself as thou dost stand;
  Thy lidless eyes tenebriously bright;
Thy wings, thy vesture, thy dishevelled hair
Dark as the Grave; thou statue of Despair,
  Thou Night essential radiating night.

Thus have I seen thee in thine actual form;
  Not thus can see thee those whom thou dost sway,
Inscrutable Enchantress: young and warm,
  Pard-beautiful and brilliant, ever gay;
Thy cup the very Wine of Life, thy rod
The wand of more voluptuous spells than God
  Can wield in Heaven; thus charmest thou thy prey.

The selfish, fatuous, proud, and pitiless,
  All who have falsified life's royal trust;
The strong whose strength hath basked in idleness,
  The great heart given up to worldly lust,
The great mind destitute of moral faith;
Thou scourgest down to Night and utter Death,
  Or penal spheres of retribution just.

O mighty Spirit, fraudful and malign,
  Demon of madness and perversity!
The evil passions which may make me thine
  Are not yet irrepressible in me;
And I have pierced thy mask of riant youth,
And seen thy form in all its hideous truth:
  I will not, Dreadful Mother, call on Thee.

Last Thou, retirèd nun and throneless queen,
  Our Lady of Oblivion, last Thou:
Of human stature, of abstracted mien;
  Upon whose pallid face and drooping brow
Are shadowed melancholy dreams of Doom,
And deep absorption into silent gloom,
  And weary bearing of the heavy Now.

Thou art all shrouded in a gauzy veil
  Sombrous and cloudlike; all, except that face
Of subtle loveliness though weirdly pale.
  Thy soft, slow-gliding footsteps leave no trace,
And stir no sound. Thy drooping hands infold
Their frail white fingers; and, unconscious, hold
  A poppy-wreath, thine anodyne of grace.

Thy hair is like a twilight round thy head:
  Thine eyes are shadowed wells, from Lethe-stream
With drowsy subterranean waters fed;
  Obscurely deep, without a stir or gleam;
The gazer drinks in from them with his gaze
An opiate charm to curtain all his days,
  A passive languor of oblivious dream.

Thou hauntest twilight regions, and the trance
  Of moonless nights when stars are few and wan:
Within black woods; or over the expanse
  Of desert seas abysmal; or upon
Old solitary shores whose populous graves
Are rocked in rest by ever-moaning waves;
  Or through vast ruined cities still and lone.

The weak, the weary, and the desolate,
  The poor, the mean, the outcast, the opprest,
All trodden down beneath the march of Fate,
  Thou gatherest, loving Sister, to thy breast,
Soothing their pain and weariness asleep;
Then in thy hidden Dreamland hushed and deep
  Dost lay them, shrouded in eternal rest.

O sweetest Sister, and sole Patron Saint
Of all the humble eremites who flee
From out life's crowded tumult, stunned and faint,
To seek a stern and lone tranquillity
In Libyan wastes of time: my hopeless life
With famished yearning craveth rest from strife;
Therefore, thou Restful One, I call on Thee!

Take me, and lull me into perfect sleep;
Down, down, far-hidden in thy duskiest cave;
While all the clamorous years above me sweep
Unheard, or, like the voice of seas that rave
On far-off coasts, but murmuring o'er my trance,
A dim vast monotone, that shall enhance
The restful rapture of the inviolate grave.

Upgathered thus in thy divine embrace,
Upon mine eyes thy soft mesmeric hand,
While wreaths of opiate odour interlace
About my pulseless brow; babe-pure and bland,
Passionless, senseless, thoughtless, let me dream
Some ever-slumbrous, never-varying theme,
Within the shadow of thy Timeless Land.

That when I thus have drunk my inmost fill
Of perfect peace, I may arise renewed;
In soul and body, intellect and will,
Equal to cope with Life whate'er its mood;
To sway its storm and energise its calm;
Through rhythmic years evolving like a psalm
Of infinite love and faith and sanctitude.

But if this cannot be, no less I cry,
Come, lead me with thy terrorless control
Down to our Mother's bosom, there to die
By abdication of my separate soul:
So shall this single, self-impelling piece
Of mechanism from lone labour cease,
Resolving into union with the Whole.

Our Mother feedeth thus our little life,
That we in turn may feed her with our death:
The great Sea sways, one interwoven strife,
Wherefrom the Sun exhales a subtle breath,
To float the heavens sublime in form and hue,
Then turning cold and dark in order due
Rain weeping back to swell the Sea beneath.

One part of me shall feed a little worm,
  And it a bird on which a man may feed;
One lime the mould, one nourish insect-sperm;
  One thrill sweet grass, one pulse in bitter weed;
This swell a fruit, and that evolve in air;
Another trickle to a springlet's lair,
  Another paint a daisy on the mead:

With cosmic interchange of parts for all,
  Through all the modes of being numberless
Of every element, as may befall.
  And if earth's general soul hath consciousness,
Their new life must with strange new joy be thrilled,
Of perfect law all perfectly fulfilled;
  No sin, no fear, no failure, no excess.

Weary of living isolated life,
  Weary of hoping hopes for ever vain,
Weary of struggling in all-sterile strife,
  Weary of thought which maketh nothing plain,
I close my eyes and hush my panting breath,
And yearn for Thee, divinely tranquil Death,
  To come and soothe away my bitter pain.

1861.

IN THE ROOM

Ceste insigne fable et tragicque comedie.
—Rabelais.

I.

The sun was down, and twilight grey
  Filled half the air; but in the room,
Whose curtain had been drawn all day,
  The twilight was a dusky gloom:
Which seemed at first as still as death,
  And void; but was indeed all rife
With subtle thrills, the pulse and breath
  Of multitudinous lower life.

II.

In their abrupt and headlong way
  Bewildered flies for light had dashed
Against the curtain all the day,
  And now slept wintrily abashed;
And nimble mice slept, wearied out
  With such a double night's uproar;
But solid beetles crawled about
  The chilly hearth and naked floor.

III.

And so throughout the twilight hour
  That vaguely murmurous hush and rest
There brooded; and beneath its power
  Life throbbing held its throbs suppresst:
Until the thin-voiced mirror sighed,
  I am all blurred with dust and damp,
So long ago the clear day died,
  So long has gleamed nor fire nor lamp.

IV.

Whereon the curtain murmured back,
  Some change is on us, good or ill;
Behind me and before is black
  As when those human things lie still:
But I have seen the darkness grow
  As grows the daylight every morn;
Have felt out there long shine and glow,
  In here long chilly dusk forlorn.

V.

The cupboard grumbled with a groan,
  Each new day worse starvation brings:
Since *he* came here I have not known
  Or sweets or cates or wholesome things:
But now! a pinch of meal, a crust,
  Throughout the week is all I get.
I am so empty; it is just
  As when they said we were to let.

VI.

What is become, then, of our Man?
  The petulant old glass exclaimed;
If all this time he slumber can,
  He really ought to be ashamed.
I wish we had our Girl again,
  So gay and busy, bright and fair:
The girls are better than these men,
  Who only for their dull selves care.

VII.

It is so many hours ago—
  The lamp and fire were both alight—
I saw him pacing to and fro,
  Perturbing restlessly the night.
His face was pale to give one fear,
  His eyes when lifted looked too bright;
He muttered; what, I could not hear:
  Bad words though; something was not right.

VIII.

The table said, He wrote so long
  That I grew weary of his weight;
The pen kept up a cricket song,
  It ran and ran at such a rate:
And in the longer pauses he
  With both his folded arms downpressed
And stared as one who does not see,
  Or sank his head upon his breast.

IX.

The fire-grate said, I am as cold
  As if I never had a blaze;
The few dead cinders here I hold,
  I held unburned for days and days.
Last night he made them flare; but still
  What good did all his writing do?
Among my ashes curl and thrill
  Thin ghosts of all those papers too.

X.

The table answered, Not quite all;
He saved and folded up one sheet,
And sealed it fast, and let it fall;
And here it lies now white and neat.
Whereon the letter's whisper came,
My writing is closed up too well;
Outside there's not a single name,
And who should read me I can't tell.

XI.

The mirror sneered with scornful spite,
(That ancient crack which spoiled her looks
Had marred her temper), Write and write!
And read those stupid, worn-out books!
That's all he does, read, write, and read,
And smoke that nasty pipe which stinks:
He never takes the slightest heed
How any of us feels or thinks.

XII.

But Lucy fifty times a day
Would come and smile here in my face,
Adjust a tress that curled astray,
Or tie a ribbon with more grace:
She looked so young and fresh and fair,
She blushed with such a charming bloom,
It did one good to see her there,
And brightened all things in the room.

XIII.

She did not sit hours stark and dumb
As pale as moonshine by the lamp;
To lie in bed when day was come,
And leave us curtained chill and damp.
She slept away the dreary dark,
And rose to greet the pleasant morn;
And sang as gaily as a lark
While busy as the flies sun-born.

XIV.

And how she loved us every one;
And dusted this and mended that,
With trills and laughs and freaks of fun,
And tender scoldings in her chat!
And then her bird, that sang as shrill
As she sang sweet; her darling flowers
That grew there in the window-sill,
Where she would sit at work for hours.

XV.

It was not much she ever wrote;
  Her fingers had good work to do;
Say, once a week a pretty note;
  And very long it took her too.
And little more she read, I wis;
  Just now and then a pictured sheet,
Besides those letters she would kiss
  And croon for hours, they were so sweet.

XVI.

She had her friends too, blithe young girls,
  Who whispered, babbled, laughed, caressed,
And romped and danced with dancing curls,
  And gave our life a joyous zest.
But with this dullard, glum and sour,
  Not one of all his fellow-men
Has ever passed a social hour;
  We might be in some wild beast's den.

XVII.

This long tirade aroused the bed,
  Who spoke in deep and ponderous bass,
Befitting that calm life he led,
  As if firm-rooted in his place:
In broad majestic bulk alone,
  As in thrice venerable age,
He stood at once the royal throne,
  The monarch, the experienced sage:

XVIII.

I know what is and what has been;
  Not anything to me comes strange,
Who in so many years have seen
  And lived through every kind of change.
I know when men are good or bad,
  When well or ill, he slowly said;
When sad or glad, when sane or mad,
  And when they sleep alive or dead.

XIX.

At this last word of solemn lore
  A tremor circled through the gloom,
As if a crash upon the floor
  Had jarred and shaken all the room:
For nearly all the listening things
  Were old and worn, and knew what curse
Of violent change death often brings,
  From good to bad, from bad to worse;

XX.

They get to know each other well,
  To feel at home and settled down;
Death bursts among them like a shell,
  And strews them over all the town.
The bed went on, This man who lies
  Upon me now is stark and cold;
He will not any more arise,
  And do the things he did of old.

XXI.

But we shall have short peace or rest;
  For soon up here will come a rout,
And nail him in a queer long chest,
  And carry him like luggage out.
They will be muffled all in black,
  And whisper much, and sigh and weep:
But he will never more come back,
  And some one else in me must sleep.

XXII.

Thereon a little phial shrilled,
  Here empty on the chair I lie:
I heard one say, as I was filled,
  With half of this a man would die.
The man there drank me with slow breath,
  And murmured, Thus ends barren strife:
O sweeter, thou cold wine of death,
  Than ever sweet warm wine of life.

XXIII.

One of my cousins long ago,
  A little thing, the mirror said,
Was carried to a couch to show,
  Whether a man was really dead.
Two great improvements marked the case:
  He did not blur her with his breath,
His many-wrinkled, twitching face
  Was smooth old ivory: verdict, Death.—

XXIV.

It lay, the lowest thing there, lulled
  Sweet-sleep-like in corruption's truce;
The form whose purpose was annulled,
  While all the other shapes meant use.
It lay, the *he* become now *it*,
  Unconscious of the deep disgrace,
Unanxious how its parts might flit
  Through what new forms in time and space.

XXV.

It lay and preached, as dumb things do,
  More powerfully than tongues can prate;
Though life be torture through and through,
  Man is but weak to plain of fate:
The drear path crawls on drearier still
  To wounded feet and hopeless breast?
Well, he can lie down when he will,
  And straight all ends in endless rest.

XXVI.

And while the black night nothing saw,
  And till the cold morn came at last,
That old bed held the room in awe
  With tales of its experience vast.
It thrilled the gloom; it told such tales
  Of human sorrows and delights,
Of fever moans and infant wails,
  Of births and deaths and bridal nights.

1867-68.

SUNDAY AT HAMPSTEAD

(AN IDLE IDYLL BY A VERY HUMBLE MEMBER
OF THE GREAT AND NOBLE LONDON MOB.)

I.

This is the Heath of Hampstead,
There is the dome of Saint Paul's;
Beneath, on the serried house-tops,
A chequered lustre falls:

And the mighty city of London,
Under the clouds and the light,
Seems a low wet beach, half shingle,
With a few sharp rocks upright.

Here will we sit, my darling,
And dream an hour away:
The donkeys are hurried and worried,
But we are not donkeys to-day:

Through all the weary week, dear,
We toil in the murk down there,
Tied to a desk and a counter,
A patient stupid pair!

But on Sunday we slip our tether,
And away from the smoke and the smirch;
Too grateful to God for His Sabbath
To shut its hours in a church.

Away to the green, green country,
Under the open sky;
Where the earth's sweet breath is incense
And the lark sings psalms on high.

On Sunday we're Lord and Lady,
With ten times the love and glee
Of those pale and languid rich ones
Who are always and never free.

They drawl and stare and simper,
So fine and cold and staid,
Like exquisite waxwork figures
That must be kept in the shade:

We can laugh out loud when merry,
We can romp at kiss-in-the-ring,
We can take our beer at a public,
We can loll on the grass and sing. . . .

Would you grieve very much, my darling,
If all yon low wet shore
Were drowned by a mighty flood-tide,
And we never toiled there more?

Wicked?—there is no sin, dear,
In an idle dreamer's head;
He turns the world topsy-turvy
To prove that his soul's not dead.

I am sinking, sinking, sinking;
It is hard to sit upright!
Your lap is the softest pillow!
Good night, my Love, good night!

II.

How your eyes dazzle down into my soul!
  I drink and drink of their deep violet wine,
And ever thirst the more, although my whole
  Dazed being whirls in drunkenness divine.

Pout down your lips from that bewildering smile,
  And kiss me for the interruption, Sweet!
I had escaped you: floating for awhile
  In that far cloud ablaze with living heat:

I floated with it through the solemn skies,
  I melted with it up the Crystal Sea
Into the Heaven of Heavens; and shut my eyes
  To feel eternal rest enfolding me. . . .

Well, I prefer one tyrannous girl down here,
  You jealous violet-eyed Bewitcher, you!
To being lord in Mohammed's seventh sphere
  Of meekest houris threescore ten and two!

III.

Was it hundreds of years ago, my Love,
  Was it thousands of miles away,
That two poor creatures we know, my Love,
  Were toiling day by day;
    Were toiling weary, weary,
    With many myriads more,
    In a City dark and dreary
    On a sullen river's shore?

Was it truly a fact or a dream, my Love?
  I think my brain still reels,
And my ears still throbbing seem, my Love,
  With the rush and the clang of wheels;
    Of a vast machinery roaring
    For ever in skyless gloom;
    Where the poor slaves peace imploring,
    Found peace alone in the tomb.

Was it hundreds of years ago, my Love,
  Was it thousands of miles away?
Or was it a dream to show, my Love,
  The rapture of to-day?
    This day of holy splendour,
    This Sabbath of rich rest,
    Wherein to God we render
    All praise by being blest.

IV.

Eight of us promised to meet here
And tea together at five:
And—who would ever believe it?—
We are the first to arrive!

Oh, shame on us, my darling;
It is a monstrous crime
To make a tryst with *others*
And be before our time!

Lizzie is off with William,
Quite happy for her part;
Our sugar in her pocket,
And the sweet love in her heart.

Mary and Dick so grandly
Parade suburban streets;
His waistcoat and her bonnet
Proving the best of treats.

And Fanny plagues big Robert
With tricks of the wildest glee:
O Fanny, *you'll* get in hot water
If you do not bring us our tea!

Why, bless me, look at that table,
Every one of them there!—
"Ha, here at last we have them,
The always behindhand pair!

"When the last trumpet-solo
Strikes up instead of the lark,
They'll turn in their sleep just grunting
Who's up so soon in the dark?"

Babble and gabble, you rabble,
A thousand in full yell!
And this is your Tower of Babel,
This not-to-be-finished Hotel. *

"You should see it in the drawing,
You'd think a Palace they make,
Like the one in the *Lady of Lyons*,
With this pond for the lovely lake!"

"I wish it wasn't Sunday,
There's no amusement at all:
Who was here Hot-cross-bun-day?
We had such an open-air ball!

"The bands played polkas, waltzes,
Quadrilles; it was glorious fun!
And each gentleman gave them a penny
After each dance was done."

"Mary is going to chapel,
And what takes her there, do you guess?
Her sweet little duck of a bonnet,
And her new second-hand silk dress."

"*We* went to Church one Sunday,
But felt we had no right there;

* (Since finished, in a fashion. The verses were written in 1863.)

For it's only a place for the grand folk
Who come in a carriage and pair.

"And I laughed out loud,—it was shameful!
But Fanny said, *Oh, what lives!*
He must have been clever, the rascal,
To manage seven hundred wives!"

"Suppose we play Hunt-the-Slipper?"
"We can't, there's the crinoline!"—"Phew!
Bother it, always a nuisance!"
"Hoop-de-dooden-do!"

"I think I've seen all the girls here,
About a thousand, or more;
But none of them half so pretty
As our own loving four."

"*Thank* you! and I've been listening
To lots of the men, the knaves;
But none of them half such humbugs
As our devoted slaves."

"Do you see those purple flushes?
The sun will set in state:
Up all! we must cross to the heath, friends,
Before it gets too late.

"We will couch in the fern together,
And watch for the moon and the stars;
And the slim tree-tops will be lighted,
So the boys may light their cigars.

"And while the sunset glory
Burns down in crimson and gold,
LAZY shall tell us a story
Of his wonderful times of old."

V.

Ten thousand years ago, *("No more than that?")*
Ten thousand years, *("The age of Robert's hat!"*
"Silence, you gods!"—"Pinch Fanny!"—"Now we're good.")
This place where we are sitting was a wood,
Savage and desert save for one rude home
Of wattles plastered with stiff clay and loam;
And here, in front, upon the grassy mire
Four naked squaws were squatted round a fire:

Then four tall naked wild men crushing through
The tangled underwood came into view;
Two of them bent beneath a mighty boar,
The third was gashed and bleeding, number four
Strutted full-drest in war-paint, *("That was Dick!")*
Blue of a devilish pattern laid on thick.
The squaws jumped up to roast the carcass whole;
The braves sank silent, stark 'gainst root and bole.
The meat half-done, they tore it and devoured,
Sullenly ravenous; the women cowered
Until their lords had finished, then partook.
Mist rose; all crept into their cabin-nook,
And staked the mouth; the floor was one broad bed
Of rushes dried with fox and bearskins spread.
Wolves howled and wild cats wailed; they snored; and so
The long night passed, shedding a storm of snow;
This very night ten thousand years ago.

VI.

Ten thousand years before, *("Come, draw it mild!*
Don't waste Conk-ology like that, my child!")
From where we sit to the horizon's bound
A level brilliant plain was spread all round,
As level and as brilliant as a sea
Under the burning sun; high as your knee
Aflame with flowers, yellow and blue and red:
Long lines of palm-trees marked out there the bed
Of a great river, and among them gleamed
A few grey tents. Then four swift horsemen streamed
Out of the West, magnificent in ire,
Churning the meadow into flakes of fire,
Brandishing monstrous spears as if in fight,
They wheeled, ducked, charged, and shouted fierce delight:
So till they reach the camp: the women there
Awaiting them the evening meal prepare;
Milk from the goats and camels, dates plucked fresh,
Cool curds and cheese, millet, sweet broiled kid's flesh.
The spear struck deep hath picketed each barb;
A grave proud turbaned man in flowing garb
Sups with a grave meek woman, humbly proud,
Whose eyes flash empire. Then the solemn crowd
Of stars above, the silent plain below,
Until the East resumes its furnace-glow;
This same night twenty thousand years ago.

VII.

Ten thousand years before, *("But if you take*
Such mouthfuls, you will soon eat up Time's cake!")
Where we are sitting rose in splendid light
A broad cool marble palace; from the height
Broad terrace-gardens stairlike sank away
Down to the floor of a deep sapphire bay.
Where the last slope slid greenly to the wave,
And dark rich glossy foliage shadow gave,
Four women—or four goddesses—leaned calm,
Of mighty stature, graceful as the palm:
One stroked with careless hand a lion's mane,
One fed an eagle; while a measured strain
Was poured forth by the others, harp and voice,
Music to make the universe rejoice.
An isle was in the offing seen afar,
Deep-purple based, its peak a glittering star;
Whence rowed a galley (drooped the silken sails),
A dragon-barque with golden burning scales.
Then four bronzed giants leapt to land, embraced
The glorious women, chanting: "Did we haste?
The Cavern-Voice hath silenced all your fears;
Peace on our earth another thousand years!"
On fruits and noble wine, with song's rich flow,
They feasted in the sunset's golden glow;
This same night thirty thousand years ago.

VIII.

Ten thousand years before, *("Another ten!*
Good Lord, how greedy are these little men!")
This place where we are sitting *("Half asleep.")*
Was in the sea a hundred fathoms deep:
A floor of silver sand so fine and soft,
A coral forest branching far aloft;
Above, the great dusk emerald golden-green;
Silence profound and solitude serene.
Four mermaids sit beneath the coral rocks,
Combing with golden combs their long green locks,
And wreathing them with little pearly shells;
Four mermen come from out the deep-sea dells,
And whisper to them, and they all turn pale:
Then through the hyaline a voice of wail,
With passionate gestures, "Ever alas for woe!
A rumour cometh down the Ocean-flow,
A word calamitous! that we shall be
All disinherited from the great sea:
Our tail with which like fishes we can swim

Shall split into an awkward double-limb,
And we must waddle on the arid soil,
And build dirt-huts, and get our food with toil,
And lose our happy, happy lives!" And so
These gentle creatures wept "Alas for woe!"
This same night forty thousand years ago.

IX.

"Are you not going back a little more?
What was the case ten thousand years before?"
Ten thousand years before 'twas Sunday night;
Four lovely girls were listening with delight,
Three noble youths admired another youth
Discoursing History crammed full of truth:
They all were sitting upon Hampstead Heath,
And monstrous grimy London lay beneath.
"The stupidest story LAZY ever told;
I've no more faith in his fine times of old."
"How do you like our prospects now, my dears?
We'll all be mermaids in ten thousand years."
"Mermaids are beautiful enough, but law!
Think of becoming a poor naked squaw!"
"But in these changes, sex will change no doubt;
We'll all be men and women turn about."
"Then these four chaps will be the squaws?—that's just;
With lots of picaninnies, I *do* trust!"
"If changes go by fifty thousand, yes;
But if by ten, they last were squaws, I guess!"
"Come on; we'll go and do the very beers
We did this night was fifty thousand years."
Thou prophet, thou deep sage! we'll go, we'll go:
The ring is round, Life naught, the World an O;
This night is fifty thousand years ago!

X.

As we rush, as we rush in the Train,
The trees and the houses go wheeling back,
But the starry heavens above the plain
Come flying on our track.

All the beautiful stars of the sky,
The silver doves of the forest of Night,
Over the dull earth swarm and fly,
Companions of our flight.

We will rush ever on without fear;
Let the goal be far, the flight be fleet!
For we carry the Heavens with us, Dear,
While the Earth slips from our feet!

XI.

Day after day of this azure May
The blood of the Spring has swelled in my veins;
Night after night of broad moonlight
A mystical dream has dazzled my brains.

A seething might, a fierce delight,
The blood of the Spring is the wine of the world;
My veins run fire and thrill desire,
Every leaf of my heart's red rose uncurled.

A sad sweet calm, a tearful balm,
The light of the Moon is the trance of the world;
My brain is fraught with yearning thought,
And the rose is pale and its leaves are furled.

O speed the day, thou dear, dear May,
And hasten the night I charge thee, O June,
When the trance divine shall burn with the wine
And the red rose unfurl all its fire to the Moon!

XII.

O mellow moonlight warm,
Weave round my Love a charm;
O countless starry eyes,
Watch from the holy skies;
O ever-solemn Night,
Shield her within thy might:
Watch her, my little one!
Shield her, my darling!

How my heart shrinks with fear,
Nightly to leave thee, dear;
Lonely and pure within
Vast glooms of woe and sin:
Our wealth of love and bliss
Too heavenly-perfect is:
Good night, my little one!
God keep thee, darling!

1863; 1865.

SUNDAY UP THE RIVER

AN IDYLL OF COCKAIGNE

En allant promener aux champs,
J'y ai trouvé les blés si grands,
Les aubépines florissant.
En vérité, en vérité,
C'est le mois, le joli mois,
C'est le joli mois de mai.

* * *

Dieu veuill' garder les vins, les blés,
Les jeunes filles à marier.
Les jeun' garçons pour les aimer!
En vérité, en vérité,
C'est le mois, le joli mois,
C'est le joli mois de mai.

—Carol of Lorraine.*

I.

I looked out into the morning,
I looked out into the west:
The soft blue eye of the quiet sky
Still drooped in dreamy rest;

The trees were still like clouds there,
The clouds like mountains dim;
The broad mist lay, a silver bay
Whose tide was at the brim.

I looked out into the morning,
I looked out into the east:
The flood of light upon the night
Had silently increased;

* From Victor Fournel's charming book, *Ce qu'on voit dans les rues de Paris.*

The sky was pale with fervour,
  The distant trees were grey,
The hill-lines drawn like waves of dawn
  Dissolving in the day.

I looked out into the morning;
  Looked east, looked west, with glee:
O richest day of happy May,
  My love will spend with me!

II.

"Oh, what are you waiting for here, young man?
  What are you looking for over the bridge?"
A little straw hat with the streaming blue ribbons
  Is soon to come dancing over the bridge.

Her heart beats the measure that keeps her feet dancing,
  Dancing along like a wave o' the sea;
Her heart pours the sunshine with which her eyes glancing
  Light up strange faces in looking for me.

The strange faces brighten in meeting her glances;
  The strangers all bless her, pure, lovely, and free:
She fancies she walks, but her walk skips and dances,
  Her heart makes such music in coming to me.

Oh, thousands and thousands of happy young maidens
  Are tripping this morning their sweethearts to see;
But none whose heart beats to a sweeter love-cadence
  Than hers who will brighten the sunshine for me.

"Oh, what are you waiting for here, young man?
  What are you looking for over the bridge?"
A little straw hat with the streaming blue ribbons;
  —And here it comes dancing over the bridge!

III.

   In the vast vague grey,
Mistily luminous, brightly dim,
The trees to the south there, far away,
Float as beautiful, strange and grand
As pencilled palm-trees, every line
Mystic with a grace divine,
In our dreams of the holy Eastern Land.

There is not a cloud in the sky;
The vague vast grey
Melts into azure dim on high.
Warmth, and languor, and infinite peace!
Surely the young Day
Hath fallen into a vision and a trance,
And his burning flight doth cease.

Yet look how here and there
Soft curves, fine contours, seem to swim,
Half emerging, wan and dim,
Into the quiet air:
Like statues growing slowly, slowly out
From the great vault of marble; here a limb,
And there a feature, but the rest all doubt.

Then the sculpturing sunbeams smite,
And the forms start forth to the day;
And the breath of the morning sweepeth light
The luminous dust away:
And soon, soon, soon,
Crowning the floor of the land and the sea,
Shall be wrought the dome of Noon.

The burning sapphire dome,
With solemn imagery; vast shapes that stand
Each like an island ringed with flashing foam,
Black-purple mountains, creeks and rivers of light,
Crags of cleft crystal blazing to the crest:
Vast isles that move, that roam
A tideless sea of infinite fathomless rest.

Thus shall it be this noon:
And thus, so slowly, slowly from its birth
In the long night's dark swoon,
Through the long morning's trance, sweet, vague, and dim,
The Sun divine above
Doth build up in us, Heaven completing Earth,
Our solemn Noon of Love.

IV.

The church bells are ringing:
How green the earth, how fresh and fair!
The thrushes are singing:
What rapture but to breathe this air!

The church bells are ringing:
  Lo, how the river dreameth there!
The thrushes are singing:
  Green flames wave lightly everywhere!

The church bells are ringing:
  How all the world breathes praise and prayer!
The thrushes are singing:
  What Sabbath peace doth trance the air!

V.

I love all hardy exercise
  That makes one strain and quiver;
And best of all I love and prize
  This boating on our river.
    I to row and you to steer,
    Gay shall be Life's trip, my dear:
    You to steer and I to row,
    All is bright where'er we go.

We push off from the bank; again
  We're free upon the waters;
The happiest of the sons of men,
  The fairest of earth's daughters.
    And I row, and I row;
    The blue floats above us as we go:
    And you steer, and you steer,
  Framed in gliding wood and water, O my dear.

I pull a long calm mile or two,
  Pull slowly, deftly feather:
How sinful *any* work to do
  In this Italian weather!
    Yet I row, yet I row;
    The blue floats above us as we go:
    While you steer, while you steer,
  Framed in gliding wood and water, O my dear.

Those lovely breadths of lawn that sweep
  Adown in still green billows!
And o'er the brim in fountains leap;
  Green fountains, weeping willows!
    And I row, and I row;
    The blue floats above us as we go:
    And you steer, and you steer,
  Framed in gliding wood and water, O my dear.

We push among the flags in flower,
  Beneath the branches tender,
And we are in a faerie bower
  Of green and golden splendour.
    I to row and you to steer,
    Gay must be Life's trip, my dear;
    You to steer and I to row,
    All is bright where'er we go.

A secret bower where we can hide
  In lustrous shadow lonely;
The crystal floor may lap and glide
  To rock our dreaming only.
    I to row and you to steer,
    Gay must be Life's trip, my dear;
    You to steer and I to row,
    All is bright where'er we go.

VI.

I love this hardy exercise,
  This strenuous toil of boating:
Our skiff beneath the willow lies
  Half stranded and half floating.
    As I lie, as I lie,
    Glimpses dazzle of the blue and burning sky;
    As you lean, as you lean,
    Faerie Princess of the secret faerie scene.

My shirt is of the soft red wool,
  My cap is azure braided
By two white hands so beautiful,
  My tie mauve purple-shaded.
    As I lie, as I lie,
    Glimpses dazzle of white clouds and sapphire sky;
    As you lean, as you lean,
    Faerie Princess of the secret faerie scene.

Your hat with long blue streamers decked,
  Your pure throat crimson-banded;
White-robed, my own white dove unflecked,
  Dove-footed, lilac-handed.
    As I lie, as I lie,
    Glimpses dazzle of white clouds and sapphire sky;
    As you lean, as you lean,
    Faerie Princess of the secret faerie scene.

If any boaters boating past
  Should look where we're reclining,
They'll say, To-day green willows glassed
  Rubies and sapphires shining!
    As I lie, as I lie,
    Glimpses dazzle of the blue and burning sky;
    As you lean, as you lean,
    Faerie Princess of the secret faerie scene.

VII.

Grey clouds come puffing from my lips
  And hang there softly curling,
While from the bowl now leaps, now slips,
  A steel-blue thread high twirling.
    As I lie, as I lie,
    The hours fold their wings beneath the sky;
    As you lean, as you lean,
    In that trance of perfect love and bliss serene.

I gaze on you and I am crowned,
  A Monarch great and glorious,
A Hero in all realms renowned,
  A Faerie Prince victorious.
    As I lie, as I lie,
    The hours fold their wings beneath the sky;
    As you lean, as you lean,
    In that trance of perfect love and bliss serene.

Your violet eyes pour out their whole
  Pure light in earnest rapture;
Your thoughts come dreaming through my soul,
  And nestle past recapture.
    As I lie, as I lie,
    The hours fold their wings beneath the sky;
    As you lean, as you lean,
    In that trance of perfect love and bliss serene.

O friends, your best years to the oar
  Like galley-slaves devoting,
This is and shall be evermore
  The true sublime of boating!
    As I lie, as I lie,
    The hours fold their wings beneath the sky;
    As you lean, as you lean,
    In that trance of perfect love and bliss serene.

VIII.

The water is cool and sweet and pure,
  The water is clear as crystal;
And water's a noble liquid, sure;—
  But look at my pocket-pistol!

Tim Boyland gave it me, one of two
  The rogue brought back from Dublin;
With a jar of the genuine stuff: hurroo!
  How deliciously it comes bubblin'!

It is not brandy, it is not wine,
  It is Jameson's Irish Whisky:
It fills the heart with joy divine,
  And it makes the fancy frisky.

All other spirits are vile resorts,
  Except its own Scotch first cousin;
And as for your Clarets and Sherries and Ports,
  A naggin is worth a dozen.

I have watered this, though a toothful neat
  Just melts like cream down the throttle:
But it's grand in the punch, hot, strong, and sweet:
  Not a headache in a bottle.

It is amber as the western skies
  When the sunset glows serenest;
It is mellow as the mild moonrise
  When the shamrock leaves fold greenest.

Just a little, wee, wee, tiny sip!
  Just the wet of the bill of a starling!
A drop of dew for the rosy lip,
  And two stars in the eyes of my darling!

'Faith your kiss has made it so sweet at the brim
  I could go on supping for ever!
We'll pocket the pistol: And Tim, you limb,
  May this *craturr* abandon you never!

IX.

Like violets pale i' the Spring o' the year
Came my Love's sad eyes to my youth;
Wan and dim with many a tear,
But the sweeter for that in sooth:
Wet and dim,
Tender and true,
Violet eyes
Of the sweetest blue.

Like pansies dark i' the June o' the year
Grow my Love's glad eyes to my prime;
Rich with the purple splendour clear
Of their thoughtful bliss sublime:
Deep and dark,
Solemn and true,
Pansy eyes
Of the noblest blue.

X.

Were I a real Poet, I would sing
Such joyous songs of you, and all mere truth;
As true as buds and tender leaves in Spring,
As true as lofty dreams in dreamful youth;
That men should cry: How foolish every one
Who thinks the world is getting out of tune!
Where is the tarnish in our golden sun?
Where is the clouding in our crystal moon?
The lark sings now the eversame new song
With which it soared through Eden's purest skies;
This poet's music doth for us prolong
The very speech Love learnt in Paradise;
This maiden is as young and pure and fair
As Eve agaze on Adam sleeping there.

XI.

When will you have not a sole kiss left,
And my prodigal mouth be all bereft?
When your lips have ravished the last sweet flush
Of the red with which the roses blush:
Now I kiss them and kiss them till they hush.

When will you have not a glance to give
Of the love in whose lustre my glances live?
  When, O my darling, your fathomless eyes
  Have drawn all the azure out of the skies:
  Now I gaze and I gaze till they dare not rise.

When will you find not a single vow
Of the myriads and myriads you lavish now?
  When your voice has gurgled the last sweet note
  That was meant from the nightingales to float:
  Now I whisper it, whisper it dumb in your throat.

When will you love me no more, no more,
And my happy, happy dream be o'er?
  When no rose is red, and no skies are blue,
  And no nightingale sings the whole year through,
  Then my heart may have no love for you.

XII.

My Love o'er the water bends dreaming;
  It glideth and glideth away:
She sees there her own beauty, gleaming
  Through shadow and ripple and spray.

Oh, tell her, thou murmuring river,
  As past her your light wavelets roll,
How steadfast that image for ever
  Shines pure in pure depths of my soul.

XIII.

The wandering airs float over the lawn,
And linger and whisper in at our bower;
    (They babble, babble all they know:)
The delicate secrets they have drawn
From bird and meadow and tree and flower;
    (Gossiping softly, whispering low.)

Some linden stretches itself to the height,
Then rustles back to its dream of the day;
    (They babble, babble all they know:)
Some bird would trill out its love-delight,
But the honey melts in its throat away;
    (Gossiping softly, whispering low.)

Some flower seduced by the treacherous calm
Breathes all its soul in a fragrant sigh;
(They babble, babble all they know:)
Some blossom weeps a tear of balm
For the lost caress of a butterfly;
(Gossiping softly, whispering low.)

Our Mother lies in siesta now,
And we listen to her breathings here;
(They babble, babble all they know:)
And we learn all the thoughts hid under her brow,
All her heart's deep dreams of the happy year:
(Gossiping softly, whispering low.)

XIV.

Those azure, azure eyes
Gaze on me with their love;
And I am lost in dream,
And cannot speak or move.

Those azure, azure eyes
Stay with me when we part;
A sea of azure thoughts
Overfloods my heart. *

XV.

Give a man a horse he can ride,
Give a man a boat he can sail;
And his rank and wealth, his strength and health,
On sea nor shore shall fail.

Give a man a pipe he can smoke,
Give a man a book he can read;
And his home is bright with a calm delight,
Though the room be poor indeed.

Give a man a girl he can love,
As I, O my Love, love thee;
And his heart is great with the pulse of Fate,
At home, on land, on sea.

* Mit deinen blauen Augen
Siehst du mich lieblich an;
Da ward mir so träumend zu Sinne
Dass ich nicht sprechen kann. [HEINE]

XVI.

My love is the flaming Sword
To fight through the world;
Thy love is the Shield to ward,
And the Armour of the Lord
And the Banner of Heaven unfurled.

XVII.

Let my voice ring out and over the earth,
Through all the grief and strife,
With a golden joy in a silver mirth:
Thank God for Life!

Let my voice swell out through the great abyss
To the azure dome above,
With a chord of faith in the harp of bliss:
Thank God for Love!

Let my voice thrill out beneath and above,
The whole world through:
O my Love and Life, O my Life and Love,
Thank God for you!

XVIII.

The wine of Love is music,
And the feast of Love is song:
And when Love sits down to the banquet,
Love sits long:

Sits long and ariseth drunken,
But not with the feast and the wine;
He reeleth with his own heart,
That great rich Vine.

XIX.

Drink! drink! open your mouth!
This air is as rich as wine;
Flowing with balm from the sunny south,
And health from the western brine.

Drink! drink! open your mouth!
This air is as strong as wine:
My brain is drugged with the balm o' the south,
And rolls with the western brine.

Drink! drink! open your mouth!
This air is the choicest wine;
From that golden grape the Sun, i' the south
Of Heaven's broad vine.

XX.

Could we float thus ever,
Floating down a river,
Down a tranquil river, and you alone with me:
Past broad shining meadows,
Past the great wood-shadows,
Past fair farms and hamlets, for ever to the sea.

Through the golden noonlight,
Through the silver moonlight,
Through the tender gloaming, gliding calm and free;
From the sunset gliding,
Into morning sliding,
With the tranquil river for ever to the sea.

Past the masses hoary
Of cities great in story,
Past their towers and temples drifting lone and free:
Gliding, never hasting,
Gliding, never resting,
Ever with the river that glideth to the sea.

With a swifter motion
Out upon the Ocean,
Heaven above and round us, and you alone with me;
Heaven around and o'er us,
The Infinite before us,
Floating on for ever upon the flowing sea.

* * * * * *

What time is it, dear, now?
We are in the year now
Of the New Creation one million two or three.
But where are we now, Love?
We are as I trow, Love,
In the Heaven of Heavens upon the Crystal Sea.

And may mortal sinners
Care for carnal dinners
In your Heaven of Heavens, New Era millions three?
Oh, if their boat gets stranding
Upon some Richmond landing,
They're thirsty as the desert and hungry as the sea!

1865.

THE NAKED GODDESS

Arcane danze
D'immortal piede i ruinosi gioghi
Scossero e l'ardue selve (oggi romito
Nido de' venti).

—Leopardi

Through the country to the town
Ran a rumour and renown,
That a woman grand and tall,
Swift of foot, and therewithal
Naked as a lily gleaming,
Had been seen by eyes not dreaming,
Darting down far forest glades,
Flashing sunshine through the shades.

With this rumour's swelling word
All the city buzzed and stirred;
Solemn senators conferred;
Priest, astrologer, and mage,
Subtle sophist, bard, and sage,
Brought their wisdom, lore, and wit,
To expound or riddle it:
Last a porter ventured—"We
Might go out ourselves to see."

Thus, upon a summer morn
Lo the city all forlorn;
Every house and street and square
In the sunshine still and bare,
Every galley left to sway
Silent in the glittering bay;
All the people swarming out,
Young and old a joyous rout,
Rich and poor, far-streaming through
Fields and meadows dark with dew,
Crowd on crowd, and throng on throng;
Chatter, laughter, jest, and song
Deafened all the singing birds,
Wildered sober grazing herds.

Up the hillside 'gainst the sun,
Where the forest outskirts run;
On along the level high,

Where the azure of the sky,
And the ruddy morning sheen,
Drop in fragments through the treen
Where the sward surrounds the brake
With a lucid, glassy lake,
Where the ample glades extend
Until clouds and foliage blend;
Where whoever turneth may
See the city and the bay,
And, beyond, the broad sea bright,
League on league of slanting light;
Where the moist blue shadows sleep
In the sacred forest deep.

Suddenly the foremost pause,
Ere the rear discern a cause;
Loiterers press up row on row,
All the mass heaves to and fro;
All seem murmuring in one strain,
All seem hearkening fixed and fain:
Silence, and the lifted light
Of countless faces gazing white.

Four broad beech-trees, great of bole,
Crowned the green, smooth-swelling knoll;
There She leant, the glorious form
Dazzling with its beauty warm,
Naked as the sun of noon,
Naked as the midnight moon:
And around her, tame and mild,
All the forest creatures wild—
Lion, panther, kid, and fawn,
Eagle, hawk, and dove, all drawn
By the magic of her splendour,
By her great voice, rich and tender,
Whereof every beast and bird
Understood each tone and word,
While she fondled and carest,
Playing freaks of joyous zest.

Suddenly the lion stood,
Turned and saw the multitude,
Swelled his mighty front in ire,
Roared the roar of raging fire:
Then She turned, the living light,
Sprang erect, grew up in height,
Smote them with the flash and blaze
Of her terrible, swift gaze;

A divine, flushed, throbbing form,
Dreadfuller than blackest storm.

All the forest creatures cowered,
Trembling, moaning, overpowered;
All the simple folk who saw
Sank upon their knees in awe
Of this Goddess, fierce and splendid,
Whom they witless had offended;
And they murmured out faint prayers,
Inarticulate despairs,
Till her haught and angry mien
Grew more gentle and serene.

Stood the high priest forth, and went
Halfway up the green ascent;
There began a preachment long
Of the great and grievous wrong
She unto her own soul wrought
In thus living without thought
Of the gods who sain and save,
Of the life beyond the grave:
Living with the beasts that perish,
Far from all the rites that cherish
Hope and faith and holy love,
And appease the thrones above:
Full of unction pled the preacher;
Let her come and they would teach her
Spirit strangled in the mesh
Of the vile and sinful flesh,
How to gain the heavenly prize,
How grow meet for Paradise;
Penance, prayer, self sacrifice,
Fasting, cloistered solitude,
Mind uplifted, heart subdued;
Thus a Virgin, clean and chaste,
In the Bridegroom's arms embraced.
Vestal sister's hooded gown,
Straight and strait, of dismal brown,
Here he proffered, and laid down
On the green grass like a frown.

Then stood forth the old arch-sage,
Wrinkled more with thought than age:
What could worse afflict, deject
Any well-trained intellect
Than in savage forest seeing
Such a full-grown human being

With the beasts and birds at play,
Ignorant and wild as they?
Sciences and arts, by which
Man makes Nature's poor life rich,
Dominates the world around,
Proves himself its King self-crowned,
She knew nothing of them, she
Knew not even what they be!
Body naked to the air,
And the reason just as bare!
Yet (since circumstance, that can
Hinder the full growth of man,
Cannot kill the seeds of worth
Innate in the Lord of Earth),
Yet she might be taught and brought
To full sovranty of thought,
Crowned with reason's glorious crown.
So he tendered and laid down,
Sober grey beside the brown,
Amplest philosophic gown.

Calm and proud she stood the while
With a certain wondering smile;
When the luminous sage was done
She began to speak as one
Using language not her own,
Simplest words in sweetest tone:
"Poor old greybeards, worn and bent!
I do know not what they meant;
Only here and there a word
Reached my mind of all I heard;
Let some child come here, I may
Understand what it can say."

So two little children went,
Lingering up the green ascent,
Hand in hand, but grew the while
Bolder in her gentle smile;
When she kissed them they were free,
Joyous as at mother's knee.
"Tell me, darlings, now," said she,
"What they want to say to me."
Boy and girl then, nothing loth,
Sometimes one and sometimes both,
Prattled to her sitting there
Fondling with their soft young hair:
"Dear kind lady, do you stay
Here with always holiday?

Do you sleep among the trees?
People want you, if you please,
To put on your dress and come
With us to the City home;
Live with us and be our friend:
Oh, such pleasant times we'll spend! . . .
But if you can't come away,
Will you let us stop and play
With you and all these happy things
With hair and horns and shining wings?"

She arose and went half down,
Took the vestal sister's gown,
Tried it on, burst through its shroud,
As the sun bums through a cloud:
Flung it from her split and rent;
Said: "This cerement sad was meant
For some creature stunted, thin,
Breastless, blighted, bones and skin."

Then the sage's robe she tried,
Muffling in its long folds wide
All her lithe and glorious grace:
"I should stumble every pace!
This big bag was meant to hold
Some poor sluggard fat and old,
Limping, shuffling wearily,
With a form not fit to see!"
So she flung it off again
With a gesture of disdain.

Naked as the midnight moon,
Naked as the sun of noon,
Burning too intensely bright,
Clothed in its own dazzling light;
Seen less thus than in the shroud
Of morning mist or evening cloud;
She stood terrible and proud
O'er the pallid quivering crowd.

At a gesture ere they wist,
Perched a falcon on her wrist,
And she whispered to the bird
Something it alone there heard;
Then she threw it off: when thrown
Straight it rose as falls a stone,
Arrow-swift on high, on high,
Till a mere speck in the sky;

Then it circled round and round,
Till, as if the prey were found,
Forth it darted on its quest
Straight away into the West. . . .
Every eye that watched its flight
Felt a sideward flash of light,
All were for a moment dazed,
Then around intently gazed:
What had passed them? Where was She,
The offended deity?
O'er the city, o'er the bay,
They beheld her melt away,
Melt away beyond their quest
Through the regions of the west;
While the eagle screamed rauque ire,
And the lion roared like fire.

That same night both priest and sage
Died accursed in sombre rage.
Never more in wild wood green
Was that glorious Goddess seen,
Never more: and from that day
Evil hap and dull decay
Fell on countryside and town;
Life and vigour dwindled down;
Storms in Spring nipped bud and sprout,
Summer suns shed plague and drought,
Autumn's store was crude and scant,
Winter snows beleaguered want;
Vines were black at vintage-tide,
Flocks and herds of murrain died;
Fishing boats came empty home,
Good ships foundered in the foam;
Haggard traders lost all heart
Wandering through the empty mart:
For the air hung thick with gloom,
Silence, and the sense of doom.

But those little children she
Had caressed so tenderly
Were betrothed that self-same night,
Grew up beautiful and bright,
Lovers through the years of play
Forward to their marriage-day.
Three long moons of bridal bliss
Overflowed them; after this,
With his bride and with a band
Of the noblest in the land,

Youths and maidens, wedded pairs
Scarcely older in life's cares,
He took ship and sailed away
Westward Ho from out the bay:
Portioned from their native shrine
With the Sacred Fire divine,
They will cherish while they roam,
Quenchless 'mid the salt sea foam,
Till it burns beneath a dome
In some new and far-off home.

As they ventured more and more
In that ocean without shore,
And some hearts were growing cold
At the emprise all too bold,
It is said a falcon came
Down the void blue swift as flame;
Every sunset came to rest
On the prow's high curving crest,
Every sunrise rose from rest
Flying forth into the west;
And they followed, faint no more,
Through that ocean without shore.

Three moons crescent fill and wane
O'er the solitary main,
When behold a green shore smile:
It was that Atlantic isle,
Drowned beneath the waves and years,
Whereof some faint shadow peers
Dubious through the modern stream
Of Platonic legend-dream.
High upon that green shore stood
She who left their native wood;
Glorious, and with solemn hand
Beckoned to them there to land.
Though She forthwith disappeared
As the wave-worn galley neared,
They knew well her presence still
Haunted stream and wood and hill.
There they landed, there grew great,
Founders of a mighty state:
There the Sacred Fire divine
Burned within a wondrous shrine
Which Her statue glorified
Throughout many kingdoms wide.
There those children wore the crown
To their children handed down

Many and many a golden age
Blotted now from history's page;
Till the last of all the line
Leagued him with the other nine
Great Atlantic kings whose hosts
Ravaged all the Mid Sea coasts:
Then the whelming deluge rolled
Over all those regions old;
Thrice three thousand years before
Solon questioned Egypt's lore. *

1866-67.

* Plato: the *Timæus*, and the *Critias*.

ART

I.

What precious thing are you making fast
　　In all these silken lines?
And where and to whom will it go at last?
　　Such subtle knots and twines!

I am tying up all my love in this,
　　With all its hopes and fears,
With all its anguish and all its bliss,
　　And its hours as heavy as years.

I am going to send it afar, afar,
　　To I know not where above;
To that sphere beyond the highest star
　　Where dwells the soul of my Love.

But in vain, in vain, would I make it fast
　　With countless subtle twines;
For ever its fire breaks out at last,
　　And shrivels all the lines.

II.

If you have a carrier-dove
　That can fly over land and sea;
And a message for your Love,
　"Lady, I love but thee!"

And this dove will never stir
　But straight from her to you,
And straight from you to her;
　As you know and she knows too.

Will you first ensure, O sage,
　Your dove that never tires
With your message in a cage,
　Though a cage of golden wires?

Or will you fling your dove:
　"Fly, darling, without rest,
Over land and sea to my Love,
　And fold your wings in her breast"?

III.

Singing is sweet; but be sure of this,
Lips only sing when they cannot kiss.

Did he ever suspire a tender lay
While her presence took his breath away?

Had his fingers been able to toy with her hair
Would they then have written the verses fair?

Had she let his arm steal round her waist
Would the lovely portrait yet be traced?

Since he could not embrace it flushed and warm
He has carved in stone the perfect form.

Who gives the fine report of the feast?
He who got none and enjoyed it least.

Were the wine really slipping down his throat
Would his song of the wine advance a note?

Will you puff out the music that sways the whirl,
Or dance and make love with a pretty girl?

Who shall the great battle-story write?
Not the hero down in the thick of the fight.

Statues and pictures and verse may be grand,
But they are not the Life for which they stand.

1865.

PHILOSOPHY

I.

His eyes found nothing beautiful and bright,
Nor wealth nor honour, glory nor delight,
Which he could grasp and keep with might and right.

Flowers bloomed for maidens, swords outflashed for boys,
The world's big children had their various toys;
He could not feel their sorrows and their joys.

Hills held a secret they would not unfold,
In careless scorn of him the ocean rolled,
The stars were alien splendours high and cold.

He felt himself a king bereft of crown,
Defrauded from his birthright of renown,
Bred up in littleness with churl and clown.

II.

How could he vindicate himself? His eyes,
That found not anywhere their proper prize,
Looked through and through the specious earth and skies.

They probed, and all things yielded to their probe;
They saw the void around the massy globe,
The raging fire within its flowery robe.

They pierced through beauty; saw the bones, the mesh
Of nerves and veins, the hideous raw red flesh,
Beneath the skin most delicate and fresh:

Saw Space a mist unfurled around the steep
Where plunge Time's waters to the blackest deep;
Saw Life a dream in Death's eternal sleep.

III.

A certain fair form came before his sight,
Responding to him as the day to night:
To yearning, love; to cold and gloom, warm light.

A hope sprang from his breast, and fluttered far
On rainbow wings; beyond the cloudy bar,
Though very much beneath the nearest star.

His eyes drew back their beams to kindle fire
In his own heart; whose masterful desire
Scorned all beyond its aim, lower or higher.

This fire flung lustre upon grace and bloom,
Gave warmth and brightness to a little room,
Burned Thought to ashes in its fight with gloom.

IV.

He said: Those eyes alone see well that view
Life's lovely surfaces of form and hue;
And not Death's entrails, looking through and through.

Bones, nerves, and veins, and flesh, are covered in
By this opaque transparency of skin,
Precisely that we should not see within.

The corpse is hid, that Death may work its vile
Corruption in black secrecy; the while
Our saddest graves with grass and fair flowers smile.

If you will analyse the bread you eat,
The water and the wine most pure and sweet,
Your stomach soon must loathe all drink and meat.

Life liveth but in Life, and doth not roam
To other realms if all be well at home:
"Solid as ocean-foam," quoth ocean-foam.

If Midge will pine and curse its hours away
Because Midge is not Everything For-aye,
Poor Midge thus loses its one summer day;
Loses its all—and winneth what, I pray?

1866.

LIFE'S HEBE

In the early morning-shine
Of a certain day divine,
I beheld a Maiden stand
With a pitcher in her hand;
Whence she poured into a cup
Until it was half filled up
Nectar that was golden light
In the cup of crystal bright.

And the first who took the cup
With pure water filled it up;
As he drank then, it was more
Ruddy golden than before:
And he leapt and danced and sang
As to Bacchic cymbals' clang.

But the next who took the cup
With the red wine filled it up;
What he drank then was in hue
Of a heavy sombre blue:
First he reeled and then he crept,
Then lay faint but never slept.

And the next who took the cup
With the white milk filled it up;
What he drank at first seemed blood,
Then turned thick and brown as mud:
And he moved away as slow
As a weary ox may go.

But the next who took the cup
With sweet honey filled it up;
Nathless that which he did drink
Was thin fluid black as ink:
As he went he stumbled soon,
And lay still in deathlike swoon.

She the while without a word
Unto all the cup preferred;
Blandly smiled and sweetly laughed
As each mingled his own draught.

And the next who took the cup
To the sunshine held it up,
Gave it back and did not taste;
It was empty when replaced:
First he bowed a reverent bow,
Then he kissed her on the brow.

But the next who took the cup
Without mixture drank it up;
When she took it back from him
It was full unto the brim:
He with a right bold embrace
Kissed her sweet lips face to face.

Then she sang with blithest cheer:
Who has thirst, come here, come here!
Nectar that is golden light
In the cup of crystal bright,
Nectar that is sunny fire
Warm as warmest heart's desire:
Pitcher never lacketh more,
Arm is never tired to pour:
Honey, water, milk, or wine
Mingle with the draught divine,
Drink it pure, or drink it not;
Each is free to choose his lot:
Am I old? or am I cold?
Only two have kissed me bold!

She was young and fair and gay
As that young and glorious day.

1866.

A POLISH INSURGENT

What would you have? said I; *
'Tis so easy to go and die,
'Tis so hard to stay and live,
In this alien peace and this comfort callous,
Where only the murderers get the gallows,
Where the jails are for rogues who thieve.

'Tis so easy to go and die,
Where our Country, our Mother, the Martyr,
Moaning in bonds doth lie,
Bleeding with stabs in her breast,
Her throat with a foul clutch prest,
Under the thrice-accursed Tartar.

But Smith, your man of sense,
Ruddy, and broad, and round—like so!
Kindly—but dense, but dense,
Said to me: "Do not go:
It is hopeless; right is wrong;
The tyrant is too strong."

Must a man have hope to fight?
Can a man not fight in despair?
Must the soul cower down for the body's weakness,
And slaver the devil's hoof with meekness,
Nor care nor dare to share
Certain defeat with the right?

They do not know us, my Mother!
They know not our love, our hate!
And how we would die with each other,
Embracing proud and elate,
Rather than live apart
In peace with shame in the heart.

No hope!—If a heavy anger
Our God hath treasured against us long,
His lightning-shafts from His thunder-clangour
Raining a century down:
We have loved when we went most wrong;
He cannot for ever frown.

* Some time after writing this I found that the great BALZAC, in *La Cousine Bette*, dwells on this very phrase, "Que voulez-vous?" as characteristic of the gallant and reckless Poles.

No hope!—We can haste to be killed,
That the tale of the victims get filled;
The more of the debt we pay,
The less on our sons shall weigh:
This star through the baleful rack of the cope
Burns red; red is our hope.

O our Mother, thou art noble and fair!
Fair and proud and chaste; thou Queen!
Chained and stabbed in the breast,
Thy throat with a foul clutch prest;
Yet around thee how coarse, how mean,
Are these rich shopwives who stare!

Art thou moaning, O our Mother, through the swoon
Of thine agony of desolation?—
"Do my sons still love me? or can they stand
Gazing afar from a foreign land,
Loving more peace and gold—the boon
Of a people strange, of a sordid nation?"

O our Mother, moan not thus!
We love you as you love as,
And our hearts are wild with thy sorrow:
If we cannot save thee, we are blest
Who can die on thy sacred bleeding breast.—
So we left Smith-Land on the morrow,
And we hasten across the West.

1863.

L'ANCIEN RÉGIME;

OR

THE GOOD OLD RULE

Who has a thing to bring
For a gift to our lord the king,
Our king all kings above?
A young girl brought him love;
And he dowered her with shame,
With a sort of infamous fame,
And then with lonely years
Of penance and bitter tears:
Love is scarcely the thing
To bring as a gift for our king.

Who has a thing to bring
For a gift to our lord the king?
A statesman brought him planned
Justice for all the land;
And he in recompense got
Fierce struggle with brigue and plot,
Then a fall from lofty place
Into exile and disgrace:
Justice is never the thing
To bring as a gift for our king.

Who has a thing to bring
For a gift to our lord the king?
A writer brought him truth;
And first he imprisoned the youth;
And then he bestowed a free pyre
That the works might have plenty of fire,
And also to cure the pain
Of the headache called thought in the brain:
Truth is a very bad thing
To bring as a gift for our king.

Who has a thing to bring
For a gift to our lord the king?
The people brought their sure
Loyalty fervid and pure;
And he gave them bountiful spoil
Of taxes and hunger and toil,

Ignorance, brutish plight,
And wholesale slaughter in fight:
Loyalty's quite the worst thing
To bring as a gift for our king.

Who has a thing to bring
For a gift to our lord the king?
A courtier brought to his feet
Servility graceful and sweet,
With an ever ready smile
And an ever supple guile;
And he got in reward the place
Of the statesman in disgrace:
Servility's always a thing
To bring as a gift for our king.

Who has a thing to bring
For a gift to our lord the king?
A soldier brought him war,
La gloire, la victoire,
Ravage and carnage and groans,
For the pious Te Deum tones;
And he got in return for himself
Rank and honours and pelf:
War is a very fine thing
To bring as a gift for our king.

Who has a thing to bring
For a gift to our lord the king?
A harlot brought him her flesh,
Her lusts, and the manifold mesh
Of her wiles intervolved with caprice;
And he gave her his realm to fleece,
To corrupt, to ruin, and gave
Himself for her toy and her slave:
Harlotry's just the thing
To bring as a gift for our king.

Who has a thing to bring
For a gift to our lord the king?
Our king who fears to die?
A priest brought him a lie,
The blackness of hell uprolled
In heaven's shining gold;
And he got as guerdon for that
A see and a cardinal's hat:
A lie is an excellent thing
To bring as a gift for our king.

Has any one yet a thing
For a gift to our lord the king?
The country gave him a tomb,
A magnificent sleeping-room;
And for this it obtained some rest,
Clear riddance of many a pest,
And a hope which it much enjoyed
That the throne would continue void:
A tomb is the very best thing
For a gift to our lord the king.

1867.

TO A PIANISTE

I saw thee once, I see thee now;
  Thy pure young face, thy noble mien,
Thy truthful eyes, thy radiant brow;
  All childlike, lovely, and serene;
Rapt in harmonious visions proud,
Scarce conscious of the audient crowd.

I heard thee when the instrument,
  Possessed and quickened by thy soul,
Impassioned and intelligent,
  Responded to thy full control
With all the treasures of its dower,
Its sweetest and its grandest power.

I saw and heard with such delight
  As rarely charms our lower sphere:
Blind Handel would not miss his sight,
  Thy beauty voiced thus in his ear;
Beethoven in that face would see
His glorious unheard harmony.

1859.

VIRTUE AND VICE

She was so good, and he was so bad:
A very pretty time they had!
A pretty time, and it lasted long:
Which of the two was more in the wrong?
He befouled in the slough of sin;
Or she whose piety pushed him in?
He found her yet more cold and staid
As wedded wife than courted maid:
She filled their home with freezing gloom;
He felt it dismal as a tomb:
Her steadfast mind disdained his toys
Of worldly pleasures, carnal joys;
Her heart firm-set on things above
Was frigid to his earthly love.

So he came staggering home at night;
Where she sat chilling, chaste, and white:
She smiled a scornful virtuous smile,
He flung good books with curses vile.
Fresh with the early morn she rose,
While he yet lay in a feverish doze:
She prayed for blessings from the Throne,
He called for "a hair of the dog" with a groan:
She blessed God for her strength to bear
The heavy load,—he 'gan to swear:
She sighed, Would Heaven, ere yet too late,
Bring him to see his awful state!
The charity thus sweetly pressed
Made him rage like one possessed.

So she grew holier day by day,
While he grew all the other way.
She left him: she had done her part
To wean from sin his sinful heart,
But all in vain; her presence might
Make him a murderer some mad night.
Her family took her back, pure saint,
Serene in soul, above complaint:
The narrow path she strictly trod,
And went in triumph home to God:
While he into the Union fell,
Our halfway house on the road to Hell.
With which would you rather pass your life,
The wicked husband or saintly wife?

1865.

THE THREE THAT SHALL BE ONE

Love on the earth alit,
Come to be Lord of it;
Looked round and laughed with glee,
Noble my empery!
Straight ere that laugh was done
Sprang forth the royal sun,
Pouring out golden shine
Over the realm divine.

Came then a lovely may,
Dazzling the new-born day,
Wreathing her golden hair
With the red roses there,
Laughing with sunny eyes
Up to the sunny skies,
Moving so light and free
To her own minstrelsy.

Love with swift rapture cried,
Dear Life, thou art my bride!
Whereto, with fearless pride,
Dear Love, indeed thy bride!
All the earth's fruit and flowers,
All the world's wealth are ours;
Sun, moon, and stars gem
Our marriage diadem.

So they together fare,
Lovely and joyous pair;
So hand in hand they roam
All through their Eden home;
Each to the other's sight
An ever-new delight:
Blue heaven and blooming earth
Joy in their darling's mirth.

Who comes to meet them now,—
She with the pallid brow,
Wreathing her night-dark hair
With the red poppies there,

Pouring from solemn eyes
Gloom through the sunny skies,
Moving so silently
In her deep reverie?

Life paled as she drew near,
Love shook with doubt and fear.
Ah, then, she said, in truth
(Eyes full of yearning ruth),
Love, thou would'st have this Life,
Fair may! to be thy wife?
Yet at an awful shrine
Wert thou not plighted mine?

Pale, paler poor Life grew;
Love murmured, It is true!
How could I thee forsake?
From the brief dream I wake.
Yet, O belovèd Death,
See how *she* suffereth;
Ere we from earth depart
Soothe her, thou tender heart!

Faint on the ground she lay;
Love kissed the swoon away;
Death then bent over her,
Death the sweet comforter!
Whispered with tearful smile,
Wait but a little while,
Then I will come for thee;
We are one family.

1863.

E. B. B. *

I.

The white-rose garland at her feet,
  The crown of laurel at her head,
Her noble life on earth complete,
  Lay her in the last low bed
For the slumber calm and deep:
"He giveth His belovèd sleep."

II.

Soldiers find their fittest grave
  In the field whereon they died;
So her spirit pure and brave
  Leaves the clay it glorified
To the land for which she fought
With such grand impassioned thought.

III.

Keats and Shelley sleep at Rome,
  She in well-loved Tuscan earth;
Finding all their death's long home
  Far from their old home of birth.
Italy, you hold in trust
Very sacred English dust.

IV.

Therefore this one prayer I breathe,—
  That you yet may worthy prove
Of the heirlooms they bequeath
  Who have loved you with such love:
Fairest land while land of slaves
Yields their free souls no fit graves.

1861.

* [Elizabeth Barrett Browning (1806-1861).]

THE LORD OF THE CASTLE OF INDOLENCE

I.

Nor did we lack our own right royal king,
The glory of our peaceful realm and race.
By no long years of restless travailing,
By no fierce wars or intrigues bland and base,
Did he attain his superlofty place;
But one fair day he lounging to the throne
Reclined thereon with such possessing grace
That all could see it was in sooth his own,
That it for him was fit and he for it alone.

II.

He there reclined as lilies on a river,
All cool in sunfire, float in buoyant rest;
He stirred as flowers that in the sweet south quiver;
He moved as swans move on a lake's calm breast,
Or clouds slow gliding in the golden west;
He thought as birds may think when 'mid the trees
Their joy showers music o'er the brood-filled nest;
He swayed us all with ever placid ease
As sways the thronèd moon her world-wide wandering seas.

III.

Look, as within some fair and princely hall
The marble statue of a god may rest,
Admired in silent reverence by all;
Soothing the weary brain and anguished breast,
By life's sore burthens all-too-much oppressed,
With visions of tranquillity supreme;
So, self-sufficing, grand and bland and blest,
He dwelt enthroned, and whoso gazed did seem
Endowed with death-calm life in long unwistful dream.

IV.

While others fumed and schemed and toiled in vain
To mould the world according to their mood,
He did by might of perfect faith refrain
From any part in such disturbance rude.
The world, he said, indeed is very good,
Its Maker surely wiser far than we;
Feed soul and flesh upon its bounteous food,
Nor fret because of ill; All-good is He,
And worketh not in years but in Eternity.

V.

How men will strain to row against the tide,
  Which yet must sweep them down in its career!
Or if some win their way and crown their pride,
  What do they win? the desert wild and drear,
  The savage rocks, the icy wastes austere,
Wherefrom the river's turbid rills downflow:
  But he upon the waters broad and clear,
In harmony with all the winds that blow,
'Mid cities, fields and farms, went drifting to and fro.

VI.

The king with constant heed must rule his realm,
  The soldier faint and starve in marches long,
The sailor guide with sleepless care his helm,
  The poet from sick languors soar in song:
  But he alone amidst the troubled throng
In restful ease diffused beneficence;
  Most like a mid-year noontide rich and strong,
That fills the earth with fruitful life intense,
And yet doth trance it all in sweetest indolence.

VII.

When summer reigns the joyous leaves and flowers
  Steal imperceptibly upon the tree;
So stole upon him all his bounteous hours,
  So passive to their influence seemed he,
  So clothed they him with joy and majesty;
Basking in ripest summer all his time,
  We blessed his shade and sang him songs of glee;
The dew and sunbeams fed his perfect prime,
And rooted broad and deep he broadly towered sublime.

VIII.

Thus could he laugh those great and generous laughs
  Which made us love ourselves, the world, and him;
And while they rang we felt as one who quaffs
  Some potent wine-cup dowered to the brim,
  And straightway all things seem to reel and swim,—
Suns, moons, earth, stars sweep through the vast profound,
  Wrapt in a golden mist-light warm and dim,
Rolled in a volume of triumphant sound;
So in that laughter's joy the whole world carolled round.

IX.

The sea, the sky, wood, mountain, stream and plain,
Our whole fair world did serve him and adorn,
Most like some casual robe which he might deign
To use when kinglier vesture was not worn.
Was all its being by his soul upborne,
That it should render homage so complete?
The day and night, the even and the morn,
Seemed ever circling grateful round his feet,
"With Thee, through Thee we live this rich life pure and sweet!"

X.

For while he loved our broad world beautiful,
His placid wisdom penetrated it,
And found the lovely words but poor and dull
Beside the secret splendours they transmit,
The heavenly things in earthly symbols writ:
He knew the blood-red sweetness of the vine,
Yet did not therefore at the revel sit;
But straining out the very wine of wine,
Lived calm and pure and glad in drunkenness divine.

XI.

Without an effort the imperial sun
With ever ample life of light doth feed
The spheres revolving round it every one:
So all his heart and soul and thought and deed
Flowed freely forth for every brother's need;
He knew no difference between good and ill,
But as the sun doth nourish flower and weed
With self-same bounty, he too ever still
Lived blessing all alike with equal loving will.

XII.

The all-bestowing sun is clothed with splendour,
The all-supporting sun doth reign supreme;
So must eternal justice ever render
Each unsought payment to its last extreme:
Thus he most rich in others' joy did seem,
And reigned by servitude all-effortless;
For heaven and earth must vanish like a dream
Ere such a soul divine can know distress,
Whom all the laws of Life conspire to love and bless.

1859.

A RECUSANT

The Church stands there beyond the orchard-blooms:
  How yearningly I gaze upon its spire!
Lifted mysterious through the twilight glooms,
  Dissolving in the sunset's golden fire,
Or dim as slender incense morn by morn
  Ascending to the blue and open sky.
For ever when my heart feels most forlorn
  It murmurs to me with a weary sigh,
How sweet to enter in, to kneel and pray
  With all the others whom we love so well!
All disbelief and doubt might pass away,
  All peace float to us with its Sabbath bell.
Conscience replies, There is but one good rest,
Whose head is pillowed upon Truth's pure breast.

1858.

ATTEMPTS AT TRANSLATION FROM HEINE

THE PILGRIMAGE TO KEVLAAR

I.

At the window stood the mother,
In bed the sick son lay;
"Will you not get up, William,
And see them marching away?"

"I am so ill, O mother,
That I cannot hear or see!
I think of my dead Maggie,
And my heart is broken in me."

"Get up; we will to Kevlaar,
Take missal and rosarie;
The Mother of God our Saviour
Will heal thy heart for thee."

They wave the broad church-banners,
They chant the holy song;
And through Cologne on the Rhine stream,
The procession draws along.

The mother follows the pilgrims,
And her sick son leadeth she;
And their voices join in the chorale:
"Blessed be thou, Marie!"

II.

The Mother of God at Kevlaar
  To-day wears her richest dress;
To-day she will be right busy,
  Such numbers come in distress.

And all the poor sick people
  Bring with them offerings meet;
They are little waxen figures,
  Many waxen hands and feet.

And who a wax hand offers,
  His hand's wound hurts no more;
And who a wax foot offers,
  His foot is healed of its sore.

To Kevlaar went many on crutches,
  Who now can dance all night;
And many now play on the viol
  Whose fingers were helpless quite.

The mother took a wax-light,
  And thereout shaped a heart:
"Take that to our dear Lord's Mother,
  And she will cure thy smart."

Sighing he took the wax heart
  And knelt to the holy form;
The tears from his eyes outstreaming,
  And the words from his heart blood-warm:

"Thou blessed among women,
  God's Virgin pure from taint,
Thou Queen of the highest Heaven,
  To thee I bring my plaint!

"I lived with my dear mother
  In the city of Cologne,
The city for many hundreds
  Of churches and chapels known.

"And next to us lived Maggie,
  She lived, she lives not now:
Marie, I bring thee a wax heart,
  My bleeding heart heal thou!

"Heal thou my heart sore wounded,
  And early and late to thee
Will I sing and play with fervour,
  Blessèd be thou, Marie!"

III.

The sick son and his mother
  Were sleeping from all ill,
When lo, the Mother of Jesus
  Came gliding in so still.

She bent down over the sick one,
  And softly laid her hand
Upon his heart; then vanished
  Smiling sweet and bland.

The mother saw all in her dreaming,
  And fain had seen yet more;
But she was roused from slumber,
  The dogs made such uproar.

There lay outstretched beside her
  Her son, and he was dead;
On the pallid features sparkled
  The light of the morning red.

The mother folded her hands then,
  She felt so wistfully;
Devoutly sang she softly:
  "Blessèd be thou, Marie!"

THE LORELEY

I know not what evil is coming,
  But my heart feels sad and cold;
A song in my head keeps humming,
  A tale from the times of old.

The air is fresh and it darkles,
  And smoothly flows the Rhine;
The peak of the mountain sparkles
  In the fading sunset-shine.

The loveliest wonderful Maiden
  On high is sitting there,
With golden jewels braiden,
  And she combs her golden hair.

With a golden comb sits combing,
  And ever the while sings she
A marvellous song through the gloaming
  Of magical melody.

It hath caught the boatman, and bound him
  In the spell of a wild sad love;
He sees not the rocks around him,
  He sees only her above.

The waves through the pass sweep swinging,
  But boatman or boat is none;
And this with her mighty singing
  The LORELEY hath done.

THE MOUNTAIN VOICE

All sadly through the stern ravine
  There rode a horseman brave:
"Ah! draw I near to my darling's arms,
  Or near to the gloomy grave?"
    The echo answer gave:
    "To the gloomy grave!"

And as the horseman onward rode
  A deep sigh heaved his breast:
"If I thus early go to the grave,
  Well, in the grave is rest!"
    The answering voice confessed:
    "In the grave is rest!"

Slowly adown the rider's cheek
  A tear of sad thought fell:
"If but in the grave there is rest for me,
  For me in the grave 'tis well!"
    Whereto the echoing knell:
    "In the grave 'tis well!"

"FOR MANY THOUSAND AGES"

For many thousand ages
  The steadfast stars above
Have gazed upon each other
  With ever-mournful love.

They speak a certain language,
  So beautiful, so grand,
Which none of the philologians
  Could ever understand.

But I have learned it, learned it
  For ever, by the grace
Of studying one grammar,
  My heart's own darling's face.

"IN THE RHINE"

In the Rhine, in the beautiful river
 The mighty shadow is thrown
With its great cathedral,
 Of holy and great Cologne.

One picture in the cathedral,
 On gilded leather wrought,
Unto my life's wild sorrow
 Hath gracious comfort brought:

The dear Madonna, with floating
 Angels and flowers above;
The eyes and the lips and the contours
 Are all just those of my love.

"THE LOTUS-FLOWER DOTH LANGUISH"

The Lotus-flower doth languish
 Beneath the sun's fierce light;
With drooping head she waiteth
 All dreamily for night.

The Moon is her true lover, *
 He wakes her with his glance:
To him she unveils gladly
 Her gentle countenance.

She blooms and glows and brightens,
 Intent on him above;
Exhaling, weeping, trembling,
 With ever-yearning love.

* In the German, Moon, *Der Mond,* is masculine; and Sun, *Die Sonne,* feminine.

"THE WORLD IS DULL"

The world is dull, the world is blind,
  And daily grows more silly!
It says of you, my lovely child,
  You are not quite a lily.

The world is dull, the world is blind,
  And judges in stupid fashion:
It knows not how sweet your kisses are,
  And how they burn with passion.

"I BLAME THEE NOT"

I blame thee not, a broken heart my lot,
O Love for ever lost! I blame thee not.
Though thou art splendid with the diamonds bright,
There falls no gleam within thy heart's deep night.

I've known this long. I saw thee in clear dream,
And saw black night within thy soul supreme,
And saw the worm still fretting at thy heart;
I saw how wretched, O my love, thou art.

Yes, thou art wretched, and I blame thee not;—
  My Love, we both must ever wretched be!
Until death's peace concludes our fatal lot,
  My Love, we both must ever wretched be!

I see the scorn which round thy pale lip weaves,
  And see thine eyes outlighten haughtily,
And see the pride with which thy bosom heaves;
  And wretched art thou still, wretched as I.

In secret round thy mouth a pain-thrill steals,
  Through tears held back thine eyes can scarcely see,
The haughty breast a bleeding heart conceals;
  My Love, we both must ever wretched be.

"THE VIOLETS BLUE OF THE EYES DIVINE"

The violets blue of the eyes divine,
And the rose of the cheeks as red as wine,
And the lilies white of the hands so fine,
They flourish and flourish from year to year,
And only the heart is withered and sere.

"THE EARTH IS SO FAIR"

The earth is so fair and the heaven so blue,
And the breeze is breathing so warmly too,
And the flowers of the meadow are gleaming through
The sparkling and glittering morning dew,
And the people are joyous wherever I view:
Yet would were I in the grave at rest
Folded close to my lost Love's breast.

"I GAZED UPON HER PICTURE"

I gazed upon her picture,
  Absorbed in dreams of gloom,
Till those beloved features
  Began to breathe and bloom.

About her lips came wreathing
  That sweet, sweet smile I knew;
The eyes were softly gleaming
  With tears as fresh as dew.

And my tears sprang then also,
  The dark cloud's rain was shed:
And, O my Love, I cannot
  Believe that thou art dead!

"A PINE-TREE STANDETH LONELY"

A pine-tree standeth lonely
  In the North on an upland bare;
It standeth whitely shrouded
  With snow, and sleepeth there:

It dreameth of a palm-tree,
  Which far in the East alone
In mournful silence standeth
  On its ridge of burning stone.

"MY DARLING, THOU ART FLOWERLIKE"

My darling, thou art flowerlike,
  So tender, pure, and fair;
I gaze on thee, and sadness
  Steals on me unaware:

I yearn to lay my hands then
  Upon thy head in prayer,
That God will keep thee ever
  Thus tender, pure, and fair.

"SAY, WHERE IS THE MAIDEN SWEET"

"Say, where is the maiden sweet,
  Whom you once so sweetly sung,
When the flames of mighty heat
  Filled your heart and fired your tongue?"

Ah, those flames no longer burn;
  Cold and drear the heart that fed;
And this book is but the urn
  Of the ashes of love dead.

"THE OLD DREAM COMES AGAIN TO ME"

The old dream comes again to me:
  With May-night stars above,
We two sat under the linden-tree
  And swore eternal love.

Again and again we plighted troth,
  We chattered, and laughed, and kissed;
To make me well remember my oath
  You gave me a bite in the wrist.

O darling with the eyes serene,
  And with the teeth so white!
The vows were proper to the scene,
  Superfluous was the bite.

"MY DARLING, WE SAT TOGETHER"

My darling, we sat together,
  We two in our frail boat;
The night was calm o'er the wide sea
  Whereon we were afloat.

The Spectre-Island, the lovely,
  Lay dim in the moon's mild glance;
There sounded sweetest music,
  There waved the shadowy dance.

It sounded sweet and sweeter,
  It waved there to and fro;
But we slid past forlornly
  Upon the great sea-flow.

"MY HEART, MY HEART IS MOURNFUL"

My heart, my heart is mournful,
  Yet joyously shines the May;
I stand by the linden leaning,
  High on the bastion grey.

The blue town-moat thereunder
  Glides peacefully along;
A boy in a boat is angling
  And whistling a careless song.

Beyond, like a well-known picture,
  All small and fair are strewed
Houses and gardens and people,
  Oxen and meadows and wood.

The maidens bleach the linen,
  And dance in the grass for glee;
The mill-wheel scatters diamonds,
  Its far hum reaches me.

Upon the hoary tower
  A sentry-box stands low;
A youth in his coat of scarlet
  There paces to and fro.

He trifles with his musket,
  Which gleams in the sunshine red;
He shoulders and presents it—
  I would he shot me dead.

QUESTIONS

By the sea, by the desert midnight sea,
Stands a youth,
His heart full of anguish, his head full of doubt,
And with sullen lips he questions the waves:—

"Oh, solve to me the Riddle of Life,
The painful primordial riddle,
Which already has racked so many heads,
Heads in hieroglyphic caps,
Heads in turbans and black berrets,
Heads in wigs, and myriad other
Poor perspiring human heads;
What is the meaning of Man?
Whence comes he? Whither goes he?
Who dwells there above in the golden stars?"

The waves murmur their everlasting murmur,
The wind sweeps, the clouds scud,
The stars glitter indifferent and cold,
And a fool awaits an answer.

"AS I EACH DAY IN THE MORNING"

As I each day in the morning
  Pass by that house of thine,
It gives me joy, thou darling,
  When you at the window shine.

Your dark brown eyes they ask me,
  As only sweet eyes can:
Who art thou, and what ails thee,
  Thou sickly foreign man?

I am a German poet,
  Well known beyond the Rhine;
When men the best names mention,
  Be sure they mention mine.

And what ails me, thou darling,
  Ails many beyond the Rhine;
When men the worst woes mention, *
  Be sure they mention mine.

"YOU LOVELY FISHER-MAIDEN"

You lovely fisher-maiden,
  Bring now the boat to land:
Come here and sit beside me,
  We'll prattle hand in hand.

Your head lay on my bosom,
  Nor be afraid of me:
Do you not trust all fearless
  Daily the great wild sea?

My heart is like the sea, dear,
  Has storm, and ebb, and flow,
And many purest pearl-gems
  Within its dim depth glow.

* Not the worst *instances* of woe; else this would be peculiar which he has just declared common: but the worst *kinds* of woe; thus claiming for his people unusual sensibility, or hinting that they are inordinately oppressed.

"THE MOON IS FULLY RISEN"

The moon is fully risen,
  And shineth over the sea;
And I embrace my darling,
  Our hearts swell free.

In the arms of the lovely maiden
  I lie alone on the strand:
"What sounds in the breeze's sighing?
  Why trembles your white hand?"

"That is no breeze's sighing,
  That is the mermaidens' song,
The singing of my sisters
  Whom the sea hath drowned so long."

WHERE?

Where shall once the wanderer weary
  Meet his resting-place and shrine?
Under palm-trees by the Ganges?
  Under lindens of the Rhine?

Shall I somewhere in the desert
  Owe my grave to stranger hands?
Or upon some lonely sea-shore
  Rest at last beneath the sands?

Ever onward! God's wide heaven
  Must surround me there as here;
And like death-lamps o'er me swinging
  Night by night the stars burn clear.

BODY AND SOUL

The poor Soul speaketh to its Clay:
I cannot leave thee thus; I'll stay
With thee, with thee in death will sink
And black Annihilation drink.
Thou still hast been my second *I*,
Embracing me so lovingly;
A satin feast-robe round my form
Doubled with ermine soft and warm.
Woe's me! I dare not face the fact—
Quite disembodied, quite abstract,
To loiter as a blessèd Naught
Above there in the realm of Thought,
Through Heavenly halls immense and frigid,
Where the Immortals dumb and rigid
Yawn to me as they clatter by
With leaden clogs so wearily.
Oh, it is horrible! Oh, stay,
Stay with me, thou beloved Clay!
The Body to the poor Soul said:
Oh, murmur not, be comforted!
We all should quietly endure
The wounds of Fate, which none can cure.
I was the lamp's wick, and to dust
Consume; but thou, the Spirit, must
Be saved with care, and lifted far
To shine in heaven, a little star
Of purest light. I am but cinder,
Mere matter, rubbish, rotten tinder,
Losing the shape we took at birth,
Mouldering again to earth in earth.
Now, fare thee well, and grieve no more!
Perchance life is not such a bore
In Heaven, as you expect up there.
If you should meet the old Great Bear
(Not Meyer-Bear *) i' the starry climes,
Greet him from me a thousand times!

* Meyerbeer, the great musician. Heine in his later years lost no opportunity for a skit at him. The poet is also alluding to his own "Atta-Troll," whose title-hero is a bear.

VANE'S STORY
AND OTHER POEMS (1881)

INSCRIBED TO THE MEMORY

OF THE

POET OF POETS AND PUREST OF MEN

PERCY BYSSHE SHELLEY

WITH THE

GRATITUDE AND LOVE AND REVERENCE

OF THE AUTHOR

VANE'S STORY

PROLOGUE.

This is the story
(To God be the glory!)
Which Vane, found in bed
When a splash of fierce red
From the sunset made strange
The street's opposite range,
Told me; who, astonished,
Had firstly admonished,
Then asked him outright,
"On the spree all last night?"

Pale looked he, and queer;
But his speech calm and clear,
And his voice, sweet and strong,
So swayed me ere long,
That I almost or quite
Believed him that night.
He named not the hall
Where he went to the ball;
Of his friends I could trace
None who knew of the case,
Nor the Jones, nor the Brown—
There are myriads in town!
The landlord avows
He went out with his spouse
After tea; slept at Bow,
At her sister's.
And so,
Shall we trust Vane? or deem
Him the dupe of a dream?
Let who will decide.
The next week he died,
And thus ended his story.
(To God be the glory!)

THE STORY.

One flamelet flickered to and fro
Above the clear vermilion glow;
The house was silent, and the street
Deserted by all echoing feet;
And that small restless tongue of light
Possest my ear and mocked my sight,
While drowsy, happy, warm, I lay
* Upon the couch at close of day,
And drowsy, dreamy, more and more,
I floated from the twilight shore
Over the vague vast sea of sleep,
Just conscious of the rest so deep;
Not sinking to the under caves,
But rocking on the surface waves.
When fitfully some muffled sound
Came from the crowded streets around,
It brought no thought of restless life
With wakeful care and passionate strife;
But seemed the booming of a bell
Sweetly ringing tumult's knell,
Slowly chiming far away
The euthanasia of the day.
And then unsummoned by my will
Came floating through this mood so still
The scenes of all my life's past range,
In perfect pictures, fair and strange,
As flowers limned in purest light
Upon a background such as might
Expand beneath some forest-screen
After the sunset, goldbrowngreen.
And then I heard on every side
The shadowy rustling slow and wide
Of night's dim curtains softly drawn
To hush the world asleep till dawn.
I heard the rustling, and my eyes
Were curtained with the curtained skies;
And I lay wrapt as in a fleece
Of warmth and purity and peace;
While consciousness within the stream
Of rippling thought and shadowy dream
Sank slowly to the deepest deep,

* Here for decorum be it said,
This couch was sofa and not bed.

Lured by the murmuring Siren, sleep;
When suddenly a little thrill
Of splendour pricked both mind and will,
And brought me tidings grand and strange;
I did not stir with outward change,
But felt with inward royal mirth,
On all this dusk of heaven and earth
The moon may rise or not to-night;
But in my soul she rises bright!

The globe of glory swelling rose
In mighty pulses, solemn throes;
And filled and overfilled me soon
With light and music, with the swoon
Of too much rapture and amaze,
A murmurous hush, a luminous haze.
How long in this sweet swoon I lay,
What hours or years, I cannot say;
Vast arcs of the celestial sphere
Subtend such little angles here.
But after the ineffable,
This first I can remember well:
A Rose of Heaven, so dewy-sweet
Its fragrance was a soul complete,
Came, touched my brow, caressed my lips,
And then my eyes in their eclipse;
And still I stirred not, though there came
A wine of fire through all my frame,
An ecstasy of joy and love,
A vision of the throne above,
A myriad-voiced triumphant psalm
Upswelling through a splendour calm;
Then suddenly, as if a door
Were shut, veiled silence as before.

The sweetest voice said, "True it is!
He does not waken at my kiss!"

I smiled: "Your kisses three and four
Just gave me Heaven, no less, no more;
I held me still, eyes shut, lest bliss
Should overflow and waste a kiss."

Then dreamily my lids I raised,
And with grand joy, small wonder, gazed,
Although the miracle I saw
Might well have made me wan with awe.
"Why have you left your golden hair,

These gorgeous dusky braids to wear?
Why have you left your azure eyes,
To gaze through deep dark mysteries?
Why have you left your robe of white,
And come in cloudy lace bedight?
Or did you think that I could fail
To know you through whatever veil?
As bird or beast, as fish or worm,
In fiendish or angelic form,
As flower or tree, as wave or stone,
Be sure I recognise My Own!"

The sweet sad voice was sad no more,
But sweeter, tenderer, than before;
"Oh, ask no questions yet," said she,
"But answer me, but answer me.

"I now have listened very long
To catch some notes of that great song
Your youth began to sing so well;
Oh, why have none yet reached me? tell!"
"And why is any lamp not bright,
With no more oil to feed its light?
Why does a robe moth-eaten fade
When she is gone whom it arrayed?
Great songs must pulse with lifeful breath,
No hymns mark time for timeless death;
One long keen wail above the bier,
Then smothered moans, then stillness drear."

"I long have listened, all aflame,
For some full echoes of the fame
Youth pledged ripe manhood to achieve:
Why must I, hearing none, still grieve?"
"And why should he who cannot spend
Not make of gold his life's chief end?
O Love, the jewels of renown,
So priceless in a monarch's crown,
What are they when his realm is lost,
And he must wander like a ghost
Alone through wilds of rocky dearth,
But pretty pebbles nothing worth?
And would you have our love's proclaim
In shouts and trumpet-peals of fame;
Or whispered as I whisper here,
Into this little pink-shell ear
Still full of echoes from the sea
Of fathomless Eternity?"

"I do not seek thy fame because
Enamoured of the world's applause,
Though even its most reckless shout
Involves some true love-praise no doubt:
But, Dearest, when fame's trumpets blare
Great hearts are battling with despair:
Better the tumult of the strife
Than stillness of lone-wasting life.
If you were working out God's will,
Could all the air around be still?"

"But I am working out God's will
Alike when active and when still;
And work we good or work we ill,
We never work against His will. . . .
All work, work, work! Why must we toil
For ever in the hot turmoil?
God wrought six days, and formed the world;
Then on the seventh His power refurled,
And felt so happy that He blest
That Sabbath day above the rest;
And afterwards, we read, He cursed
The work He thought so good at first;
And surely Earth and Heaven evince
That He has done but little since.

* "Well, I, who am a puny man,
And not a God who all things can,
Have also worked: not six short days
Of work refulgent with self-praise,
Of work 'all-good,' whose end was blest
With infinite eternal rest:
No, I have worked life after life
Of sorrow, sufferance and strife,
So many ages, that I ask
To rest one lifetime from the task,
To spend these years (forlorn of thee)
Sequestered in passivity;
Observing all things God hath made,
And of no ugliest truth afraid,
But having leisure time enough
To look at both sides of the stuff. . . .
With Shelley to his ocean-doom,
With Dante to his alien tomb;

* The last chapter of George Sand's *Lélia* may seem to be the source of the following section: in fact, however, I chanced to read that work just after, and not before, this section was written.

With Wallace, Raleigh, Sidney, Vane,
All to the axe's bloody stain;
With Socrates until the cup
Of hemlock lifted calmly up,
With Jesus to the fatal tree
After the garden's agony,
With Mohammed in flight and fight,
With Burns in all his fate's deep night,
With Joan to the fiery screen,
With Charlotte to the guillotine,
With Campanella all the while
And Tasso in their dungeons vile,
With Swift slow-dying from the top,
With Rabelais to the curtain's drop,
Cervantes prisoner and slave,
Columbus on the unknown wave,
And Luther through his lifelong war;
With these, and with how many more,
Since poor Eve fell, and as she fell
Of course pulled Adam down as well,—
In these, and in how many more,
Have I outbattled life's stern war,
Endured all hardships, toiled and fought,
Oppressed, sore-wounded, and distraught,
While inwardly consumed with thought;
How long! how long!—Mankind no whit
The better for the whole of it!
And *I*, look at me, do I need
The little rest I claim, indeed,
With body dwindled, brain outworn,
Soul's pith dried up, and heart forlorn? . . .
And so I rest me, half-content
That all my active power is spent:
No new campaign till after cure!
Meanwhile I passively endure
The wounds bequeathed by so much strife,
The hopelessness of present life:
And this is much; what further can
Be looked for from a wreck of man?
I bear in silence and alone
What maddened me at first, I own."

"The wounds bequeathed by so much strife,
The hopelessness of present life."
She dwelt upon these words again
With such a look of wistful pain
As made my heart all creep and stir
With pity, not for self, for her.

"O my true love!"she said (the while
Her poor lips sought and failed to smile),
"O love! your laugh is like a knell;
Your phantasy is horrible,
Thus calmly plunged a glittering knife
Into the core of your own life!"
And there she broke down; all the grief,
Love, pity powerless for relief,
Yearning to suffer in my stead,
Revulsion against fatal dread,
Long swelling mighty in her soul
O'erflooded now beyond control.
She gave a little laughing cry,
Choked sharply off; then heavily
Flung herself down upon my breast
With passionate weeping unreprest;
A night-dark cloud upon some bleak
And thunder-furrowed mountain peak
Pouring itself in rain and fire;
For now through all the black attire
Heaving about her heaving frame
Fermented flashes of swift flame;
Not tempest-lightnings, but indeed
Auroral splendours such as speed
Battling with gloom before the day,
And herald its triumphant sway.
Her instincts in that mighty hour
Of insurrection grasped at power;
And her true self arrayed in light,
Azure and golden, dazzling-bright,
Was struggling through the mask of night.

The mask remained,—for some good cause
Well emphasised by Heavenly laws;
She sobbed herself to self-control,
Represt the heavings of her soul;
Then stood up, pallid, faint, distraught,
Facing some phantom of dread thought.

"Another spasm like this," I said,
"Will kill me! When we both are dead
I'll use my very first new breath
To thank you for the blissful death,
The torture-rapture utterless,
You dear life-giving murderess!"
I laughed; and yet the while I gazed
Upon her standing wan and dazed:
Would I had bitten out my tongue

Ere any word of mine had stung
With such an unforeboded smart
That purest and most loving heart!

"And do you never kneel and pray
For comfort on your lonely way?
And have you no firm trust in God
To lighten your so-heavy load?"
The voice how strange and sad! the mien
How troubled from its pure serene!
"You good Child! I beseech no more
That one and one may make up four,
When one and one are my assets
And four the total of my debts:
Nor do I now with fervour pray
To cast no shadow in broad day:
Nor even ask (as I asked once)
That laws sustaining worlds and suns
In their eternal path should be
Suspended, that to pleasure me
Some flower I love,—now drooping dead,
May be empowered to lift its head."

"Ah, good pure souls have told me how
You laughed at prayer as you laugh now,
And turned all holy things to mirth,
And made a mock of heaven and earth;
And sometimes seemed to have no faith
In God, in true life after death."
"But God exists, or not, indeed,
Quite irrespective of our creed;
We live, or live not, after death,
Alike whatever be our faith;
And not a single truth, in brief,
Is modified by our belief.
And if God *does* subsist and act,
Though some men cannot learn the fact,
Who but Himself has made mankind,
Alike the seers and the blind?
It may be that for some good cause
He loves to rest deep-veiled in laws;
And better likes us who don't ask
Or seek to get behind the mask,
Than those our fellow-insect fry
Who creep and hop and itch and pry,
The Godhead's lice, the swarming fleas
In Jove's great bed of slumbrous ease?"

"They said you scorned all wise restraints,
And loved the sinners, not the saints;
And mocking these, still dwelt with those
The friends who are the worst of foes."

"They told you something like the truth,
These dear tale-bearers full of ruth.
How proffer mere coarse human love
To hearts sole-set on things above?
And furthermore, although of old
Wolves ravaged dreadfully the fold,
Yet now Christ's tender lambs indeed
Securely frisk, unstinted feed.
To us poor goats they freely give
The dreariest tracts, but they—they live
In pastures green, by rivers clear,
Quite sleek and happy even here:
And when these lambs that frisk and leap
Are all staid, stout, and well-clothed sheep,
The shepherd, having taken stock,
Will lead away the whole white flock
To bleat and batten in galore
Of Heavenly clover evermore!
The dear saints want no earthly friend,
Having their Jesus: but, perpend;
What of the wild goats? what of us,
A hundred times more numerous,
Poor devils, starving wretched here
On barren tracts and wild rocks drear,
And in the next life (as they tell)
Roasted eternally in Hell?"

"But when you join the multitude
Of sinners, is it for their good;
To hale them from the slough of sin,
Or but to plunge your own soul in?"
"And what they are, must I not be?
The dear Lord made them Who made me?
If God *did* make us, this is sure,
We all are brothers, vile and pure.
I've known some brilliant saints who spent
Their lives absorbed in one intent,
Salvation each of his own soul;
The race they ran had just one goal,
And just one modest little prize,
A wicket gate in Paradise,

A sneaking-in there through the wall
To bliss eternal; that was all.
Some of them thought this bliss would too
Be spiced by the contrasting view
Of Hell beneath them surging crammed
With all the tortures of the damned.
Their alms were loans to poor God lent,
Interest infinity-per-cent.,
(And God must be hard-up indeed
If of such loans He stands in need);
Their earnest prayers were coward cries,
Their holy doctrines blasphemies;
Their faith, hope, love, no more, no less,
Than sublimated selfishness.

"Now my gross, earthly, human heart
With man and not with God takes part;
With men, however vile, and not
With seraphim I cast my lot:
With those poor ruffian thieves, too strong
To starve amidst our social wrong,
And yet too weak to wait and earn
Dry bread by honest labour stern;
With those poor harlots steeping sin
And shame and woe in vitriol-gin:
Shall these, so hardly dealt with here,
Be worse off in a future sphere;
And I, a well-fed lounger, seek
To 'cut' them dead, to cringe and sneak
Into that bland *beau monde* the sky,
Whose upper circles are so high? . . .
If any human soul at all
Must die the second death, must fall
Into that gulph of quenchless flame
Which keeps its victims still the same,
Unpurified as unconsumed,
To everlasting torments doomed;
Then I give God my scorn and hate,
And turning back from Heaven's gate
(Suppose me got there!) bow, *Adieu!*
Almighty Devil, damn me too!"*

As lightnings from dusk summer skies,
Mirth dazzled from her brow and eyes;
A charming chiming silvery laughter

* This was written before Mr. J. S. Mill published a similar declaration. It will be noticed, however, that while the philosopher treated the matter with his habitual lofty earnestness, the flippant rhymester but makes it a subject for mockery and laughter.

Accompanied my speech, and after
Still tinkled when the speech was done
Its symphony of faëry fun:
And then her lips superbly smiled.
"*You* are the child, the naughty child,
Screaming and kicking on its back,
And choking with convulsions black,
At these old-bogey tales of Hell
Its hard-pressed priestly nurses tell!"
And gaylier, sweetlier yet she laughed,
Till I was drunken, dizzy, daft.
"You wicked holy one!" I cried,
"You changeling seraph! you black-eyed
Black-hearted scoffer! Heaven itself
Has only made you worse, mad elf,
[Than when you plagued me here of old
With infinite witchcraft! Was I told
You once demurely begged *I am*
To serve some sauce up with the Lamb,
As without condiment such food
Was apt to pall however good? . . .] *
Well, I confess that I deserve
Your arrowy laugh, your lip's grand curve,
For foaming out in such a rage
Of boyish nonsense at my age,
Anent this stupid Hell and Heaven
Some half-believe one day in seven.
Let all who stickle for a Hell
Have it; they deserve it well. . . .
Not often in these latter years
Am I, my darling, moved to tears,
Or joyous laughter or hot scorn,
While plodding to the quiet bourne;
'Tis you have brought me back a part
Of my old youthful passionate heart."

"And do you feel no bitter grief
Of penitence for unbelief?
No stings of venomous remorse
In tracing backward to its source
This wicked godless lifetime's course?"

"I half remember, years ago,
Fits of despair that maddened woe,
Frantic remorse, intense self-scorn,
And yearnings harder to be borne

* [The six lines bracketed here were included when the poem was first published in the *National Review* in 1866, but were later omitted by Thomson.]

Of utter loneliness forlorn;
What passionate secret prayers I prayed!
What futile firm resolves I made!
As well a thorn might pray to be
Transformed into an olive-tree;
As well a weevil might determine
To grow a farmer hating vermin;
The *I am that I am* of God
Defines no less a worm or clod.
My penitence was honest guile;
My inmost being all the while
Was laughing in a patient mood
At this exteme solicitude,
Was waiting laughing till once more
I should be sane as heretofore;
And in the pauses of the fits
That rent my heart and scared my wits,
Its pleasant mockery whispered through,
Oh, what can Saadi have to do
With penitence? and what can you?
Are Shiraz roses wreathed with rue?

"Now tell me, ere once more we turn
To things which us alone concern,
Of all the prosperous saints you see
Has none a kindly word for me?"
"First SHELLEY, parting for above,
Left you a greeting full of love."

"The burning Seraph of the Throne!
Not for my worship deep and lone
Of him, but for my love of you,
He loves and greets me; in his view
I stand all great and glorified,
The bridegroom worthy of the bride
For whom the purest soul in Heaven
Might wait and serve long lifetimes seven,
And other seven when these were past,
Nor deem the service long at last,
Though after all he failed for ever
In his magnificent endeavour."

"Then that dear Friend of yours, who came
Uncouthly shrinking, full of shame,
Hopeless and desolate, at first,
Dismayed that he was not accurst;
But when his essence shone out clear
Was found the noblest of our sphere;

Beautiful, faithful, valiant, wise,
With tenderest love that may suffice
When once with equal power unfurled
To sway and bless a whole bad world:
Is it for my own sake that *he*
Bows down, Sir, half-adoring me?"

"The great deep heart of purest gold,
Ever o'erflowing as of old
From the eternal source divine
With Heaven's most rich and cordial wine!
Enough: the loneliest on earth,
Famishing in affection's dearth,
Who found but two such friends above
Would banquet evermore on love."

"Now ask me what you wish to ask;
Your slave is eager for her task."
"Then, firstly, I, who never mix
With our vile nether politics,
Have also ceased for many years
To study those of your high spheres.
Who now is, under God and Fate,
The Steward of the world-estate,
The Grand Vizier, Prime Minister,
Or (if you will) sole Manager
Of this bewildering Pantomime
Whose scenes and acts fill Space and Time?"

"I have heard many and many a name;
The laws seem evermore the same,
The operation of the laws
Reveals no variance in the cause."

"A learned politician, you!
Well, any name perchance will do;
And we will take an old one, say
That Demiurgos still bears sway.
I want a prayer to reach his throne,
And you can bear it, you alone;
For neither God nor fiend nor man
(Nay, scarcely any woman) can
Resist that voice of tenderest pleading,
Or turn away from it unheeding.
Not in this mystic mask of night,
But in your dazzling noonday light;
Not with this silent storm of hair,
But crowned with sunbeams you shall fare,

Not with these darkest Delphian eyes,
But with your luminous azure skies;
For powers of solemn awe and gloom
Love loveliness and joy and bloom.
Only your voice you must not change;
It is not, where all else is, strange;
The sweetest voice in all the world,
The soul of cosmic music furled
In such a little slender sound,
Delighting in its golden bound;
The evening star of melody,
The morning star of harmony;
When I can catch its faintest tone
In sighing breeze, in dim wave's moan,
I feel you near, my Love, my Own."

"And who shall guide me to the throne
Whose place is unto all unknown?"
"By one at least the path is known:
* To Demogorgon's awful throne,
Down, down, through all the mysteries
He led the Oceanides:
Where Demogorgon dwelleth deep
There Demiurgos watch doth keep,
Though Vesta sleeps æonian sleep:
SHELLEY himself shall be your guide,
Since I must still on earth abide:
Down, down, into the deepest deep;
Down, down, and through the shade of sleep;
Down, down, beyond the cloudy strife
Of interwoven death and life;
Down, down, unto the central gloom
Whose darkness radiates through the tomb
And fills the universal womb.

"Then he shall leave thee lonely there,
And thou shalt kneel and make thy prayer,
A childish prayer for simple boon:
That soon and soon and very soon
Our Lady of Oblivious Death
May come and hush my painful breath,
And bear me thorough Lethe-stream,
Sleeping sweet sleep without a dream;
And bring you also from that sphere
Where you grow sad without me, Dear;
And bear us to her deepest cave
Under the Sea without a wave,

* *Prometheus Unbound*, act. ii., scene 3, *et seq.*

Where the eternal shadows brood
In the Eternal Solitude,
Stirring never, breathing never,
Silent for ever and for ever;
And side by side and face to face,
And linked as in a death-embrace,
Leave us absorbing thus the balm
Of most divinely perfect calm,
Till ten full years have overflowed
For each wherein we bore the load
Of heavy life upon this earth
From birth to death from death to birth:
That when this cycle shall be past
We may wake young and pure at last,
And both together recommence
The life of passion, thought and sense,
Of fear and hope, of woe and bliss;—
But in another world than this.

"For I am infinitely tired
With this old sphere we once admired,
With this old earth we loved too well;
Disgusted more than words can tell,
And would not mind a change of Hell.
The same old solid hills and leas,
The same old stupid patient trees,
The same old ocean blue and green,
The same sky cloudy or serene;
The old two-dozen hours to run
Between the settings of the sun.
The old three hundred sixty-five
Dull days to every year alive;
Old stingy measure, weight and rule,
No margin left to play the fool;
The same old way of getting born
Into it naked and forlorn,
The same old way of creeping out
Through death's low door for lean and stout;
Same men with the old hungry needs,
Puffed up with the old windy creeds;
Old toil, old care, old worthless treasures,
Old gnawing sorrows, swindling pleasures:
The cards are shuffled to and fro,
The hands may vary somewhat so,
The dirty pack's the same we know
Played with long thousand years ago;
Played with and lost with still by Man,—
Fate marked them ere the game began;

I think the only thing that's strange
Is our illusion as to change.

"This is the favour I would ask:
Can you submit to such a task?"

"All you have told me I will do,
Rejoicing to give joy to you:
Oh, I will plead, will win the boon,
That we may be united soon. . . .
But sameness palls upon you so,
That to relieve you I will go."

"By no means! wait a little, Dear!
The change is in your being here.
Besides, I have not finished yet—
How stupid of me to forget!
Sh! I shall think of it just now. . . .
Your kiss, my Angel, on my brow!
Your kiss that through the dullest pain
Flashed inspiration on my brain!"

Her face was fulgent with clear bliss;
She bent down o'er me with the kiss
As bends a dawn of golden light
To kiss away the earth's long night.
The splendour of her beauty made
Me blind, and in the rapturous shade
From head to foot my being thrilled
As if with mighty music filled,
To feel that kiss come leaning down
Upon me like a radiant crown.
Her royal kiss was on my brow
A burning ruby, burning now
As then, and burning evermore;
A Star of Love above the roar
And fever of this life's long war:
And suddenly my brain was bright
With glowing fire and dancing light,
A rich intoxicating shine
Like wave on wave of noble wine,
The Alcahest of joy supreme
Dissolving all things into dream.

So when at length I found a tongue,
Bell-clear and bold my voice outrung:
"Dearest, all thanks were out of place
For this thine overwhelming grace.

The kiss of tenderness, the kiss
Of truth, you gave me erst; but this
Is consecration; to the man
Who wears this burning talisman
The veil of Isis melts away
To woven air, the night is day,
That he alone in all the shrine
May see the lineaments divine:
And fate the marble Sphinx, dumb, stern,
Terror of Beauty cold, shall yearn
And melt to flesh, and blood shall thrill
The stony heart, and life shall fill
The statue: it shall follow him
Submissive to his every whim,
Ev'n as the lion of the wild
Followed pure Una, meek and mild.

"Now, I can tell you what we two
Before we part this night will do.
There is a dance—I wish it were
Some brilliant night-fête rich and rare,
With gold-and-scarlet uniforms
Far-flashing through the music-storms;
Some Carnival's last Masquerade,
Wherein our parts were fitly played.
This is another sort of thing,
The mere tame weekly gathering
Of humble tradesmen, lively clerks,
And fair ones who befit such sparks:
Few merry meetings could look duller;
No wealth, no grandeur, no rich colour.
Yet they enjoy it: give a girl
Some fiddle-screech to time her twirl,
And give a youth the limpest waist
That wears a gown to hold embraced;
Then dance, dance, dance! both girl and boy
Are overbrimmed and drunk with joy;
Because young hearts to love's own chime
Beat passionate rhythms all the time.

"This is the night, and we will go,
For many of the *Class* I know;
Young friendly fellows, rather rough,
But frank and kind and good enough
For this bad world: how all will stare
To see me with a dark Queen there!
I went last winter twice or thrice,
As dull as lead, as cold as ice,

Amidst the flushed and vivid crowd
Of youths and maidens laughing loud;
For thought retraced the long sad years
Of pallid smiles and frozen tears
Back to a certain festal night,
A whirl and blaze of swift delight,
When we together danced, we two!
I live it all again! . . . Do you
Remember how I broke down quite
In the mere polka? . . . Dressed in white,
A loose pink sash around your waist,
Low shoes across the instep laced,
Your moonwhite shoulders glancing through
Long yellow ringlets dancing too,
You were an angel then; as clean
From earthly dust-speck, as serene
And lovely and beyond my love,
As now in your far world above.

"You shall this night a few more hours
Be absent from your heavenly bowers;
With leave or not, 'tis all the same,
I keep you here and bear the blame.
Your Star this night must take its chance
Without you in the spheral dance,
For you shall waltz and whirl with me
Amidst a staider companie;
The Cherubim and Seraphim
And Saintly Hosts may drown their hymn
With tenfold noise of harp and lyre;
The sweetest voice of all the quire
Shall sing to me, shall make my room,
This little nutshellful of gloom,
A Heaven of Heavens, the best of all,
While I am dressing for the Ball! . . .

"What book is this I held before,
The gloaming glooming more and more,
Eyes dreamed and hand drooped on the floor?
The *Lieder*—Heine's—what we want!
A lay of Heine's you shall chant;
Our poor Saint Heinrich! for he was
A saint here of the loftiest class,
By martyrdom more dreadly solemn
Than that of Simeon on the column.

God put him to the torture; seven
Long years beneath unpitying heaven,
The body dead, the man at strife
With all the common cares of life:
A living Voice intense and brave
Issuing from a Mattress-grave.
At length the cruel agony wrung
Confessions from that haughty tongue;
Confessions of the strangest, more
Than ever God had bargained for;
With prayers and penitential psalms
That gave the angels grinning qualms,
With jests when sharp pangs cut too deep
That made the very devils weep.
Enough of this! the Monarch cried;
Fear gave what mercy still denied;
Torture committed suicide
To quench that voice; the victim died
Victorious over Heaven and Doom;
The Mattress-grave became a tomb
Deep in our Mother's kindly womb,
Oblivion tranced the painful breath,
The Death-in-Life grew perfect Death."

"Is it the mere quaint German type,
Or is it from some blackened pipe?
The volume seems, without a joke,
A volume of tobacco-smoke!"

"The choice is difficult in sooth;
But sing that song of love and ruth
The Princess Ilse sang his youth:
And sing it very softly sweet,
As not to ravish all the street;
And sing it to what air you will,
Your voice in any tune must thrill. . . .
Yet stay, there was a certain hymn
Which used at Sunday School to brim
Our hearts with holy love and zeal,
Our eyes with tears they yearned to feel:
Mild Bishop Heber shall embrace
Wild Heine by sweet music's grace,
The while you sing the verses fair
To *Greenland's icy mountains'* air;
A freezing name! but icy mountains
Were linked with Afric's sunny fountains."

Ich bin die Prinsessin Ilse, *
Und wohne im Ilsenstein;
Komm mit nach meinem Schlosse,
Wir wollen selig sein.
"Dear Princess, I will come with thee
Into thy cavern's mystery,
And both of us shall happy be."

In meinen weissen Armen,
An meiner weissen Brust,
Da sollst du liegen und träumen
Von alter Märchenlust.
"In your white arms, on your white breast,
I'll lie and dream in perfect rest,
With more than faëry blessings blest."

Es bleiben todt die Todten,
Und nur der Lebendige lebt;
Und ich bin schön und blühend,
Mein lachendes Herze bebt.
"Yes, dead the dead for ever lie;
But you my Love and your Love I
Are of the souls that cannot die."

Doch dich soll mein Arm umschlingen,
Wie er Kaiser Heinrich umschlang;—
Ich hielt ihm zu die Ohren,
Wenn die Trompet erklang.
"Roll drum, plead lute, blare trumpet-call;
Our ears shall be fast closed to all
Beneath divine Oblivion's pall."

Oh what a quaintly coupled pair
The poem and the music were!
The Sunday School's old simple air,
The heathen verses rich and rare!

* * * *

Wan ghosts have risen from the grave
To flit across the midnight wave;

---

* [The four quatrains in German are extracted from Heine's poem "Die Ilse." Edgar Alfred Bowring's 1898 translation of the relevant stanzas runs as follows: "I am the princess Ilse, / And dwell in Ilsenstein; / Come with me to my castle, / And there 'midst pleasures be mine. (. . .) Within my arms so snowy, / Upon my snowy breast, / Shalt thou repose, and dream there / Of olden legends blest. (. . .) None live except the living, / The dead are dead and gone; / And I am fair and blooming, / My laughing heart beats on. (. . .) But thee shall my arm hold warmly, / As Kaiser Henry it held; / I held him fast imprison'd, / When loudly the trumpet note swell'd."]

Pale phantoms started from the tomb
To hurry through the wildwood gloom;
Cold corpses left their wormy bed
To mingle in high feasts, 'tis said;
But never since old Noah's flood
Turned Eden into sand and mud,
(Relieving thus the Heavenly guard
From its long spell of duty hard?) *
Has any Angel left the sphere
Of Heaven to dance with mortals here:
Though earthly angels crowd each ball,
Since women are such angels all.

My partner was no icy corse,
No phantom of a wild remorse,
No Lamia of delirious dream,
No nymph of forest, sea, or stream:
A soul of fire, a lovely form
Lithe to the dance and breathing warm;
A face that flushed with cordial pleasure,
Dove-feet that flew in perfect measure;
A little hand so soft and fine,
Whose touch electric thrilled through mine;
A heart that beat against my breast
Full pulses of triumphant zest;
Deep eyes, pure eyes, as dark as night,
Yet full of liquid love and light
When their moon-soul came floating through
The clouds of mystery into view,
And myriad star-rays glittering keen
Were tempered in its mystic sheen;
Soft lips full curved in ruddy glow,
And swift as young Apollo's bow,—
What arrowy laughters flashing free
With barbs of pleasant mockery
Pierced through and through the whirling rout,
And let thought in where life flew out,
And made the world a happy dream
"Where nothing is, but all things seem!"

* The Holy Bible unfortunately tells us nothing of this. Readers may, however, refer to our auxiliary Bible, "Paradise Lost," Book xi., Michael's prophecy of the Flood. But Milton was really too careless about the fate of the guard. Was it recalled in time, or did it perish at its post? Did the deluge sweep over that gate, "With dreadful faces thronged, and fiery arms?" Let us hope not. It would be sad to think that the "flaming sword" was extinguished with a hiss; and that the "Cherubim" were drowned like the other animals, without even the salvation of a single live specimen in the Ark. Probably, however, being abundantly and superabundantly furnished with wings, they all flew away to Heaven when the waters began sweeping the Mount of Paradise "Down the great river to the opening gulf."

The splendid beauty of her face,
Her dancing's proud and passionate grace,
Her soul's eternal life intense
Lavishly poured through every sense,
Intoxicated all the air,
Inspiring every dancer there:
Never again shall that old Hall
Spin round with such another Ball;
The human whirlwind might have whirled
It through the heights of air and hurled
It down at last into the sea,
Nor yet disturbed the revelry.
The violin and the violoncello,
The flute that withered little fellow,
The red-faced cornet always mellow,
Our noble Orchestra of four,
Played as they never played of yore,
Played as they will play nevermore,
As if the rushing air were cloven
By all the legions of Beethoven.

In one of the eternal trances
(Five minutes long) between two dances,
The Brown whom one meets everywhere
Came smug and grinning to me there,
And "May I have the pleasure,—honour?"
A glance (encouraging) upon her.

"My dear good Brown, you understand
This lady's from a foreign land,
And does not comprehend a word
You speak so well: nay, I have heard
That one may search all England through,
And not find twenty scholars who
Can speak or write her language clearly,
Though once our great men loved it dearly.
The little of it I know still
(Read well, write badly, speak so ill!)
I first learnt many years ago
From her, and one you do not know,
A restless wanderer, one of these
You call damned doubtful refugees,
Enthusiasts, whom while harboured here
All proper folk dislike and fear."

Brown muttered, "I've a little knowledge
Of French,—the Working Man's New College."

"Ah, yes; your French is doubtless good,
And French we know is understood
By polished people everywhere;
But then her land, though rich and fair,
Lies far beyond the continents
Of civilised accomplishments;
And she could sooner learn to speak
Persian or Sanskrit, Norse or Greek,
Than this delightful brilliant witty
Tongue of delightful Paris city,
* (*'The devils' paradise, the hell*
Of angels,'—Heine loved it well!).
And finally, my dearest Brown,
The customs of her folk would frown
Austere rebukes on her if she
Dared dance with any one but me!"

Brown went and whispered strange remarks
To eager girls and staring clerks. . . .
We are caught up and swept away
In the cyclone-gallop's sway
And round and round and round and round
Go whirling in a storm of sound.

But in the next brief perfect trance
That followed the impassioned dance,

* Mich ruft der Tod. . . .

* * * *

Glaub mir, mein Kind, mein Weib, Mathilde,
Nicht so gefährlich ist das wilde
Erzürnte Meer und der trotzige Wald,
Als unser jetzige Aufenthalt!
Wie schrecklich auch der Wolf und der Geier,
Haifische und sonstige Meerungeheuer:
Viel grimmere, schlimmere Bestien enthält
Paris, die leuchtende Hauptstadt der Welt,
Das singende, springende, schöne Paris,
Die Hölle der Engel, der Teufel Paradies—
Das ich dich hier verlassen soll,
Das macht mir verrückt, das macht mir toll!

LETZTE GEDICHTE: *Babylonische Sorgen.*

The title suggests, and may have been specially suggested by, that great verse of Jeremiah li. 7: "Babylon hath been a golden cup in the Lord's hand, that made all the earth drunken: the nations have drunken of her wine; therefore the nations are mad."

So Béranger, in his *Jean de Paris*:

Quel amour incroyable,
Maintenant et jadis,
Pour ces murs dont le diable
A fait son paradis!

And he who knew his Paris best, Balzac the Terrible: "Cette succursale de l'enfer."—*Melmoth Reconcilié.*

Again, "Paris a été nommé un enfer. Tenez ce mot pour vrai."—*La Fille aux Yeux d'or.* (*Histoire des Treize.*)

And yet again, "Ce Paris qualifié d'antichambre de l'enfer."—*Balzac, to the Abbé Eglé.*

The Jones whom one too rarely sees
Came rushing on me like a breeze:
"What miracle! what magic might!—
But have you seen yourself to-night?"

"Oh yes! twin-mirrored in the skies
Of these my Lady's glorious eyes!
In our rude days of kingly fear,
If any monarch drawing near
The palace saw so bright and clear
His picture in the windows shine,
He well might say, *Auspicious sign*
That still this noble home is mine!"

"But you are half as tall again,
And stately as a King of Men;
And in the prime of health and youth,
Younger by twenty years, in sooth;
Your face, the pale and sallow, glows
As fresh as any morning rose;
Your voice rings richly as a bell,
Resonant as a trumpet-swell;
Your dull and mournful dreamy eyes
Now dazzle, burn, and mesmerise:
Thus gazed, thus spoke, thus smiled, thus trod,
Apollo the immortal God!"

"Dear Jones, as usual, you are right;
I stand revealed Myself to-night,
The God of Poesy, Lord of Light. . . .
But you would learn now whence the change:
Listen; it is and is not strange.

"There was a Fountain long ago,
A fountain of perpetual flow,
Whose purest springlets had their birth
Deep in the bosom of the earth.
Its joyous wavering silvery shaft
To all the beams of morning laughed,
Its steadfast murmurous crystal column
Was loved by all the moonbeams solemn;
From morn to eve it fell again
A singing many-jewelled rain,
From eve to morn it charmed the hours
With whispering dew and diamond showers;
Crowned many a day with sunbows bright,
With moonbows halo'd many a night;
And so kept full its marble urn,

All fringed with fronds of greenest fern,
O'er which with timeless love intent
A pure white marble Goddess leant:
And overflowing aye the urn
In rillets that became a burn,
It danced adown the verdant slope
As light as youth, as gay as hope,
And 'wandered at its own sweet will;'
And here it was a lakelet still,
And there it was a flashing stream;
And all about it was a dream
Of beauty, such a Paradise
As rarely blooms beneath our skies;
The loveliest flowers, the grandest trees,
The broadest glades, the fairest leas;
And double music tranced the hours,—
The countless perfumes of the flowers,
The countless songs of swift delight
That birds were singing day and night.

"But suddenly there fell a change;
So suddenly, so sad, so strange!
The fountain ceased to wave its lance
Of silver to the spheral dance;
The runnels were no longer fed,
And each one withered from its bed;
The stream fell stagnant, and was soon
A bloated marsh, a pest-lagoon;
The sweet flowers died, the noble trees
Turned black and gaunt anatomies;
The birds all left the saddened air
To seek some other home as fair;
The pure white Goddess and her urn
Were covered with the withered fern,—
The red and yellow fans outworn,
And red and yellow leaves forlorn,
Slow drifting round into a heap
Till the fair shapes were buried deep:
The happy Eden rich and fair
Became a savage waste, a lair
Where Silence with broad wings of gloom
Brooded above a nameless tomb. . . .
And thus it was for years and years;
And only there were bitter tears
Beneath those dark wings shed alway
Instead of the bright fountain's play,
And in the stead of sweet bird-tones
Low unheard solitary moans.

"Ah, sudden was that ruin sad;
As sudden, resurrection glad!
Unheralded one quiet night
There came an Angel darkly bright,
An Angel from the Heavenly Throne,
Or else that Goddess carved in stone
Enraptured into life by power
Of her most marvellous beauty's dower:
And from her long robe's sweeping pride
The dead leaves all were scattered wide;
And from a touch of her soft hand,
Without one gesture of command,
All suddenly was rolled away
A mighty stone, whose broad mass lay
Upon the urn, as on a tomb
There lies a stone to seal its gloom:
And straightway sprang into the night
That joyous Fountain's shaft of light,
Singing its old unwearied tune
Of rapture to the quiet moon,
As strong and swift and pure and high
As ere it ever seemed run dry:
For never since that Long-ago
Had its deep springlets ceased to flow;
But shut down from the light of day
Their waters sadly oozed away
Through pores of the dim underearth,
Bereft of splendour, speed, and mirth;
Yet ever ready now as then
To leap into the air again."

"Ah yes," said Jones, "I understand."
Then with his smile of sadness bland,
"*My* fountain never got a chance
To spring into the sunlight's glance,
And wave its mystic silver lance
In time with all the starry dance;
Yet I believe 'tis ever there
Heart-pulsing in its secret lair,
Until the Goddess some fine day
Shall come and roll the stone away. . . .
Nor have you startled me; I knew
Quite well it was a Goddess too."

"Because so well you know and speak
Her esoteric Persian-Greek."

"Or shall we say (a truth of wine,
If falsehood in the nectar-shine),
Because a beauty so divine
Has stirred no envy, grudge, or pine
In any girl's or woman's breast,
But only love and joyous zest?—
For if the beauty dazzling thus
Were nubile and not nebulous?"

"This beauty is more real far
Than all the other beauties are;
And such a beauty's bridal kiss
Transcends all other bridal bliss;
And such a marriage-love will last
When all the other loves are past.
You know this well, dear friend of mine,
When drinking nectar and not wine."

"I know it,—know it not: we rhyme
The petals of the Flower of Time;
And rhyming strip them off, perplext
For every leaflet by the next
Is contradicted in its turn;
And thus we yearning ever yearn,
And ever learning never learn;
For while we pluck, from hour to hour
New petals spring to clothe the flower,
And till we strip the final one
Can final answer fall to none. . . .
To strip and strip the living bloom,
Nor learn the oracle of Doom
Until the fulgent Flower o' the Day
Is altogether stripped away;
Then with the dead stem leave the light,
And moulder in eternal night!"

"The sad old truth of earthly wine;
The joyous fable in the shine
Of nectar at the feast divine! . . .
Love a near maid, love a far maid,
But let Hebe be your barmaid;
When she proffers you the cup,
Never fear to drink it up;
Though you see her crush her wine
From a belladonna vine,
Drink it, pouring on the clods
Prelibation to the gods.

Reck this rede unto the end:
It is my good night, good friend."

* * * *

The music 'gan again arise;
A music of delicious sighs,
A music plaintive with a grief
More exquisite than all relief;
Music impassioned, but subdued
To a sweet sad dreamy mood. . . .
And now a swift and sudden stream
Of melody breaks through the dream:
The still air trembles, and the whole
Night-darkness fills with life and soul,
And keen stars listen throbbing pale
The drama of the nightingale. . . .
The nightingale is now a thrush. . . .
And now a soaring skylark. . . . Hush!
Never a song in all the world!
But low clouds floating soft and furled,
And rivers winding far away,
And ripples weaving faëry spray,
And mists far-curving swelling round
Dim twilight hills that soon are drowned,
And breezes stirring solemn woods,
And seas embracing solitudes;
Interminable intervolving,
Weaving webs for redissolving;
The intertwining, interblending
Of spirals evermore ascending;
The floating hither, wheeling thither,
Without a whence, without a whither;
And still we whirl and wheel and float,
But how the dancers are remote!

"Is that the wonderful waltz-tune,
Or is it the full-shining moon?
And are those notes, so far and far?
Each seems to me a brilliant star!
Can we be dancing in the ball,
And yet not see the earth at all? . . .
The starry notes are round us whirling,
Beneath the great moon-waltz is twirling;
And thus without our own endeavour
May we float and float for ever?"

"When six long days of toil are past,
The holy Sabbath comes at last."

Oh better than a battle won,
And better than a great deed done,
And better than a martyr's crown,
And better than a king's renown,
And better than a long calm life
With lovely bairns and loving wife,
And better than the sweetest thought
That tearful Memory ever brought
From searching with her rapturous woe
Within the moonlit Long-ago,
And better than the stillest sleep
To him who wakes to moan and weep,
And better than the trance of death
To him who yearning suffereth;
Better than this, than these, than all
That mortals joys and triumphs call,
Was last night's Meeting, last night's Ball!

* * * * *

The tongue of flame had ceased to play,
The steadfast glow long died away;
The house was grave-still, and the street
Re-echoed to no wandering feet;
And still and chill as any stone
* I lay upon the couch alone,
Drest to the white kid-gloves in all
The dress I put on for the Ball:
And there, that glorious flower you see,
She fixed it in my breast for me;
Could such a flower of flowers have birth
Upon our worn-out frigid earth?
That golden-hearted amethyst
Her own hand held, her own mouth kissed.

The clocks struck one and two and three,
And each stroke fell as aimed at me;
For none should muse or read or write
So late into the awful night,
None dare awake the deep affright
That pulseth in the heart of night,
None venture save sleep-shrouded quite
Into the solemn dead of night,

* (It may not be amiss to vouch
The previous note anent this couch.)

None wander save in dreams of light
Through the vast desert of black night;
And none at three be dressed at all,
Unless mere night-clothes dress you call
Or underlinen of a pall;
Therefore, my friend, in bidding you
And all the rest a long adieu,
For I am weary, Alleleu!—
Yourself and all I re-advise,
Early to bed and early to rise,
Is the way to be healthy, wealthy, and wise!

EPILOGUE.

(Grossness here indeed is regnant,
But it is the grossness pregnant;
HEINE growled it, ending thus
His wild *Book of Lazarus*;
Modern swansong's final note,
Hoarse death-rattle in the throat.
Swan was white or black?—*Our* candour!
Black or white no swan's a gander.)

"Glory warms us in the grave!
Stupid words, that sound so brave!
Better warmth would give to us
Molly Seagrim amorous,
Slobbering kisses lips and tongue,
And yet reeking from the dung. *
Better warmth would likewise dart
Through the cockles of one's heart,
Drinking mulled wine, punch, or grog,
Until helpless as a log,
In the lowest den whose crowd is
Thieves and drabs and ragged rowdies,
Mortgaged to the gallows-rope,
But who meanwhile breathe and hope,
And more enviable far
Than the son of Thetis are.
Yes, Pelides was a judge;—
Better live the poorest drudge
In the upper world, than loom
On the Stygian shore of gloom
Phantom-Leader, bodiless roamer,
Though besung by mighty Homer."

1864.

* *Eine Kuh-magd*—Any farm-wench; but Heine, who knew Fielding, probably had Molly Seagrim in his mind.

WEDDAH
AND
OM-EL-BONAIN

NOTE.—I found this story, and that of the short piece following, which merit far better English versions than I have been able to accomplish, in the *De l'Amour* of De Stendhal (Henri Beyle), chap. 53, where they are given among "Fragments Extracted and Translated from an Arabic Collection, entitled *The Divan of Love*, compiled by Ebn-Abi-Hadglat." From another of these fragments I quote a few lines by way of introduction: "The Benou-Azra are a tribe famous for love among all the tribes of Arabia. So that the manner in which they love has passed into a proverb, and God has not made any other creatures so tender in loving as are they. Sahid, son of Agba, one day asked an Arab, Of what people art thou? I am of the people who die when they love, answered the Arab. Thou art then of the tribe of Azra? said Sahid. Yes, by the master of the Caaba! replied the Arab. Whence comes it, then, that you thus love? asked Sahid. Our women are beautiful and our young men are chaste, answered the Arab."

On this theme HEINE has a poem of four unrhymed quatrains, *Der Azra*, of which the sense without the melody may be given in English:—

Daily went the wondrous-lovely
Sultan's daughter to and fro there
In the evening by the fountain,
Where the waters white were plashing.

Daily stood the youthful captive
In the evening by the fountain,
Where the waters white were plashing;
Daily grew he pale and paler.

And one evening the princess
Stepped to him with sudden question:
"I would know your name, young captive,
And your country and your kindred."

Then the slave replied: "My name is
Mohammed, I come from Yemen,
And my kindred are the Azra,
They who when they love must perish."

PART I.

I.

Weddah and Om-el-Bonain, scarcely grown
To boy and girlhood from their swaddling bands,
Were known where'er the Azra tribe was known,
Through Araby and all the neighbouring lands;
Were chanted in the songs of sweetest tone
Which sprang like fountains 'mid the desert sands:
  They were so beautiful that none who saw
  But felt a rapture trembling into awe.

II.

Once on a dewy evetide when the balm
Of herb and flower made all the air rich wine,
And still the sunless shadow of the palm
Sought out the birthplace of the day divine,
These two were playing in the happy calm.
A young chief said: In these be sure a sign
  Great God vouchsafes; a living talisman
  Of glory and rich weal to bless our clan.

III.

Proud hearts applauded; but a senior chief
Said: Perfect beauty is its own sole end;
It is ripe flower and fruit, not bud and leaf;
The promise and the blessing meet and blend,
Fulfilled at once: then malice, wrath, and grief,
Lust of the foe and passion of the friend,
  Assail the marvel; for all Hell is moved
  Against the work of Allah most approved.

IV.

Thus beauty is that pearl a poor man found;
Which could not be surrendered, changed, or sold,
Which he might never bury in the ground,
Or hide away within his girdle-fold;
But had to wear upon his brow uncrowned,
A star of storm and terrors; for, behold,
  The richest kings raged jealous for its light,
  And just men's hearts turned robbers at the sight.

V.

But if the soul be royal as the gem,
That star of danger may flash victory too,
The younger urged, and bring the diadem
To set itself in. And the other: True;
If all Life's golden apples crown one stem,
Fate touches none; but single they are few:
  And whether to defeat or triumph, this
  One star lights war and woe, not peaceful bliss.

VI.

But nothing recked the children in that hour,
And little recked through fifteen happy years,
Of any doom in their surpassing dower:
Rich with the present, free from hopes and fears,
They dwelt in time as in a heavenly bower:
Their life was strange to laughter as to tears,
  Serenely glad; their partings were too brief
  For pain; and side by side, what thing was grief?

VII.

Amidst their clan they dwelt in solitude,
Not haughtily but by instinctive love;
As lion mates with lion in the wood,
And eagle pairs with eagle not with dove;
The lowlier creatures finding their own good
In their own race, nor seeking it above:
  These dreamt as little of divided life
  As that first pair created man and wife.

VIII.

The calm years flowed thus till the youth and maid
Were almost man and woman, and the spell
Of passion wrought, and each was self-dismayed;
The hearts their simple childhood knew so well
Were now such riddles to them, in the shade
And trouble of the mists that seethe and swell
  When the large dawn is kindling, which shall grow
  Through crimson fires to steadfast azure glow.

IX.

That year a tribe-feud, which some years had slept
Through faintness, woke up stronger than before;
And with its stir young hearts on all sides leapt
For battle, swoln with peace and plenteous store;
Swift couriers to and fro the loud land swept
Weaving thin spites to one vast woof of war:
  And Weddah sallied forth elate, ranked man,
  A warrior of the warriors of his clan.

X.

Ere long flushed foes turned haggard at his name;
The beautiful, the terrible: for fire
Burns most intensely in the clearest flame;
The comeliest steed is ever last to tire
And swiftest footed; and in war's fierce game
The noblest sword is deadliest in its gyre:
   His gentle gravity grew keen and gay
   In hottest fight as for a festal day.

XI.

And while he fought far distant with his band,
Walid the Syrian, Abd-el-Malek's son;
Renowned already for a scheme long planned
With silent patience, and a sharp deed done
When its ripe fruit leaned ready for his hand,
And liberal sharing of the fruit well won;
   Came south to greet the tribe, and knit anew
   Old bonds of friendship and alliance true.

XII.

He had full often from the poets heard
Of these two children the divinely fair;
But was not one to kindle at a word,
And languish on faint echoes of an air;
By what he saw and touched his heart was stirred,
Nor knew sick longings and the vague despair
   Of those who turn from every nearest boon
   To catch like infants at the reachless moon.

XIII.

But when one sunset flaming crimson-barred
He saw a damsel like a shape of sleep,
Who moved as moves in indolence the pard;
Above whose veil burned large eyes black and deep,
The lairs of an intense and slow regard
Which made all splendours of the broad world cheap,
   And death and life thin dreams; fate-smitten there
   He rested shuddering past the hour of prayer.

XIV.

Be heaven all stars, we feel the one moon's rise:
Who else could move with that imperial grace?
Who else could bear about those fateful eyes,
Too overwhelming for a mortal face?
Beyond all heed of questions and surprise
He stood a termless hour in that same place,
   Convulsed in silent wrestling with his doom;
   Haggard as one brought living from the tomb.

XV.

And she had shuddered also passing by,
A moment; for her spirit though intent
Was chilled as conscious of an evil eye;
But forthwith turned and o'er its one dream bent;
A woman lilting as she came anigh:
But to destroy on earth was Weddah sent;
  There where he is brave warriors fall before him,
  Where he is not pine damsels who adore him.

XVI.

And thus with purpose like a trenchant blade
Forged in that fierce hour's fire, the Syrian chief
Began new life. When next the Council weighed
The heavy future charged with wrath and grief,
He spoke his will: I ask to wed the maid,
The child of Abd-el-Aziz: and, in brief,
  I bring for dowry all our wealth and might,
  Unto our last heart's blood, to fight your fight.

XVII.

All mute with marvelling sat. Her sire then said:
From infancy unto my brother's son
She has been held betrothed: our Lord can wed
Full many a lovelier, many a richer one.
But quite in vain they reasoned, flattered, pled;
This was his proffer, other he had none:
  A boy and girl outweighed the Azra tribe?
  'Twas strange! His vow was fixed to that sole bribe.

XVIII.

And as their couriers came in day by day
Pregnant with portents of yet blacker ill;
And all their urgence broke in fuming spray
Against the rock of his firm-planted will;
The baffled current took a tortuous way,
And drowned a happy garden green and still,
  O'erwhelming Abd-el-Aziz with that gibe,
  A boy and girl outvalue all our tribe?

XIX.

He loved his daughter, and he loved yet more
His brother's son; and now the whole tribe prest
The scale against them: there was raging war,
Too sure of hapless issue in his breast;
Sea-tossed where rocks on all sides fanged the shore.
She heard him moaning: Would I were at rest,
  Ere this should come upon me, in the grave!
  Her poor heart bled to hear him weep and rave.

XX.

She flung herself all yearning at his feet;
The long white malehair dashed her brow with tears;
But her tears scalded him; her kisses sweet
Were crueller than iron barbs of spears;
He had no eyes her tender eyes to meet;
Her soft caressing words scarce touched his ears
But they were fire and madness in his brain:
Yet while she clasped he mutely clasped again.

XXI.

At length he answered her: A heavy doom
Is laid upon me; now, when I am old,
And weak, and bending toward the quiet tomb . . .
Can it then be, as we are sometimes told,
That woman, nay, that young girls in their bloom,
Lovely, beloved, and loving, have been bold
To give their lives, when blenched the bravest man,
For safety of their city or their clan?

XXII.

She trembled in cold shadow of a rock
Leaning to crush her where she knelt fast bound;
She grew all ear to catch the coming shock,
And felt already quakings of the ground;
Yet firmly said: Your anguish would not mock
Your daughter, O my Father: pray expound
The woeful riddle; and whate'er my part,
It is your very blood which feeds this heart.

XXIII.

He told her all: the perils great and near;
The might of Walid; and the friendship long
Which bound them to his house, and year by year
With mutual kindnesses had grown more strong
His offer, his demand, which would not hear
A word in mitigation right or wrong.
Her young blood curdled: bring him to our tent,
That I may plead; perchance he will relent.

XXIV.

He came; and found her sitting double-veiled,
For grief was round her like a funeral stole.
She pleaded, she o'erwhelmed him, and she failed;
For still the more her passion moved his soul,
The more he loved her; when his heart most quailed,
His purpose stretched most eager for the goal:
I stake myself, house, friends, all, for the tribe
Which gives me you; but for no meaner bribe.

XXV.

So her face set into a stony mask,
And heavy silence crushed them for an hour
Ere she could learn the words to say her task:
Let only mutes appeal to Fate's deaf power!
Behold I pledge myself to what you ask,
My sire here sells me for the settled dower:
 The sheikhs can know we are at one; I pray
 That none else know it ere the wedding-day.

XXVI.

Which shall be when next moon is on the wane
As this to-night: my heart is now the bier
Of that which we have sacrificed and slain;
My own poor Past, still beautiful and dear,
Cut off from life, wants burial; and though vain
Is woman's weeping, I must weep I fear
 A little on the well-beloved's tomb
 Ere marriage smiles and blushes can outbloom.

XXVII.

He left them, sire and daughter, to their woe;
Himself then sick at heart as they could be:
But set to work at once, and spurred the slow
Sad hours till they were fiery-swift as he:
With messengers on all sides to and fro,
With ravelled webs of subtle policy,
 He gave the sheikhs good earnest of what aid
 They had so cheaply bought with one fair maid.

XXVIII.

Thus he took Araby's one peerless prize,
And homeward went ungrudging all the cost;
Though she was marble; with blank arid eyes,
Weary and hopeless as the waste they crossed
When neither moon nor star is in the skies,
And water faileth, and the track is lost.
 He took such statue triumphing for wife,
 Assured his love would kindle it to life.

XXIX.

She had indeed wept, wept and wailed that moon,
But had not buried yet her shrouded Past;
Which ever lay in a most deathlike swoon,
Pallid and pulseless, motionless and ghast,
While Fate withheld from it death's perfect boon:
She kept this doleful mystery locked up fast;
 Her form was as its sepulchre of stone,
 Her heart its purple couch and hidden throne.

XXX.

She went; and sweeter voiced than cooing dove
Hassan the bard his farewell ode must render:
We had a Night, the dream of heaven above,
Wherein one moon and countless stars of splendour;
We had a Moon, the face of perfect love,
Wherein two nights with stars more pure and tender:
  Our Night with its one moon we still have here;
  Where is our Moon with its twin nights more dear?

PART II.

I.

As Weddah and his troop were coming back
From their first foray, which success made brief,
Scouts met him and in sharp haste turned his track
On special mission to a powerful chief,
Who wavered still between the white and black,
And lurked for mere self-profit like a thief.
  This errand well fulfilled, at last he came
  To flush her tear-pearls with the ruby fame.

II.

Into the camp full joyously he rode,
Leading his weary escort; as for him,
The love and trust that in his bosom glowed
Had laughed away all weariness of limb.
The sheikhs, his full report heard, all bestowed
Well-measured praises, brief and somewhat grim;
  As veterans scanning the enormous night
  In which this one star shone so bravely bright.

III.

Then Abd-el-Aziz rose and left the tent,
And he accompanied with eager pace;
And marked not how his frank smiles as he went
Were unreflected in each well-known face;
How joyous greetings he on all sides sent
Brought hollow echoes as from caverned space:
  His heart drank sweet wine 'mid the roses singing,
  And thought the whole world with like revels ringing.

IV.

He entered with his uncle, and his glance
Sank disappointed. But the old man wept
With passion o'er him, eyeing him askance;
And made him eat and drink; and ever kept
Questioning, questioning, as to every chance
Throughout his absence; keen to intercept
  The fatal, But my cousin? ready strung
  Upon the tense lips by the eager tongue.

V.

At length it flew, the lover's wingèd dart;
He sped it wreathed with flowers of hope and joy,
It pierced with iron point the old man's heart,
Who quivering cried: You are, then, still a boy!
Love, love, the sweet to meet, the smart to part,
Make all your world of pleasure and annoy!
  Is this a time for dalliance in rose bowers?
  The vultures gather; do they scent sweet flowers?

VI.

It is a time of woe and shame, of strife
Whose victory must be dolorous as defeat:
The sons of Ishmael clutch the stranger's knife
To stab each other; every corpse you meet
Has held a Moslem soul, an Arab life:
The town-serfs prisoned in stark fort and street
  Exult while countless tents that freely roam
  Perish like proud ships clashing in the foam.

VII.

We might learn wisdom from our foes and thralls!
The mongrels of a hundred barbarous races,
Who know not their own sires, appease their brawls,
Leave night and sunward set their impure faces,
To bay in concert round old Syrian walls,
And thrust their three gods on our holy places:
  We have one Sire, one Prophet, and one Lord,
  And yet against each other turn the sword.

VIII.

Thus long he groaned with fevered bitterness,
Till, Say at least, my Father, she is well!
Stung prudence out of patience: Surely yes!
The children of the faith whom Azrael
Hath gathered, do they suffer our distress?—
But smitten by that word the lover fell,
  As if at such rash mention of his name
  That bird of God with wings of midnight came.

IX.

Deep in the shadow of those awful plumes
A night and day and night he senseless lay;
And Abd-el-Aziz cowered 'mid deeper glooms,
Silent in vast despair, both night and day:
It seemed two forms belonging to the tombs
Had been abandoned in that tent; for they
  Were stark and still and mute alike, although
  The one was conscious of their double woe.

X.

At last death left the balance, and the scale
Of wretched life jarred earth: and in the morn
The lover woke, confused as if a veil
Of heavy dreams involved him; weak and worn
And cold at heart, and wondering what bale
Had wounded him and left him thus forlorn:
  So still half-stunned with anguish he lay long,
  Fretful to rend the shroud that wrapt his wrong.

XI.

He turned; and on the pillow, near his head,
He saw a toy, a trifle, that gave tongue
To mute disaster: forthwith on his bed
The coiled-snake Memory hissed and sprang and stung:
Then all the fury of the storm was shed
From the black swollen clouds that overhung;
  The hot rain poured, the fierce gusts shook his soul,
  Wild flashes lit waste gloom from pole to pole.

XII.

He hardly dared to touch the petty thing,
The talisman of this tremendous spell:
A purse of dark blue silk; a golden ring,
A letter in the hand he knew so well.
Still as he sought to read new gusts would fling
Wet blindness in his vision, and a knell
  Of rushing thunder trample through his brain
  And tread him down into the swoon again.

XIII.

He read: Farewell! In one sad word I weave
More thoughts than pen could write or tongue declare.
No other word can Om-el-Bonain leave
To Weddah, save her blessing; and her prayer.
That he will quail not, though his heart must grieve,
That all his strength and valour, skill and care,
  Shall be devoted loyally to serve
  The sacred Tribe, and never self-ward swerve.

XIV.

For verily the Tribe is all, and we
Are nothing singly save as parts of it:
The one great Nile flows ever to the sea,
The waterdrops for ever change and flit;
And some the first ooze snares, and some may be
The King's sweet draught, proud Cairo's mirror; fit
  For all each service of the stream whose fame
  They share, by which alone they have a name.

XV.

And since I know that you cannot forget,
And am too sure your love will never change,
I leave my image to your soul: but yet
Keep it as shrined and shrouded till the strange
Sad dream of life, illusion and regret,
Is ended; short must be its longest range.
  Farewell! Hope gleams the wan lamp in a tomb
  Above a corpse that waits the final doom.

XVI.

This writing was a dear but cruel friend
That dragged him from the deep, and held him fast
Upon life's shore, who would have found an end,
Peace and oblivion. Turn from such a past
To such a future, and unquailing wend
Its infinite hopeless hours! he shrank aghast:
  Yet in this utmost weakness swore to make
  The dreadful sacrifice for her dear sake.

XVII.

But when he stood as one about to fall,
And would go weep upon her tomb alone,
And Abd-el-Aziz had to tell him all,
The cry of anguish took a harsher tone:
Rich harem coverlets for funeral pall,
For grave a Syrian marriage couch and throne!
  A human rival, breathing mortal breath,
  And not the star-cold sanctity of Death!

XVIII.

This truth was as a potent poison-draught,
Fire in the entrails, wild fire in the brain,
Which kindled savage strength in him who quaffed
And did not die of its first maddening pain.
It struck him like the mere malignant shaft
Which stings a warrior into sense again,
  Who lay benumbed with wounds, and would have died
  Unroused: the fresh wound makes him crawl and hide.

XIX.

A month he wandered in wild solitude;
And in that month grew old, and yet grew strong:
Now lying prone and still as death would brood
The whole long day through and the whole night long;
Now demon-driven day and night pursued
Stark weariness amidst the clamorous throng
  Of thoughts that raged with memory and desire,
  And parched, his bruised feet burning, could not tire.

XX.

When he came back, o'ermastered by his vow
To serve the Tribe through which he was unblest,
None gazed without remorse upon his brow,
None felt his glance without an aching breast:
Magnificent in beauty even now,
Ravaged by grief and fury and unrest,
  He moved among them swift and stern of deed,
  And always silent save in action's need.

XXI.

And thus went forth, and unrejoicingly
Drank deep of war's hot wine: as one who drinks
And only grows more sullen, while yet he
Never the challenge of the full cup shrinks;
And rises pale with horror when the glee
Of careless revellers into slumber sinks,
  Because the feast which could not give him joy
  At least kept phantoms from their worst annoy.

XXII.

The lion of the Azra is come back
A meagre wolf! foes mocked, who mocked no more
When midnight scared them with his fresh attack
After the long day's fighting, and the war
Found him for ever wolf-like on their track,
As if consumed with slakeless thirst of gore:
  Since he was cursed from slumber and repose,
  He wreaked his restlessness on friends and foes.

XXIII.

The lightnings of his keen sword ever flashed
Without a ray of lightning in his glance;
His blade where blades were thickest clove or clashed
Without a war-cry: ever in advance
He sought out death; but death as if abashed
Adopted for its own his sword and lance,
  And rode his steed, and swayed aside or blunted
  The eager hostile weapons he affronted.

XXIV.

Once in the thick of battle as he raged
Thus cold and dumb amidst the furious cries,
Hassan the bard was near to him engaged,
And read a weird in those forlorn fixed eyes;
And singing of that combat they had waged
Gave voice to what surpassed his own surmise:
For our young Lion of the mateless doom
Shall never go a cold corpse to the tomb!

XXV.

Awe silenced him who sang, and deep awe fell
On those who heard it round the campfire's blaze:
But when they questioned he had nought to tell;
The vision had departed from his gaze.
The verse took wing and was a mighty spell;
Upon the foe new terror and amaze,
To friends redoubled force; to one alone,
The hero's self, it long remained unknown.

XXVI.

While Weddah in the South with fiery will
Bore conquest wheresoe'er his banner flew,
Walid with royal heart and patient skill
Upon the Syrian confines triumphed too.
They never met: each felt a savage thrill
Which jarred his inmost being through and through
As still fresh fame the other's fame enlarged:
Each wished his rival in the ranks he charged.

XXVII.

And when the foemen sued at length for peace
To victors surfeited with war's alarms,
Save him who knew all rest in rest must cease,
They said: O warriors, not by your own arms,
Though they are mighty! may their might increase!
But more by Om-el-Bonain's fatal charms,
Possessing both who lost her and who won,
Have we been baffled, vanquished, and undone.

XXVIII.

Whence Hassan sang his sudden daring ode
Of Beauty revelling in the storm of fight:
For if the warriors into battle rode,
Their hearts were kindled by her living light;
Either as sun that in pure azure glowed,
Or baleful star in deep despair's black night:
And whether by despair or joy she lit
Intenser fires perplexed the poet's wit.

XXIX.

And would you know why empires break asunder,
Why peoples perish and proud cities fall;
Seek not the captains where the steedclouds thunder,
Seek not the elders in the council hall;
But seek the chamber where some shining wonder
Of delicate beauty nestles, far from all
  The turmoil, toying with adornments queenly,
  And murmuring songs of tender love serenely.

XXX.

The clashing cymbals and the trumpet's clangour
Are peacefuller than her soft trembling lute;
The armies raging with hot fire of anger
Are gentler than her gentle glances mute;
The restless rushings of her dainty languor
Outveer the wind, outspeed the barb's pursuit:
  Well Hassan knows; who sings high laud and blessing
  To this dear fatal riddle past all guessing.

PART III.

I.

The war was over for the time; and men
Returned to heal its wounds, repair its waste,
And thus grow strong and rich to fight again.
And Weddah, cold in victory's sun, embraced
The uncle whom his glory warmed; and then,
Gathering his spoil of gems and gold in haste,
  Rode forth: the clansmen wondered much to find
  His famous favourite steed was left behind.

II.

He set out in the night: none knew his goal,
Though some might fix it in their secret thought.
He could no longer stifle or control,
In calm by battle's fever undistraught,
The piteous yearning of his famished soul
Which unappeasably its food besought;
  Fretting his life out like an infant's cry,
  Let us but see her once before we die!

III.

When he returned not, soon the rumour spread,
That he had vanished now his work was done;
The prophecy had been fulfilled; not dead,
But in the body borne beyond the sun,
He lived eternal life. He heard this said
Himself in Walid's city, where as one
  Who sojourns but for traffic's sake he dwelt;
  And hearing it, more surely shrouded felt.

IV.

Courteous and humble as beseemeth trade,
While ever on the watch, some gems he sold:
Men said, this young man is discreet and staid,
Yet fair in dealing, nor too fond of gold.
He smiled to hear his virtues thus arrayed,
A smile that gloomed to frowning; but controlled
  The haughty spirit surging in his breast;
  The end in view, what mattered all the rest?

V.

The end in reach: for now the favourite slave
Of Om-el-Bonain, as he knew full well;
A frank-eyed girl, whose bosom was a wave
Whereon love's lotus lightly rose and fell;
Drew near to him, attracted by his grave
Unsceptred majesty, and by the spell
  Of his intense and fathomless regard,
  Splendid in gloom as midnight myriad-starred.

VI.

She haggled for a trinket with her tongue
To veil the eager commerce of her eyes;
Those daring smugglers when the heart is young,
For contraband of passion. His disguise
In talk with her but loosely round him hung;
She glimpsed a secret and an enterprise;
  Love's flower, unsunned by hope, soon fades; she grieves,
  Yet still returns to scent the rich dead leaves.

VII.

Till sick at heart and desperate with delay
He ventured all, abruptly flinging down
The weary mask: if death must end the play,
Better at once: I learn that in your town
Dwells Om-el-Bonain, whom you know men say,
Upon her eye-flash dropped a decent frown:
  She is my mistress, and great Walid's wife—
  The word his heart sought, stabbed in with a knife.

VIII.

Your mistress is my cousin; and will be
The friend of who shall tell her I am here.
But if I may not trust your secrecy,
Tell Walid, tell not her: and have no fear
That I will harm you for harm done to me,
Unaimed at her. The life I hold not dear
   Might dower you well. But with a passionate oath
   The eager girl swore loyalty to both.

IX.

Then hurried from him to her lady sweet,
And thrilled her frozen heart with burning pang:
For life resigned and torpid in defeat
To new contention with its fate upsprang,
This sword of hope found lying at her feet
While love's impetuous clarion summons rang:
   Weddah alive: alive and here! Beware!
   If you now mock, Hell mock your dying prayer!

X.

I saw a merchant: never chief or king
Of form so noble visited our land;
He wore a little ring, a lady's ring,
On the last finger of a feared right hand;
Some woe enormous overshadowing
Made beauty terrible that had been bland;
   He was convulsed when he would speak your name,
   From such abysses of his heart it came.

XI.

Now whether this be Weddah's self or not,
My Lady in her wisdom must decide.
The lady's questions ploughed the self-same spot
Over and over lest some grains should hide
Of this vast treasure fallen to her lot:
Swear by the Prophet's tomb I may confide
   In you as in myself until the end;
   And Om-el-Bonain lives and dies your friend.

XII.

Brave Amine swore, and bravely held the vow.
Her mistress kept her babbling all that eve,
A pleasant rill. And on the morrow: Now
Go bid him tell all friends that he must leave
In seven days; so much we must allow,
So many starving hours of bliss bereave!
   His travels urge him in his own despite;
   He gives a farewell feast on such a night:

XIII.

And in the meanwhile he shall fully learn
What is to follow. When this message came,
The thick dark in him 'gan to seethe and burn
Till soul and body fused in one clear flame.
His guests all blinked with wonder to discern
This glowing heart of joy; and flushed with shame
  Unmerited for having thought him cold,
  Who made their old feel young, their young feel old.

XIV.

The long week passed; the morning came to crown
Or kill the lovers' hope. It was a day
Well chosen, for some guests of high renown
Left Walid, who would speed them on their way;
And festal tumult filled the sunny town.
The merchant in departure strolled astray
  Amongst the groups about the palace heaving
  To glimpse the rich procession form for leaving.

XV.

And when it left, absorbing every eye;
A stream of splendours rolling with the din
Of horn and tabor under that blue sky;
Came Amine carelessly and led him in,
With chat of certain anklets she would buy;
And led him lounging onwards till they win
  A storeroom where her mistress daily spent
  Some matin hours on household cares intent.

XVI.

Large chests were ranged around it, one of which
They had made ready with most loving care;
Lurked apertures among the carvings rich,
Above its deep soft couch, for light and air:
Behold your prison cell, your palace niche,
The jewel casket of my Lady fair!
  I lock you in; from her must come your key:
  Love's captives pay sweet ransom to get free!

XVII.

She found her mistress fever-flushed, and told
Their full success: Our prisoner is secure;
A lion meek as lambkin of the fold,
Prepared your harshest torments to endure!
But, dearest Lady, as you have been bold,
Be prudent, prudent, prudent, and assure
  Long life to bliss. Now with your leave I go
  To be well seen of all the house below.

XVIII.

She took another stairway for descent,
And sauntered round to the front courtyard gate,
Chatting and laughing lightly as she went
With various groups, all busy in debate
On those departed guests: and some were shent
For meanness maugre retinue and state,
And some extolled for bounteous disposition,
And all summed up with judgment-day precision.

XIX.

Of all her fellow-slaves it seemed but one,
Whose breast was tinder for love's flame would she
Vouchsafe a spark, had spied the venture run:
Soho, my flirting madam, where is he
You brought in here an hour since with your fun?
A happy rogue, whoever he may be!
Have you already tired of this new dandy,
Or hid him somewhere to be always handy?

XX.

The stupid jealous creature that you are!
Where were your eyes, then, not to know his face?
For weeks back he has dealt in our bazaar,
And now is on the road to some new place.
He had an emerald and diamond star
I thought might win my poor dear Lady's grace;
She would not even look at it, alack!
I packed him off for ever with his pack.

XXI.

Thus these long-hapless lovers for awhile,
Enringed with dreadful fire, safe ambush found,
Screened by its very glare; a magic isle
By roaring billows guarded well till drowned;
A refuge spot of green and liquid smile
Whose rampart was the simoom gathering round:
If darkness hid them, it was thunder gloom
Whose light must come in lightnings to consume.

XXII.

And even as Iskander's self, for whom
The whole broad earth sufficed not, found at last
Full scope vouchsafed him in the narrow tomb;
So he long pining in the desert vast
As in a dungeon, found now ample room,
Found perfect freedom and content, shut fast
Alive within that coffer-coffin lonely,
Which gave him issue to that chamber only.

XXIII.

They knew what peril compassed them about,
But could not feel the dread it would inspire;
Imperious love shut other passions out,
Or made them fuel for his altar fire.
At first one sole thought harassed them with doubt;
To kill her lord and flee? Then tribe and sire
  Would justly curse them; for in every act
  He had been loyal to the evil pact.

XXIV.

He had indeed wronged them; for well he knew
Their love from infancy, their plighted troth,
When merciless in mastery he drew
From her repugnant lips the fatal oath:
That love avenged the wrong of love was due;
But still his blood was sacred to them both;
  The tender husband and the proved ally
  They dare not harm; must death come, they could die.

XXV.

Die! Often he would dream for hours supine
Upon his lidded couch, Life's dream is over;
I wait the resurrection in this shrine:
Anon an angel cometh to uncover
The inmost glories of the realm divine,
Because though dead I still am faithful lover;
  My spirit drinks its fill of bliss, and then
  Sinks back into this twilight trance again.

XXVI.

Like bird above its young one in the nest
Which cannot fly, he often heard her singing;
The thrill and swell of rapture from her breast
In fountains of delightful music springing:
It seemed he had been borne among the blest,
Whose quires around his darksome couch were ringing;
  Long after that celestial voice sank mute
  His heartstrings kept sweet tremble like a lute.

XXVII.

She heard his breathing like a muffled chime,
She heard his tranquil heart-beats through the flow
Of busy menials in the morning time;
Far-couched at night she felt a sudden glow,
And straight her breathing answered rhyme for rhyme
His softest furtive footsteps to and fro:
  And none else heard? She marvelled how the sense
  Of living souls could be so dull and dense.

XXVIII.

Once early, early, ere the dawn grew loud,
She stole to watch his slumber by its gleam;
And blushing with a soft laugh-gurgle bowed
And sank as in the bosom of a stream,
An ardent angel in a rosy cloud
Resolving the enchantment of his dream:
  Where there is room for thee, is room for us;
  So may I share thy death-sarcophagus!

XXIX.

She grew so lovely, ravishing, and sweet,
Her brow so radiant and her lips so warm;
Such rich heart-music stirred her buoyant feet,
And swayed the gestures of her lithe young form,
And revelled in her voice to bliss complete;
That Walid whirled with his great passion's storm,
  Befooled with joy, went doting down his hell:
  Oh, tame and meek, my skittish wild gazelle!

XXX.

Thus these, sings Hassan, of their love's full measure
Drank swiftly in that circle of swift fire;
A veil of light and ardour to their pleasure
Till it revealed their ashes on one pyre:
Some never win, some spend in youth this treasure,
And crawl down sad age starvelings of desire:
  These lavished royal wealth in one brief season,
  But Death found both so rich he gave them reason.

PART IV.

I.

The tender almond-blossom flushed and white
Sank floating in warm flakes through lucid air;
The rose flung forth into the sea of light
Her heart of fire and incense burning bare;
The nightingale thrilled all the breathless night
With passion so intense it seemed despair:
  And still these lovers drank love's perfect wine
  From that gold urn of secrecy divine.

II.

Then Fate prepared the end. A grey old man,
Bowed down with grief who had not bent with time,
Made way to Walid in the full divan:
His son, great-hearted and in youth's hot prime,
Was now a fugitive and under ban
For an indignant deed of sinless crime;
  A noble heirloom pearl the suppliant brought
  To clear the clouded face ere he besought.

III.

This pearl in Walid's mood of golden joy
Shone fair as morning star in rosy dawn;
He called his minion, Motar: Take this toy
Unto your Lady where she sits withdrawn,
With my love-greeting, and this message, boy:
Were this a string of such, a monarch's pawn,
  A pearl for every note, it would not pay
  That song I heard you singing yesterday.

IV.

They had been leaning for an hour perchance,
Motionless, gazing in each other's eyes;
Floating in deep pure joy, whose still expanse
Rippled but rarely with long satiate sighs;
Their souls so intermingled in the trance,
So far away dissolved through fervent skies,
  That it was marvel how each fair mute form
  Without its pulse and breath remained life-warm.

V.

When rapid footsteps almost at the door
Stung her to vigilance, and her fierce start
Shook Weddah, and that lion of proud war
Must flee to covert like a timid hart:
But drunken with the message he now bore
The saucy youth flew in, Fate's servile dart,
  Without announcement; and espied, what he,
  Still subtle though amazed, feigned not to see.

VI.

The message with the goodly pearl he gave:
She could for wrath have ground it into dust
Between her richer teeth, and stabbed the slave
Who brought it; but most bitterly she must
Put on sweet smiles of pleasure, and the knave
With tender answer full of thanks entrust.
  He lingered: Our kind lady will bestow
  Some little mark of bounty ere I go?

VII.

Her anger cried: Only the message dear
Has saved the messenger from punishment;
If evermore as now you enter here
You shall be scourged and starved and prison-pent.
He cowered away from her in sullen fear,
And darted from the room; and as he went
  The sting of her rebuke was curdling all
  His blood of vanity to poison gall.

VIII.

He hissed in Walid's ear the seething spite:
My Lord's pearl by my Lady's was surpassed;
In that rich cedar coffer to the right
I saw the treasure being hidden fast;
A gallant, young and beautiful and bright.
Unmothered slave, be that foul lie your last!
  And clove the scandal with his instant sword
  Strong Walid: Motar had his full reward.

IX.

When Weddah, plunged from glory into gloom,
Heard that last speech of Om-el-Bonain there,
A sudden ominous sense of icy doom
Assailed his glowing heart with bleak despair.
The moment that false slave had left the room
She sprang to seize her lover in his lair:
  She bowed all quivering like a storm-swept palm;
  He rose to meet her solemn, pale and calm.

X.

He clasped her with strong passion to his breast,
He kissed her with a very tender kiss:
Soul of my soul! what lives men call most blest
Can be compared to our brief lives in bliss?
But one wild year of anguish and unrest;
Three moons of perfect secret love! Were this
  My dying hour, I thankfully attest
  Of all earth's dooms I have enjoyed the best.

XI.

What, weeping, thou, such kiss-unworthy tears!
The glory of the Azra must not weep,
Whom mighty Weddah worships, for cold fears;
But only for strong love, in stillness deep,
Secluded from all alien eyes and ears.
And now to vigil, and perchance to sleep,
  Enshrined once more: be proud and calm and strong;
  Your second visitor will come ere long.

XII.

And scarcely was all said when Walid came,
Full gently stealing for a tiger-spring;
His love and fury, hope and fear and shame,
All mad with venom from that serpent's sting,
Like wild beasts huddled in a den of flame
Within the cool white palace of a king:
  She rose to greet; he deigned no glance of quest,
  But went and lolled upon that cedar chest.

XIII.

I come like any haggler of the mart,
Who having sent a bauble seeks its price:
Will you forgive the meanness of my part,
And one of these fair coffers sacrifice?
A clutch of iron fingers gript her heart
Till it seemed bursting in the cruel vice:
  And yet she quivered not, nor breathed a moan:
  Are not myself and all things here your own?

XIV.

I thank you for the bountiful award;
And choose, say this whereon I now sit here?
Take any, take them all; but that, my Lord,
Is full of household stuff and woman's gear.
I want the coffer, not what it may hoard,
However rich and beautiful and dear.
  And it is thine, she said; and this the key:
  Her royal hand outheld it steadfastly.

XV.

Swift as a double flash from thunder-skies
The angel and the devil of his doubt
Flamed from the sombre windows of his eyes:
He went and took the key she thus held out,
And turned as if he would unlock his prize.
She breathed not; all the air ran blood about
  A swirl of terrors and wild hopes of guilt;
  Calm Weddah seized, then loosed, his dagger-hilt.

XVI.

But Walid had restrained himself, and thought:
Shall I unlock the secret of my soul,
The mystery of my Fate, that has been brought
So perfectly within my own control?
That were indeed a work by folly wrought:
For Time, in this my vassal, must unroll
  To me, and none but me, what I would learn;
  I hold the vantage, undiscerned discern.

XVII.

He summoned certain slaves, and bade them bear
The coffer he had sealed with his own seal
Into a room below with strictest care;
And followed thoughtful at the last one's heel.
At noontide Amine found her mistress there,
Benumbed with horror, deaf to her appeal;
   The sightless eyes fixed glaring on that door
   By which her soul had vanished evermore.

XVIII.

Beneath the cedar whose noonshadow large,
Level from massive trunk, outspread halfway
Adown a swardslope to the river marge,
Where rosebowers shone between the willows grey,
The wondering bearers bore their heavy charge;
And where the central shadow thickest lay
   He bade them delve a pit, and delve it deep
   Till watersprings against their strokes should leap.

XIX.

Then waved them to a distance, while he bowed
Upon the coffer, hearkening for a space:
If truth bought that poor wretch his bloody shroud,
I bury thus her guilt and my disgrace;
And you, as by the whole earth disavowed,
Sink into nothingness and leave no trace:
   If not, it is a harmless whim enough
   To sepulchre a chest of household stuff.

XX.

With face encircled by his hands, which leaned
Upon the wood, he challenged clear and slow:
The hollow sound, his full hot breath thus screened
Suffused his visage with a tingling glow;
His pulse, his vesture's rustling intervened
And marred the silence: he drew back, and so
   Knelt listening yet awhile with bated breath:
   The secret lay as mute and still as death.

XXI.

Above there in her chamber Weddah might
Have leapt forth suddenly their foe to kill.
Ev'n here with hazard of swift fight and flight
Escaped or perished as a warrior still;
But thus through him her name had suffered blight:
He locked his breath and nerves with rigid will.
   So Walid first let sink his key unused,
   Then signed the slaves back: they wrought on, he mused.

XXII.

Against the dark bulk swelled the waters thin;
The stones and earth were trampled to a mound.
He then broke silence, stern and sad: Within
That coffer ye have buried, sealed and bound,
Lies one of the most potent evil djinn,
Whose hate on me and mine hath darkly frowned;
He sought to kill your mistress: Hell and Doom
And Allah's curse all guard this dungeon-tomb!

XXIII.

And Walid never spoke of this again,
And none dared ask him; for his brow grew black,
His eye flamed evil and appalling when
Some careless word but strayed upon a track
That might from far lead to it: therefore men
Spoke only of the thing behind his back.
The cedar shadow centred by that mound
Was sacredly eschewed as haunted ground.

XXIV.

But one pale phantom, noon and night and morn,
Was ever seen there; quiet as a stone,
Huddled and shapeless, weeping tears forlorn
As silent as the dews; her heart alone
And not her lips, whose seal was never torn,
Upbraiding sluggish death with constant moan.
Hushed whispers circled, piteous eyes were wet;
The captive djinnee holds her captive yet.

XXV.

Thus Walid learned too well the bitter truth,
His home dissolved, its marvellous joy a cheat;
Yet gave no sign to her: for there was ruth
Of memories gall itself left subtly sweet;
And consciousness of wrong against her youth,
And surfeit of a vengeance so complete:
He could not stab her bleeding heart; her name
With his own honour he kept pure from shame.

XXVI.

She thought Death dead, or prisoned in deep Hell
As sole assuager of the human lot:
But when the evening of the seventh day fell
Walid alone dared tread the fatal spot:
She crouched as who would plunge into a well,
Livid and writhed into a desperate knot;
Her fingers clutched like talons in the mould:
Thus the last time his arms about her fold.

XXVII.

As if to glut the demon with her doom,
And break the spell, there where her corse was found
He had it buried; and a simple tomb
Of black-domed marble sealed the dolorous mound;
And there was set to guard the cedar gloom
A triple cirque of cypress-trees around:
  Thus Love wrought Destiny to join his slaves
  Weddah and Om-el-Bonain in their graves.

XXVIII.

True Amine, freed and richly dowered, no less
Had served until the end her lady dear;
And shrouded for the grave that loveliness
Whose noon-eclipse left life without its peer:
Then sought the Azra in her lone distress,
And tended Abd-el-Aziz through the sere
  Forlorn last days; and married in the clan,
  And bore brave children to a valiant man.

XXIX.

Great Walid lived long years beyond this woe,
And still increased in wealth and power and glory;
A loyal friend, a formidable foe;
Each Azra was his mother's child saith story;
And he saw goodly children round him grow
To keep his name green when Death took him hoary:
  So prosperous, was he happy too? the sage
  Cites this one counsel of his reverend age:

XXX.

Have brood-mares in your stables, my young friend,
And women in your harem, but no wife:
A common daggerblade may pierce or rend,
A month bring healing; this, the choicest knife
In Fate's whole armoury, wounds beyond amend,
And with a scratch can poison all your life;
  And it lies naked in your naked breast
  When you are drunk with joy and sleep's rich rest.

XXXI.

As surely as a very precious stone
Finds out that jeweller who doth excel,
So surely to the bard becometh known
The tale which only he can fitly tell:
A few years thence, and Walid's heart alone
Had thrilled not to a talisman's great spell,
  His deathstone set in Hassan's golden verse;
  Here poorly copied in cheap bronze or worse.

XXXII.

He ends: We know not which to most admire;
The lover who went silent to his doom;
The spouse obedient to her lord's just ire,
The mistress faithful to her lover's tomb;
The husband calm in jealousy's fierce fire,
Who strode unswerving through the doubtful gloom
To vengeance instant, secret and complete,
And did not strike one blow more than was meet.

XXXIII.

With stringent cords of circumstance dark Fate
Doth certain lives here so entoil and mesh
That some or all must strangle if they wait,
And knife to cut the knots must cut quick flesh:
The first strong arm free severs ere too late;
Fresh writhings would but tangle it afresh:
To die with valiant fortitude, to kill
As priest not butcher; so much scope has will.

XXXIV.

These perished, and he slew them, in such wise
That all may meet as friends and free from shame,
Whether they meet in Hell or Paradise.
If he has won long life and power and fame,
Our darlings too have won their own set prize,
Conjoined for evermore in true love's name:
The Azra die when they do love, of old
Was graven with the iron pen, on gold.

XXXV.

May Allah grant eternal joy and youth
In fateless Heaven to one and all of these.
And for himself a little grain of ruth
The bard will beg, this once, while on his knees;
Who cannot always see the very truth,
And does not always sing the truth he sees,
But something pleasanter to foolish ears
That should be tickled not with straws but spears.

1868-69.

TWO LOVERS

Their eyes met; flashed an instant like swift swords
  That leapt unparrying to each other's heart,
Jarring convulsion through the inmost chords;
  Then fell, for they had fully done their part.

She, in the manner of her folk unveiled,
  Might have been veiled for all he saw of her;
Those sudden eyes, from which he reeled and quailed;
  The old life dead, no new life yet astir.

His good steed bore him onward slow and proud:
  And through the open lattice still she leant;
Pale, still, though whirled in a black rushing cloud,
  As if on her fair flowers and dreams intent.

Days passed, and he passed timid, furtive, slow:
  Nights came, and he came motionless and mute;
A steadfast sentinel till morning-glow,
  Though blank her window, dumb her voice and lute.

She loved: the Cross stretched rigid arms to scare
  Her soul from the perdition of that love;
She saw Christ's wounds bleed when she knelt in prayer,
  And frown abhorrent all the saints above.

He loved: the Crescent hung with sharp cold gleam,
  A scimitar to cleave such love in twain;
The Prophet menaced in his waking dream,
  Livid and swoln with wrath that great brow-vein.

Each sternly true to the immortal soul,
  Crushed down the passion of the mortal heart;
Which bled away beneath the iron control,
  But inwardly: they die; none sees the smart.

Thus long months went, until his time came round
  To leave that city terrible and dear;
To go afar on soulless business bound,
  Perchance for absence of a whole dead year.

No word: but as she knelt to pray one night,
  What was that silk thing pendant from the Cross?
Half of a talisman of chrysolite:
  Farewell! Full triumph stunned like fatal loss.

A sacred jewel-charm of sovereign power
  'Gainst demons haunting soul and sense and brain,
'Gainst madness: had it not until that hour
  Despite love's impious frenzy kept him sane?

Now let her look forth boldly day by day;
  He will not come to wound her with his eyes;
Now at the open lattice darkling stay,
  Only the stars are watching from the skies;

Now with clear spirit let her sing and pray;
  No human presence clouds her Lord's full light:
Now let her weep and moan and waste away,
  With broken heart a-bleeding day and night.

Thin as a spectre, haggard, taciturn,
  He reached his native city; there did all
He had to do: indifferent yet stern,
  As one whose task must end ere evening-fall.

Then sank, and knew that Azrael was near:
  The hard dull rage of impotent remorse
Burned into passion that consumed old fear:
  He loathed his unlived life, his unspent force.

"Must we be sundered, then, beyond the grave,
  By that which here has sundered us? Not so!
I can be lost with her I cannot save,
  And with these Christian dogs to deep Hell go."

A priest baptized the sinking renegade,
  A priest assured him of the Heaven he spurned;
His wealth for many a mass thereafter paid;
  And many a Moslem his example turned.

A friend had sworn to do his last behest;
  To be his swift and faithful messenger:
His own half talisman from his true breast
  Would seal the truth of all things told to her.

The funeral over, while the stars yet shone
 Though pale in the new dawn, this friend forth-spurred;
Brief rests, long stages, hurried fiercely on;
 Hating the errand, loyal to his word.

Twenty days' travel done in thrice three days,
 He reached her city, found her mansion there;
A crowd before it busy with amaze,
 Cries from within it wounding the sweet air.

She was no more since that day's sun had set;
 But wonder outran grief; for ere she died
Infinite yearning, fathomless regret,
 Flooded her soul and drowned its faith and pride.

"Shall I be happy with the saints above,
 While he is burning in the paynim Hell?
Here I have cheated him of all my love,
 But there with him I can for ever dwell."

So she renounced the Cross and threefold God,
 And died in Islam; whence the bruit was great.
Silent the friend his backward journey trod,
 Silent, and shrouded with the sense of Fate.

Thus in the very hour supreme of death
 These two great hearts first dared live perfect life;
Drew inspiration with their failing breath,
 Snatched victory as they sank down slain in strife.

And thus Fate mocked them, who when life was sweet
 Had kept apart, both famished to the core;
Let them draw near and in the death-point meet,
 But to diverge for ever, evermore.

Yet both died happy in self-sacrifice;
 A dolorous happiness, yet true and deep:
And Gods and Fate and Hell and Paradise
 Perchance are one to their eternal sleep.

Poor human hearts, that yearn beyond the tomb,
 Wherein you all must moulder into dust!
What has the blank immitigable gloom
 Of light or fervour to reward your trust?

Live out your whole free life while yet on earth;
Seize the quick Present, prize your one sure boon;
Though brief, each day a golden sun has birth;
Though dim, the night is gemmed with stars and moon.

Love out your cordial love, hate out your hate;
Be strong to grasp a foe, to clasp a friend:
Your wants true laws are; thirst and hunger sate:
Feel you have been yourselves when comes the end.

Let the great gods, if they indeed exist,
Fight out their fight themselves; for they are strong:
How can we puny mortals e'er assist?
How judge the supra-mortal right and wrong?

But if we made these gods, with all their strife,
And not they us: what frenzy equals this;
To starve, maim, poison, strangle our poor life,
For empty shadows of death's dark abyss?

This man and maiden claim a brother's tear,
Martyrs of sweet love, killed by bitter faith;
Defrauded by the Gods of glad life here,
And mocked by Doom in their heroic death.

1867.

BERTRAM TO THE MOST NOBLE AND BEAUTIFUL LADY GERALDINE

I.

Lady! this night for the first time my eyes,
My bodily eyes, drank in with sateless thirst
Thy noblest beauty; as when desert skies
By the full moon late-risen are immerst
In pure and solemn splendour. Not surprise
But breathless awe filled all my soul when first
You floated vision-strange before its sight;
O long-lost Star! O well-known unknown Light!

II.

Amid the murmurous hum and dusty glare,
With which those restless throngs confused the room,
I moved and gazed, with little thought or care,
So that the hours slipt smoothly through Life's loom,
Weaving gay vesture for an old despair;
When the unearthly sense of some great doom
Approaching near possessed me, and I thrilled
With tremors too mysterious to be stilled.

III.

Rapt by that revelation from the crowd,
My eyes were lifted,—to behold your face!
While, like a silver-burning summer-cloud,
Slow-soothed by dreamful airs through azure space,
You floated past me, glorious, tranquil, proud;
Borne gliding on with such serenest grace
By slow sweet music, that it seemed to be
Voicing thine own soul's inward harmony.

IV.

Forthwith I knew Thee, whom I had not sought
Since Youth high-hoping found no outward meed,
And, ignorant that high hope its own bliss wrought,
Left Faith to die, and nursed the bitter weed
Which blooms in poisonous gauds of heartless thought.
O sole fulfilment of my heart's great need!
Vision revealing how and whence it pined!
Blessed redeemer of my sinking mind!

V.

Thy Presence was its own most adequate
  Proclaimer, full-credentialled, to my soul:
An instant, and I recognized my Fate,
  Yielding with solemn joy to its control.
I have been wandering in this intricate
  And gloomy maze of Life, without a goal,
Baffled and hopeless; but my future way
Lies straight and clear through life and death for aye.

VI.

And more:—as moonlight up some sombre stream
  May flow in silence, a refulgent river,
Enchanting the dull line with gracious beam
  Till far back toward its fount outleaps the quiver
Of free waves joyous, living in the gleam;
  Even so your Apparition did deliver
My long-dead years from blank Lethean night,
And all lived forth in your celestial light

VII.

All glorious dreams that beautified and blest
  My fervent youth were realised in Thee;
Young longings, nobler far in their unrest
  Than later moods of scornful stagnancy,
Again could heave and agitate my breast;
  My mind, long world-filled, was empowered to see
That Life has sacred mysteries unrevealed,
And grander trusts than Earth and Time can yield.

VIII.

And all this Past was thus redeemed from death,
  Through its pure prescience of Thyself alone;
Shining in splendours of unclouded faith,
  Breathing in pants of love. Yes, I had known
Thee well in hours long faded; when your breath
  Thrilled all my frame, and when your dark eyes shone
With holy passion and exalted bliss,
Throughout my spirit tranced in ecstasies.

IX.

Yet it was not the eyes, large, solemn, deep—
  The several features of the noble face;
Nor wealth of hair, flung down in long-curved sweep,
  Flashing like rippling sunbeams, whose embrace
Doth in so warm a glow of beauty steep
  That harmony severe of stately grace
Which moulds thy form; nor was it that full form
In its serene perfection breathing warm:—

X.

Not in all these can I find all the spell
Which thrilled such instant recognition, wild
Yet doubtless as an holy oracle,
Throughout my being torpid and defiled.
Why should I fear this joyous truth to tell,
Which Love has murmured to his last-born child?—
Unaided by the mean of bodily sense,
Souls can reciprocate deep influence.

XI.

O music, flow for ever soft and sweet
Through subtler mazes, that in timeless dream
I may for ever watch her dove-quick feet
Circling in light adown thy shadowy stream,
And calm-robed form float, swaying to the beat
Of the long languid pulses; while outgleam
Her face and round arms radiant through the whirls,
Grand neck, white shoulders, queenly golden curls.

XII.

Desire, by its own wild intensity,
Was baffled,—I stood trembling, panting, pale;
And every eager step approaching Thee
Sank back: how spirits nearing Heaven must quail!
Till some strong inspiration carried me,
Half-dumb, to gasp my pleading,—and prevail;
To sue, and stand dance-ready at thy side,
Intoxicate with love and bliss and pride.

XIII.

Oh, glory of the dance sublimed to this!
Oh pure white arm electric that embraced
Ethereal-lightly my unbounded bliss!
Oh, let me die on but another taste
Of that warm breath ambrosial, and the kiss
Of those whirl-wanton ringlets; interlaced,
Quick frame with frame borne on; my lips the while
Within a neck-bend of that heavenly smile!

XIV.

Did music measure that delirious dancing?
I heard it not; I know not what strange sway
Kept us among those spectral figures, glancing
As its poor harmonies might rule their way.
I was o'erfilled with music more entrancing,
But wild, how wild! I could have fled astray,
Footing the buoyant æther's moonlight sea,
For ever and for ever linked with Thee.

XV.

Most pure and beautiful! what stayed my lips,
  When parched with thirsting near such ænomel,
From clinging unto thine for bee-like sips?
  From pasturing o'er thy brow's white asphodel?
Sealing thine eyes in passion's dear eclipse,
  With pressure on the full blue-veined swell,
And thrillings o'er the silken lashes fine,
Mid interdraughts of their deep violet wine?

XVI.

Yet, O Belovèd, though thus love-distraught,
  Blame not my spirit; for I felt You there
So holy-pure, that self-condemning thought
  Blighted my passionate worship with despair:
Half shrank I from each touch, although it brought
  Such rapture with it as I scarce could bear,
As if from harp strings ready tuned above,
To vibrate forth seraphic bliss and love.

XVII.

I felt You as a flower, my hand I knew
  With touch the lightest-tender still must harm;
Or gem so lucenter than morning dew,
  That my least breath must sully its pure charm:
The cold white moon cresting night's cloudless blue
  Above dark moorland, far from town and farm,
Or few wan stars dim-steadfast in dim skies,
Are not so dowered with awe-fraught sanctities.

XVIII.

Ay, while I thought: Could I seize one caress,
  But one grand grape from this full-fruited vine;
Grasp the rich ripeness, press and press and press,
  Till drunk with its last drain of glorious wine;
Staking the Future's infinite barrenness
  'Gainst one transcendent moment's bliss divine!—
Even then, my wildered spirit knelt subdued
Beneath thy pure calm noble maidenhood.

XIX.

Subdued by Thee,—and yet exalted more!
  Calmed by perfection of resolve and pride!
The future was drear-barren as a shore
  Wave-wasted by an ever wintry tide:
But now! Shall he, whose sanest hopes may soar
  To win the empire's Empress for his bride,
Purloin a jewel from her crowned brow?
Be kingly, heart! the throne awaits us now.

XX.

Thou wert the farther from me, as so near;
  Veiled awful, at a distance dim and great,
In that supernal spiritual sphere
  To which Love lifts, that he may isolate
The truest lovers from their union here:
  Hence their eternal Bridal, consecrate
By perfect reverence; for the Loved must be
An ever-new Delight and Mystery.

XXI.

Did aught of these tempestuous agitations
  In irrepressible gust or lightning-burst
Perturb thy heaven of starry contemplations
  In depths of moonlit quietude immerst?
I long for answer; but no meditations
  Can realise those memories, all disperst
In such wild seething mists of joy, hope, fear:—
Oh, that the question now could reach thine ear!

XXII.

But when I saw the end must come indeed,
  When laggard pairs were failing from the dance,
Surely my curbless thoughts found words to plead:—
  "Forgive, sweet Maiden!—Time and Circumstance
Are lightning-swift, and I must match their speed.
  Believe me, that I speak in heavenly trance
Diviner truth than souls can reach or prove
When uninspired by seraph-sighted Love.

XXIII.

"The Vision sways me; I must speak or die:
  Life of my life! I see, I know, I feel;
The inspiration cannot err or lie;
  Passion doth its own truth with pure fire seal;—
God from the depths of all Eternity
  Created us One Soul, in woe or weal,
In life and death, in union or apart:
Whisper but 'Yea,' assuring my sure heart!

XXIV.

"You tremble pallid, with the same new birth
  Of Love, the pure eternal Seraph-child!
Flooding with fulness all our deadly dearth,
  Is it not strange and fierce and rapture-wild?
I have dim memory that in yon poor earth
  Where late I grovelled hopeless and defiled
A mortal thing called Love with doubt and pain
Is reared: scarce one his sole true Bride can gain.

XXV.

"But time is very brief:—Shall we away
Into the great calm Night besprinkled o'er
With silver throbbing stars? My Dearest, say!
And yet, so rich in years is Evermore
That hurry were mean thrift: we well can stay,
Who long have stayed, some few brief time-lives more;
Being so certain from this hour sublime
Of coming Union, perfect, beyond Time."

XXVI.

Were such words borne exultant on my breath?
Memory, which cannot oversoar the deep
That yawns between two lives in sombre death,
Nor even that 'twixt wakefulness and sleep,
Brings no sure tidings: yet, unmoved in faith,
Though sick with failing from that glorious steep
Whence all the Promised Land was seen so clear,
I plod Time's desert with more hope than fear.

XXVII.

Yes, though I now feel faint and spiritless,—
For when such fire of rapture burns down low
We shivering cower, unmanned by chill distress,
Over the embers while the bleak winds blow;
With dismal dread that such rich blessedness
Will never more within our cold hearts glow;
Till in the bitter dark we almost deem
That vanished glory a delusive dream:—

XXVIII.

Yet have I even now deep confidence
In those great oracles of solemn bliss
Uttered so clearly to my spirit's sense
By heavenly Love who pure and perfect is;
Yet must I cherish them with reverence
Though scornful voices from our world-abyss
Proclaim the madness of both Him and them:
This staff sustains,—may fruit yet crown its stem!

XXIX.

Perchance we never more till death shall meet:
You dwell on far high places of the earth,
'Midst well-befitting pomp; beneath your feet
I labour humbly, not assured from dearth,—
The hard-won bread itself most bitter-sweet.
Were I your peer in wealth and worldly birth
You still might justly scorn my love and me;
Yet none the less must I live loving Thee.

XXX.

It is my fate; your soul hath conquered mine;
And I must be your slave and glory in
The bondage whether cruel or benign.
Still let me cherish hopes even here to win
By strenuous toil the far-off Prize divine;
And feed on visions, not so shadowy-thin,
Of gaining You beneath a nobler sun
Should I in this life's battle be undone.

XXXI.

And with my passionate love for evermore
Is blended pure and reverent gratitude;
Nor can I this full sacrifice deplore
Though You should scorn me whom You have subdued,
Or know not what devotion I outpour.
Ah, from this timeless night what boundless good
Your Presence hath bestowed on me!—no less
That I am stung with my unworthiness.

XXXII.

Dark winter ruled a desert of drear frost;
Spring's breath stole softly o'er its ice and snow;
All life revives which had so long been lost,
Trees green, flowers bloom, birds sing, and fountains flow;
The realm is laughing wide from coast to coast.
Dear May of its redemption! while we know
It seemed unworthy of thy Spring-love tender,
That love yet fits it for full Summer splendour.

XXXIII.

Henceforth my life shall not unearnest prove;
It hath an ardent aim, a glorious goal:
Numb Faith re-lives; You from your sphere above
Have planted and must nourish in my soul
That priceless blessing, pure and fervent love,
O'er which no thought of self can have control.
If with these boons come ever-longing pain,
It shall be welcomed for the infinite gain.

XXXIV.

Be pain unnoticed in a doom like this!
I see eyes gazing on my weary night
Like cold strange stars from out the world-abyss;
They gaze with scorn or pity: but their sight
Is banished from my inward golden bliss,
Floating divinely in the noonday light
Of Thee round whom I circle—O far Sun,
Through mirk and shine alike the earth's true course is run!

January 1857.

THE FADELESS BOWER

I.

Athwart the gloom of haunted years,
  Whose phantoms mock my lonely woe,
I gaze, and see through glimmering tears
  A Vision of the Long-ago:
From out the waste verge dim and far
How purely gleams that single star!

II.

Shine forth, sole star!—The dear old bower
  And I therein alone with Her,
In that rich summer's crowning hour,
  Whose quiet breathings scarcely stir
The woof of leaves and tendrils thin
Through which faint moonlight ripples in.

III.

I have this moment told my love;
  Kneeling, I clasp her hands in mine:
She does not speak, she does not move;
  The silent answer is divine.
The flood of rapture swells till breath
Is almost tranced in deathless death.

IV.

Had He whom, 'midst the whirlwind's roar,
  That fiery chariot's living light
Far through the Heaven of Heavens upbore,
  Consuming space with meteor-flight,
God's glory dazzling on his gaze,—
Had *he* then breath for prayer or praise?

V.

The bower is very dim and still;
  But clustering in the copses near
Sweet nightingales impassioned thrill
  The night with utterance full and clear
Of love and love's harmonious jars,
As glorious as the shining stars.

VI.

My lips still lie upon her hand,
Quivering and faint beyond the kiss;
The heavens before my soul expand
Athrob with dazzling light and bliss;
He in his fiery car sublime
Soared not more swiftly out of Time.

VII.

Behold her as she standeth there,
Breathless, with fixed awe-shadowed eyes
Beneath her moon-touched golden hair!
Her spirit's pure humilities
Are trembling, half would disavow
The crown I bring to crown her brow.

VIII.

Unworthy crown; and yet her life
Was set on gaining it alone:
And now in triumph without strife
Led upward to the queenly throne,
She falters from the sceptre's weight,
While flushed with high-wrought pride elate.

IX.

The simple folds of white invest
Her noble form, as purest snow
Some far and lovely mountain-crest
Faint-flushed with all the dawn's first glow;
Alone, resplendent, lifted high
Into the clear vast breathless sky.

X.

The bower is hushed and still as death;
The moonlight melting through its gloom
Is mingled with the languid breath
Of roses steeped in liquid bloom,
That bare their inmost hearts this night
To drink in deep the dew and light.

XI.

So Thou, my Rose, my perfect Queen
Of Beauty, float and breathe, nor move,
In this enchanted air serene,
Unfolding all thy heart to love;
Drink in this dew of heavenly wine,
This light which is a soul divine.

XII.

The Vision fades . . . ah, woe, woe, woe!—
While dreamed that summer's sun-tranced hours
The ghastly Hand was creeping slow
Through all their maze of leaves and flowers,
And tore my Rose off when her breath
Was sweetest: O remorseless Death!—

XIII.

Could that one hour have been drawn out
Until the end of Time's whole range!
We rapt away, so sphered about,
And made eternal, free from change;
In heart and mind, in soul and frame
Preserved for evermore the same!

XIV.

The life of that great town afar
Would breathe its murmur vast and dim,
With all the multitudinous jar
Sublimed into a solemn hymn,
Mysterious, soothing, evermore,
As heaven may hear our harsh Life-roar:

XV.

The overtrading passion-flower
Gaze ever on the starry sky
With all its constellated bower
Of large and starlike blooms, which lie
Amidst their golden fruit beset
With leaves and tendrils dark-dew-wet:

XVI.

And I for ever kneel there still,
With lifted eyes whose yearning sight
Could never drink its perfect fill
From those dear eyes of love and light,
In which to me thy thoughts shine clear
As yon high stars in yon blue sphere:

XVII.

Entranced above the worded Yes,
All flushed and pale with rapturous shame,
In that dim moonlit quietness
You stand for evermore the same,
Fairer than heaven, the Queen who now
Is trembling as I crown her brow.

XVIII.

Some ardent Seraph from above,
  Some Angel ever growing young,
Would find this Eden of our love,
  Sequestered all the worlds among;
With silent pinions gliding bright
Into our calm enchanted night.

XIX.

And, ushered by the chant divine
  Of yonder deathless nightingales,
Through all the tree-shades reach our shrine;
  And softly drawing back the veils
Of foliage let some fuller stream
Of moonlight bathe thy beauty's dream.

XX.

And gazing long, until his form
  Might seem as fixed in trance as we,
Serenely perfect breathing warm,
  Would sigh a sigh of mystery,
Half vague regrets, half longings sweet;
Then slow with lingering plumes retreat:

XXI.

Murmuring, "It is a goddess born,
  But left with mortals from her birth,
None knew that she was thus forlorn;
  Till this one youth of all the earth,
Inspired to see her as divine,
Knelt down in reverence at her shrine.

XXII.

"Her native instincts roused to life
  Leap up to claim the worship due,
Are breaking with imperial strife
  The bonds of earthly custom through;
Yet still remains some sweet half-fear
At entrance to the unknown sphere.

XXIII.

"But, oh, what glory, triumph, bliss,
  The sudden revelation wrought!
What power had that young mortal's kiss
  To thrill her thus beyond all thought?
She shares with him the Heavenly throne
Which he hath made indeed her own.

XXIV.

"And hence while every other earth
  Rolls circling through the vast abyss
With interchange of death and birth,
  And night and day, and woe and bliss,
One sphere is kept for these alway
Above all growth and all decay.

XXV.

"And here she blooms, a budded rose,
  Whose crimson fire of life new-lit
Is ever fervent to unclose
  The many-petalled wealth of it,
Embalmed from reaching to that prime
Which fades so soon in sultry Time.

XXVI.

"New dawn, far fairer than the noon;
  Hope, kinglier than thy crowning day;
Young spring's green promise fresh and boon,
  No wealthiest summer's fruit can pay;
Dreamland, so rich beyond life's bounds;
Silence, more sweet than all sweet sounds!

XXVII.

"While he who once was mean and poor
  Is climbing strenuous toward the throne,
He breathes a loftier joy be sure
  Than when the prize is made his own,
When reft of hope and valiant strife
He paces lordly-level life.

XXVIII.

"O happy bud, for ever young,
  For ever just about to blow!
O happy love, upon whose tongue
  The Yes doth ever trembling grow!
O happiest Twain, whose deathless bower
Embalms you in life's crowning hour!" . . .

XXIX.

The Seraph-murmurs die out low,
  As fades the Vision, fades the Bower.
The bower *has* faded long ago;
  The roses and the passion-flower
Have rotted in the sodden mould;
The new place quite forgets the old.

XXX.

Ah, Alice, if I dream and dream,
  What else is left me in this life?
New faces all about me teem,
  New hopes and woes and loves are rife:
I overlived my own self, Dear,
In lingering when you left me here.

XXXI.

And so my heart must soar away
  To where alone its treasure is:
Despite my dream that we should stay
  Entranced in unfulfilling bliss,
What fiery longings burn my breast
To reach, to gain, to be possessed!

XXXII.

Then fade, dim dream! and Sorrow, cease!
  While I can trust, where'er you be,
That you are waiting my release
  To live out to its depth with me,
In bowers or dens through noble spheres
The love suspended all these years.

1858.

GARIBALDI REVISITING ENGLAND

I.

This day all the eyes of our millions
  Are fixed on the south, where the light
Of the waves of the Channel laughs fearless
  Round the thunder-clouds stored with our might;
This day the great heart of the people
  Is throbbing expectant, upstirred
By a pride and a joy and a sorrow
  The voice of those thunders should word.

II.

For what is this mighty heart glowing?
  For what do these earnest eyes scan?
It glows for a hero and martyr,
  They look for a patriot, a Man;
For a hero supreme in the battle,
  A martyr no griefs could subdue,
A patriot the soul of his country,
  A man to the people all-true:

III.

For him who as grandly defended
  As grandly MAZZINI ruled Rome;
For him who gave Sicily, Naples,
  To those who had bartered his home;
For him who on sad Aspromonte
  Was pierced by a countryman's ball,—
Tu Brute! this Cæsar worst-wounded
  In soul yet forgiveth it all.

IV.

Oh, let us, we people of England,
  We millions the worst and the best,
Give welcome true, solemn, and thoughtful,
  Befitting the worth of our guest.
All titles and wealth which the monarch
  Could proffer this man is above;
The people alone can reward him
  In his own golden coin, loyal love.

V.

Nor let us forget in the shoutings
  And feasts of the triumph they plan,
That he comes not alone in his glory;
  The Nation is here in the Man:
Enceladus Italy, risen
  With earthquake, but pausing distrest;
The left arm still brutally fettered,
  And Peter's rock crushing the breast.

Evviva a te, magnanimo
  Ribelle! A la tua fronte
Più sacri lauri crebbero
  Le selve d' Aspromonte.

* * *

Chi vinse te? Deh, cessino
  I vanti disonesti:
Te vinse amor di patria,
  E nel cader vincesti.

Evviva a te, magnanimo
  Ribelle e precursore!
Il culto a te de' posteri,
  Con te d' Italia e il cuore!

Io bevo a 'l dì che fausto
L' eterna Roma schiuda
Non a' Seidni ignobili
A i Tigellini a i Giuda,

Si a libertà che vindice
Dell' umano pensiero
Spezzi la falsa cattedra
Del successor di Piero.

* * *

Sii maledetto:—e d' odio
Con inesauste brame
I fratricidi il premano
Onde Aspromonte è infame.

* * *

Odio di dei Prometeo,
Arridi a' figli tuoi:
Solcati anche dal fulmine,
Pur l' avvenir siam noi.

—GIOSUÈ CARDUCCI: *DOPO ASPROMONTE.*

1864.

EUROPE'S ROUGE ET NOIR

(AFTER MENTANA) *

There has been a slight run on the black, we know;
But those who have thereby won,
Lost very much more not long ago,
And, their desperate martingales clearly show,
Will lose all before they've done.

ca. 1867.

* [The Battle of Mentana was fought on 3 Nov. 1867, in Garibaldi's unsuccessful effort to reclaim Rome for the capital of a united Italy.]

THE JOLLY VETERANS

I.

Come rest, come rest, my leal old friends,
Loll at ease round the old round table;
Now the sun descends and our duty ends,
We'll have mirth as long as we're able.

CHORUS.

Then for all the rich blood we have ever outpoured
Let us pour in the red wine fairly;
Though our hands have warred till weak for the sword,
They can wield round the wine-cup rarely.

II.

We have marched, we have fought, in the sweltry sun
All the day since reveillé's blaring;
Now the march is done and the field is won
We've a right to rest and good faring.
Then for all, &c.

III.

See a rich warm light in the west still glows
Though the sun has sunk before us,
Though the grey shades close on the earth's repose,
And the black night gathers o'er us.
Then for all, &c.

IV.

Though our voices break as our songs we troll,
Though our eyes and our limbs fail weary,
Let each trusty soul have his pipe and his bowl,
And the last few hours shall be cheery.
Then for all, &c.

V.

Till the thick night wraps both the vale and the steep
Where through bad luck and good we fought fair, boys;
Till we sink in the deep, in the long still sleep,
Which shall drown all troubles and care, boys.
Then for all, &c.

VI.

And what reck we, when that sleep is out,
What may come with the dawn of the morrow?
We shall rise fresh and stout, with the old hearts, no doubt,
To confront toil and danger and sorrow.
Then for all, &c.

1857.

A CAPSTAN CHORUS

I.

Rolling along, bowling along,
  Over the seas we go;
And we heave up our anchor singing our song,
  With a Yeo, cheery men, yeo!
      Yeo, cheery men, yeo!

II.

The wind and the waves they will beat us about,
  And the rocks lie a-waiting below;
But our yards they are trim and our timbers are stout;
  Sing a Yeo, cheery men, yeo!
      Yeo, cheery men, yeo!

III.

Monstrous and terrible growls the old sea
  When storms make his white rage grow;
Grim death lurks then in his heart for we;
  But Yeo, cheery men, yeo!
      Yeo, cheery men, yeo!

IV.

For well are we nursed on his broad boon breast
  When his rage shall overblow,
Fed full of the free bold life which is best;
  Sing a Yeo, cheery men, yeo!
      Yeo, cheery men, yeo!

V.

How he swings him along 'neath his ocean of air
  In his great heart's careless flow!
How we win his love when his wrath we dare!
  Sing a Yeo, cheery men, yeo!
      Yeo, cheery men, yeo!

VI.

Rolling along, bowling along,
  Over the seas we go;
And we heave up our anchor singing our song,
  With a yeo, cheery men, yeo!
      Yeo, cheery men, yeo!

1857.

POLYCRATES
ON WATERLOO BRIDGE

Let no mortals dare to be
Happier in their lives than we:
Thus the jealous gods decree.

This decree was never heard,
Never by their lips averred,
Yet on high stands registered.

I have read it, and I fear
All the gods above, my Dear,
All must envy us two here.

Let us, then, propitiate
These proud satraps of sole Fate;
Our hearts' wealth is all too great.

Say, what rich and cherished thing
Can I to the river fling
As a solemn offering?

O belovèd Meerschaum Pipe,
Whose pink bloom would soon be ripe,
Must thou be the chosen type?

Cloud-compeller! Foam o' the Sea,
Whence rose Venus fair and free
On some poet's reverie!

In the sumptuous silken-lined
Case where thou hast lain enshrined
Thou must now a coffin find!

And, to drag thee surely down,
Lo! I tie my last half-crown:
We shall have to walk through town.

Penny toll is paid, and thus
All the bridge is free to us;
But no cab, nor even a 'bus!

Far I fling thee through the gloom;
Sink into thy watery tomb,
O thou consecrate to Doom!

May no sharp police, while they track
Spoils thrown after some great "crack,"
Ever, ever bring thee back!

No mudlarkers, who explore
Every ebb the filthy floor,
Bring thee to the day once more!

No sleek cook—I spare the wish;
Dead dogs, cats, and suchlike fish,
Surely are not yet a dish? . . .

Gods! the dearest, as I wis,
Of my treasures offered is;
Pardon us our heavenly bliss!

What Voice murmurs full of spleen?
Not that Pipe, but——Ssss! how mean
All the gods have ever been!

1865.

SHAMELESS

Kew Gardens.

That irreverent scoundrel grinned as he passed;
And perhaps we *did* look silly!
As I on you those sheep's-eyes cast,
Which you cast back willy-nilly:

While both my hands patted your dear little hand,
As if in a fit of abstraction;
And you let it lie at their command,
Quite unaware of the action!

A deaf mute, say, for the first time sees
A youth and a damsel dancing,
With their bows, twirls, shuffles, and one-two-threes,
Retreating and advancing.

He hears not the music, he finds no cause
For such bewildering antic;
He thinks the poor creatures obey no laws,
But are certainly daft or frantic.

So one who has felt not the love which rules
And stirs, the harmonious passion,
Must deem us lovers demented fools
To act in so queer a fashion.

I have heard that this theme in the assonant rhyme
Has been sung with a beauty entrancing:
The Spaniards have ever been sublime
In passionate love and dancing.

1865.

THE FIRE THAT FILLED MY HEART OF OLD

I.

The fire that filled my heart of old
  Gave lustre while it burned;
Now only ashes grey and cold
  Are in its silence urned.
Ah! better was the furious flame,
  The splendour with the smart:
I never cared for the singer's fame,
  But, oh! for the singer's heart
      Once more—
  The burning fulgent heart!

II.

No love, no hate, no hope, no fear,
  No anguish and no mirth;
Thus life extends from year to year,
  A flat of sullen dearth.
Ah! life's blood creepeth cold and tame,
  Life's thought plays no new part:
I never cared for the singer's fame,
  But, oh! for the singer's heart
      Once more—
  The bleeding passionate heart!

1864.

WITHERED LEAVES

I.

Let the roses lie, dear,
Let them lie;
They are all thrown by, dear,
All thrown by:
What should they do now but quickly die?

II.

Yester morn they flourished
Fresh and fair;
Dew and sunlight nourished,
Bloomed they there,
Blushing as their sweetness felt the air.

III.

Yester eve he tore them
From the tree;
Stars that glimmered o'er them,
Two or three,
Set not ere they perished, woe is me!

IV.

Scarcely seem they dead yet—
Death is new;
See the petals red yet,
Scent and dew,
All as when in life they blushing grew.

V.

Touch them yet I dare not
While they show
As if dead they were not;
Ah! I know
Dreams of life in death but madden woe.

VI.

Let them lie and wither,
As is right;
I may then steal hither
In the night;
Find them wan and shrivelled in death's blight;

VII.

Gather each leaf slowly
From its nook;
Hoard them up as holy
In the Book
Wherein Memory now for Hope must look.

1857.

THE CYPRESS AND THE ROSES

Roses and roses year by year
Do I plant and cherish here,
With many a wistful sigh and tear,
Cradling new in the self-same bier
Where the dead be.
Hope and care and love betrayed!
Blighted buds, they all, all fade
In the constant deadly shade
Of this cypress tree.

One black cypress shade will blight
Myriads of roses of delight;
One stern cypress will outlast
Ages of roses withering fast,
Too well I see.
What is left me now to do?
What, but sink at the dark root too;
Let the baleful gloom and rue
Kill also me.

1858.

MEETING AGAIN

Your eyes were burning with wild love and woe;
They seared my inmost heart:
We knew, we knew too well that I must go,
Yet could not bear to part.

We did not blame each other; that worst gall
Of common sin was spared;
Nor vindicate ourselves: confessing all,
In silence each despaired.

One yearning overwhelmed all strength and hope,—
That then and there we might
Sink down, embracing, under heaven's cope,
Engulfed in death's deep night.

And now again, after long bitter years,
We are allowed to meet,
And mingle henceforth all our sighs and tears
While these two hearts shall beat:

I from that fearful world where I was cast
Among the multitude,
To expiate the inexpiable Past
By constant doing good:

You from the sterner solitary life,
By woe and sin possessed,
And waging with them constant deadly strife
Within thine own poor breast.

Ah! can you really love me, whom you know
So weak and foul of yore?
Dear heart! *I* feel that evil long-ago
But makes me love you more.

Yet still that longing almost swayeth me—
That we should sink down deep,
And side by side, from life's sore burthen free,
Sleep death's eternal sleep.

1860.

TWO SONNETS

I.

"Why are your songs all wild and bitter sad
  As funeral dirges with the orphans' cries?
Each night since first the world was made hath had
  A sequent day to laugh it down the skies.
Chant us a glee to make our hearts rejoice,
  Or seal in silence this unmanly moan."
My friend, I have no power to rule my voice:
  A spirit lifts me where I lie alone,
And thrills me into song by its own laws;
  That which I feel, but seldom know, indeed
Tempering the melody it could not cause.
  The bleeding heart cannot for ever bleed
Inwardly solely: on the wan lips too
Dark blood will bubble ghastly into view.

II.

Striving to sing glad songs, I but attain
  Wild discords sadder than Grief's saddest tune;
As if an owl with his harsh screech should strain
  To over-gratulate a thrush of June.
The nightingale upon its thorny spray
  Finds inspiration in the sullen dark;
The kindling dawn, the world-wide joyous day
  Are inspiration to the soaring lark;
The seas are silent in the sunny calm,
  Their anthem-surges in the tempest boom;
The skies outroll no solemn thunder psalm
  Till they have clothed themselves with clouds of gloom.
My mirth can laugh and talk, but cannot sing;
My grief finds harmonies in everything.

1860.

A SONG OF SIGHING

I.

Would some little joy to-day
Visit us, heart!
Could it but a moment stay,
Then depart,
With the flutter of its wings
Stirring sense of brighter things.

II.

Like a butterfly astray
In a dark room;
Telling:—Outside there is day,
Sweet flowers bloom,
Birds are singing, trees are green,
Runnels ripple silver sheen.

III.

Heart! we now have been so long
Sad without change,
Shut in deep from shine and song,
Nor can range;
It would do us good to know
That the world is not all woe.

IV.

Would some little joy to-day
Visit us, heart!
Could it but a moment stay,
Then depart,
With the lustre of its wings
Lighting dreams of happy things,
O sad my heart!

1868.

"ALLACE! THAT SAMYN SWEIT FACE!" *

I.

"Allace! that samyn sweit face!"
Bitter tears have drowned the shine
Wont to laugh in azure eyne;
Fear hath blanched the laughing lips,
And they tremble trying to speak;
Pain hath cast a wan eclipse
On the round and rosy cheek;
Grief hath greyed the locks; and how
Care hath wrinkled that smooth brow!
"Allace! that samyn sweit face!"
Sweet then, yet sweeter now!

II.

"Allace! that samyn sweit face!"
Eyes have lost the light of youth,
But have kept their loving truth;
Lips that tremble while they speak
Speak the words that ravish me;
And the forpined hollow cheek,
Oh, it breaks my heart to see!
Hair yet witnesseth a vow;
Loyalty is on the brow:
"Allace! that samyn sweit face!"
Sweet then, yet sweetest now!

III.

"Allace! that samyn sweit face!"
Could one kindle up those eyes,
Think you, with a love-surprise?
Could a rain of kisses turn
Those poor lips to bloom once more?
Would those wan cheeks swell and burn
Fed with joys of heretofore?
Would caressing hands allow
Not a furrow on that brow?
"Allace! that samyn sweit face!"
Dear then, yet dearest now!

1865.

* "In 1549 was printed at St. Andrews a curious work entitled 'Vedderburn's Complainte of Scotlande,' in which are preserved the titles of no less than thirty-seven songs."—*The Book of Scottish Song*, by Alex. Whitelaw: Preface, p. v. Among the thirty-seven titles is this most pathetic one, "Allace! that samyn sweit face."

DAY

Waking one morning
In a pleasant land,
By a river flowing
Over golden sand:—

Whence flow ye, waters,
O'er your golden sand?
We come flowing
From the Silent Land.

Whither flow ye, waters,
O'er your golden sand?
We go flowing
To the Silent Land.

And what is this fair realm?
A grain of golden sand
In the great darkness
Of the Silent Land.

1866.

NIGHT

He cried out through the night:
    "Where is the light?
    Shall nevermore
    Open Heaven's door?
    Oh, I am left
    Lonely, bereft!"

He cried out through the night:
    It spread vaguely white,
    With its ghost of a moon
    Above the dark swoon
    Of the earth lying chill,
    Breathless, grave still.

He cried out through the night:
    His voice in its might
    Rang forth far and far,
    And then like a star
    Dwindled from sense
    In the Immense.

He cried out through the night:
    No answering light,
    No syllabled sound;
    Beneath and around
    A long shuddering thrill,
    Then all again still.

1864.

MATER TENEBRARUM

I.

In the endless nights, from my bed, where sleepless in anguish I lie,
I startle the stillness and gloom with a bitter and strong cry:
O Love! O Belovèd long lost! come down from thy Heaven above,
For my heart is wasting and dying in uttermost famine for love!
Come down for a moment! oh, come! Come serious and mild
And pale, as thou wert on this earth, thou adorable Child!
Or come as thou art, with thy sanctitude, triumph and bliss,
For a garment of glory about thee; and give me one kiss,
One tender and pitying look of thy tenderest eyes,
One word of solemn assurance and truth that the soul with its love never dies!

II.

In the endless nights, from my bed, where sleepless in frenzy I lie,
I cleave through the crushing gloom with a bitter and deadly cry:
Oh! where have they taken my Love from our Eden of bliss on this earth,
Which now is a frozen waste of sepulchral and horrible dearth?
Have they killed her indeed? is her soul as her body, which long
Has mouldered away in the dust where the foul worms throng?
O'er what abhorrent Lethes, to what remotest star,
Is she rapt away from my pursuit through cycles and systems far?
She is dead, she is utterly dead; for her life would hear and speed
To the wild imploring cry of my heart that cries in its dreadful need.

III.

In the endless nights, on my bed, where sleeplessly brooding I lie,
I burden the heavy gloom with a bitter and weary sigh:
No hope in this worn-out world, no hope beyond the tomb;
No living and loving God, but blind and stony Doom.
Anguish and grief and sin, terror, disease and despair:
Why throw not off this life, this garment of torture I wear,
And go down to sleep in the grave in everlasting rest?
What keeps me yet in this life, what spark in my frozen breast?
A fire of dread, a light of hope, kindled, O Love, by thee;
For thy pure and gentle and beautiful soul, it must immortal be.

1859.

A REQUIEM

Thou hast lived in pain and woe,
Thou hast lived in grief and fear;
Now thine heart can dread no blow,
Now thine eyes can shed no tear:
  Storms round us shall beat and rave;
  Thou art sheltered in the grave.

Thou for long, long years hast borne,
Bleeding through Life's wilderness,
Heavy loss and wounding scorn;
Now thine heart is burdenless:
  Vainly rest for ours we crave;
  Thine is quiet in the grave.

We must toil with pain and care,
We must front tremendous Fate,
We must fight with dark Despair:
Thou dost dwell in solemn state,
  Couched triumphant, calm and brave,
  In the ever-holy grave.

1858.

PROMETHEUS

(AFTER GOETHE.)

Overcast thy heaven, Zeus,
With thunder-clouds;
And practise, like a boy
Beheading thistles,
On broad oaks and mountain-tops;
You must yet leave me
My solid earth,
And my hut, which you built not,
And my hearth, whose glow
You envy me.

I know nothing poorer
Under the sun than you gods!
Miserably feeds
On tribute of sacrifice
And breath of prayer,
Your Majesty;
And would starve were not
Children and beggars
The fools of hope.

When I was a child,
And knew not how to help myself,
I raised to the sun my erring glance,
As if on high had been
An ear to hear my plaint,
A heart, like my own,
To compassionate the distressed.

Who helped me
Against the Titanic insolence?
Who delivered me from death?
From slavery?
Hast thou not all thyself accomplished,
Inviolate glowing heart?
And didst glow, young and good, and duped,
Grateful for deliverance
To the Sleeper above there?

I honour thee? Wherefore?
Hast thou ever soothed the pangs
Of the oppressed?
Hast thou ever dried the tears
Of the afflicted?
Have I not been forged to manhood *
By Time the omnipotent
And eternal Destiny,
My Lords and thine?

Didst thou really think
I should hate life,
And flee to the deserts,
Because not all
My dream-blossoms ripened?
Here sit I, form men
After my image,
A race resembling me,
To suffer, to weep,
To enjoy and rejoice,
Careless of you,
As I myself!

* Forged, in the original *geschmiedet, smith-ed,* wrought with fire and hard hammering; a term magnificently correct.

FROM THE "WEST-ÖSTLICHER DIVAN."

(AFTER GOETHE.) *

Lady, say what mean those whispers?
What so softly moves your lips?
Whispering to your own self there,
Sweeter than the sweet wine sips!
Think you to your mouth's twin sisters
Thus to draw another pair!
    I will kiss! will kiss! I murmured.

Look! how in the doubtful darkness
All in bloom the branches glow;
Downward glitters star on star;
Greening through the leafage low
Rubies by the thousand sparkle:
Yet from all thy soul is far.
    I will kiss! will kiss! I murmured.

Even thus, afar, thy lover
Proveth now the bitter-sweet,
Feeleth an unblissful bliss.
Solemnly you vowed to greet
At the full moon, greet each other;
Now the very moment is.
    I will kiss! will kiss! I murmur.

* [This poem is a translation of "The Book of Suleika," XLIV.]

[AFTER HEINE.]

CHILDHOOD

(TO HIS SISTER.)

My child, we both were children,
  And merry days we saw,
We used to creep into the fowl-house
  And hide there under the straw.

And then we set up a crowing;
  The people who passed on the road—
Cock-a-doodle-doo!—they thought it
  Was really a cock that crowed.

The cases that lay in our courtyard,
  We fitted them up with care;
And made a magnificent mansion,
  And lived together there.

And the cat of our next-door neighbour
  Came to visit us too;
We gave our best bows and courtseys
  With compliments fine and new.

As to her health we asked her,
  With friendly and earnest air;
Many old cats have we since asked
  The like with the like deep care.

And often we sat discussing,
  As if we were old and grey;
Bemoaning how things were better,
  Better indeed, in our day.

How Love, Truth, Faith had vanished,
  And left the world all bad;
How the price of coffee was shameful,
  And money was not to be had! . . .

Past, past, are the sports of our childhood,
  And all rolls past in sooth,—
The World, and Time, and Money,
  And Faith, and Love, and Truth.

A VOICE FROM THE NILE AND OTHER POEMS (1884)

[POSTHUMOUS]

A VOICE FROM THE NILE

I come from mountains under other stars
Than those reflected in my waters here;
Athwart broad realms, beneath large skies, I flow,
Between the Libyan and Arabian hills,
And merge at last into the great Mid-Sea;
And make this land of Egypt. All is mine:
The palm-trees and the doves among the palms,
The corn-fields and the flowers among the corn,
The patient oxen and the crocodiles,
The ibis and the heron and the hawk,
The lotus and the thick papyrus reeds,
The slant-sailed boats that flit before the wind
Or up my rapids ropes hale heavily;
Yea, even all the massive temple-fronts
With all their columns and huge effigies,
The pyramids and Memnon and the Sphinx,
This Cairo and the City of the Greek
As Memphis and the hundred-gated Thebes,
Sais and Denderah of Isis queen;
Have grown because I fed them with full life,
And flourish only while I feed them still.
For if I stint my fertilising flood,
Gaunt famine reaps among the sons of men
Who have not corn to reap for all they sowed,
And blight and languishment are everywhere;
And when I have withdrawn or turned aside
To other realms my ever-flowing streams,
The old realms withered from their old renown,
The sands came over them, the desert-sands
Incessantly encroaching, numberless
Beyond my water-drops, and buried them,
And all is silence, solitude, and death,
Exanimate silence while the waste winds howl
Over the sad immeasurable waste.

Dusk memories haunt me of an infinite past,
Ages and cycles brood above my springs,
Though I remember not my primal birth.
So ancient is my being and august,
I know not anything more venerable;
Unless, perchance, the vaulting skies that hold

The sun and moon and stars that shine on me;
The air that breathes upon me with delight;
And Earth, All-Mother, all-beneficent,
Who held her mountains forth like opulent breasts
To cradle me and feed me with their snows,
And hollowed out the great sea to receive
My overplus of flowing energy:
Blessèd for ever be our Mother Earth.

Only, the mountains that must feed my springs
Year after year and every year with snows
As they have fed innumerable years,
These mountains they are evermore the same,
Rooted and motionless; the solemn heavens
Are evermore the same in stable rest;
The sun and moon and stars that shine on me
Are evermore the same although they move:
I solely, moving ever without pause,
Am evermore the same and not the same;
Pouring myself away into the sea,
And self-renewing from the farthest heights;
Ever-fresh waters streaming down and down,
The one old Nilus constant through their change.

The creatures also whom I breed and feed
Perpetually perish and dissolve,
And other creatures like them take their place,
To perish in their turn and be no more:
My profluent waters perish not from life,
Absorbed into the ever-living sea
Whose life is in their full replenishment.

Of all these creatures whom I breed and feed,
One only with his works is strange to me,
Is strange and admirable and pitiable,
As homeless where all others are at home.
My crocodiles are happy in my slime,
And bask and seize their prey, each for itself,
And leave their eggs to hatch in the hot sun,
And die, their lives fulfilled, and are no more,
And others bask and prey and leave their eggs.
My doves they build their nests, each pair its own,
And feed their callow young, each pair its own,
None serves another, each one serves itself;
All glean alike about my fields of grain,
And all the nests they build them are alike,
And are the self-same nests they built of old
Before the rearing of the pyramids,

Before great Hekatompylos was reared;
Their cooing is the cooing soft and sweet
That murmured plaintively at evening-tide
In pillared Karnak as its pillars rose;
And they are happy floating through my palms.

But Man, the admirable, the pitiable,
These sad-eyed peoples of the sons of men,
Are as the children of an alien race
Planted among my children, not at home,
Changelings aloof from all my family.
The one is servant and the other lord,
And many myriads serve a single lord:
So was it when the pyramids were reared,
And sphinxes and huge columns and wrought stones
Were haled long lengthening leagues adown my banks
By hundreds groaning with the stress of toil
And groaning under the taskmaster's scourge,
With many falling foredone by the way,
Half-starved on lentils, onions, and scant bread;
So is it now with these poor fellaheen
To whom my annual bounty brings fierce toil
With scarce enough of food to keep-in life.
They build mud huts and spacious palaces;
And in the huts the moiling millions dwell,
And in the palaces their sumptuous lords
Pampered with all the choicest things I yield:
Most admirable, most pitiable Man.

Also their peoples ever are at war,
Slaying and slain, burning and ravaging,
And one yields to another and they pass,
While I flow evermore the same great Nile,
The ever-young and ever-ancient Nile:
The swarthy is succeeded by the dusk,
The dusky by the pale, the pale again
By sunburned turbaned tribes long-linen-robed:
And with these changes all things change and pass,
All things but Me and this old Land of mine,
Their dwellings, habitudes, and garbs, and tongues:
I hear strange voices; * never more the voice
Austere priests chanted to the boat of death
Gliding across the Acherusian lake,
Or satraps parleyed in the Pharaoh's halls;
Never the voice of mad Cambyses' hosts,
Never the voice of Alexander's Greece,
Never the voice of Cæsar's haughty Rome:

* "and Nilus heareth strange voices."—*Sir Thomas Browne.*

And with the peoples and the languages,
With the great Empires still the great Creeds change;
They shift, they change, they vanish like thin dreams,
As unsubstantial as the mists that rise
After my overflow from out my fields,
In silver fleeces, golden volumes, rise,
And melt away before the mounting sun;
While I flow onward solely permanent
Amidst their swiftly-passing pageantry.

Poor men, most admirable, most pitiable,
With all their changes all their great Creeds change:
For Man, this alien in my family,
Is alien most in this, to cherish dreams
And brood on visions of eternity,
And build religions in his brooding brain
And in the dark depths awe-full of his soul.
My other children live their little lives,
Are born and reach their prime and slowly fail,
And all their little lives are self-fulfilled;
They die and are no more, content with age
And weary with infirmity. But Man
Has fear and hope and phantasy and awe,
And wistful yearnings and unsated loves,
That strain beyond the limits of his life,
And therefore Gods and Demons, Heaven and Hell:
This Man, the admirable, the pitiable.

Lo, I look backward some few thousand years,
And see men hewing temples in my rocks
With seated forms gigantic fronting them,
And solemn labyrinthine catacombs
With tombs all pictured with fair scenes of life
And scenes and symbols of mysterious death;
And planting avenues of sphinxes forth,
Sphinxes couched calm, whose passionless regard
Sets timeless riddles to bewildered time,
Forth from my sacred banks to other fanes
Islanded in the boundless sea of air,
Upon whose walls and colonnades are carved
Tremendous hieroglyphs of secret things;
I see embalming of the bodies dead
And judging of the disembodied souls;
I see the sacred animals alive,
And statues of the various-headed gods,
Among them throned a woman and a babe,
The goddess crescent-horned, the babe divine.
Then I flow forward some few thousand years,

And see new temples shining with all grace,
Whose sculptured gods are beautiful human forms.
Then I flow forward not a thousand years,
And see again a woman and a babe,
The woman haloed and the babe divine;
And everywhere that symbol of the cross
I knew aforetime in the ancient days,
The emblem then of life, but now of death.
Then I flow forward some few hundred years,
And see again the crescent, now supreme
On lofty cupolas and minarets
Whence voices sweet and solemn call to prayer.
So the men change along my changeless stream,
And change their faiths; but I yield all alike
Sweet water for their drinking, sweet as wine,
And pure sweet water for their lustral rites:
For thirty generations of my corn
Outlast a generation of my men,
And thirty generations of my men
Outlast a generation of their gods:
O admirable, pitiable Man,
My child yet alien in my family.

And I through all these generations flow
Of corn and men and gods, all-bountiful,
Perennial through their transientness, still fed
By earth with waters in abundancy;
And as I flowed here long before they were,
So may I flow when they no longer are,
Most like the serpent of eternity:
Blessèd for ever be our Mother Earth.

November 1881.

RICHARD FOREST'S MIDSUMMER NIGHT

I.

The sun is setting in pale lucid gold,
  From out that strange sweet green
The heavens through half their lucid breadth unfold,
  Unfathomably serene.

The moon is risen, formless, vague and wan,
  Until the glory wane;
Less moon as yet than thin white cloud, whereon
  Young yearning eyes fix fain.

The splendour ripples on the broad calm bay
  Where still some white sails gleam
Like sea-birds in the offing far away,
  Suspended as in dream.

The wavelets whisper on the soft sands wide,
  Soothing their thread of foam,
The silver fringe of the advancing tide,
  Nearer and nearer home.

The hammers ringing on the building ships
  Are ceasing from their chime;
Our toils are closing in this sweet eclipse
  Of tranquil vesper-time.

O day slow-dying in the golden west,
  O far flushed clouds above,
O slowly rising moon, your infinite rest
  Brings infinite longing love.

II.

But what come forth with the dark,
  With the dusk of the eve and the night?
When the lessening sails of that single barque
  Shall be wholly lost to sight,
And the latest song of the latest lark
  Shall be mute in the mute moonlight.

All the stars come forth on high
  Like spirits that cast their shrouds,
And the solemn depths of the darkening sky
  Are filled with their radiant crowds,
And Hesper, lovely as Love's own eye,
  Shines beneath purple clouds;

And the maidens and youths on earth,
  On the shores of the sands and the piers,
Like a sudden bountiful beautiful birth,
  In the flower of their happy years,
With babble and laughter and musical mirth
  Under the silent spheres.

With the silent stars above,
  And the maidens and youths below
With their murmurs sweeter than voice of the dove,
  By the calm sea's plash and flow,
All the soft warm air breathes bliss and love
  In the sunset's after-glow.

For the burning hours are past,
  And the toils of the day are done,
And the peace of the night is come at last,
  And the moon succeeds the sun;
And the pulses of Heaven and Earth throb fast,
  All the thousands throbbing as one.

III.

Oh, a myriad stars may shine,
  But ever the one sole Moon,
The Queen of the stars and the night divine,
  The Queen most fair and boon,
For her mystical shine is Love's best wine,
  And her midnight Love's own noon.

I have heard that the smallest star
  Is a much more mighty sphere,
Than the regnant moon in her silver car
  That we love and worship here;
But behold, the star it is faint and far,
  While our moon is bright and near.

Let the star in its distant skies
  Burn glorious and great,
A sun of life to the far-off eyes
  In the planets that swell its state;
But it sways not the tides of our seas as it rides,
  Nor the tides of our human fate.

So, there on the shining sand,
  And there on the long curved pier,
Fair ladies circle fulgent and grand,
  Each in her proper sphere;
But the sun so far is a little star,
  While my Love is near and dear:

Is near and dear and bright,
  The Queen of my Heavens above,
The pure sweet light of my darkest night,
  My Lotus, my Lily, my Dove;
And my pulses flow and thrill and glow
  In the sway of Her splendid love.

IV.

Farewell, fair margent of the sea,
  Fair city of the noble bay;
I seek my Love who looks for me,
  Not far away, not far away,
Over the hill of wood and lea,
  And near that other bay adown
  The winding valley lone and lown.

The valley with its tethered kine,
  The orchard plots and fields of grain,
So tranquil in the broad sunshine,
  More tranquil now the high stars reign,
And tranquil most and most divine
  When over it comes floating soon
  The mystic splendour of the moon.

The cottage nestles sheltered well
  Among rich apple-trees, embowered
In its side-nook of dimpled dell;
  Roses and jasmine starry-flowered
Clothe all its front; the tide's long swell
  Sounds up the valley slow and calm,
  To ebb away a dying psalm.

Through clouds of delicate blossom white
  The red tiles burn with steadfast glow,
Or through green leaves and apples bright
  And hoary stems a-slanting low,
When morning crowns the eastern height;
  The blue smoke quivering up the air
  Its slender breath of household prayer;

The sweet flowers flush and glow and yearn,
  With wild bees humming in their bloom,
The lane comes winding like a burn
  Through banks of golden gorse and broom,
And edged with grass and fringed with fern;
  The rapturous larks are singing high
  In all the regions of the sky.

But that is day, these days of June
  A-verging into hot July,
And this is night, more rich and boon,
  Although its hours so swiftly fly:
O light of lovers, gracious moon,
  My own Moon waits me full of love,
  Brighter than all heaven's stars above.

V.

Ere the road curves up through the shade
  With its transverse moonlight bars,
While above in the leafy gloom of the glade
  Hang the glittering fruits of the stars;
Let me pause for a moment and turn and look down
Beyond all the villa clumps duskily brown,
And beyond all the pale yellow lamps of the town;

To the sea and the noble bay
  Lulled asleep in the broad moonshine;
To the shore where our youths and our maidens stray
  On the sands and the pier's long line,
Like a swarm of bees that suspend their flight
To gather the honey of love and delight
In the heart of the azure-leaved Flower of the Night.

Like a swarm of buzzing bees
  Whose busy murmurs float
On the wide-wafting wings of the southerly breeze,
  Merged into one vague note:
They are drunk with the honey of love and of bliss,
And they throb with the stars of the azure abyss,
And the air is as soft as a tremulous kiss.

I shall find Her all alone
  At the wicket of garden and lane,
Or out of the porch by the rose o'ergrown
  She will glide all flushed and fain:
So gather your honey, you bees that swarm,
I drink-in my nectar all golden and warm
From a flower-cup the fairest in colour and form.

VI.

Do I love you more for your own grand sake,
  Or more for the bliss you bring to me?
You big black arms of the elms that make
  The little white arms cling to me.

Do I love you more for your own sweet sake,
  Or more for my heart's desire to me?
You flowers of the night whose perfumes make
  The sweetest breath suspire to me.

Do I love you more for your own dear sake,
  Or more for the joys that rill through me?

You nightingales whose voices make
  The dearest soft voice thrill through me.

Do I love you more for your own bright sake,
  Or more for the joys that stream on me?
You stars of the heaven whose glances make
  The brightest moist eyes beam on me.

Do I love you more for your own dear sake,
  Or more for the bliss possessing me?
You whispering waves of the sea that make
  The dear lips mute caressing me.

Do I love you more for your own pure sake,
  Or more for the Heavens you declare to me?
You naked moon, whose splendours make
  The soul of her pure love bare to me.

Oh, I love you all for your own love's sake,
  And my love of my Love and her love to me,
Dear earth and sea and heavens that make
  This life as the life above to me.

VII.

She is not there at the rustic gate,
  Nor in the garden, nor in the porch:
Lucy! the hour is not yet late,
  The moon, our this night's signal torch,
The beacon-fire of our heart's desire,
    Over the wooded promontory
    Shines on our bay in all her glory.

Good Father nods in his old arm-chair,
  A-dozing over his evening pipe,
The old brown jug at his elbow there
  Half-full of the old ale humming-ripe;
For his work is done with the set o' the sun,
    And he settles down content and placid,
    Sweetness without one drop of acid.

And our little Mother upright sits,
  Under her glasses glancing keen
And listening sharp as she knits and knits;
  Nothing unheard, nothing unseen;
Her work is not done with the set o' the sun,
    And she never nods and she never dozes
    Until her head in the bed reposes.

Or else the dear old couple play
  Some game they have played this thirty year;
Cribbage, and how she pegs away!
  Perhaps Don Pedro when I appear,
And Lucy and I must join and try
    Which shall prove the more prompt and able,
    Or youth or eld at the old oak-table.

But Lucy, Lucy, where is She?
  Not in the garden, not at the gate,
Not in the porch a-looking for me,
  Not at the parlour-lattice in wait!
Can she sew or read and take no heed
    How the stars are bright and the moon is shining,
    And I am without here longing and pining?

O Lucy, Lucy! can you dream
  O'er the loves in a book with your own Love near?—
Out from the back-shade darts a gleam;
  Lucy is here! Lucy is here!
Dancing light in her eyes of a wicked surprise,
    White rose in her hair, red rose in her fingers,
    How she hastens! and how she lingers!

Oh, the smile of your mouth!—but I want my own kiss!
  Oh, the flush of your face!—but your head on my breast!
Oh, the rose in your yellow hair fragrant with bliss!
  Oh, the rose in your hand by my own hand caressed!
O dear form I enlace in this perfect embrace,
    My Love all a-tremble with passion and yearning,
    While under my kisses the pure neck is burning!

VIII.

Oh, how the nights are short,
  These heavenly nights of June!
The long day all amort
With toil, the time to court
  So stinted in its boon!

In winter brief work-days,
  Long rest-nights dark and cold,
Dank mists and miry ways,
Black boughs and leafless sprays,
  No sweet birds singing bold.

I find this order strange,
  And not at all the right;
Not thus would I arrange:
May I propose a change
  In seasons, day and night?

Cold days, warm nights, be long,
  Cold nights, warm days, be brief:
Warm nights of scent and song,
Nights long as love is strong,—
  Oh, Love should have relief!

Yet some days we would spare,
  Long days of love and rest,
So long, so rich, so rare,
When but to breathe the air
  Is to be fully blest.

When deep in fern we lie
  With golden gorse above;
Deep sapphire sea and sky,
Ringing of larks on high,
  Our whole world breathing love.

Long days of perfect rest!
  Long days of infinite bliss!
Your head upon my breast;
Possessing and possessed,
  Dissolving in a kiss.

IX.

Oh, how the nights are short,
  These heavenly nights of June!
The long hot day amort
With toil, the time to court
  So stinted in its boon!

But three or four brief hours
  Between the afterglow
And dawnlight; while the flowers
Are dreaming in their bowers,
  And birds their song forego;

And in the noon of night,
  As in the noon of day,
Flowers close on their delight,
Birds nestle from their flight,
  Deep stillness holdeth sway:

Only the nightingales
  Yet sing to moon and stars,
Although their full song fails;
The corn-crake never quails,
  But through the silence jars.

So few brief hours of peace;
  And only one for us,
Alone, in toil's surcease,
To feed on love's increase:
  It is too cruel thus!

Did little Mother chide
  Because our sewing dropped
And we sat dreamy-eyed?
Dear Mother, good betide,
  The scolding must be stopped.

Dear Mother, good and true,
  All-loving while you blame,
When spring brings skies of blue
And buds and flowers anew,
  I come in with my claim!

I claim my Love, my Own,
  Yet ever yours the while,
Under whose care hath grown
The sweetest blossom blown
  In all our flower-loved isle.

The Spring renews its youth
  And youth renews its Spring:
Love's wildest dreams are truth,
Magic is sober sooth;
  Charm of the Magic Ring!

X.

As we gaze and gaze on the sleeping sea
  Beneath the moon's soft splendour,
The wide expanse inspires a trance
  Most solemn and most tender.

The heavens all silent with their stars,
  The sweet air hardly breathing,
The liquid light of ripples bright
  Wreathing and interwreathing.

The tide self-poised now at the full,
  Scarce swaying, almost soundless;
The sea between twin skies serene,
  Calm, fathomless and boundless.

What specks are we in this vast world,
  Our little lives how fleeting!
While star on star is throbbing far,
  What matter two hearts beating?

How many many million years
  Those living lights supernal
Shone ere our birth on this small earth!
  Yet they are not eternal.

How many many million years,
  When we have passed death's portal,
Those stars shall shine as now divine!
  Yet they are not immortal.

Deep as may be the deepest sea,
  Yet deeper is our love, dear;
Our souls dilate with bliss as great
  As all the heavens above, dear.

We float in dream until we seem
  With all these worlds revolving;
Our love intense, our bliss immense,
  Throughout the whole dissolving.

A calm profound and infinite
  Within us as without us;
Our pulses beat in union sweet
  With all the Life about us.

We are the whole World yet ourself
By some divine illusion;
The I in Thee and Thou in Me
By mystic interfusion.

Our soul-tides poising at the full,
Scarce swaying, tranced in glory,
Have reached the clime of timeless time
Amid the transitory.

We have not spoken now so long,
But mute in still caressing,
Without one kiss have breathed the bliss
Too perfect for expressing.

XI.

Good night; good night! how truly hath been sung,
It is good night then only when the tongue
Need never say Good night;
When hearts may beat together till the morrow
Dawns on long hours fulfilled of bliss not sorrow,
And eyes that close for darkness, frayed and stung
By the so less sweet light.

Good night; good night! I leave you to sweet sleep
And lovely dreams of love divinely deep;
May this be your good night:
My straining arms reluctantly surrender
Into the arms of sleep divinely tender
My Dearest thus, to safely surely keep
Until the morn shines bright.

Good night; good night! I leave you and go back
Into the silent city; and, alack!
Can this be my good night?
Yet Love, Bliss, Memory, radiant Hope are burning
In brain all throbbing and in heart all yearning,
As moon and stars in skies that else were black
With glorifying might.

Good night; good night! If parting when so brief
Is yet so bitter, what would be our grief
With Good-bye for Good night!—
Farewell! for weeks, for months, for years, for ever!
Alas for Lovers whom the Fates thus sever!
Where can they look for comfort or relief?
Oh, worse than mortal blight!

Good night; good night! for more than twenty hours!
The sleeping time of all the birds and flowers,
For whom it is good night;
The waking time of all the sun's wide glory:
Ere yet the moon has crowned yon promontory
To-morrow evening, back to Eden's bowers
I come with swerveless flight.

Good night; good night! my Life, my Love, my Bliss!
But one more last embrace, one more last kiss,
To sweeten sour Good night:
O dear Heavens, have her in your holy keeping!
O moon and stars, watch tenderly her sleeping!
O sun, thou regent of our World-abyss,
Awake her to delight!

December 1881.

INSOMNIA

"Sleepless himself to give to others sleep."
"He giveth His beloved sleep."

I.

I heard the sounding of the midnight hour;
The others one by one had left the room,
In calm assurance that the gracious power
Of sleep's fine alchemy would bless the gloom,
Transmuting all its leaden weight to gold,
To treasures of rich virtues manifold,
New strength, new health, new life;
Just weary enough to nestle softly, sweetly,
Into divine unconsciousness, completely
Delivered from the world of toil and care and strife.

II.

Just weary enough to feel assured of rest,
Of Sleep's divine oblivion and repose,
Renewing heart and brain for richer zest
Of waking life when golden morning glows,
As young and pure and glad as if the first
That ever on the void of darkness burst
With ravishing warmth and light;
On dewy grass and flowers and blithe birds singing,
And shining waters, all enraptured springing,
Fragrance and shine and song, out of the womb of night.

III.

But I with infinite weariness outworn,
Haggard with endless nights unblessed by sleep,
Ravaged by thoughts unutterably forlorn,
Plunged in despairs unfathomably deep,
Went cold and pale and trembling with affright
Into the desert vastitude of Night,
Arid and wild and black;
Foreboding no oasis of sweet slumber,
Counting beforehand all the countless number
Of sands that are its minutes on my desolate track.

IV.

And so I went, the last, to my drear bed,
Aghast as one who should go down to lie
Among the blissfully unconscious dead,
Assured that as the endless years flowed by
Over the dreadful silence and deep gloom
And dense oppression of the stifling tomb,
He only of them all,
Nerveless and impotent to madness, never
Could hope oblivion's perfect trance for ever:
An agony of life eternal in death's pall.

V.

But that would be for ever, without cure!—
And yet the agony be not more great;
Supreme fatigue and pain, while they endure,
Into Eternity their time translate;
Be it of hours and days or countless years,
And boundless æons, it alike appears
To the crushed victim's soul;
Utter despair foresees no termination,
But feels itself of infinite duration;
The smallest fragment instant comprehends the whole.

VI.

The absolute of torture as of bliss
Is timeless, each transcending time and space;
The one an infinite obscure abyss,
The other an eternal Heaven of grace.—
Keeping a little lamp of glimmering light
Companion through the horror of the night,
I laid me down aghast
As *he* of all who pass death's quiet portal
Malignantly reserved alone immortal,
In consciousness of bale that must for ever last.

VII.

I laid me down and closed my heavy eyes,
As if sleep's mockery might win true sleep;
And grew aware, with awe but not surprise,
Blindly aware through all the silence deep,
Of some dark Presence watching by my bed,
The awful image of a nameless dread;
But I lay still fordone;
And felt its Shadow on me dark and solemn
And steadfast as a monumental column,
And thought drear thoughts of Doom, and heard the bells chime One.

VIII.

And then I raised my weary eyes and saw,
By some slant moonlight on the ceiling thrown
And faint lamp-gleam, that Image of my awe,
Still as a pillar of basaltic stone,
But all enveloped in a sombre shroud
Except the wan face drooping heavy-browed,
With sad eyes fixed on mine;
Sad weary yearning eyes, but fixed remorseless
Upon my eyes yet wearier, that were forceless
To bear the cruel pressure; cruel, unmalign.

IX.

Wherefore I asked for what I knew too well:
O ominous midnight Presence, What art Thou?
Whereto in tones that sounded like a knell:
"I am the Second Hour, appointed now
To watch beside thy slumberless unrest."
Then I: Thus both, unlike, alike unblest;
For I should sleep, you fly:
Are not those wings beneath thy mantle moulded?
O Hour! unfold those wings so straitly folded,
And urge thy natural flight beneath the moonlit sky.

X.

"My wings shall open when your eyes shall close
In real slumber from this waking drear;
Your wild unrest is my enforced repose;
Ere I move hence you must not know me here."
Could not your wings fan slumber through my brain,
Soothing away its weariness and pain?
"Your sleep must stir my wings:
Sleep, and I bear you gently on my pinions
Athwart my span of hollow night's dominions,
Whence hour on hour shall bear to morning's golden springs."

XI.

That which I ask of you, you ask of me,
O weary Hour, thus standing sentinel
Against your nature, as I feel and see
Against my own your form immovable:
Could I bring Sleep to set you on the wing,
What other thing so gladly would I bring?
Truly the poet saith:
If that is best whose absence we deplore most,
Whose presence in our longings is the foremost,
What blessings equal Sleep save only love and death?

XII.

I let my lids fall, sick of thought and sense,
But felt that Shadow heavy on my heart;
And saw the night before me an immense
Black waste of ridge-walls, hour by hour apart,
Dividing deep ravines: from ridge to ridge
Sleep's flying hour was an aërial bridge;
But I, whose hours stood fast,
Must climb down painfully each steep side hither,
And climb more painfully each steep side thither,
And so make one hour's span for years of travail last.

XIII.

Thus I went down into that first ravine,
Wearily, slowly, blindly, and alone,
Staggering, stumbling, sinking depths unseen,
Shaken and bruised and gashed by stub and stone;
And at the bottom paven with slipperiness,
A torrent-brook rushed headlong with such stress
Against my feeble limbs,
Such fury of wave and foam and icy bleakness
Buffeting insupportably my weakness
That when I would recall dazed memory swirls and swims.

XIV.

How I got through I know not, faint as death;
And then I had to climb the awful scarp,
Creeping with many a pause for panting breath,
Clinging to tangled root and rock-jut sharp;
Perspiring with faint chills instead of heat,
Trembling, and bleeding hands and knees and feet;
Falling, to rise anew;
Until, with lamentable toil and travel
Upon the ridge of arid sand and gravel
I lay supine half-dead and heard the bells chime Two;

XV.

And knew a change of Watchers in the room
Without a stir or sound beside my bed;
Only the tingling silence of the gloom,
The muffled pulsing of the night's deep dread;
And felt an image mightier to appal,
And looked; the moonlight on the bed-foot wall
And corniced ceiling white
Was slanting now; and in the midst stood solemn
And hopeless as a black sepulchral column
A steadfast shrouded Form, the Third Hour of the night.

XVI.

The fixed regard implacably austere,
Yet none the less ineffably forlorn.
Something transcending all my former fear
Came jarring through my shattered frame outworn:
I knew that crushing rock could not be stirred;
I had no heart to say a single word,
But closed my eyes again;
And set me shuddering to the task stupendous
Of climbing down and up that gulf tremendous
Unto the next hour-ridge beyond Hope's farthest ken.

XVII.

Men sigh and plain and wail how life is brief:
Ah yes, our bright eternities of bliss
Are transient, rare, minute beyond belief,
Mere star-dust meteors in Time's night-abyss;
Ah no, our black eternities intense
Of bale are lasting, dominant, immense,
As Time which is their breath;
The memory of the bliss is yearning sorrow,
The memory of the bale clouds every morrow
Darkening through nights and days unto the night of Death.

XVIII.

No human words could paint my travail sore
In the thick darkness of the next ravine,
Deeper immeasurably than that before;
When hideous agonies, unheard, unseen,
In overwhelming floods of torture roll,
And horrors of great darkness drown the soul,
To be is not to be
In memory save as ghastliest impression,
And chaos of demoniacal possession. . . . .
I shuddered on the ridge, and heard the bells chime Three.

XIX.

And like a pillar of essential gloom,
Most terrible in stature and regard,
Black in the moonlight filling all the room
The Image of the Fourth Hour, evil-starred,
Stood over me; but there was Something more,
Something behind It undiscerned before,
More dreadful than Its dread,
Which overshadowed it as with a fateful
Inexorable fascination hateful,—
A wan and formless Shade from regions of the dead.

XX.

I shut my eyes against that spectral Shade,
Which yet allured them with a deadly charm,
And that black Image of the Hour, dismayed
By such tremendous menacing of harm;
And so into the gulf as into Hell;
Where what immeasurable depths I fell,
With seizures of the heart
Whose each clutch seemed the end of all pulsation,
And tremors of exanimate prostration,
Are horrors in my soul that never can depart.

XXI.

If I for hope or wish had any force,
It was that I might rush down sharply hurled
From rock to rock until a mangled corse
Down with the fury of the torrent whirled,
The fury of black waters and white foam,
To where the homeless find their only home,
In the immense void Sea,
Whose isles are worlds, surrounding, unsurrounded,
Whose depths no mortal plummet ever sounded,
Beneath all surface storm calm in Eternity.

XXII.

Such hope or wish was as a feeble spark,
A little lamp's pale glimmer in a tomb,
To just reveal the hopeless deadly dark
And wordless horrors of my soul's fixed doom:
Yet some mysterious instinct obstinate,
Blindly unconscious as a law of Fate,
Still urged me on and bore
My shattered being through the unfeared peril
Of death less hateful than the life as sterile:
I shuddered on the ridge, and heard the bells chime Four.

XXIII.

The Image of that Fifth Hour of the night
Was blacker in the moonlight now aslant
Upon its left than on its shrouded right;
And over and behind It, dominant,
The shadow not Its shadow cast its spell,
Most vague and dim and wan and terrible,
Death's ghastly aureole,
Pregnant with overpowering fascination,
Commanding by repulsive instigation,
Despair's envenomed anodyne to tempt the Soul.

XXIV.

I closed my eyes, but could no longer keep
Under that Image and most awful Shade,
Supine in mockery of blissful sleep,
Delirious with such fierce thirst unallayed;
Of all worst agonies the most unblest
Is passive agony of wild unrest:
Trembling and faint I rose,
And dressed with painful efforts, and descended
With furtive footsteps and with breath suspended,
And left the slumbering house with my unslumbering woes.

XXV.

Constrained to move through the unmoving hours,
Accurst from rest because the hours stood still;
Feeling the hands of the Infernal Powers
Heavy upon me for enormous ill,
Inscrutable intolerable pain,
Against which mortal pleas and prayers are vain,
Gaspings of dying breath,
And human struggles, dying spasms yet vainer:
Renounce defence when Doom is the Arraigner;
Let impotence of Life subside appeased in Death.

XXVI.

I paced the silent and deserted streets
In cold dark shade and chillier moonlight grey;
Pondering a dolorous series of defeats
And black disasters from life's opening day,
Invested with the shadow of a doom
That filled the Spring and Summer with a gloom
Most wintry bleak and drear;
Gloom from within as from a sulphurous censer
Making the glooms without for ever denser,
To blight the buds and flowers and fruitage of my year.

XXVII.

Against a bridge's stony parapet
I leaned, and gazed into the waters black;
And marked an angry morning red and wet
Beneath a livid and enormous rack
Glare out confronting the belated moon,
Huddled and wan and feeble as the swoon
Of featureless Despair:
When some stray workman, half-asleep but lusty,
Passed urgent through the rainpour wild and gusty,
I felt a ghost already, planted watching there.

XXVIII.

As phantom to its grave, or to its den
Some wild beast of the night when night is sped,
I turned unto my homeless home again
To front a day only less charged with dread
Than that dread night; and after day, to front
Another night of—what would be the brunt?
I put the thought aside,
To be resumed when common life unfolded
In common daylight had my brain remoulded;
Meanwhile the flaws of rain refreshed and fortified.

XXIX.

The day passed, and the night; and other days,
And other nights; and all of evil doom;
The sun-hours in a sick bewildering haze,
The star-hours in a thick enormous gloom,
With rending lightnings and with thunder-knells;
The ghastly hours of all the timeless Hells:—
Bury them with their bane!
I look back on the words already written,
And writhe by cold rage stung, by self-scorn smitten,
They are so weak and vain and infinitely inane. . . .

XXX.

"How from those hideous Malebolges deep
I ever could win back to upper earth,
Restored to human nights of blessed sleep
And healthy waking with the new day's birth?"—
How do men climb back from a swoon whose stress,
Crushing far deeper than all consciousness,
Is deep as deep death seems?
Who can the steps and stages mete and number
By which we re-emerge from nightly slumber?—
Our poor vast petty life is one dark maze of dreams.

March 1882.

HE HEARD HER SING

We were now in the midmost Maytime, in the full green flood of the Spring,
When the air is sweet all the daytime with the blossoms and birds that sing;
When the air is rich all the night, and richest of all in its noon
When the nightingales pant the delight and keen stress of their love to the moon;
When the almond and apple and pear spread wavering wavelets of snow
In the light of the soft warm air far-flushed with a delicate glow;
When the towering chestnuts uphold their masses of spires red or white,
And the pendulous tresses of gold of the slim laburnum burn bright,
And the lilac guardeth the bowers with the gleam of a lifted spear,
And the scent of the hawthorn flowers breathes all the new life of the year,
And the linden's tender pink bud by the green of the leaf is o'errun,
And the bronze-beech shines like blood in the light of the morning sun,
And the leaf-buds seem spangling some network of gossamer flung on the elm,
And the hedges are filling their fretwork with every sweet green of Spring's realm;
And the flowers are everywhere budding and blowing about our feet,
The green of the meadows star-studding and the bright green blades of the wheat.

An evening and night of song. For first when I left the town,
And took the lane that is long and came out on the breeze-swept down,
The sunset heavens were all ringing wide over the golden gorse
With the skylarks' rapturous singing, a revel of larks in full force,
A revel of larks in the raptures surpassing all raptures of Man,
Who ponders the blessings he captures and finds in each blessing some ban.
And then I went on down the dale in the light of the afterglow,
In that strange light green and pale and serene and pathetic and slow
In its fading round to the north, while the light of the unseen moon
From the east comes brightening forth an ever-increasing boon.
And there in the cottage my Alice, through the hours so short and so long,
Kept filled to the brim love's chalice with the wine of music and song:
And first with colossal Beethoven, the gentlest spirit sublime
Of the harmonies interwoven, Eternity woven with Time;
Of the melodies slowly and slowly dissolving away through the soul,
While it dissolves with them wholly and our being is lost in the Whole;
As gentle as Dante the Poet, for only the lulls of the stress
Of the mightiest spirits can know it, this ineffable gentleness:
And then with the delicate tender fantastic dreamer of night,
Whose splendour is starlike splendour and his light a mystic moonlight,
Nocturn on nocturn dreaming while the mind floats far in the haze
And the dusk and the shadow and gleaming of a realm that has no days:
And then she sang ballads olden, ballads of love and of woe,
Love all burningly golden, grief with heart's-blood in its flow;

Those ballads of Scotland that thrill you, keen from the heart to the heart,
Till their pathos is seeming to kill you, with an exquisite bliss in the smart.

And then we went out of the valley and over the spur of the hill,
And down by a woodland alley where the sprinkled moonlight lay still;
For the breeze in the boughs was still and the breeze was still in the sprays,
And the leaves had scarcely a thrill in the stream of the silver rays,
But looked as if drawn on the sky or etched with a graver keen,
Sharp shadows thrown from on high deep out of the azure serene:
And a certain copse we knew, where never in Maytime fails,
While the night distils sweet dew, the song of the nightingales:
And there together we heard the lyrical drama of love
Of the wonderful passionate bird which swelleth the heart so above
All other thought of this life, all other care of this earth,
Be it of pleasure or strife, be it of sorrow or mirth,
Saving the one intense imperious passion supreme
Kindling the soul and the sense, making the world but a dream,
The dream of an aching delight and a yearning afar and afar,
While the music thrills all the void night to the loftiest pulsating star:—
"Love, love only, for ever; love with its torture and bliss;
All the world's glories can never equal two souls in one kiss."

And when I had bidden farewell to my Love at the cottage door,
For a night and a day farewell, for a night and a day and no more,
I went down to the shining strand of our own belovèd bay,
To the shore of soft white sand caressed by the pure white spray,
In the arms of the hills serene, clothed from the base to the crest
With garments of manifold green, curving to east and to west;
And high in the pale blue south where the clouds were white as wool,
Over the little bay-mouth the moon shone near the full;
And I walked by the waves' soft moan, for my heart was beyond control,
And I needed to be alone with the night and my love and my soul,
And I could not think of sleep in the moonlight broad and clear,
For a music solemn and deep filled all my spirit's sphere,
A music interwoven of all that night I had heard,
From the music of mighty Beethoven to the song of the little brown bird.

And thus as I paced the shore beneath the azure abyss,
And my soul thrilled more and more with a yearning and sadness of bliss,
A voice came over the water from over the eastern cape,
Like the voice of some ocean daughter wailing a lover's escape,—
A voice so plaintive and distant, as faint as a wounded dove,
Whose wings are scarcely resistant to the air beneath and above,
Wavering, panting, urging from the farthest east to the west,
Over some wild sea surging in the hope forlorn of its nest;
A voice that quivered and trembled, with falls of a broken heart,
And then like that dove reassembled its forces to play out its part;
Till it came to a fall that was dying, the end of an infinite grief,

A sobbing and throbbing and sighing that death was a welcome relief:
And so there was silence once more, and the moonlight looked sad as a pall,
And I stood entranced on the shore and marvelled what next would befall.

And thus all-expectant abiding I waited not long, for soon
A boat came gliding and gliding out in the light of the moon,
Gliding with muffled oars, slowly, a thin dark line,
Round from the shadowing shores into the silver shine
Of the clear moon westering now, and still drew on and on,
While the water before its prow breaking and glistering shone,
Slowly in silence strange; and the rower rowed till it lay
Afloat within easy range deep in the curve of the bay:
And besides the rower were two; a Woman, who sat in the stern,
And Her by her fame I knew, one of those fames that burn,
Startling and kindling the world, one whose likeness we everywhere see;
And a man reclining half-curled with an indolent grace at her knee,
The Signor, lord of her choice; and he lightly touched a guitar;—
A guitar for that glorious voice! Illumine the sun with a star!
She sat superb and erect, stately, all-happy, serene,
Her right hand toying unchecked with the hair of that page of a Queen;
With her head and her throat and her bust like the bust and the throat and the head
Of Her who has long been dust, of her who shall never be dead,
Preserved by the potent art made trebly potent by love,
While the transient ages depart from under the heavens above,—
Preserved in the colour and line on the canvas fulgently flung
By Him the Artist divine who triumphed and vanished so young:
Surely there rarely hath been a lot more to be envied in life
Than thy lot, O FORNARINA, whom RAPHAEL'S heart took to wife.

There was silence yet for a time save the tinkling capricious and quaint,
Then She lifted her voice sublime, no longer tender and faint,
Pathetic and tremulous, no! but firm as a column it rose,
Rising solemn and slow with a full rich swell to the close,
Firm as a marble column soaring with noble pride
In a triumph of rapture solemn to some Hero deified;
In a rapture of exultation made calm by its stress intense,
In a triumph of consecration and a jubilation immense.
And the Voice flowed on and on, and ever it swelled as it poured,
Till the stars that throbbed as they shone seemed throbbing with it in accord;
Till the moon herself in my dream, still Empress of all the night,
Was only that voice supreme translated into pure light:
And I lost all sense of the earth though I still had sense of the sea;
And I saw the stupendous girth of a tree like the Norse World-Tree;
And its branches filled all the sky, and the deep sea watered its root,
And the clouds were its leaves on high and the stars were its silver fruit;
Yet the stars were the notes of the singing and the moon was the voice of the song,
Through the vault of the firmament ringing and swelling resistlessly strong;
And the whole vast night was a shell for that music of manifold might,

And was strained by the stress of the swell of the music yet vaster than night.
And I saw as a crystal fountain whose shaft was a column of light
More high than the loftiest mountain ascend the abyss of the night;
And its spray filled all the sky, and the clouds were the clouds of its spray,
Which glittered in star-points on high and filled with pure silver the bay;
And ever in rising and falling it sang as it rose and it fell,
And the heavens with their pure azure walling all pulsed with the pulse of its swell,
For the stars were the notes of the singing and the moon was the voice of the song
Through the vault of the firmament ringing and swelling ineffably strong;
And the whole vast night was a shell for that music of manifold might,
And was strained by the stress of the swell of the music yet vaster than night:
And the fountain in swelling and soaring and filling beneath and above,
Grew flushed with red fire in outpouring, transmuting great power into love,
Great power with a greater love flushing, immense and intense and supreme,
As if all the World's heart-blood outgushing ensanguined the trance of my dream;
And the waves of its blood seemed to dash on the shore of the sky to the cope
With the stress of the fire of a passion and yearning of limitless scope,
Vast fire of a passion and yearning, keen torture of rapture intense,
A most unendurable burning consuming the soul with the sense:—
"Love, love only, for ever; love with its torture of bliss;
All the world's glories can never equal two souls in one kiss:
Love, and ever love wholly; love in all time and all space;
Life is consummate then solely in the death of a burning embrace."

And at length when that Voice sank mute, and silence fell over all
Save the tinkling thin of that lute, the deep heavens rushed down like a pall,
The stars and the moon for a time with all their splendours of light,
Were quenched with that Voice sublime, and great darkness filled the night. . . .
When I felt again the scent of the night-flowers rich and sweet,
As ere my senses went, and knew where I stood on my feet,
And saw the yet-bright bay and the moon gone low in my dream,
The boat had passed away with Her the Singer supreme;
She was gone, the marvellous Singer whose wonderful world-wide fame
Could never possibly bring her a tithe of her just acclaim.
And I wandered all night in a trance of rapture and yearning and love,
And saw the dim grey expanse flush far with the dawning above;
And I passed that copse in the night, but the nightingales all were dumb
From their passionate aching delight, and perhaps whoever should come
On the morrow would find, I have read, under its bush or its tree
Some poor little brown bird dead, dead of its melody,
Slain by the agitation, by the stress and the strain of the strife,
And the pang of the vain emulation in the music yet dearer than life.
And I heard the skylarks singing high in the morning sun,
All the sunrise heavens ringing as the sunset heavens had done:
And ever I dreamed and pondered while over the fragrant soil,
My happy footsteps wandered before I resumed my toil:—
Truly, my darling, my Alice, truly the whole night long
Have I filled to the brim love's chalice with the wine of music and song.

I have passed and repassed your door from the singing until the dawn
A dozen times and more, and ever the curtains drawn;
And now that the morn is breaking out of the stillness deep,
Sweet as my visions of waking be all your visions of sleep!
Could you but wake, O my dearest, a moment, and give one glance,
Just a furtive peep the merest, to learn the day's advance!
For I must away up the dale and over the hill to my toil,
And the night's rich dreams grow pale in the working day's turmoil;
But to-night, O my darling, my Alice, till night it will not be long,
We will fill to the brim love's chalice with the wine of music and song;
And never the memory fails of what I have learnt in my dream
From the song of the nightingales and the song of the Singer supreme:—
"Love, love only, for ever; love with its torture and bliss;
All the world's glories can never equal two souls in one kiss:
Love, love ever and wholly; love in all time and all space;
Love is consummate then solely in the death of a burning embrace."

February 1882.

THE POET AND HIS MUSE

I sighed unto my Muse, "O gentle Muse,
Would you but come and kiss my aching brow,
And thus a little life and joy infuse
Into my brain and heart so weary now;
Into my heart so sad with emptiness
Even when unafflicted by the stress
Of all our kind's poor life;
Into my brain so feeble and so listless,
Crushed down by burthens of dark thought resistless
Of all our want and woe and unresulting strife.

"Would you but come and kiss me on the brow,
Would you but kiss me on the pallid lips
That have so many years been songless now,
And on the eyes involved in drear eclipse;
That thus the barren brain long overwrought
Might yield again some blossoms of glad thought,
And the long-mute lips sing,
And the long-arid eyes grow moist and tender
With some new vision of the ancient splendour
Of beauty and delight that lives in everything.

"Would you but kiss me on the silent lips
And teach them thus to sing some new sweet song;
Would you but kiss my eyes from their eclipse
With some new tale of old-world right and wrong:
Some song of love and joy or tender grief
Whose sweetness is its own divine relief,
Whose joy is golden bliss;
Some solemn and impassioned antique story
Where love against dark doom burns out in glory,
Where life is freely staked to win one mutual kiss.

"Would you but sing to me some new dear song
Of love in bliss or bale alike supreme;
Some story of our old-world right and wrong
With noble passion burning through the theme:
What though the story be of darkest doom,
If loyal spirits shining through its gloom
Throb to us from afar?
What though the song with heavy sorrows languish,
If loving hearts pulse to us through its anguish?
Is not the whole black night enriched by one pure star?"

And lo! She came, the ever-gentle Muse,
Sad as my heart, and languid as my brain;
Too gentle in her loving to refuse,
Although her steps were weariness and pain;
Although her eyes were blank and lustreless,
Although her form was clothed with heaviness
And drooped beneath the weight;
Although her lips were blanched from all their blooming,
Her pure face pallid as from long entombing,
Her bright regard and smile sombre and desolate.—

"Sad as thy heart and languid as thy brain
I come unto thy sighing through the gloom,
I come with mortal weariness and pain,
I come as one compelled to leave her tomb:
Behold, am I not wrapt as in the cloud
Of death's investiture and sombre shroud?
Am I not wan as death?
Look at the withered leafage of my garland,
Is it not nightshade from the sad dim far land
Of night and old oblivion and no mortal breath?

"I come unto thy sighing through the gloom,
My hair dishevelled dank with dews of night,
Reluctantly constrained to leave my tomb;
With eyes that have for ever lost their light;
My vesture mouldering with deep death's disgrace,
My heart as chill and bloodless as my face,
My forehead like a stone;
My spirit sightless as my eyes are sightless,
My inmost being nerveless, soulless, lightless,
My joyous singing voice a harsh sepulchral moan.

"My hair dishevelled dank with dews of night,
From that far region of dim death I come,
With eyes and soul and spirit void of light,
With lips more sad in speech than stark and dumb:
Lo, you have ravaged me with dolorous thought
Until my brain was wholly overwrought,
Barren of flowers and fruit;
Until my heart was bloodless for all passion,
Until my trembling lips could no more fashion
Sweet words to fit sweet airs of trembling lyre and lute.

"From the sad regions of dim death I come;
We tell no tales there for our tale is told,
We sing no songs there for our lips are dumb,
Likewise our hearts and brains are graveyard mould;
No wreaths of laurel, myrtle, ivy or vine,
About our pale and pulseless brows entwine,
And that sad frustrate realm
Nor amaranths nor asphodels can nourish,
But aconite and black-red poppies flourish
On such Lethean dews as fair life overwhelm.

"We tell no tales more, we whose tale is told;
As your brain withered and your heart grew chill
My heart and brain were turned to churchyard mould,
Wherefore my singing voice sank ever still;
And I, all heart and brain and voice, am dead;
It is my Phantom here beside your bed
That speaketh to you now;
Though you exist still, a mere form inurning
The ashes of dead fires of thought and yearning,
Dead faith, dead love, dead hope, in hollow breast and brow."

When It had moaned these words of hopeless doom,
The Phantom of the Muse once young and fair,
Pallid and dim from its disastrous tomb,
Of Her so sweet and young and *débonnaire*,
So rich of heart and brain and singing voice,
So quick to shed sweet tears and to rejoice
And smile with ravishing grace;
My soul was stupefied by its own reaping,
Then burst into a flood of passionate weeping,
Tears bitter as black blood streaming adown my face.

"O Muse, so young and sweet and glad and fair,
O Muse of hope and faith and joy and love,
O Muse so gracious and so *débonnaire*,
Darling of earth beneath and heaven above;
If Thou art gone into oblivious death,
Why should I still prolong my painful breath?
Why still exist, the urn
Holding of once-great fires the long dead ashes,
No sole spark left of all their glow and flashes,
Fires never to rekindle more and shine and burn?

"O Muse of hope and faith and joy and love,
Soul of my soul, if Thou in truth art dead,
A mournful alien in our world above,
A Phantom moaning by my midnight bed;
How can I be alive, a hollow form
With ashes of dead fires once bright and warm?
What thing is worth my strife?
The Past a great regret, the Present sterile,
The Future hopeless, with the further peril
Of withering down and down to utter death-in-life.

"Soul of my soul, canst Thou indeed be dead?
What mean for me if I accept their lore;
Thy words, O Phantom moaning by my bed,
'I cannot sing again for evermore'?
I nevermore can think or feel or dream
Or hope or love—the fatal loss supreme!
I am a soulless clod;
No germ of life within me that surpasses
The little germs of weeds and flowers and grasses
Wherewith our liberal Mother decks the graveyard sod.

"I am half-torpid yet I spurn this lore,
I am long silent yet cannot avow
My singing voice is lost for evermore;
For lo, this beating heart, this burning brow,
This spirit gasping in keen spasms of dread
And fierce revulsion that it is not dead,
This agony of the sting:
What soulless clod could have these tears and sobbings,
These terrors that are hopes, these passionate throbbings?
Dear Muse, revive! we yet may dream and love and sing!"

February 1882.

THE SLEEPER

The fire is in a steadfast glow,
  The curtains drawn against the night;
Upon the red couch soft and low
  Between the fire and lamp alight
She rests half-sitting, half-reclining,
Encompassed by the cosy shining,
  Her ruby dress with lace trimmed white.

Her left hand shades her drooping eyes
  Against the fervour of the fire,
The right upon her cincture lies
  In languid grace beyond desire,
A lily fallen among roses;
So placidly her form reposes,
  It scarcely seemeth to respire.

She is not surely all awake,
  As yet she is not all asleep;
The eyes with lids half-open take
  A startled deprecating peep
Of quivering drowsiness, then slowly
The lids sink back, before she wholly
  Resigns herself to slumber deep.

The side-neck gleams so pure beneath
  The underfringe of gossamer,
The tendrils of whose faery wreath
  The softest sigh suppressed would stir.
The little pink-shell ear-rim flushes
With her young blood's translucent blushes,
  Nestling in tresses warm as fur.

The contour of her cheek and chin
  Is curved in one delicious line,
Pure as a vase of porcelain thin
  Through which a tender light may shine;
Her brow and blue-veined temple gleaming
Beneath the dusk of hair back-streaming
  Are as a virgin's marble shrine.

The ear is burning crimson fire,
  The flush is brightening on the face,
The lips are parting to suspire,
  The hair grows restless in its place
As if itself new tangles wreathing;
The bosom with her deeper breathing
  Swells and subsides with ravishing grace.

The hand slides softly to caress,
  Unconscious, that fine-pencilled curve
"Her lip's contour and downiness,"
  Unbending with a sweet reserve;
A tender darkness that abashes
Steals out beneath the long dark lashes,
  Whose sightless eyes make eyesight swerve.

The hand on chin and throat downslips,
  Then softly, softly on her breast;
A dream comes fluttering o'er the lips,
  And stirs the eyelids in their rest,
And makes their undershadows quiver,
And like a ripple on a river
  Glides through her breathing manifest.

I feel an awe to read this dream
  So clearly written in her smile;
A pleasant not a passionate theme,
  A little love, a little guile;
I fear lest she should speak revealing
The secret of some maiden feeling
  I have no right to hear the while.

The dream has passed without a word
  Of all that hovered finely traced;
The hand has slipt down, gently stirred
  To join the other at her waist;
Her breath from that light agitation
Has settled to its slow pulsation;
  She is by deep sleep re-embraced.

Deep sleep, so holy in its calm,
  So helpless, yet so awful too;
Whose silence sheds as sweet a balm
  As ever sweetest voice could do;
Whose trancèd eyes, unseen, unseeing
Shadowed by pure love, thrill our being
  With tender yearnings through and through.

Sweet sleep; no hope, no fear, no strife;
  The solemn sanctity of death,
With all the loveliest bloom of life;
  Eternal peace in mortal breath:
Pure sleep from which she will awaken
Refreshed as one who hath partaken
  New strength, new hope, new love, new faith.

January 1882.

MODERN PENELOPE

(RIDDLE SOLVED.)

What did she mean by that crochet work?
The work that never got done,
Lolling as indolent as a Turk,
Looking demure as a Nun:
What subtle mystery might lurk
(Of course there must be one)
In that Penelope web of work,
The work that never got done?

She lolled on the low couch just under the light
So very serene and staid:
We had some other guests that night,
One sang, another played,
A couple discovered the stars were bright,
Of course a youth and a maid,
I watched her knitting under the light
So very serene and staid.

I knew that she was a rogue in her heart,
As roguish as ever could be,
And she knew that I knew, yet would not dart
A single glance at me,
But seemed as it were withdrawn apart
Amid the companie,
A nun in her face with a rogue in her heart
As roguish as ever could be.

I like a riddle when its knot
Involves a pretty girl,
I puzzle about, now cold, now hot,
Through every loop and twirl,
For the question is “Who” as well as “What”?
And the answer is thus a pearl,
And really you cannot study the knot,
Unless you study the girl.

With a graceful lazy kittypuss air
She fingered the net and the ball:
At first she started to work on the square,
And then she undid all:
To make it round was next her care,
But the progress was strangely small,

With a graceful lazy kittypuss air
    Trifling with net and ball.

About her lips a quiet smile
    Came hovering, then took rest:
A butterfly in the selfsame style
    Will choose some sweet flower's breast:
Her eyes were drooping all the while,
    But the drooping lids expressed
The satisfaction of a smile
    Like a butterfly at rest.

Her hands kept floating to and fro
    Like a pair of soft white doves,
In gentle dalliance coy and slow
    Around a nest of Loves:
And against my chair her couch was low,
    And six was the size of her gloves,
They were charming those hands there to and fro
    Like a pair of soft white doves.

Her fair face opened like a flower,
    And a sigh thrilled the smile on her lips,
And her eyes shone out with a dazzling power
    From the dream of their half-eclipse
As she welcomed the trill of "A summer shower"
    With plausive finger-tips—
Oh! her eyes so bright, and her face like a flower,
    And the exquisite smile of her lips!

Those hands kept floating soft and white
    Our hearts to mesmerise,
Those dark eyes keep half-veiled their light
    To lure and lure our eyes;
That web is but a subtle sleight
    To mesh us by surprise:
Do I not read your riddle right,
    Penelope the wise?

O you nun in face with the rogue in your heart
    As roguish as ever can be,
You have played an immensely wiser part
    Than the old Penelope:
You have caught twin loves in the toils of your art,
    And neither will ever get free:
You have won the game of a heart for a heart,
    And when shall the settling be?

1882.

AT BELVOIR

Sunday, July 3, 1881.

A BALLAD, HISTORICAL AND PROPHETIC.

("In maiden meditation, fancy free.")

My thoughts go back to last July,
    Sweet happy thoughts and tender;—
"The bridal of the earth and sky,"
    A day of noble splendour;
A day to make the saddest heart
    In joy a true believer;
When two good friends we roamed apart
    The shady walks of Belvoir.

A maiden like a budding rose,
    Unconscious of the golden
And fragrant bliss of love that glows
    Deep in her heart infolden;
A Poet old in years and thought,
    Yet not too old for pleasance,
Made young again and fancy-fraught
    By such a sweet friend's presence.

The other two beyond our ken
    Most shamefully deserted,
And far from all the ways of men
    Their stealthy steps averted:
Of course our Jack would go astray,
    Erotic and erratic;
But Mary!—well, I own the day
    Was really too ecstatic.

We roamed with many a merry jest
    And many a ringing laughter;
The slow calm hours too rich in zest
    To heed before and after:
Yet lingering down the lovely walks
    Soft strains anon came stealing,
A finer music through our talks
    Of sweeter, deeper feeling:

Yes, now and then a quiet word
 Of seriousness dissembling
In smiles would touch some hidden chord
 And set it all a-trembling:
I trembled too, and felt it strange;—
 Could I be in possession
Of music richer in its range
 Than yet had found expression?

The cattle standing in the mere,
 The swans upon it gliding,
The sunlight on the waters clear,
 The radiant clouds dividing;
The solemn sapphire sky above,
 The foliage lightly waving,
The soft air's Sabbath peace and love
 To satisfy all craving.

We mapped the whole fair region out
 As Country of the Tender,
From first pursuit in fear and doubt
 To final glad surrender:
Each knoll and arbour got its name,
 Each vista, covert, dingle;—
No young pair now may track the same
 And long continue single!

And in the spot most thrilling-sweet
 Of all this Love-Realm rosy
Our truant pair had found retreat,
 Unblushing, calm and cosy:
Where seats too wide for one are placed,
 And yet for two but narrow,
It's "Let my arm steal round your waist,
 And be my winsome marrow!"

Reclining on a pleasant lea
 Such tender scenes rehearsing,
A freakish fit seized him and me
 For wildly foolish versing:
We versed of this, we versed of that,
 A pair of mocking sinners,
While our lost couple strayed or sat
 Oblivious of their dinners.

But what was strange, our maddest rhymes
    In all their divagations
Were charged and over-charged at times
    With deep vaticinations:
I yearn with wonder at the power
    Of Poetry prophetic
Which in my soul made that blithe hour
    With this hour sympathetic.

For though we are in winter now,
    My heart is in full summer:
Old Year, old Wish, have made their bow;
    I welcome each new-comer.
"The King is dead, long live the King!
    The throne is vacant never!"
Is true, I read, of everything,
    So of my heart for ever!

My thoughts go on to next July,
    More happy thoughts, more tender;
"The bridal of the earth and sky,"
    A day of perfect splendour;
A day to make the saddest heart
    In bliss a firm believer;
When two True Loves may roam apart
    The shadiest walks of Belvoir.

There may be less of merry jest
    And less of ringing laughter,
Yet life be much more rich in zest
    And richer still thereafter;
The love-scenes of that region fair
    Have very real rehearsing,
And tremulous kisses thrill the air
    Far sweetlier than sweet versing;

The bud full blown at length reveal
    Its deepest golden burning;
The heart inspired with love unseal
    Its inmost passionate yearning:
The music of the hidden chord
    At length find full expression;
The Seraph of the Flaming Sword
    Assume divine possession.

January 1882.

A STRANGER

I.

It is not surely, this, a little thing,
  That day and night and every Sabbath day
Throughout these months of winterless glad Spring,

March mild as April, April sweet as May,
  And May as rich as June in common years,
It has been given me upon my way,

Given to me and all my village peers,
  But most to me as my full heart knows well,
Brimming my eyes with tender wistful tears

And throbbing with strange awe ineffable,
  To meet and pass, to follow with slow pace,
Or on the street or in our quiet dell

Or through the fields, that Lady of all grace
With sweet sad eyes and noble mournful face.

II.

We know not who she is or whence she came,
  She and her little boy with her own eyes
And brow and patient smile, whose Christian name

Without the surname tells us where he lies
  With her heart buried in the self-same grave:
The larks were singing in the soft blue skies,

And even some few violets were brave
  To breathe faint sweetness on the bland warm air,
Good Valentine such benediction gave,

When she arrived with him, her anxious care,
  Her only joy, her terrible dark grief:
In early April he was lying there;

The Spring all blithe with bud and flower and leaf
And scent and song above his Spring so brief.

III.

Only the Christian name upon the stone
  Above the date of birth and date of death;
Two syllables of everlasting moan,

Immortal sorrow breathing mortal breath,
  Continual weeping that would fain not weep,
Sad comforting that vainly comforteth

The deadly anguish graven far more deep
  Upon the heart than on the marble cold,
"For so He giveth His belovèd sleep."

Yet with a lofty patience she controlled
  The outward signs of anguish; eve and morn
Tending that little bed of sacred mould

And others near it that were left forlorn;
Praying, I think, to sleep herself outworn.

IV.

Her sorrow flowed with blessings from above;
  Her heart of joy and hope was in that tomb,
But not her heart of sympathy and love:

While her young flower was fading from its bloom
  She had been wonderfully sweet and kind;
And now that it was buried in the gloom

Her own sore suffering did but closelier bind
  Her heart to other hearts in all distress;
The little angel in her sad soul shrined

Was a true angel of pure gentleness
  And soft compassion and unwearying will
To soothe and aid and with all solace bless:

Our joys and sorrows take our nature still;
Hers wrought bright good from her own darkest ill.

V.

Tenderness, worship, bliss in yearning pain!—
  To see her young and fair and more than fair,
Amidst us yet not of us, sole remain

As sanctified already unaware;
  To see the peacefulness of pure white brow
Beneath the smoothness of the rich brown hair;

The cloistral solitude without the vow;
  The self-renunciation mild and meek
With meekness that is ever glad to bow,

Evading honours such as others seek,
  Yet in its stooping cannot help but rise;
To hear that soft slow voice its good words speak;

To feel the fascination of those eyes,
Solemn and dark and deep as midnight skies.

VI.

I did not wonder she could be so pure
  Amidst our petty cares and sordid strife,
But how our common meanness could endure

Beneath the lofty radiance of her life;
  Until I saw how, fine and soft and clear
As starbeams quivering through the darkness rife,

Her effluence shone on souls all dull and drear:
  Then as the Moon in moving through the Night
Bears round her ever her own hemisphere

Of tranquil beauty and entrancing light
  By solemn shadows more mysterious made,
Her regnant beauty turned all darkness bright

Or glorified mysteriously its shade;
Fair Queen most queenly as in Night arrayed.

VII.

Oh, joyless joy of this most bounteous June,
  For with the Maytide She is gone, is gone!
All men adore and love the one sole Moon;

But she of all on whom her light has shone,
  Of all her pure and gracious light has blest,
Discerns no mortal save Endymion,

To him alone unveils her virgin breast,
  On him alone outpours her love divine.
What shall we do who undistinguished rest?

Shall we against her solemn choice repine?
  Or shall we rather lift our souls above
To hold her ever in a crystal shrine,

The perfect beauty of Heaven's brooding Dove,
The sacred vision of Heaven's reachless Love?

March 1882.

LAW *v.* GOSPEL

The Gospel and the Law of late
Have been at sad dissension
Before the Judge and Magistrate:
Old Satan's last invention.
Of course the Law upholds the Law,
The Gospel over-ruling;
And those who have St. Paul in awe
Must seek more modern schooling.

The Gospel says, Swear not at all;
The Law, or good or bad law,
Says, You must swear, whatever befall,
Or else I fine you, Bradlaugh.
Whereon he goes and swears himself
In solemn legal banter;
His fellow-members on the shelf
Deposit him instanter.

And then we have that narrow sect
Of most Peculiar People,
Who by the Book their way direct,
And not by the Church steeple.
They read how Asa sought not God,
But doctors, being sickly;
And therefore slept beneath the sod
With his forefathers quickly.

St. James enjoins, When one is ill,
Send for an elder straightway;
Anoint and pray (no doctor's bill!)
And thus elude Death's gateway.
So said so done; and then report
Of death of son or daughter,
And parents sentenced by the Court
To prison for manslaughter.

And now a new and noisy set—
The Army of Salvation—
Our equal-minded justice fret
With constant botheration:
For sometimes they obstruct the way,
And sometimes cause a riot;
Too much of zeal—too much, we say,
Why can't the fools keep quiet?

The dean and canons in their stalls
Are placid as stalled cattle,
And never rush out from St. Paul's
To give the devil battle.
In streets and lanes to brawl and fight
Is far too low and rowdy;
No, if he wants a spar, invite
Him home to Mrs. Proudie.

On Tuesday, March, the fourteenth day,
Before Sir Thomas Owden,
A youth was brought who blocked the way,
Already over-crowden—
Threadneedle-street—the wild *War Cry,*
This well-dressed youth was selling:
A camel and a needle's eye—
The rest requires no telling.

Sir Thomas said he understood
How men in shabby raiment,
To get a living, bad or good,
Should do this thing for payment;
But he could never understand
How any young man, dressed all
In decent clothes, could join the band,
Like this young Henry Restall.

"It's not to get a living, sir,"
This youth spoke fast and faster;
"I have been called to minister—
I work for God, my Master."
Sir Thomas answered (much I grieve
If you don't find it *bon sens)*
He never could be made believe
In such outrageous nonsense.

This hardened youth he made reply,
"We have reformed some thousand
Poor drunkards;" Sir T. winked full sly,
And sneezing sneered, *"Der Tausend!"*
And for a fortnight did remand,
Upon his good behaviour,
That youth, who now should understand
He mustn't cry his Saviour.

Just think of Simon Peter thus,
And all the zealous dozen,
Brought up before Asinius,
Our Owden's great fore-cousin.
He would have quickly stopped their prate
On a police-court summons;
We should have no Archbishop Tait,
No pious House of Commons!

'Tis true they were but fishermen
And suchlike, poor and humble;
And thus might earn a living then
Approved by every Bumble.
But preach a Gospel *not* for pelf!
Absurd to Owden thinkers!—
Just keep your Good News to yourself,
And cease reforming drinkers!

March 1882.

THE OLD STORY
AND
THE NEW STOREY

(House of Commons, *Thursday, March 23.*)

For whosoever hath, to him shall be given, and he shall have more abundance: but whosoever hath not, from him shall be taken away even that he hath.—Matthew xiii. 12.

The Old Story says: We've another
    Young prince who will wed like a man;
Let us give him, because of his mother,
    An extra ten thousand per ann.
She has barely enough for herself, sirs;
    Not five hundred a week is his sum;
Some of you have vastly more pelf, sirs;
    Let our vote be unanimous, come!

The New Storey * says—(It is mentioned
    How, hating such meanness to hear,
The noble array of the pensioned
    Assailed him with laughter and jeer)—
He says: Public money should solely
    For good public service be spent.
(Dear lords, what a doctrine unholy!
    Why it saps at your rights to your rent!)

He says: What I urge 'gainst a wasteful
    And unjust proposal like this
Must to many of you be distasteful,
    And the wherefore too palpable is;
Since one hundred and ten of your body,
    And one hundred and twenty-six peers,
For no service, or service of shoddy,
    Keep bleeding us numberless years.

He says: This ten thousand per annum
    You would lavish on one wealthy pair—
Many hundred a grandad and grannam
    Would keep in a comfort too rare;

* Mr. Storey, M.P. for Sunderland.

Or in Sunderland—that's my own borough—
A small place—laugh on!—would secure
Education quite free and quite thorough
Without any rate on the poor.

He says: These same princes as dummies
In army and navy fill posts,
While veterans, scorched up like mummies,
Must starve in the cold like their ghosts.
He says: Sweep away lordly flunkeys,
If you really this money must clutch,
Those bedizened and posturing monkeys—
Your Gold Sticks in Waiting and such.

He says—But fine ears we won't batter
With more of his speech unpolite;
So we'll give our own view of the matter,
And *our* view of course is the right.
We say: When your State-ship you're building,
If you *will* have a gilt figure-head,
Of course you must pay for the gilding;
We say—there's no more to be said.

It is true that the head a ship carries
In proportion costs little when built;
It is true that this head never marries
And breeds little heads to be gilt.
It is true—but sane words are a treasure
Too precious for subjects like these—
Having set up such heads at your pleasure,
You can set them aside when you please.

April 1882.

DESPOTISM TEMPERED BY DYNAMITE

There is no other title in the world
So proud as mine, who am no law-cramped king,
No mere imperial monarch absolute,
The WHITE TSAR worshipped as a visible God,
As Lord of Heaven no less than Lord of Earth—
I look with terror to my crowning day.

Through half of Europe my dominions spread,
And then through half of Asia to the shores
Of Earth's great ocean washing the New World;
And nothing bounds them to the Northern Pole,
They merge into the everlasting ice—
    I look with terror to my crowning day.

Full eighty million subjects worship me—
Their father, high priest, monarch, God on earth;
My children who but hold their lives with mine
For our most Holy Russia dear and great,
Whose might is concentrated in my hands—
    I look with terror to my crowning day.

I chain and gag with chains and gags of iron
The impious hands and mouths that dare express
A word against my sacred sovranty;
The half of Asia is my prison-house,
Myriads of convicts lost in its Immense—
    I look with terror to my crowning day.

I cannot chain and gag the evil thoughts
Of men and women poisoned by the West,
Frenzied in soul by the anarchic West;
These thoughts transmute themselves to dynamite;
My sire was borne all shattered to his tomb—
    I look with terror to my crowning day.

My peasants rise to their unvarying toil,
And go to sleep outwearied by their toil,
Without the hope of any better life.
But with no hope they have no deadly fear,
They sleep and eat their scanty food in peace—
    I look with terror to my crowning day.

My palaces are prisons to myself;
I taste no food that may not poison me;
I plant no footstep sure it will not stir
Instant destruction of explosive fire;
I look with terror to each day and night—
    With tenfold terror to my crowning day.

May 1882.

POEMS UNCOLLECTED BY THOMSON (1852-1882)

A PROEM

"Carouse in the Past."
—Robert Browning's *Saul.*

We will drink anew of old pleasures;
In the golden chalice of song
We will pour out the wine-like treasures
Of memories hidden long.

Old memories, hidden but cherished,
In a heart-nook deep and calm;
They have not faded and perished
Like the old friends they embalm.

We will call them forth from their darkness
As we call forth a rare old wine
Which the long rich years have mellowed
Till the flavour is divine.

In a glorious intoxication
Will we revel while such drink may last;
And dead to the leaden-houred Present,
Live in golden hours of the Past.

1854.

LOVE SONG

Breathe onward, soft breeze odor laden,
And gather new sweets on your way,
For a happy and lovely young maiden
Will inhale thy rich perfume this day.
And tell her, oh! breeze, softly sighing,
When round her your soft pinions wreathe,
That my love-stricken soul with thee vieing
All its treasures to her would outbreathe.

Flow onward, ye pure sparkling waters,
In sunshine with ripple and spray,
For the fairest of earth's fair young daughters
Will be imaged within you this day.
And tell her, oh! murmuring river,
When past her your clear billows roll,
That thus, too, her fairest form ever
Is imaged with truth in my soul.

1854.

THE APPROACH TO ST. PAUL'S

Eastwards through busy streets I lingered on;
Jostled by anxious crowds, who, heart and brain,
Were so absorbed in dreams of Mammon-gain,
That they could spare no time to look upon
The sunset's gold and crimson fires, which shone
Blessing keen eyes and wrinkled brows in vain.
Right in my path stood out that solemn Fane
Whose soaring cupola of stern grey stone
Lifteth for awful beacon to the sky
The burning Cross: silent and sole amid
That ceaseless uproar, as a pyramid
Isled in its desert. The great throngs pressed by
Heedless and urgent: thus Religion towers
Above this sordid, restless life of ours.

1855.

THE DREAMER

Sing the old song while the dear child is sleeping,
Sing it most sweetly and tenderly low;
Not to awake her again to her weeping;
Let the soft notes through her dream gently flow.
What, though the passionate tears were down-streaming
From eye-balls long parched, when she lay down to rest:
Poor thing, she now is most tranquilly dreaming;
Her life is again with His dear presence blest.

See, o'er her wan face what joy brightly flushes;
Beneath the dark lids how her eyes swell and gleam!
The sweet smile is drowned in the glow of love-blushes!
Yes! he companions her now in the dream.
Darling! her lips murmur softly and slowly,—
What sacred vows and confessions of love?
Is not this Dream-life most blessèd and holy
Less of the earth than of Heaven above?

No, do not draw down the white lawny curtain:
The moonlight sleeps still on her hair, on her face;
Mystical blending of shadow uncertain
With lustre as holy as Heaven's blessèd grace.
It stirs not her slumber, but chastened and tender—
Our musical murmur half-thrilling its breast
Pervades with a blissful entrancement of splendour
That dim world of dreams where her soul findeth rest.

Sing the old song still with low-voicèd sweetness,
To harmonise well with her brief dream of bliss,
Blending therewith to ecstatic completeness:—
The poor pallid lips, are they trembling a kiss!
So may the words and the scenes of her vision
To her tranced spirit more exquisite grow;
With beauty and glory and rapture Elysian
Subtly attuned to our soft music's flow:

And she may, alas, when she wakes with the morrow
  To bitter reality, hopeless and lone,
Remember far more to sooth anguish and sorrow
  Of the dream and the dream-words of him who is gone:
And so, when we sing the old song in her hearing,
  May she with wonder and secret joy find
The dear words, the bliss of her dream re-appearing
  With the loved music that flows through her mind.

Perhaps she now hears him an old love-lay singing;
  Does it not thrill in her eager, fixed face?
Or hears the old Church-bells in golden chimes ringing
  The union that cannot in this world take place.
But sleep, darling, sleep; oh, dwell long in that heaven,
  The strange, solemn dream-land so holy and calm,
Which God hath in mercy to such as thee given;
  Where all stricken hearts may find wound-healing balm.

1855.

SUGGESTED BY MATTHEW ARNOLD'S
"STANZAS FROM THE GRANDE CHARTREUSE"

That one long dirge-moan sad and deep,
  Low, muffled by the solemn stress
Of such emotion as doth steep
  The soul in brooding quietness,
Befits our anguished time too well,
Whose Life-march is a funeral knell.

Dirge for a mighty Creed outworn—
  Its spirit fading from the earth,
Its mouldering body left forlorn:
  Weak idol! feeding scornful mirth
In shallow hearts; divine no more
Save to some ignorant pagan poor;

And some who know how by Its light
  The past world well did walk and live,
And feel It even now more bright
  Than any lamp mere men can give;
So cling to It with yearning faith,
Yet own It almost quenched in death:

While many who win wealth and power
  And honours serving at Its shrine,
Rather than lose their worldly dower
  Proclaim their dead thing "Life divine;"
And sacrifice to coward lust
Their own souls' truth, a people's trust.

And will none mourn the mighty Dead,—
  Pillar of heavenly fire and cloud,
Which through this life's wild desert led
  For whole millenniums each grand crowd
Of sages, bards, saints, heroes, all
Whose names we glory to recall?

None mourn Him, dead, with deep-moved soul,
  Whom, living, all our sires adored?
None feel the heavy darkness roll
  Stifling about us, when the Lord
Leaves us to walk by our own light,
That one pale speck in boundless Night?—

That earthly lamp when sun and star,
  When all the heavenly lights are lost:
Does it shed radiance round afar?
  Our pathway is by deep gulfs cross'd:
It fathoms none. We lift it high:
It casts not one beam on the sky.

If He thus died as no more fit
  To lead the modern march of thought,
Supreme,—commanding, guiding it,
  With noblest love and wisdom fraught;
He was at least Divine; and none
Of human souls can lead it on.

We pine in our dark living tomb,
  Waiting the God-illumined One
Who, only, can disperse the gloom;
  Completing what the Dead begun,
Or farther leading us some space
Toward our eternal resting-place.

But Israel wanders shepherdless,
  Or gloom-involved unmoving lies,
And in despair's stark sinfulness
  Reviles the promised Paradise
It cannot reach—Father divine!
Let us not long thus hopeless pine.

Still the deep dirge-notes long and low
  Breathe forth strange anguish to recall—
Could we forget—our direst woe:
  A proud strong Age fast losing all
Earth has of heaven; bereft of faith;
And living in Eternal Death.

And loudly boastful of such life:
  Blinded by our material might,
Absorbed in frantic worldly strife,
  Unconscious of the utter Night
Whose palpable and monstrous gloom
Is gathering for our spirits' tomb.

We feel as gods in our own hearts;
  Seeming to conquer Time and Space;
Wealth gorging our imperial marts;
  Earth pregnant, from the fierce embrace
Our matter-lusting spirits press,
With unexampled fruitfulness.

God, answering well our worldly prayer,
  Our hearts' chief prayer through all the hours
Of selfish joy and sordid care,
  Comes down to us in golden showers:
God turns to Mammon at our cry;
Our souls wealth-crushed, dross-stifled lie.

Those few, how rich! while this great mass,
  Myriads with equal greed for gold,
Sink in such want and woe, alas!
  As never can on earth be told:
These starve, and those yet wealthier rise;
Meanwhile in both the spirit dies.

Hear now the thrilling dirge-notes peal
  The anguished cry in thunder rolls:—
The few yet left who think and feel,
  Who yearn with strenuous soaring souls
For more than earth or time can grant;
Where, where shall they appease their want?

Black disbelief, substantial doubt
  Wreathe—blent into one louring cloud
Through which Heaven's light can scarce shine out—
  Round all the Faiths: all in such shroud
Fade ghostlike to th' entombing Past:
Our Heaven is wildly overcast.

Yet each Creed, senile, sick, half-dead,
  With bitter spite and doting rage
Reviles all others. Whoso, led
  By thirst of love to pilgrimage,
Seeks now old God-given Wells of Life,
Finds drought-dry centres of vain strife;

And turns away in blank despair,
  To scoff or weep as fits his mood.
O God in Heaven, hear our prayer!
  We know Thou art, Allwise, Allgood,
Yet sink in godless misery:
Oh, teach us how to worship Thee!

PART II.

The great Form lies there nerveless still:
  But as we fix our longing gaze
It grows in grandest beauty, till
  We worship in entranced amaze;
Such holy love and wisdom seem
To be there rapt in heavenly dream.

Oh, if He may once more awake!
  Oh, if it be not death, but sleep!—
And He from that dread slumber break
  Refreshed and strong, full-powered to sweep
The darkness from our path again;
Once more the Guiding Star of men!

Yet—though it be death—view It well.
  The brow, how nobly high and broad!
What love on those shut lips might well!
  This Form sublimely templed God:
And, if not perfect, is a shrine
Approaching well the most Divine.

Do not turn hastily away
  From mighty death to petty life;
Gaze in deep reverence on the clay
  With such a soul's expression rife:
Read here, read long, the features worn
By One incarnate Heavenly-born.

So may we hope to recognise
  That Greater One who shall succeed
This death-bound Monarch, who now lies
  In mute appealing for our need:
God cannot long desert His earth;
In the Old's death the New has birth.

What say we?—we know well this truth,
  There is no death for the Divine;
Which lives in ever-perfect youth:
  The Form alone—its earthly shrine—
Is subject to earth's mortal sway;
Sickens, and dies, and rots away.

Thus each Form in its turn expires,
  No more with all revealed Truth rife,—
Which even at that time inspires
  Some new and nobler form with life,
Grander and vaster to express
More of Its infinite heavenliness.

Thus has it been since Time's first birth,
  Thus must it be for evermore:
Still lie, moth-eaten, on the earth
  Old garments which this Spirit wore;
Till, soiled and rent, they were off-thrown,
And wider-flowing robes put on.

They could not grow with His great growth,
  Pauseless though slow throughout the years;
And vainly worshippers—so loath
  To leave what lengthened use endears—
May still the empty robes adore;
Their virtue was from Him who wore.

Let none say the Divine is dead,
  Although this Form be soul-less quite:
The Heavenly Sun doth ever shed
  His lifeful heat, His saving light;
Never our earth doth lose His ray,
Save when she turns herself away.

Let none say the Divine is dumb,
  Although His voice no more we hear:
It is that we are deaf become.
  For measured to each eye and ear
His glory shines, His voice outspeaks;
To each He gives the most it seeks.

Our spirits may for ever grow;
  And He will fill them as before,
And still their measure overflow
  With His unlessened infinite More:
He gives us all we can receive;
He teaches all we can believe.

The pure can see Him perfect-pure;
  The strong feel Him, Omnipotence;
The wise, All-wise; He is obscure
  But to the gross and earth-bound sense:
Alas for us with blinded sight
Who dare to cry, There is no light!

PART III.

Nay, ask us not to rise and leave
  Him from whom power and life seem gone;
Say not that it is weak to grieve;
  Duty does *not, now,* urge us on:
In vain ye urge; too well we know
We cannot by our own strength go.

Vainly ye choose you Saviours now
  Of men,—however good and wise
Be those your mean faith would endow
  With power to which no man can rise:
No best men living lure our faith
From the Divine though veiled in death.

Vainly ye wander every way
  Throughout the earth in search of Heaven,
Changing your useless path each day
  With each new transient impulse given
By human guides, who still agree
In naught but fallibility.

We should know better from the lore
  Of worldly wisdom—keen mistrust—
On which our minds so love to pore;
  Nor leave for any child of dust
This One Divine: to Him adhere
Till the diviner One appear.

My brothers, let us own the truth,
  Bitter and mournful though it be,—
That we, who spent our dreary youth
  In foul and sensual slavery,
Are all too slavish, too unmanned,
For Conquerors of the Promised Land.

In unprogressive wanderings
  We plod the desert to and fro;
And fiery serpents' mortal stings,
  Earthquake and sword and weary woe
And pestilence deal fearful death
Amongst us for our want of faith.

Far-scattered o'er the Waste forlorn
  Our bones shall whiten through the years,
And startle pilgrims yet unborn;
  Our noblest captains, priests and seers,
Dark death shall one by one remove,
For lack of wisdom, faith, or love.

Yet be we patient, meek and pure,
  Unselfishly resigned to God's
Mysterious judgments; and endure
  Our sore scarce-intermitted loads
Of grief and weary pain, imbued
With sternly passive fortitude:

And pray that those who shall succeed
  Prove worthy of a happier life
Than we dare ask for as our meed;
  That they a constant noble strife
Victorious against Ill may wage,
And gain the glorious heritage.

Cease now to cry and storm, and move,
  By such tumultuous toil opprest
As, without guidance, vain must prove:
  When God keeps still can ye not rest?
When He sends night so dark and deep,
Why shrink from renovating sleep?

Sleep, to His care resigned, a space;
  That when He rises in His might
To lead our hosts from this dire place,
  We may have strength and heart to fight
All evils that would bar our way,
And march unfaltering all the day.

Yes, let us stay in loving grief,
  Which patient hope and trust yet cheer,
Silent beside our silent Chief,
  Till His Successor shall appear;
Till death's veil fall from off His face,
Or One anointed take His place.

Nay,—our adoring love should have
  More faith than to believe that He,
Before Another comes to save,
  Can leave us in blind misery
Without a Guide: God never can
So utterly depart from man.

We will move onward!—let us trust
  That there is life and saving power
In this dear Form which seems but dust.
  Arise, arise! though darkness lower,
Earnest, bold-hearted, cease to mourn;
It shall before our hosts be borne.

Triumphantly He ever led
  Our faithful armies while alive;
What though His form be cold and dead,
  His Spirit doth that death survive:
We conquer by that Soul this Form
Enshrined, not ill, while free and warm.

Thus men have honoured fellow men,
  Who dying left a lofty fame;
And won most glorious victories then
  By inspiration of a Name:
If in men's names such life abode,
Shall there not in *His*,—Son of God.

A dawn-light creeps throughout the gloom,
  Sullenly sinks the storm of wrath;
Life blossoms in our desert tomb;
  Mysteriously we find a path
Which leadeth on to Paradise.
Thus to our love's faith He replies!

But, while the dirge still rolls away
  In passionate thunders wildly blent
With mournful moanings, let us pray—
  Still on our Holy War intent—
"O God, revive the seeming Dead;
Or send Another in His stead!

"The wintry midnight drear is past,
  But still the dawn gleams grey and cold;
Dread phantoms haunt each restless blast,
  Our stumblings still are manifold:
Oh, let Thy cloudless Sun rise soon,
And flood us with His summer noon!"

July 1855.

TASSO TO LEONORA

FROM HIS DUNGEON;
IN MISERY AND DISTRACTION.

"Ha! thy frozen pulses flutter
With a love thou dar'st not utter. . . .
Lady, whose imperial brow
Is endiademed with woe!
* * *
All the wide world beside us
Show like multitudinous
Puppets passing from a scene;
What but mockery can they mean?"
SHELLEY—*Misery; a Fragment.*

Noblest Lady, throned above
All my soaring hopes of love;
Could you read my fate's dark truth,
You would give me scornless ruth.

Dawn by dawn I wake to say,—
I *will* drive all thought away
Of Her I cannot hope to win;
Vain regret is coward sin.

Yet each night I yearn to be
Wandering far alone with thee,
Through still Dreamland's dimmest grove
Moonlit by thy heavenly love.

Ah, the long days dark and cold!
Life, bereft of thee, unsouled—
Save for Memory!—crawls on slow,
One sick swoon of barren woe.

Ah, the long nights dreadly still!
When sleep flies my frantic will;
When through filmy dreams its sting
Consciousness darts quivering.

But when rich Sleep's nectared balm
Bathes my weary heart in calm;
Life, Strength, Joy are all re-found,
With thy pure love glory-crowned.

Thus thou hast my soul unsphered;
Waking life is dead and weird;
Deathlike trance is life:—ah me!
All our being seems to be
Interfused with mockery.

Yes—as Love is truer far
Than all other things; so are
Life and Death, the World and Time,
Mere false shows in some great Mime,
By dreadful mystery sublime.

Do not scorn me, Sweet, I crave;
Perhaps this woe may somewhat rave:
Yet how should It?—I can feel
Truth itself at times less real.

Do not scorn me,—for behold!
Near and nearer swiftly rolled
Solemn glooms of that great Night
No false Day shall dawn to blight.

Then the everlasting sleep,
Shall our souls in rapture steep,
Then in tranced Eternity
Thou shalt be made One with me!

Play our parts out in this Mime!—
Spectres mocking spectral Time,
Whose grim mockery keeps us hurled
Reeling through our spectral World.

What a Theatre expands!
For its Stage all seas and lands;
By the moon and high stars lit;
Vaulted by the Infinite.

Heavens! and I must bear a part,
With my restless passionate heart
Coffined in this foul dead den
From the surging seas of men.

Well . . . we all must act our time
On the unreal Stage sublime;
None of us is what he seems,
Dramatising frenzy-dreams.

By such monsters fleered, stung, tost,
In such wildering mazes lost;
How superbly serious all
Threads the restless, senseless brawl
Of our rabid Carnival!

Noble, beautiful, serene,
Thou must play the part of Queen;
Crowned with unreal gems and gold,
Phantom purples round thee rolled

Sweep with stately step the stage;
Act great passions, love and rage,
With yon crowd of half-souled things
Masked as nobles, princes, kings.

I must act a wretch forlorn,
Wealthless, rankless, lowly born;
Cursed more with a soul and sense
Bounteous, regal, too intense:

Ay, a woeful Wretch indeed;
Say a starved incarnate Need,
Ever with consummate art
In his strange half-tragic part
Living on an empty heart!

Well, Dear, brief must be our task;
Little matters in what mask
We may rant our mimic rage
On our unsubstantial Stage.

So, Sweet Love, sustain your rôle,
Freeze the pulses of your soul;
Fair, grand, queenly dignified,
Case yourself in marble pride.

I—the while,—by evidence
Of my purest love intense,
Sure that when the Play is o'er
You are mine for evermore—

I will madly waste and moan,
Pouring out against thy throne
All my life of love,—flung back
In wild foam o'er gulfs of black.

Let some hollow princely mask,
In thine Alpine sunshine bask;
Blight me with well-feignèd scorn
Let me pine and rage forlorn:

Have it counted lunacy,
My audacious love for Thee!
In a lazar-dungeon thrust,
Make me mad to prove you just.

Brava, Dearest! noble, grand!
Played with wondrous self-command!
O great Theatre world-filled,
Whom her spell holds rapt and thrilled,
Shout the plaudits too long stilled!

I, too,—do not I act well
All the horrors of this Hell?
Act so well, Love, that I feel
Sometimes as if all were real!

What a sickly, foolish fear!
Love soon re-assures me, Dear:
I must ape such anguish vile
With an inward settled smile.

Do I seem to writhe with pain
Under thy assumed disdain?
Do I seem, indeed, to be
Far too mean for hope of thee?

Do I really seem to brood
In this dark den's solitude,
Frenzied by the fœtid gloom
Of such hideous living tomb?

Do I seem to cringe, and crave
Mercy from the poor dull slave,
Who, disguised in sceptered power,
Acts thy brother for the hour?

Yet I scorn him: and serene,
Far above this mimic scene
With its shows of Space and Time,
Dwell with thee in love sublime.

Ah! your part so grand and fine
Must be harder yet than mine;
Bitter, but to *seem,* in sooth,
False to love's eternal truth:
Ah! you have my saddest ruth.

Still, our parts are so forth writ
In this Mime whose venomed wit
Our poor wits so far transcends.
On its acting life depends,
Wild it is, but soon it ends.

Joy! the Play must soon be done!
Then the lamps called Stars and Sun
Shall be quenched in perfect gloom
By the grand foreclosing Doom;

Then the Stage of land and sea
Shall down-vanish utterly;
Then the fretted azure roof
Roll off like a burning woof;

Then the serried multitude
Surge out in a vast dim flood;—
All, all fade and vanish quite,
Leaving void and silent Night.

Then, once more alone, my Sweet,
We shall in the strange dark meet:
You will doff your tinselled pride,
I shall throw my rags aside.

Then in silent darkness deep
Comes the everlasting sleep,
Comes the inexpressive bliss
Of our union's perfectness!

Time's loud turbid stream shall flow,
With its perils, strife and woe,
Far from where our Soul then lies
Tranced in still Eternities:

Tho', soft breathed from far away,
Its dim soothing murmurs may
Lull us to profounder rest,
Swaying with the Ocean's breast.

For we seek home after this;
Clinging with a fonder kiss
For the parting which so pained,
For the cold neglect you feigned.

We two only,—Woman, Man,
Wedded ere the Mime began,
Heaven-created Man and Wife
For our whole true timeless life:

Soul of soul and heart of heart;
Each alone a wretched part,
Lifeless, useless, maimed, unright,
Ever yearning to unite

In the perfect spheral Whole,
Living, self-sufficient Soul,
Swayed through Æther crystalline
Circling restful in the shine
Of the central Sun Divine. . . .

What, although this trance at times
Must be broken by such mimes?
What, though we must earn by these
Our reposeful ecstasies?

Dearest, all the false cold days,
With their bitter mocking Plays,
Swiftly die to glorious Night
When we meet in new delight.

So two actors, Man and Wife,
Mimic freely rage and strife,
Suffering, terror, madness, death
Whatsoe'er the fable saith:

Earning thus wherewith to feed
That which is their life indeed,—
Long, calm, rich with love intense,
Secret from the shallow sense
Of the blatant audience.

Ah, my weak bewildered heart!
Do I act my monstrous part
With too earnest lifelike truth?—
Darling, bless me with thy ruth.

Yes, at times my heart is torn
By thy well-pretended scorn:
Soothe this foolish heart of mine
With some secret loving sign.

Perhaps it feeleth Love to be
Of such sacred verity,
That thy merely feigned untruth
Frets it like a serpent-tooth.

Grant it some dear secret sign
Which no other can divine,—
But a word, a flower, to prove
That you are my own, own Love.

Act thy strange part not so well;—
Even now, with pangs of Hell,
I dread that your neglect is true,
Doubting you, my Soul's Soul, *you!*

But I strangle such base doubt. . . .
How the drear plot lingers out!
What a Chaos, baffling thought;
Real with spectral interwrought! . . .

Lo, the wondrous Universe!
Hear its mystic powers rehearse
Sweet and subtle melodies,
Vast and solemn harmonies.

Glorious shifting sceneries, see;
And the dome's infinity,
Lamp'd by all the rhythmic quires
Of those unconsuming fires!

Mark the stony Fate that broods,
Mark the angel multitudes,
Watching for the tragic range
Of impassioned strife and change.

O sublimest Theatre!
Vexed with the insensate stir
Of this doleful Mime distraught,
By such pigmy puppets wrought.

Pigmies: and they feel it well,
While their hollow vauntings swell:
How uneasily they roam
Through its grandeurs, not at home!—

Restless in its crystal calms,
Trembling at its thunder-psalms,
Cowering from its noon-poured light,
Shuddering through its scenic night.

How their poor rants quail and die
Far beneath its solemn sky!
How their clouds of passion all,
Tumid grandeurs, burst and fall
From its deep-based mountain-wall!

Blood and filth defile the Stage,
Filth of lust and blood of rage;
Which they will not understand
Are but self-pollution, and
Suicide at second-hand.

Every one there, bad or good,
Is by all misunderstood,
Knowing not himself,—yet strives
To scheme the law for countless lives.

Each is different from each,
None hears right another's speech:
Yet all fume and fight for aye,
With anguish, hatred, death, dismay,
To make others be as they.

Every step they take perplext
Taints the freedom of the next;
Every thought and word and deed
Curbeth all that shall succeed:

Yet they still must move, nor pause,
By the Drama's rigorous laws;
Yet no true Life can there be
Save in thoughts and deeds quite free.

There work foolish Hate and Ill,
Eager, subtle, fierce of will;
Good and Love, alas, behold,
Flagging, wavering, languish cold.—

Love!—O Seraphs looking down,
Who of all that wear the crown,
That have won the sacred kiss
Which should symbol Love's pure bliss,
Even dream what true Love is?

Sternly real the galling pain
Of the vanquished bondman's chain;
But the Victor's diadem
Ever lacks its crowning gem.

Nearly all the noblest parts
Ruined by bad heads or hearts;
Those in whom redemption lies
Chained, with cankering energies,
From sublime activities.

Each aspiring burst, swayed back,
Soon plods round the old drear track;
Hope dies,—strangled in the knot
Of such ever-ravelled plot.

Did no sequent acts extend
On unto a perfect End
Far beyond these brief life-days,
What a hopeless, ghastly maze!

Yes! did'st Thou not light the scene,
Leonora, O my Queen!
One deep sigh would rend my heart,
"Oh, that I had had no part!" . . .

As it is,—to keep, perchance,
Sane amid the dizzy dance—
Muse I this fixed truth sublime,
All is but a mocking Mime.

Yet foul demons in my ear
Hiss most wordless hints of fear,—
That this hideous dream's wild strife
Is our soul's substantial life!

How the moment's thought appals!—
That these stifling dungeon-walls
Are of real during stone;
That I fester here alone;
That you cannot be my own!

No; it is a fiendish lie.
God our Father reigns on high:
You are truer than my faith. . . .
Oh, were life untwined from death!

But, you cannot scorn me, Dear,
Though I sink in doubt and fear?
You too know, this mad Mime done,
We shall evermore be one?

Cling, cling fast to this dear faith,
Rock of life in sea of death:
Our mazed web of doom is wrought
Under God's directing thought.

For were life no flitting dream,
Were things truly what they seem,
Were not all this World-scene vast
But a shade in Time's stream glass'd;

Were the moods we now display
Less phantasmal than the clay,
In which our poor spirits clad
Act this Vision, wild and sad,
I must be mad, mad,—how mad!

November 1856.

A CHANT

While the trees grow,
While the streams flow,
While the winds blow,
  We will be free!
Free as trees growing,
Free as streams flowing,
Free as winds blowing,
  Evermore free!

1857.

A FESTIVAL OF LIFE

The One remains, the many change and pass;
Heaven's light for ever shines, Earth's shadows fly;
Life, like a dome of many-coloured glass,
Stains the white radiance of Eternity,
Until Death tramples it to fragments. . . .
—SHELLEY'S *Adonais.*

The wind, in long gusts roaring,
Over the sea-waste hurled with passionate might
The torrent-rush of ponderous rain down-pouring
Through that unbounded darkness of wild night. . . .
I gazed into the tumult; seeing naught;
But mastered by it into solemn thought,
Such as can seldom brood in garish day,—
Whose myriad sounds and forms and hues
Their sparkling sensual wine infuse,
Till the soul drowses in its drunken clay.
Night scorns to pamper fleshly ears and eyes
With earth's poor store of fleeting luxuries,
Appealing to the Soul alone
In its stupendous Monotone,
Austerely murmuring spells of timeless mysteries.

Long sightlessly outgazing
I stood, when through the cloven dark, behold,
A dome of purest crystal lifted, blazing
With living splendours—purple, jasper, gold,
And crowning all, serenely arched on high,
A solemn depth of sapphire like a sky.
Far-piercing tremulous lines of watery light
And sheeted lustres wild and riven,
Like sunset glories tempest-driven,
It pours against the streaming gloom of night.
Sustaining this aërial canopy
White marble columns gleam unsteadfastly;
Yet by its hovering poise in air,
It seems self-borne to revel there,
Surmounting furious blasts over the lurid sea.

I stand by it envaulted. . . .
The palace thrills throughout from dome to floor
In swells of jubilant harmony, exalted
By the storm's intermittent clash and roar:
How the full volumes of orchestral sound
Outsurge continuously and sweep around!
As clouds by winds, see, swayed by their sweet measure,
All floating, gliding, sinking, heaving,
The countless Masquers interweaving
An Iris-coloured maze of dizzy pleasure
About the sea-like floor of marble green,
All waved with multitudinous waves, whose sheen
And restless shades the vision cheats;
They seem to flow beneath the feet
Which thrid that graceful dance of festive life serene.

Around the shorelike border,
Opening to arched recess and far aisle dim,
The feast-spread tables range in stately order.
What golden bowls, a-tremble to the brim,
Beneath the lamps in constellations shine
With jewels and the jewel-gleams of wine!
What fruits are clustered into glorious piles
Throughout the feast's magnificence,
On whose uncumbered affluence
Flowers shed the grace of their ethereal smiles!
Round the broad tables sumptuous couches flow,
Soft as June clouds, suffused with many a glow,
Of crimson, amber, violet dark:
Deep-dyed from each recess's arc
The massy curtains fall, down-sweeping full and low.

And children sport there tameless. . . .
O happy, happy children! happier far,
Possessed by unsought joyance free and aimless,
Than those tall masks with laboured pleasures are.
Through feast and dance they flit with shining faces,
Wreathing, unwreathing, in capricious chases,
With ringing laughters at their own swift wiles.
And yet a few, of strange grave mood,
Pace in shadowy solitude
Those many-columned labyrinthine aisles,
Which, opening through the oriels, link to zone
The gem-bright feast with dark grey caverned stone:
Though scarcely man or woman dares
That dusk instinct with lightning-glares,
Down whose far desert vistas waves and tempest moan.

The dome's broad-soaring lustres
Are poised upon one massive coil of gold;
A ruby-crested serpent, starred with clusters
Of flashing gems; its mighty bulk outrolled
In cyclic rest for ever; while, consumed,
The End in the Beginning lies entombed:
Gorgeous the symbol of Eternity!
The grand pilastered sweep of wall
Lives and glows around the hall,
Divinely pictured; earth and sea and sky
Have yielded the best grandeurs and delights
Of all their rolling seasons, days and nights,
To make these fields of space expand
Into an infinite Wonder-land
By their infinitude of dream-surpassing sights.

Sculptures serenely gracious
From out the flowing draperies' regal dyes,
Around the banquet-circle cool and spacious,
Gleam half-revealed to my enchanted eyes.
How can the festival flow undelayed
Amidst the heavenly visions here displayed?
How is it not rapt still, in breathless trance?—
What scenes of rock, field, sky and sea,
Flung round in infinite harmony!—
That wood where uncouth creatures sport and dance
In the weird dimness streaked with silvern rays:
That Eden quivering in the noontide blaze,
Nymphs languid in its fountain-bowers:
That sea-built City's domes and towers
Consuming in the Sunset's slow-breathed fiery haze!

"Evohe! our high Palace!
We dance, we dance, with dance-exulting feet!
We grow immortal, draining bowl and chalice
Of this life-burning wine-blood nectar-sweet,
And banqueting on this ambrosial food!
While ever and anon, in rapturous mood
Outstealing from the revel, pair by pair
Hide far within some dim recess,
And, faint with fervid eagerness,
Unlock the wildering wealth of love they share!
What though black Night inspheres us,—storm and rain
Assaulting this fair Heaven with fury vain?
Our-music-storm poured strong and fast
Can balance well the outer blast,
And yon resplendent dome for evermore sustain!"

With clash of wine-cups ringing,
So rose from flower-crowned feasters swaying there
The fervent Pæan, swelled with choral singing
By many a gallant Knight and lady fair.
What strength of wisdom and sure self-reliance
Could make *these* bold to fling such gay defiance
To all the dreadful Powers of ancient Night?—
These—pigmies swarming in the deep
Beneath their own dome's burning sweep;
These—motes invisible beneath Heaven's height!
But ere was ended the impetuous song,
A tremor ran electric through the throng:
With pallid cheek and restless eye,
With urgent voices loud and high,
Fear made them more and more the vauntful strains prolong.

"Ha! what a burst of thunder!
How the swift lightnings blanched our splendours pale!
Reweave the links of dance, too long asunder!
Let loose again the music's lifeful gale! . . .
But who are these, this never-bidden Pair,
Unnoticed while our joy-song dimmed the air?
Who are these masked in such mysterious wise?
What twain of all our company
Are missing from the revelry?—
They have assumed this melancholy guise
To shed fantastic wildness on our sport.
All here! then who are Ye, not of our court?
Whence come ye? wherefore thus invade
Our blissful brightness with the shade
Of sombre masks and robes, and joy-contemning port?"

Silent and dark and solemn,—
While the mixed tumult of amazement died
In deep hushed awe,—firm-planted as the column
Of dusky-splendid porphyry at their side,
The Strangers stood, absorbing all the scene
With slow calm eyes and wonder-baffling mien;
Two awful Spirits of the outer Night!
For age-like moments that ensued
The Saturnalian multitude
Was frozen into marble undelight;
Continued numb with terror,—lost and drowned
In that weird breathless agony profound,
Like a Nightmare's stifling pain
Crushing, maddening heart and brain,
When utter, monstrous Silence yawns like death around,

Till life, resurgent, tingled
In burning blood through every shrunken vein;
And one deep panting from all breasts commingled
To mark remission of that deadly strain
And over tension of the subtle strings
Whose music is the life of living things. . . .
Again with joy and power from secret caves
The full dance-harmonies outstreaming
Woke the Masquers from their dreaming,
Again they floated on the buoyant waves.
And all, it seemed, with fiercer yearning thirst,
Triumphant o'er the pallid swoon now burst,
Seized the fiery cup of bliss
Mantling high to greet their kiss;
And in delirious draughts awe doubt, and fear immerst.

The dim voluptuous languor
Of clouds surcharged with perfumes, slow and dense,
Uprolled from precious burnings, veiled the clangour,
The harmonised confusion grown intense,
Reckless, and surging with a wild desire
Most keenly hungered when most fed, like fire;
—Veiled the vast revel, even from their seeing,
Whose Bacchic frenzy broken loose
Was now the element profuse
That breathed it into such portentous being.
And few of all involved in this rich screen
Saw now the Strangers of mysterious mien;
Whose dark intolerable eyes
Burned through the tumult and disguise,
Commanding like Omniscience all the wildered scene.

But power to me was given
To see, to pierce the gloomy robes austere,
Which (as our world's gross night hides Hell and Heaven,
From mortals sick with longing, wild with fear)
Concealed these Two in undistinguished shade.
I saw the Vision of a Queen, arrayed
In midnight purple laced with snowy cloud,
Which as her bosom heaved shone far
With purest jewels, star on star. . . .
Grand Queen; dread Pythoness: her tall form bowed:
Transcendent beauty lost in desolate grace:
Her long dark hair thrown down about a face
So pale with awful mysteries
Of perfect love and woe and bliss,
That my own heart grew wild panting for her embrace.

But, Heaven be our protection
Against the Demon standing at Her side!—
By what dread lunacies of blind affection,
Or monstrous Destiny to Her allied!
Infernal Horror!—His rent forehead crowned
With hideous snakes writhing and interwound,
A many crested coil distinguishless;
While through black cloud with red fire seared
His vast and fleshless frame appeared
Momently shuddering into Nothingness.
On His disfeatured face was stamped a grin
Of unimagined foulness, hate and sin,
Anguish, greed, and rage and scorn,
And fiendish triumph most forlorn. . . .
Thus stood They side by side amidst the festal din.

Wilder and ever wilder
The revel surged beneath its glowing dome;
And still the outside rage grew ever wilder,
As if all powers that have in Night their home,
Lightning and thunder, rain and stormy blast,
Held *their* wild revel in its sightless vast. . . .
Then those Two Shapes were moved from stony rest;
And, keeping still their sable shroud,
Moved forward mingling with the crowd;
Each with a strange keen eagerness represt.
He seized an agèd yet carousing Knight;
She kissed a young girl's forehead drooping white;
These dancing linked in languid grace,
Those hurrying forth with swerveless pace,
Soon through a curtained portal passed from out our sight.

There rose shrill lamentation
From revellers fixed awaiting their return;
Inexplicable grief and consternation
Possessed them,—dread yet keen desire to learn
The fate of those led forth so suddenly;
And tremulous murmurings spread. . . . Then all might see
Those Shapes mysterious coming back alone. . . .
The Silence gave one reckless shout,
"The Knight was old and wearied out,
The Maid was sick and faint some hours agone:
These have but ushered them to rest and peace,
In sooth full kindly—But why therefore cease
The banquet and the dance? Away!
Every moment of delay
Is squandered from our joy's brief unreturning lease."

The rude spell fearless-hearted
Swayed back the riant feast-joy's ebbing flood:
But one—the Lover of the girl departed—
Approached the Woman desperately, and sued
With passion such as will not be denied
For reunition with his promised bride.
She led him forth in Her divine embrace;
And then returned without the boy,
Inspired by some exalted joy,
Which shone with holy splendour in Her face,
And bounded in Her port and heaved Her breast. . . .
But of the remnant every one represt
In silence of uneasy thought
The wonder that within him wrought:
The mystery had power to awe down open quest.

Thenceforth a voice of wailing,
Of grief that spurned all comfort, still increast,
For dear ones lost for ever, countervailing
The shouted songs and laughters of the feast;
Whose wine ran like a mountain rill, which grows
In strong and swift abundance as it flows.
For the dread Strangers thinned the joyous rout;
With stern and Fateful ministry
Removing almost momently
Man, woman, child, youth, maid,—selected out
By some inscrutable and lawless law.
Many to Her went willingly, I saw;
And fascinated by the bliss
Of Her tender, holy kiss,
Welcomed with solemn joy their doom's mysterious awe.

But it was shameful, fearful,
To mark of those He gestured to His side
How many shrank, with ravings wildly tearful
Of idiot pleas; while stalwart feastmen cried
"Grant us but one more hour of wine-fired glee!
Others may fail; but we, Iacchus! we
Could mount high revels with the mounting sun."
A few with high-wrought calmness grand
Took His stretched imperious hand,
And seemed, though then all powerless and undone,
To cope with His Omnipotence of Fate,
Yielding at once with undissembled hate.
But trembling wretches clustered near,
Already summoned forth by Fear
To time-destroying pangs no doom could aggravate.

O infinite tempest raging!
O awful Visitants from Heaven and Hell!
These mortals scorn and mock your dark presaging,
And wreak high feast-strains on their own deep knell.
See, through the clouds of incense wildly glancing,
What Mœnads with wild cries are wildly dancing!
All masks off-torn, their white limbs flash and shine,
Flung out tossing through the whirls;
Dishevelled tresses, wanton curls,
A-flame with flowers and dripping crimson wine,
Brush naked bosoms with their fiery trace,—
White, perfect breasts, full-swelled to the embrace
Which those wild eyes of humid light
Fiercely passionate now invite:—
The Palace, through their whirlwind, seems to reel in space.

Alas, how sad and dreary
Waned the whole scene there as the Night grew late!
When many of the Masquers, sick and weary,
Lay longing that those Ministers of Fate
Would choose them for removal: when of all
Whom They had taken from the festival
No one returned; though mourners fiercely craved
The never answering Shapes of Black
To bring them, but a moment, back,
And on the threshold of the Night-storm waved
Their feeble torches, quenched as soon as lit,
Seeking lost darlings through the Infinite:
And when at times some dreadful ghost,
Imaging the loved and lost,
Would through the startled feast with bodeful gestures flit. . . .

The lamps were quickly failing;
The pictures were weird shadows on the wall;
In the grey stone-cold dawn-gleams unprevailing
The draperies seemed a vast funereal pall
Flapping about the corpselike sculptures wan:
The floor, the cupola which glimmering shone,
The rain-dark marbles, in the tempest thrilled:
Where late the noble feast was spread
Lay scattered flower-blooms dim and dead,
'Mid stains of sullen-oozing wine outspilled
From urns and goblets shattered and o'erthrown,
And fragments in a sick confusion strown;
And lost in all the ghastly waste,
On couches tottering and displaced,
Flushed victims of the orgy, helpless, senseless, prone.

Yet evermore those Strangers
Went gathering in their harvest; and no less,
As men who face to face with deadly dangers
Inebriate their terror and distress,
A few kept up the revel with a madness
Of reeling, shrieking glee which was not gladness.
Till—portents of the near approaching Doom—
Wailings, laughters, wild and fierce,
Through the storm-swung darkness pierce,
And spectres people the dull flickering gloom. . . .
A deep foreboding hush pervades the place:
To that dis-covered Twain in one wild race
All reel along the quaking floor:
There grows a mighty booming roar,
As I am rapt away into the outer space.

With storm and fire and thunder
These rearward billows of Night's Ocean dash
Against the Palace: it is rent asunder,
Rent, shattered, with an instantaneous crash.
On, undelayed, exultingly they sweep,
Whirling its fragments through their wild waste deep:
Precipitant in their stupendous sway
The glowing fragments crystalline,
Gold, jewels, precious marbles, shine
Like showering meteors; high and far away,
Portentous, the Snake's blazing wheel is borne,
In dalliance with the lightnings whose fierce scorn
Smites into view wan wailing shades . . .
The whole Night-Chaos hurrying fades
Over the livid sea, before the dismal morn.

"O utter desolation!
O blighted beauty, splendour, triumph, bliss!
Alas, the gay and thoughtless congregation
Flung out unsheltered to the dark Abyss!
Bright Vision faded! never more can shine
A joy-insphering Palace so divine."
Lamenting thus, I sank in sleep or swoon. . . .
I wake—The isle and ocean spread
Level and bare: but overhead
The solemn Heaven of sapphire-burning noon
Has bent its dome's immeasurable height;
A few calm clouds o'erfraught with living light
Melt in the quivering crystalline;
Beneath the Eternal Sun divine,
Insphering half the world in glory and delight.

This is the Vision solely,
Trancing all aspiration with content!
Beauty all-perfect, blessedness all-holy,
Are veiled beyond that crystal firmament.
The breathless concave yearneth to the Hymn
Of all the Hosts of Stars and Seraphim;
The Hallelujah's raptured Monotone,
To whose vast swell the world-strown Sea
Of Æther throbs eternally,
Circling the footstool of that nameless Throne
Whose veil's far shadow floods this noon with light. . . .
—O self-sequestered Earth! O gross, weak sight!
For which beneath such heavenly day
Yawneth fathomless for aye
A spectre-haunted gulf of Sphere-completing Night.

February 1857.

A SERGEANT'S MESS SONG

With our arms round the waists of the charming girls,
Through the galop-sweeps and the swift waltz-whirls,
While our beards are brushed by their dancing curls,
Dance, boys, dance!

With the old black pipe and the steaming glass,
And a toast to the health of each sonsie lass,
And a right jolly set the toast to pass,
Drink, boys, drink!

For we have our hold of the world to-day,
And must snatch our share of it while we may,
Before they bury us out of the way:
Dance, boys, dance!

So we'll smoke our pipe, and we'll drink our glass,
And we'll play our game, and we'll hug our lass;
And as for the rest—why the devil's an ass:
Drink, boys, drink!

[1857?]

THE PURPLE FLOWER OF THE HEATHER

I.

On the grey lone keep stood the Lady fair,
With the lonely stream beneath;
New-numbed with horror, moaning there,
Her eye-balls fixed in a death-like stare
Across the darkening heath.

II.

They leapt from their boat in the grim grey air,
They strode on stern and slow;
By the wrinkled waters cold and bare,
Under the great clouds rolling there,
All ruggedly rimmed with a fierce red glare
From the stormy sunset low.

III.

They stood foot to foot on the lone dark heath,
Eye fixed on eye:
A pause—and each blade has left its sheath
To clash and to flash its keen cold death
Under the turbid sky.

IV.

Adown the long straight fir-tree aisles
The long gusts sing and roar;
The reeds all sigh through their shivering files
To the sad stream creeping weary miles
Across the barren moor.

V.

The gale sweeps down through southern lands;
Some stars peer faint and grey,
On two stern shadows—weary hands
Of tireless rage—with sullen brands
Still urging deadly fray.

VI.

For they fight on still, though they bleed and gasp,
With sweep and ward and pierce;
And the long glaives quiver in their clasp,
As tree-boughs quiver in a tempest's grasp
Because the grasp is fierce.

VII.

The moon came slowly up the sky
  To see a mournful sight:
The one the other kneeleth by
To tear his heart forth ere he die—
"Great God hath judged your life's deep lie!
  Confess, now, recreant knight!"

VIII.

Some faint words thrilled the waiting air—
  "I speak—to pardon you.
Sealed lips must ope for their own last prayer;
Your outrage now is washed out, fair—
Though with my blood not yours—I swear
  Both she and I were true."

IX.

Slow, slow, the moon moved through the sky
  All night above that plain;
Still gazing down with her cold wan eye
On one all wild with agony
  Beside another slain.

X.

"His form is cold as the earth beside,
  His blood is cold as the dew.
O cursèd, cursèd jealous pride!
O, lost for ever, noblest bride!
O, dear, dear friend, that I had died
  Ere death had come to you!"

XI.

Slow, slow, the moon moved through the sky,
  About that turret's gloom;
Staring mad with her lidless eye
The Lady, who with groan nor sigh,
But pale and stark and stonily,
  Leant staring for her doom.

1857.

THE DOOM OF A CITY

A FANTASIA.

PART I.

THE VOYAGE

I.

From out the house I crept,
The house which long had caged my homeless life:
The mighty City in vast silence slept,
Dreaming away its tumult, toil, and strife:
But sleep and sleep's rich dreams were not for me,
For me, accurst, whom terror and the pain
Of baffled longings, and starved misery,
And such remorse as sears the breast,
And hopeless doubt which gnaws the brain
Till wildest action blind and vain
Would be more welcome than supine unrest,
Drove forth as one possest
To leave my kind and dare the desert sea;
To drift alone and far,
Dubious of any port or isle to gain,
Ignorant of chart and star,
Upon that infinite and mysterious main
Which wastes in foam against our shore;
Whose moans and murmurs evermore,
Insupportably sublime,
Haunting the crowded tumult of our Time,
Suspend its hurrying breath—
Like whispers of sad ghosts and spirits free
From worlds beyond our life and death,
The unknown awful realm where broods Eternity.

II.

I paced through desert streets, beneath the gleam
Of lamps that lit my trembling life alone;
Like lamps sepulchral which had slowly burned
Through sunless ages, deep and undiscerned,
Within a buried City's maze of stone;
Whose peopling corpses, while they ever dream
Of birth and death of complicated life
Whose days and months and years
Are wild with laughters, groans, and tears,
As with themselves and Doom
They wage, with loss or gain, incessant strife,
Indeed, lie motionless within their tomb,
Lie motionless and never laugh or weep,
All still, and buried deep
For ever in death's sleep,
While burn the quiet lamps amidst the breathless gloom.

III.

My boat lay waiting there,
Upon the moonless river
Whose pulse had ceased to quiver
In that unnatural hush of brooding night.
I thought, Free breezes course the billowy deep!
And rowed on panting through the feverous air,
Leaving the great main waters on my right
For that canal which creeps into the sea
Across the livid marshes wild and bare.
So, slowly faded back from sight,
As doth a dream insensibly
Fade backward on the ebbing tide of sleep,
That city which had home nor hope for me,
That stifling tomb from which I now was free.

IV.

Like some weak life whose sluggish moments creep
Diffused on worthless objects, yet whose tide
With dull reluctance hard to understand
Refrains its death-in-life from death's full sleep,
The river's shallow waters oozed out wide,
Inclosing dreary flats of barren sand;
So merged at last into the lethal waste
That bounds of sea and stream could not be traced.

V.

Long languidly I rowed,
With sick and weary pain,
Between the deepest channel's bitter weeds
Whose rankness salt slime feeds;
And so out blindly thro' the dismal main,
Now shaken with a long hoarse growling swell.
And soon the Tempest as a king who had slept
The sleep of worn-out frenzy, while his slaves
Cowered still in stupor till he woke again
Refreshed for carnage—from his torpor leapt,
Breathed swarthy pallor through the dense low sky,
And hurrying swift and fell
Outspeeded his own thunder-bearing glooms;
Then prone and instantaneous from on high
Plunged down in one tremendous blast,
Which crashed into white dust the heaving waves
And left the ocean level when it past. . . .
There was a moment's respite; silence reigned,
Such shuddering silence as may once appal
The universe of tombs,
Ere the last trumpet's clangour rend them all:
And I sank down, one frail and helpless man
Alone with desolation on the sea,
To pray while any sense of prayer remained
Amidst the horrors overwhelming me.

VI.

How shall I tell that tempest's thunder-story?
The soldier plunged into the Battle-stress,
Struggling and gasping in the mighty flood,
Stunned with the roar of cannon, blind with smoke,
'Midst yells and tramplings drunk and mad with blood,
What knows he of the Battle's spheric glory?
Of heavenly laws that all its evil bless
Of sacred rights of justice which invoke
Its sternest pleading of the tranquil eye
Triumphant o'er its chaos of the Mind
Commanding all, serene and unsubdued,
Which having first with wisest care designed
Works to the end with vigilant fortitude;
And from that field so drenched with angry blood
Shall reap the golden harvest, VICTORY?

VII.

There was a stupor stung with pain and fear,
Amidst the strangling surf flung on and on;
There was bewilderment above all dread,
Delirious calm and desperate joy austere
Of revelling through the tempest lorn and lone.
My boat and I with dizzy swiftness sped,
In strange salvation from the certain doom,
Along the urgent ridges over-reeling
And gathering up their ruins as they fled;
And down into the depths of scooped-out gloom
Whose crystal walls glowed black in the revealing
Of lightning-kindled foam; and up again,
Perched on the giddy balance of two waves
Which fiercely countering mingle with the shock,
And rush aloft confused, and tower and rock
Foaming with wild convulsion, till amain
The mass heaves down from struggling, self-destroyed,
And leaves us shuddering in a gulfy void.
Confused and intermingled, fire, sea, air,
Wrought out their ravage; for the thunders there
Were echoing in the dreadly stormless caves
And shook the deep foundations of the seas;
The air was like an ocean, drenched with spray
Whose meteor-flakes outflashed tumultuously
Against the sinking heaven's black incline,
When sudden lightnings seemed to burst their way
Up through the deep to flood and fire its brine,
Ingulfing for each moment all the Night,
The blackness and the howling rage in light
More lurid and appalling, a World-pyre. . . .
But heart and brain were overwrought; and soon,
All vision reeling from my powerless eyes,
I lay in quiet mercy-granted swoon
As senseless as the boat in which I lay:
And we two things through all the agonies
    Of night, tornado, sea, and fire,
Were drifted passive on our fearful way.

VIII.

I know not for what time I lay in trance,
Nor in what course the tempest hurled us on.
At length to scarce-believed deliverance
I woke; and saw a sweet slow silent dawn
Upgrowing from the far dim grey abyss,
So slow, it seemed like some celestial flower
Unfolding perfect petals to its prime,
And feeling in its secret soul of bliss
Each leaf a loveliness for many an hour,
With amaranthine queenship over time.
It grew: its purple splendours flecked and starred
With golden fire spread floating up the steep
Until they sole possessed the mighty sweep
Of crystal lucent æther: its regard,
The blessing of a light of peace and love,
Charmed with a gradual spell the sullen mood
Of the sea-giant, until all-subdued
No more his huge bulk livid shook and hove
The meteor-threatenings of his tawny mane,
No more growled lingering wrath and turbulent pain;
But calm and glad th' unmonstered monster lay
Beneath the royal sun's perfected sway.

IX.

And there was Land. Where seemed a bank of clouds
Piled in the South, now nobly, one by one,
The pinnacles of lofty mountain-peaks
Flamed keen as stars, enkindled by the sun;
Emerging as with life from out their shrouds
Of silvern haze far-cleft with roseate streaks:
And far beneath them, down along the shore,
A wave of low round hills gleamed pure and pale.
    But soon—like any human life,
The golden promise of whose dawn doth fail
Into the same drear noon of barren strife
Of which our hearts were weary-sick of yore—
        The day grew chill and dark;
And through its sullen hours the wintry gale
        Beat restlessly my bark,
Beside that coast-line drifting to and fro
Upon the ocean's vapour-shrouded flow.

X.

I saw grey phantoms, fading as they fled,
Glide hurrying in loose rank
O'er livid backgrounds of the upper sky,
Whose vast and thunderous threat'ning overfrowned
Abysses strangely dread—
Cold, glassy gulfs, each like an evil eye
Of serpent-malice which is dead and blank
To every sight but woe and agony.
The fascination of their wan green glance
Was fixed upon the hills which, at the foot
Of that stern wall of mountain lifted proud
Above the firmament of level cloud,
Lay stretched out cold and mute,
In leaden bulk, beneath the long expanse
Of dark and desert sky, whose brooding gloom
Was blanched with cruel pallor here and there—
Pallor of wrath or dread, instinct with doom.
There stretched they far, a dark and silent host,
Like monsters stranded from their deep sea-lair
Benumbed with terror cowering;
Still unrecovered from the storm whose ire
Had drowned them in wild floods of pitiless fire,
Or prescient of some deadlier tempest lowering.

XI.

At intervals, opposing the sun's track,
Circling about the North
Shone strangely blazoned forth
Wild rainbow-fragments on the sweeping rack,
The gale's rent symbol on rent banners borne.
For ever and anon the sun gazed down
From dizzy summits of the cloud-crags black;
Or where the wind had torn
Vast jaggèd rifts athwart their mass
(Behind whose heavy frown
Faint smiles of soothing like a robe of grass
Had fallen from him on the frozen hills),
He gazed out powerless o'er the rain-grey sea:
No eye which sorrows fills
With constant bitter tears,
Drowning all life and lustre, joy and pride,
Can gaze more faint and wan and hopelessly
Into the homeless world, and waste of years

Spread out between it and the grave's sweet sleeping;
Can let the dark lid sink upon its weeping
        More often, fain to hide
The chilling desolation blurred with strife
Which, seen or unseen, maps its future life.

XII.

    Ere sunset came a storm of rain
    Ploughing up the barren main
    With fierce and vital energy,
While brief bright lightnings flashed incessantly.
And then the South stood up, one solid wall
Of battlemented cloud, in which the mountains
And hills were fused together out of sight:
The sinking sun from his intense fire-fountains
Poured out against its heaven-absorbing might
    Seas of lurid purple light
And fulvous meteors, surging and devouring
    The shattered crests, the crumbling slopes,
    The massive walls, the riven copes,
In fortitude of glowing bronze far-towering.

XIII.

From all the secret caverns of the air
Night's gloomy phantoms issuing, gathered dense
To blot and stifle out the pageant there;
The murmur of their motions breathing wide
Through that new silence thrilled upon the sense;
When, gazing southward, I became aware
Of some slow movement by the dim sea-side,
As of a wind arousing from its lair
To rend the settled vapours. I descried,
After an interval of rapt suspense,
By what faint gloaming yet was left of day,
Two startling lamps uplifted slowly glide
From out the thick and dun immensity,
Fronting a long dark line like some array
Of men that came in silent mystery,
Across the undulations of the shore
Long-winding coil on coil unbrokenly,
To celebrate weird rites and sorceries hoar,
Shrouded in gloom beside the moaning sea.

XIV.

I knew, but would not know,
I knew too well, but knowledge was despair.
It came on vast and slow,
And dipt those baleful meteors in the brine;
Whence soon it lifted them with hideous cries
That flung strange horror through the shuddering air.
Haling its length in many a monstrous twine,
It bore on steadfastly those loathsome eyes,
Set in the midst of intertangled hair
Like sea-weed in whose jungle have their lair
All foul and half-lived things:
With such a gleam as haunts the rotting graves
They fixed upon me their malignant stare;
Shallow and slimy, fiendish, eyes of death.
It neared me soon with fiendish wallowings
Athwart the heaving and repugnant waves;
Then paused a moment, and with one harsh roar
Heaved up its whole obscene and ghastly bulk,
To rankle in my memory evermore.
With hissing shrieks and bursts of strangled breath,
Torn by some agonising pang, it fell,
And lay upon the sea a vast dead hulk;
But raised yet once the huge and formless head
Whence blood-dark foam was showering; and those eyes
Glared blinking on me with the hate of Hell,
Before it turned reluctantly and fled.
Down, down, convicted by the holy skies,
Away, away, O God! it hurtled forth;
To cower in frozen caverns of the deep;
To haunt—a nightmare in that ghastly sleep—
The death and desolation of the North.

XV.

A man forlorn has wandered, cursed from rest,
Through Time's dead waste, and savage howling seas,
Bearing a fateful Horror in his breast,
Formless and dim, but mighty to disease;
Devouring, poisoning, stifling his pure life.
And suddenly, when Hope can hope no more,
He feels its coils unwinding from his heart,
And rich vitality with glorious strife
Surging through veins all shrunk and numb before:
But also sees the Incubus depart,
Coil after coil reluctant dragged away

As were a serpent's from its strangled prey;
And thus in his first health is clearly shown
What still was hidden from his lunacy,
The full obscene and deadly ghastliness
Of that which held and ruled him to this day:
Abhorrence almost chills him into stone,
And that great blow which struck the prisoner free
Hath nearly slain him by its mighty stress.
Such was my agony of joy that hour,
When saved for ever from the monster's power.

XVI.

The sky was spacious warm and bright,
The clouds were pure as morning snow;
In myriad points of living light
The sea lay laughing to and fro.
Above the hills a depth of sky,
Dim-pale with heat and light intense,
Was overhung by clouds piled high
In mountain-ranges huge and dense;
Whose rifts and ridges ran aloft
Far to their crests of dazzling snow,
Whence spread a vaporous lustre soft
Veiling the noontide's azure glow.
Through mists of purple glory seen
Those dim and panting hill-waves lay,
Absorbed into the heavens serene,
Dissolving in the perfect day.
But when the sun burned high and bare
In his own realm of solemn blue,
The clouds hung isolated there,
Dark purple grandeurs vast and few;
Like massive sculptures wrought at large
Upon that dome's immensity,
Like constant isles whose foamlit marge
Rose high from out that sapphire sea.

And all the day my boat sped on
With rapid gliding smooth as rest,
As if by mystic dreamings drawn
To some fair haven in the West;
Flew onward swift without a gale
As if it were a living thing,
And spread with joy its snow-white sail
As spreads a bird its snow-white wing;
Flashed on along the lucid deep

Dividing that most perfect sphere,
A vault above it glowing steep,
A vault beneath it no less clear;
Within whose burning sapphire-round
The clouds, the air, the land, the sea,
Lay thrilled with quivering glory, drowned
In calm as of Eternity.

PART II.
THE CITY

I.

Anear the dying of that royal day
Those amber-vested hills began to swerve;
And soon a lofty Pharos, gleaming white
Upon its isle set darkly in the light,
Beckoned us onward to the spacious bay
Encompassed broadly by their noble curve.
And so at length we entered it; and faced
The thin dark lines of countless masts, all traced
Upon the saddest sunset ever seen—
Spread out like an interminable waste
Of red and saffron sand, devoured by slow
Persistent fire; beneath whose desolate glow
A City lay, thick-zoned with solemn green
Of foliage massed upon the steeps around.
Between those mast-lines flamed the crystal fires
Of multitudinous windows; and on high
Grand marble palaces and temples, crowned
With golden domes and radiant towers and spires,
Stood all entranced beneath that desert sky,
Based on an awful stillness. Dead or dumb,
That mighty City through the breathless air
Thrilled forth no pulse of sound, no faintest hum
Of congregated life in street and square:
Becalmed beyond all calm those galleons lay,
As still and lifeless as their shadows there,
Fixed in the magic mirror of the bay
As in a rose-flushed crystal weirdly fair.
A strange, sad dream: and like a fiery pall,
Blazoned with death, that sky hung over all.

II.

Where, eastward from the town, the shore was low,
I drew at length my shallop up the sand,—
The quiet and gloomless twilight gathering slow;
And took my way across the lonely strand,
And onward to the City, lost in thought.
Who shall his own wild life-course understand?
From terror through great terrors I am brought
To front my fate in this mysterious land.
In my old common world, well fenced about
With myriad lives that fellowed well my own,
Terror and deadly anguish found me out
And drove me forth to seek the dread Unknown;
Through all whose terrors I have yet been brought,
Though hopeless, helpless, utterly alone.
May yet my long wild night be blessed with morn?
Some revelation from the awful Throne
Awaits me surely: if my life, torn free
From dire Egyptian bondage, has been led
In safety through the all-devouring sea;
If, lost in foodless deserts, it was fed
Though murmuring ever; hath it truly trod
Such paths for nothing? Shall it not be brought
To stand awe-stricken 'neath some Mount of God
Wrapt in thick clouds of thunder fire and gloom,
And hear the Law of Heaven by which its doom
To good or evil must be henceforth wrought?

III.

The moon hung golden, large, and round,
Soothing its beauty up the quiet sky
In swanlike slow pulsations, while I wound
Through dewy meads and gardens of rich flowers,
Whose fragrance like a subtle harmony
Was fascination to the languid hours.
A tender mist of light was interfused
Upon the hills and waters, woods and leas,
Throughout the gloomless gloaming; and I mused
Dim thoughts deep-floating in delicious dream,
Until the long stern lines of cypress trees,
Amidst whose plumes funereal there did seem
To creep with quivering sobs a moaning breath,
Awed back my heart to life—to life and death.
Far in the mystic moonlight lay outspread,
In trance of solemn beauty still and weird,

That Camp and City of the ancient dead;
And far around stood up in dense array
Those monumental marbles ever reared
By men still battling with the powers of Life
To those released before them from its sway:
Victors or vanquished in the fearful strife,
What matters?—ah, within our Mother's breast,
From toil and tumult, sin and sorrow free,
Sphered beyond hope and dread, divinely calm;
They lie, all gathered into perfect rest;
And o'er the trance of their Eternity
The Cypress waves more holy than the palm.

IV.

A funeral train was gathered round a bier:
The reverend priest with lifted hands and face,
Appealing silently to Heaven's grace
For this young soul called early from our sphere;
And white-robed maidens pale, whose hands scarce held
What further symbol flowers they had to shed
Upon their sweet lost sister,—awe and dread
Numbing their noisier grief, they stood compelled
To meet Death's eyes which wither youth from Life;
And leaning sole against a tree apart,
As one might lean just stricken to the heart,
A youth, wrought calm by woe's self-slaying strife—
His head was sunken nerveless on his breast,
He stood a dumb blind statue of Despair.
While all yet moved not, I approached them there,
Murmuring: They bring this maiden to her rest
Beneath the pure sad moon, in thoughtful night,
Rather than in the garish day whose King
Rides through the Heavens for ever triumphing
Throned above ruth in never-darkened light;
That ere the blank dawn chills them they may gaze,
And see her soul as some white cloud on high
Floating serenely up the star-strewn sky. . . .
My steps were now close near them, when amaze
Convulsed me with a swooning suddenness—
What people dwell within this Silent Land,
Who thus have placed, through day and night to stand,
This Scene complete in all its images
Of Life in solemn conference with Death,
Amidst the wide and populous solitude
Of Death's own realm?—a people of strange mood.
For all,—the maidens meek with bated breath
And eyes weighed down by awe and fear and sorrow,

The priest appealing to the Heavens above,
The youth whose mortal night could hope no morrow,
The sweet young girl new riven from his love,—
All save the flowers, the withered flowers alone,
Were carven weirdly in unconscious stone.

V.

Beneath my gaze was spread the princely mart.
From out the folded hills came broad the stream
Whose pulse flowed lifefull through the City's heart—
The City dead in ever-voiceless dream.
From all her stately mansions, reared apart
'Midst lawns and gardens, came no lamplight gleam,
No cheerful glow and smoke of household fire;
No festal music dying through the night,
Sad in its death as joyous in its birth;
No serenades intoning soft desire,
To which young hearts in secret throb delight;
No noise of banded revellers issuing forth
With shouts and songs and jars,
Who find the pale moon reeling jollily
And twinkling laughters in the high cold stars.
Between the hills and sea
Only a dark dead dearth
Of soulless silence yawned in dreadful mystery.

VI.

My limbs were shuddering while my veins ran fire,
And hounded on by dread
No less than by desire,
I plunged into the City of the Dead,
And pierced its Mausolean loneliness—
Between the self-sufficing palaces,
Broad fronts of azure, fire and gold, which shone
Spectrally pallid in the moonlight wan;
Adown great streets; through spacious sylvan squares,
Whose fountains plashing lone
Fretted the silence with perpetual moan;
Past range on range of marts which spread their wares
Weirdly unlighted to the eyes of heaven,
Jewels and silks and golden ornaments,
Rich perfumes soul-in-soul of all rare scents,
Viols and timbrels,—O wild mockery!
Where are the living shrines for these adornings?
Shall love-tormented phantoms hither hie,
Resolvèd that the tomb be no more mute,

And thrill their heart-sick plaints from lyre and lute
To plead against fair phantoms' cruel scornings;
Wakening dim ghosts of buried melodies
To shiver out beneath the scornful skies,
And wander homeless till they fail of breath
About this desert realm of timeless death?

VII.

What saw I in the City, which could make
All thought a frenzy and all feeling madness?
What found I in the City for whose sake
Blank death were welcome as a restful gladness?
I hold it truth, that what the stars and moon
Can gaze upon with clear and steadfast eyes,
Still soaring as of old to reach their noon,
Serenely regnant in unwithered skies;
That scene should never fill a human being
With hopelessness of horror in the seeing.
Can souls be blighted where the mere trees grow?
Can lives be frozen where the dead streams flow?
Can Man be prostrate where the fleeting mountains
Stand up and fling abroad their joyous fountains?
Could oceans, hills, stars, heavens, those imageries
And shadows of our sole realities,
Endure but for a moment undestroyed
Were we extinct—Eternity left void?
O truth beyond our sin and death's concealing!—
The ghastliest den, worst Hell of pain and fear,
In which a spirit can have will, thought, feeling,
Is to that spirit no unnatural sphere;
Nor justifies that spirit for the death
Of firm self-trust, of love and hope and faith.

VIII.

What found I in the City, then, which turned
My deep and solemn hope to wild despair?
What mystery of horror lay inurned
Within the royal City great and fair?
What found I?—Dead stone sentries stony-eyed,
Erect, steel-sworded, brass-defended all,
Guarding the sombrous gateway deep and wide
Hewn like a cavern through the mighty wall;
Stone statues all throughout the streets and squares,
Grouped as in social converse or alone;
Dim stony merchants holding forth rich wares
To catch the choice of purchasers of stone;

Fair statues leaning over balconies,
Whose bosoms made the bronze and marble chill;
Statues about the lawns, beneath the trees;
Firm sculptured horsemen on stone horses still;
Statues fixed gazing on the flowing river
Over the bridge's sculptured parapet;
Statues in boats, amidst its sway and quiver
Immovable as if in ice-waves set:—
The whole vast sea of life about me lay,
The passionate, heaving, restless, sounding life,
With all its tides and billows, foam and spray,
Arrested in full tumult of its strife
Frozen into a nightmare's ghastly death,
Struck silent from its laughter and its moan;
The vigorous heart and brain and blood and breath
Stark, strangled, coffined in eternal stone.

IX.

Look away there to the right—How the bay lies broad and bright,
All athrob with murmurous rapture in the glory of the moon!
See in front the palace stand, halls and columns nobly planned;
Marble home for marble dwellers is it not full fair and boon?
See the myriads gathered there in that green and wooded square,
In mysterious congregation,—they are statues every one:
All are clothed in rich array; it is some high festal day;
The solemnity is perfect with that pallid moon for sun.
See the theatre ranged high to its dome of deep blue sky;
Tier on tier of serried statues glare impassioned on its stage,
On its background of deep night, on its sculptured Chorus white,
On its lofty sculptured actors locked in deadly tragic rage:
Perhaps the drama was *too* great,—Titans, Furies, eyeless Fate
Brooded in such sulphurous darkness thunderswollen o'er its doom,
That the multitude abide overwrought and petrified,
Waiting till satyric sun-bursts rend away the crushing gloom.
Turn, and o'er the river mark that huge structure scowling dark:
It is black stone seamed with crimson, hopeless death with cruel gore:
In it stony jailers guard stony prisoners evil-starred;
Dungeoned thus within their dungeon, they are calm and groan no more.
Note the temples every one—How the great gods are undone!
Not a steer or goat or doveling for their holy hunger dies:
Cold, long quenched their sacred fires; dull, long dumb their flattering quires;
All the very priesthood staring at rich gifts with stolid eyes!
Not a maid whose yielding charms can enrich a god's bold arms;
Yet perchance they dwell contented though thus shorn of wealth and state:
Nectar-and-ambrosia-blest, they may bask in perfect rest,
Since (with marble joints and larynx) Man rests unimportunate!
Ha! search eagerly around—every vault beneath the ground,

Every mansion, every chariot, every galley, everywhere;
And for ever, ever find all this blissful human kind
Lifted up from clay's corruption into marble firm and fair:
Fear and shame and anguish stilled, every evil passion killed,
Crooked forms and ugly faces grown transcendent works of art;
While the grand or lovely mood of the fair and young and good
Is beatified in beauty that can nevermore depart. . . .
And the full moon gazeth down on the smokeless lampless town,
In a solemn trance of triumph, with her choir of radiant stars;
For their peace is vext no more by a curse-and-shriek-swelled roar,
By ferocities, obscenities, inebriate brawls and jars:
Nay, the very grass and trees, and the disencumbered breeze,
And the stainless river-waters, and the broad bright glittering bay,—
Do they all joy that the strife of our sordid restless life
Is now locked in adamantine bonds of perfect peace for aye?
Ever-loved and gracious Earth, Mystic Mother of our birth,
This is cruel, bitter, terrible, this joy in our dead rest!
Canst Thou still leap forth and run, glory-speeded round the Sun,
O Thou Niobe of World-stars, with Thy fairest and Thy best—
With Thy vigorous youthful darling lying stone-cold on Thy breast!

X.

The Palace gates stand open wide and free;
The King and Queen and all their company,
Transfigured in full splendour of their pride,
Came flowing forth in one refulgent tide,
While trumpets rang their silver-throated blare
Of jubilation through the sunny air;
Swept onward slowly 'neath the azure skies
Between the myriads of adoring eyes,
And poured into the Theatre's dense sea
Of many-billowed life triumphantly;
As some grand river in the sunset shine
May pour its boon of gold and crimson wine,
Brimming the fulness of the purpled ocean
Which heaves and sparkles, murmuring proud emotion.
Gathered together, all awaited there
Such scenic storms as purify life's air;
Whose scathless lightnings shimmer wildly grand,
Whose lofty thunders soothe sure peace more bland;
And now, without a throb, without a breath,
They wait, all frozen into icy death.

XI.

O marble Monarch, far more awful now
Than when thy crown begirt a throbbing brow!
No tyrant ever lived so dire and dread
As He who sways the sceptre in thy stead;
Never before on earth did any state
Beneath oppression cower thus desolate,
Thus utterly resigned to crushing Fate!
SILENCE broods ghastly on the dead realm's throne:
Whatever life, in prayer, or sigh, or moan,
Would shake the Nightmare of his tyranny,
Shudders with anguish, horror, lunacy,
To feel its scorned and strangled pleadings creep
Like homeless spectres through the vacant deep,
And wither into nothingness at last—
Devoid of refuge, unrelieved, aghast.

XII.

The Palace gates indeed stand open wide:
Perchance the stately sepulchre may hide
Some single life amidst the desolation,
Preserved alone in mystical salvation,
Entranced apart in holy contemplation?
Pace up the steps, tread through the hall,—and see
In scattered groups all lounging listlessly
Those armoured gallants of the Royal Guard—
Poor fellows! they have found it sadly hard
To make their stately moments speed along,
Though spurred with wine and gaming, jest and song,
Cruelly mulcted of their sumptuous share
In the great festival proceeding there.

XIII.

Haste on, haste on; awaken from their tomb
The ghostly echoes, swarming through the gloom,
Haunting your footsteps, gathering rank on rank,
Rustling demoniac through the deadly blank;
Better, far better that the air be rife
With weird deliriums of demoniac life,
Than void with utter idiotic death.
Haste on, with burning blood and breathless breath;—
How clear are all things round the rapid flight!
Shrouded in gloom or washed with pale moonlight,

The chemistry of terror thus intense
Burns them all lurid on the shrinking sense.—
See the mild maiden letting loose her soul
In tears and blushes o'er the tender scroll
Which plains his anguish since they two were parted,
And raves that she, poor thing, is stony-hearted.
Hurry from room to room, from hall to hall;
And mark the effigies on every wall—
Warriors and minstrels, nobles, kings, and priests,
Adoring, conquering, feasting royal feasts;
Olympian forms, ladies divinely fair
With lily-sceptred hands and flower-crowned hair;
See each and all ev'n as you hurry past
Burst into sudden life, and swarming fast
Join in the tingling chase through death and night,
While clamorous echoes voice their mad delight.

XIV.

Most sweet young Mother! thou hadst ample pleasure
Left quiet alone here with thine infant treasure;
Which, poised unsurely on its feeble limbs,
Across the sea-strange marble toward thee swims,—
One foot half-lifted, while the arms outplead
For thine extended arms to help its need:
It stands, thou kneelest; never on thy breast
Shall it fall forward in triumphant rest.

XV.

Far in his lofty turret whence the bay
And half of Heaven's vault were seen alway;
The bay, the distant ocean, and with these
Broad scope of temples, streets, and palaces,
The theatre, the square; the moving throngs,
Whose converse-murmurs flashing into songs
And laughters winged with joy were wont to rise
And wander bird-like through the sun-tranced skies,
Rippling deliciously the languid air;
Alone, yet not alone, the Sage dwelt there.
Doubtless his individual life required
In seeming solitude to be inspired
By constant intercourse with general life,
And with the universal Spirit rife
In Man and Nature,—One in all their forms,
Alike contented with its worlds and worms,
Through all its countless masks alike resplendent,
The Breath of Life, eternal and transcendent.

XVI.

He sits, the full-length statue of a Sage,
Amid the busts of those of every age
Who handed on the torch of Wisdom, bright
With growing splendour, 'thwart the billowy night
Of shoreless Ignorance. Before him lies
The roll which telleth on what mysteries
He shed its lustre till they shone out clear:
I trace its periods by the moonlight here.
It is with swelling reverence dedicate,
"Unto the King magnifical and great;
The bounteous Sun by whom we live and move
And flourish ever: Who commands our love
Even more throughly than our perfect awe;
Swaying His burning Throne by Heavenly law,
While lifted far—by nature as by birth—
Above the petty statutes of our earth:
Who while His warmth createth and sustaineth
Rich life in all, lights all; and no less deigneth
To feed abundantly with life and light
What humble spheres may strive to temper night
In realms left dark while His imperial sway
Vouchsafeth happier realms their boon of day:
To Him, by Whom our heritage is grown
The flower o' the World; to Him whose godlike throne
Shall ever stand beside its subject sea,
Fulgent with valour, arts and equity,
Based on a princely people's love and bliss:
CHRYSANDROS, TYRANT OF COSMOPOLIS!"

XVII.

Follow the problems which he hath resolved
Though heretofore in clouds of doubt involved:
"Shall this fair World consume in course of time?
Our Earth is young? or old? or in her prime?"
Whereto the Theses proud, less said than sung
In liberal phrases of his golden tongue:
"This glorious Universe shall live for ever;
By all decay and death diminished never,
Nor added to by constant birth and growth;
But in the balanced interchange of both,
Ascending slowly by successive stages
Of nobler Good and Beauty through the Ages;
Until its infinite Æther and the Whole

Of stars and spheres that through it flashing roll
Shall be informed with conscious Life and Soul:
The All, one perfect Sphere, breathing one breath
Of cosmic Life too pure for birth or death. . . .
Our Earth has scarcely ceased to be a child,
Sweet in its grace, but ignorant and wild:
She putteth on about these very years
The bloom of maidenhood, whose smiles and tears
Are all of Love: She openeth out her heart
In throbs of passionate rapture, to impart
The dearest secrets of her treasured beauty
To Man, her Lord; constrained by yearning duty
Which he shall recompense with wiser love:
How blest are we all previous men above,
Born in this Spring of her millennial Youth!—
O gracious Truth, divine and tranquil Truth,
As I long years have worshipped only Thee,
Thou hast at length unveiled Thy face to me,
That I may ever of Thy priesthood be!"

XVIII.

I trace not further in the tingling scroll
The steps by which he reached this glorious goal.
It is too horrible:—alone, alone,
I make mad dalliance with the empty flesh,
Whose form is whole, whose ghastly bloom is fresh;
And by my side, that hater of the soul—
The grinning, the accursèd Skeleton!
It is too horrible—O dreadful God,
          Thou know'st—only Thou,
What dismal paths my shuddering feet have trod;
Yet never knew I agony until now;
Never,—O Thou who heardst me when I said
Coldly and quietly, with confirming heart,
"I take thee, Misery, for my faithful Bride:
Despair hath smoothed the secret marriage-bed
Wherein we two, embracing close, may hide,
          And wreak our stern unwitnessed vow—
Never in life, nor after death, to part.
I love thee for the love which only Thou
          Dost bear me: Thy caresses
Sting my faint heart, Thy kisses on my brow
Are fire and numbing frost, Thy tingling tresses
Like serpents creep about me even now.
O my enamoured Darling, deadly sweet!
          Sorcery smitten Sorceress!

Queen of lurid loveliness!
Most tender-hearted Ministrant of Ill!
My life, my soul is lying at your feet;
Possess me, use me, at your own wild will!"

XIX.

O fool, fool, fool! cherishing fatal madness!
Mad with self-consciousness of guilt and woe,
Mad with the folly of the world's much gladness
While it was no less sunk in guilt and woe;
I shut myself up from the lives around me,
Eating my own foul heart—envenomed food;
And while dark shadows more and more enwound me,
Nourished a dreary pride of solitude;
The cords of sympathy which should have bound me
In sweet communion with earth's brotherhood,
I drew in tight and tighter still around me,
Strangling my best existence for a mood.
What—Solitude in midst of a great City,
In midst of crowded myriads brimmed with Life!—
When every tear of anguish or of pity,
When every shout of joy and scream of strife,
When every deed and word and glance and gesture,
Every emotion, impulse, secret thought
Pent in the soul from all material vesture,
Through all those myriads spread and interwrought;
Inspiring each the air with its own spirit,
Rayed forth as light is from a fount intense
The universal Æther forced to bear it,
A certain though mysterious influence
Affecting duly every other creature
That breathed its breath of life; for good or ill,
For pain or pleasure, acting on each nature,
Beyond the consciousness, despite the will.
Dire Vanity! to think to break the union
That interweaveth strictly soul with soul
In constant, sane, life-nourishing communion:
The rivers ever to the ocean roll,
The ocean-waters feed the clouds on high
Whose rains descending feed the flowing rivers:
All the world's children must how quickly die
Were they not all receivers and all givers!

XX.

But this is Solitude, O dreadful Lord!
My spirit starves in this abysmal air—
          Of every human word,
Of sigh and moan, of music and of prayer,
Of passionate heart-beats felt though never heard,
          So utterly stript bare:
The awful heavens are tranquil and divine,
Serene and saintly in their purple deep
          The moon and young stars shine;
No living souls beneath their influence leap,
No other eyes are fixed on them with mine:
          Men said that Death and Sleep
Are brothers;—yes, as lurid lightnings may
Be kindred to the glory of calm day,
Or darkness of the restful night-tide boon
To darkness of the sun eclipsed at noon. . . .
The Soul is murdered; and her world bereft
          By some dire doom still left,
A fadeless corpse whose perfect form is rife
"With ghastly affectations of true life."

XXI.

How long, how long, I cowered beside the Sage;
Whose head was lifted, fronting full the skies
In tranquil triumph from his victory lone.
Beneath that broad brow rough with thought and age,
The pitiless light-beams glittered on his eyes,
Like fatal swords flashed keen against a stone
To sharpen them for piercing to the heart,—
How was his triumph smitten, pierct, and slain!
          But cowering there apart,
Upon those swelling eyeballs, that stern head,
I ever gazed; while in my burning brain
          A cold thought soothing spread:
As one who drains a poison-chalice slowly,
In fixed and infinite longing to be dead;
So let my yearning vision cleave amain
To this grand marble image melancholy,
Till I have drunken in to the last drain
That poisonous Spirit of Death which fills it wholly. . . .
The flesh that crept like worms is growing numb;
The raging fire of blood is dying cold;
The rout of fiendish thoughts are almost dumb:

The heavens fade like a Vision cycles-old,
Where from dead eyes gaze thoughts uncomprehended:
Thank God, I soon shall cease to be alone;
My mad discordant life is nearly blended
With all this realm's unsuffering death of stone.

PART III.
THE JUDGMENTS

I.

A multitudinous roaring of the ocean!
Voices of sudden and earth-quaking thunder
From the invisible mountains!
The heavens are broken up and rent asunder
By curbless lightning-fountains,
Streaming and darting through that black commotion,
In which the moon and stars are swallowed with the sky.
Throughout the Mausolean City spread
Drear palpitations, long-drawn moan and sigh;
And then—an overwhelming whirlwind blast?
Or else, indeed, the irrepressible cry
Of all its statues waking up aghast!
Doth God in final Judgment come thus heralded?

II.

I saw Titanic forms dark, solemn, slow,
Like thunderclouds imperious o'er the wind,
Sweep far with haughty tramplings to and fro;
I heard great voices peal and trumpets blow:
Strange fragments of their chanting shook my mind.

"If the owl haunts doleful ruins and lives in the sombre night,
Could it joy in the cheerful homes of men, could it love the noonday light?
If the serpent couches in jungles and deserts of burning sand,
Would it rather cast its slough in the peopled corn-rich land?
If the great bear prowls alone in desolate wastes of ice,
Could it joy to range in herded power through a tropic Paradise?
If the vulture gorges on carrion and all abhorrent things,
Would it rather slake with fruits and wine the rush of its obscene wings?
*   *   *   *   *   *   *

"We sought through the archives of Fate, through all the records of Doom,
Records of noontide refulgence, records of lightning-seared gloom:
And lo, we have never found while the highth and the depth we explored,
We have never yet traced out Punishment or Reward.

* * * * * * *

"Peace may be happy and sweet; bitter and heart-rending Strife;
Sin is corruption and death, Virtue is health and life:
But every being is placed in that sphere, in that crisis, that spot,
Which alone its own nature demands and asserts for its lot:
As itself from itself its web the spider spins out,
Doth each all the net of relations which weave it about:
The sun shines the sun by the lustre he lavishes forth;
For his might and his life and his light circles round him the earth:
All the World—this infinite azure robe sphere-spangled sublime,
In which God walks forth revealed and veiled to the creatures of Space and Time,
Is all interwoven in one (each atom, each star, as each soul,
Evolving so duly the threads of its work for its part in the Whole):
With a woof and warp of might and light and mysteries all is wrought,
For the many-figured, many-hued being and passion and thought.

* * * * * * *

"Here hath a spirit full bliss to breathe ever-bland golden air;
Here hath a spirit wild hurrying storms of doubt, dread, anguish, despair:
For the world-realms are swept on their path for ever, through day and night;
And their course is advanced no less, no more, in the gloom than in the light:
And the journey is infinite truly,—through every various clime
Do the countless myriads wander on, through every season of time;
Cool water for him in the desert-blaze, red fire for him in the frost,
Languor for him in the summer-peace, fierce heart for the tempest-tost:
While all whence they know not whither they know not wend;
Who appraiseth the means and progress, who conceiveth the end?
But we swear by the Life Eternal, we swear by Eternal Death,
We swear by the Fate supreme which rules in every pulse and breath;
That strong or weak, simple or wise, polluted or most holy,
Each each day is fed with the food befitting him fully and solely."

III.

Again deep peace, again the stars and moon:
  I stood between the theatre and square,
  Beholding as before the statues there
Unstirred and silent in the lethal swoon.

Lo! in the empyréan grew a light—
  A great and awful Splendour, through its shroud
  Of fold on fold of massy thundercloud
Intensely burning down with steadfast might.

Wherefrom a Voice descended vast and lone;
  Of thunder-dreadfulness, of sea-fierce anger,
  Yet in its lofty silver-volumed clangour
Chanting an unimpassioned monotone:

"WHEN ALL THE WINE IS POISONED IT MUST BE
  DESTROYÈD UTTERLY;
THE VESSELS ALSO WHICH CONTAINED IT MUST
  BE BURNED AND GROUND TO DUST."

Instantly shudderings shook the stony crowd;
  Some rigid arms with writhing spasms were lifted,
  Some dungeon-throats with frenzy-spasms rifted
By hideous strangled voices shrieking loud:

"Abominable Fate,
We hurl thee back thy hate!
The poison and the wine—
Our sins and souls are thine!
Ah! pangs of utter death
  Stifle our breath—
Hear us; we plead; hear us; oh, wait!"

No answer came save trumpet-voices blaring
Death and destruction as in furious fray;
And while those forms gasped out their cry despairing
They sank down crumbling into dusty spray.
Then, as the trumpet clamours died away,
Did crash on crash in clear succession sound,
Like lingering peals of thunder; each the knell
Of house or column falling to the ground
In sudden ruin, as those statues fell.
And next, as if the solid hills were all
Disseated now to glide tremendously
Over the town and plunge athwart the sea,
A mass of gloom enveloped in its pall
Temple and palace, basement, dome and spire;
Then o'er the marble crowd submerging came:
Its black oppression burned throughout my frame,
A torture of intolerable fire.
Yet when at length its ponderous bulk was rolled
Over the shrinking waters out of sight,
The City and the steadfast statues white
Stood all unchanged about me; but, behold,
The uttered condemnation had been wrought
Upon the ruined fragments,—they were naught.

IV.

That cloud-consuming fire still held the sky,
  Blotting its worlds out wholly; while the sphere
  Seemed listening breathless in an awful fear,
Till that great Voice again rang forth on high:

"When now the sapless tree bears bloom nor fruit,
    Why linger trunk and root?
Let it be hewn away and fire-destroyed;
    And in its place left void
A living tree be set to spread and rise,
Responsive to the bounty of the skies."

The sentence smote some statues like a sword;
  With nerveless gestures pitiful to see
  They moaned their helpless hopeless litany,
"We lived, we lived, O great and dreadful Lord!"

Then as they crumbled into dust away,
The Answer speeded from the hills behind,—
A noise of rushing like a mighty wind:
The ashen fire-flood in a tempest grey
Hissed through the City and the wan array;
And hurrying o'er the sea, as if its might
With grim joy hasted to fulfil such trust,
Swept all the human and palatial dust
To irretrievable Chaos, Death and Night.

And when that deadly storm of fire was past,
A Voice came roaring like its final blast:

"Whose virtue cannot pay their Life's expense,
    Whose souls are lost in sense,
They are no more; themselves with God have willed,—
    their Æon is fulfilled."

V.

Once more that fire possessing sole the sky,
Once more deep silence o'er the lessened throng
Of waiting statues; and it lasted long
Ere that great Voice again pealed forth on high:

"When he who had a Palace and its power,
Well-favoured for his dower,
Has proved unjust and proud, has spent its treasures
On selfish pomps and pleasures;
He must descend from his exalted place:
Yet, if in deep disgrace
He do not sink still deeper, till his breath
Be wholly quenched in death;
But learn to build again his kingly heart,
The throne awaits him and the kingly part."

Ah! what a multitude of statues then
Were shaken by the thunder of this doom!—
"O Lord! all perish if Thou wilt consume
In justice! Lord have mercy on frail men!"

Ev'n as the crash of smitten structures roared
The answering Judgment-terrors filled the sky:
Inexorably swift it streamed and poured
A red-fire deluge from that cloud on high,
Which drowned the City and the multitude,
Devouring all the space from hills to sea.
Hissing and roaring the resistless flood
Plunged through the trembling earth, in haste to flee
With its vast ravage; and the earth gaped wide
To swallow in that cup of wrath amain,
Then gnashed her seared and riven jaws to hide
What shook her yet with shuddering throbs of pain.
How many had become the torrent's prey,
Swept down abrupt into some lower sphere!
But of the rest—can vision cheat me here?
What forms are these amidst the wan array
Of human marble? Strange new stony forms—
These serpents, panthers, wolves, these apes and swine,
Vultures and hawks and owls, with sheep and kine,
And many others, brutes and birds and worms,
Couched in unutterably piteous rest,
The sorcery of that Judgment-fire attest.

VI.

No more wild agonies shook the steadfast Earth;
  That night of cloud, unable to sustain
  Its soul of fire, was withering; when again
Upon the silence that great Voice flowed forth:

"When he who should have travelled all the day,
    Has lingered on his way
To sport with idlers; or in common fear
    Of lone paths steep and drear,
Has turned aside to pace down crowded roads
    Of rich and gay abodes;
He must plod this day's journey on the morrow
    With weary rue and sorrow,
Ere he can win his happy home, and greet
The dear friends waiting for his laggard feet."

Whereunto statue-voices low implored:
"Free human fellowship is very sweet;
Bitter with our own kind as foes to meet—
Heavy the load of uncompanioned life!
Alas, we are so weary-sick of strife!
Grant us awhile Thy perfect peace, O Lord!"

The humble plaining of that saddest prayer,
Relapsing into stony silentness,
So filled my heart that I was unaware
Until surrounded by its sway and stress,
How the deep Ocean rushing from its lair
Bellowed against the hillslopes planted broad;
Whilst fierce from sea-vast cloudglooms in the air,
Blazoned with dreadful sentences of God
In writhed and quivering lightnings wrought, the rain
Intense of swerveless thunderbolts streamed down,
Crashing amidst the ruins of the town,
And shrieking through the loud inundent main.

VII.

The flood below, the flood above ebbed soon
Completely; fair and still the green earth lay,
Beneath a heaven surcharged with tenfold day,
More holy-sweet of lustre than the moon.
I gazed: the statues stood there as before,
Like dateless boulders by the old sea-shore:
But of the City's vast palatial pride
Of all the works of Man on every side—
The theatre's stupendous cirque of tiers,
The pharos and the galleons and the piers,
Remained no vestige; save that here and there,
Bathed in the sea of crystal-lucent air,
Some fragment wall, some column cleft stood dim,
More like strange rocks than structures reared by Him.
Had that swift deluge been the stream of Time,
And every billow some vast age sublime,
Over the vacant City flowing ever
Until a mind should swoon in the endeavour
Such infinite cycles of its course to mete,
ERASURE had been scarcely more complete.

VIII.

The cloud was vanished from the perfect sky;
  Heaven, earth and sea all floated from my sight,
  Bathed in a dimness of exceeding light
Too pure, intense, and calm for mortal eye.

And yet I saw as we may see in trance,—
  Saw how a gradual change beatified
  The statues who had never yet replied
When those dread Judgments took dread utterance.

As Memnon woke to music with the dawn,
  They in the solemn splendour seemed to rouse
  From death to life, with glory on their brows;
A calm grand life, eyes shut and breath undrawn.

The crystal sea of sky then streamed away,
  The inmost Heavens revealed themselves abroad:
  A Throne . . . the Vision of the Living God . . .
Ravished and blind upon the earth I lay.

Once more a Voice descended vast and lone,
  The Voice of Infinite Love Omnipotent;
  Sweeter than life or death, it swelled and blent
The Universe all tuned into one tone:

"The soldier who has fought the noble fight,
    Persistent for the right,
Enduring all and daring all to prove
    His glad unpurchased love
And faithfulness, in triumph and defeat:
    What doom for him is meet?

The Battle, with the day it filled, is done;
    The field is lost or won:
Let Night then greet him well with joy and rest
    By holy visions blest;
That on the Morrow he may rise up strong
    Hopeful and fresh and young,
His sharp wounds healed, to do and dare once more
    Heroic as before,—
But with a loftier rank, with nobler power,
    With far more generous dower.
And so for ever through the Nights and Days
While he remaineth lord of his own praise,
he may go on, exalted more and more,
Till final triumph crown the fateful war;
Till Love and Life and Bliss (which once was Faith)
Have vanquished wholly Evil, Falsehood, Death;
The loftiest station that his soul can fill,
The utmost sway commensurate with his will,
The All of Wisdom that he can believe,
Of Love and Goodness that he can receive,
Are then his dower from the reachless Throne
And Him who reigns eternally thereon."

IX.

I heard it all,—there prostrate on the ground;
  I floated in the Voice as in a sea,
  Or as a cloud may float dissolvingly
Within the sapphire noontide's burning bound.

And when it ebbed it left my shrinking soul
  To shudder back into its cave of clay,
  Blind, hopeless, one dead atom fallen astray
From vital union in and with the Whole.

After a time, from such fierce consciousness
  Of personal being as is lunacy—
  As not to know is perfectly to be—
I was withdrawn by human utterances:

"O Lord! let us be hidden, let us die!
  Thy love and wisdom are too infinite!
  We throb unpeaceful in Thy perfect light,
Star-specks of gloom no Sun can glorify.

"Were we less dark than our old midnight sphere,
  Transplant us not into Thy blinding day.
  Lord, we adore Thee, Perfect, Sole, for aye—
Our sins and weakness crush our spirits here!"

X.

No answer sounded. I arose and stood.
  The gates of Heaven were shut, the Vision gone:
  But still undimmed miraculously shone
That tenfold noon of glareless sanctitude.

They stood—the Spirits who had conquered life;
  Erect, yet pleading, hands uplifted, there;
  Glorious—yet wan with that divine despair:
Was *this* the crowning issue of the strife?

The noble faces slowly turned to where
  The dim hills floated, exquisitely drawn
  Or interfused, like breathless streaks of dawn,
Upon the breathless ocean of wide air.

Thereon uplifted stood a lofty band;
  Some burning with the glory of their wings;
  Some golden-crowned and purple-robed like Kings;
Some clad in white, a palm-branch in the hand;

Some like stern warriors armed with shield and sword;
  Some swaying crystal cups in which the fire
  Of red wine quivered; while a radiant quire
Striking their harps sang loud with sweet accord.

XI.

"Dear Friends, come! we wait for you;
Strong and wise and pure and true.
Why, alas, ascend so few?

"Where are the myriads that should now be here?
How have they wasted all the lavish dower
With which God fitted them to rule their sphere—
The Passion and the Vision and the Power?
For ever hoping, disappointed ever,
We know too well the constant tragic doom:
Vision hath seen, with scarce a work-endeavour,
Then closed its eyes for more voluptuous gloom;
Passion hath disenshrined the awful soul,
Its large heart tempting fatal fleshly lusts;
And Power hath shaken off divine control,
To gorge itself with universal trusts.

"For the undone Many, ruth,
Ye have conquered, true to truth;
Dare our wine of Joy and Youth.

"The tree whose trunk and branches dark and bare
Withstood the storms of Winter, planted strong;
Doth glorify itself in summer's air
With leaf and fruit and nested bird's blithe song:
The earth-realm labouring blind and dumb and cheerless,
Yet ever onward, through the reign of night;
Leaps forth with joy majestically fearless
Into the pure new heaven of morning light.
Again stern Winter with its storms shall come,
But find the tree grown stronger 'gainst its wrath;
Again the night-gloom, weary, blind and dumb,
But find the realm far forward on its path.

"Then, dear Friends, come, come away!
Now is Summer, now is Day;
Joy assumes imperial sway!"

XII.

As when the warm spring-breezes overblow
  Some silent, frozen, melancholy main,
  Its waters heave and throb and rend their chain,
And singing in the sunbeams flash and flow:

So with the breathing of that gracious song
  Those Spirits burst their trance of silent sadness;
  Their bosoms heaved with glorious life and gladness;
Clear-eyed, erect, full-voiced, advanced their throng:

"O Brothers of this Heaven supreme and glorious!
  O Sisters of this greeting full of love!
Into what a dawn of perfect day victorious,
  Do ye usher us, and welcome us above!
The World o'erflows with life serene and tender;
  The air, the light is all celestial wine;
Our inmost soul is interfused with splendour
  And harmony divine!

"As birds the boundless azure sky-deep winging,
  As breezes flowing round and round the earth,
As flowers into the vernal welcome springing,
  As fountains leaping seaward bright with mirth;
Our thoughts throughout Infinity float chainless,
  Our souls encompass spheres of life sublime,
Our beings thrill and glow with new life stainless,
  Our swift joy laughs at Time!

"The worlds go wheeling far their cycled courses,—
  From the fathomless Unbirth of the Abyss,
By golden laws attuning counter-forces
  Built up into the noonday Heaven of Bliss:
And pervading all, sustaining all, enwreathing
  With its infinite embrace beneath, above,
The Æther—the Divine eternal breathing
  Of Life and Light and Love!"

XIII.

So singing they advanced with measured pace;
  And like a silver morning-mist were drawn
  Slow floating up the hillside wood and lawn,
Unto that high seraphical embrace.

All stood triumphant, beautiful, divine,
  Between the heaven and earth; all stood there bright;
  Informed, transfigured with the holy light
As crystal cups with sacramental wine.

I would have stood there evermore and gazed
  Entranced in adoration, consciousless,
  Upon that beauty of all holiness
In human forms embodied and upraised.

Alas! the universal light too soon
  Was fading, flowing backward to its fount,
  Until they stood upon that sombre mount
Sole-shining o'er the dark earth as a moon.

And still the glory-stream flowed back to God;
  And they with it were floated up the sky;
  Whose gates shut blank against my straining eye,
And left the earth a dark and soulless clod—

Left all the earth like some most desolate shore
  Wherefrom has ebbed the free and living tide;
  And left me stranded on its dark waste wide,
A wreck to be recovered nevermore.

O Life! this is thy deepest woe of all—
  That as a soul regains its heaven of birth,
  The body drags it swooning back to earth,
Stunned, hopeless, blind with its tremendous fall.

XIV.

When I arose the ever ancient Night
  Filled with his sombre pomp the earth and sky:
No memories of that doom of dire affright
Perturbed the calm; and undismayed on high
  The moon and stars where they had shone before
Shone on in cold and stern sublimity.
The hills loomed dark upon the silent shore,

Round which the waves in thoughtful monotone
Rolled their old voice of *Ever—evermore.*
A royal City dwelt upon this throne,—
And what now left of all its wealth and pride?
A few strange groups of pallid-gleaming stone!
But Nature cares not for the ruin wide,
Her dreaming beauty glows in perfect bloom:
Most cold, imperial, unlamenting Bride,
Her Lord and Bridegroom scarcely in the tomb . . .
The moon sank slowly down from heaven's crest;
Pale radiance lined and flecked the eastern gloom;
A stir, a breathing thrilled the world's deep rest;
No wakening bird, half-wakened, here and there
Uttered uncertain warning from its nest;
But spread a cold and fresh and fragrant air,
That seemed with lifeful breath to cleanse away
The grosser shades and vapours everywhere,
And all memorials of the night's dismay,
That pure and odorous the earth might greet
The first divine embraces of the Day,
Now hurrying up the heavens with fiery feet,
The crown of burning gold upon his head,
Cloud-robed with gold and purple, light and heat. . . .
Ages on ages in their course have shed
Ruin of fire and tempest on the earth,
Uncounted æons of her sons are dead;
Yet she exults with aboriginal mirth,
Nor feels her frame grow weak, her blood grow cold,
But pure and strong and young as at her birth
When first God's hand her glorious path outrolled:
For day by day He seals her with His sign—
Night's tomb is rent, the gates of heaven unfold
To let the ever-youngest Dawn divine,
Bathe her in balms of sempiternal youth.
I think no human soul which here doth pine
In personal anguish and with general ruth,
Without these Dawn-evangels fresh from God
Could feel its immortality a truth.
Dear are all dawns; but this that coming trod
The eastern heavens to kiss the earth's pale brow
With heavenly benedictions, when the rod
Of the Avenging Justice was but now
Withdrawn from penal smitings dire!—what speech
That mortals use, what words of lofty vow
Or soaring chant can emulate and reach
The awe, the bliss, the gratitude, the love,
That saving dawn brought with it from above?

XV.

What a dawn ascendeth fair through the pure and silent air,
Fain to greet with holy rapture what a glorious virgin Earth!
From her sins and fears and woes, from her memories, by the throes
Of a fierce regeneration born anew in perfect birth!
But what forms, what forms are they, there between the sea-loved bay
And the spiritual hills with the woods that clothe their feet;
Human forms erect in power, beasts that crouch and birds that cower,
But all wrought in fadeless marble, white and shining, pure and sweet?
Lo! as ever more and more broadening out the dawn doth soar,
Kindling emerald purple golden quivering splendours round her way;
What a flush—as if of Life kindling with triumphant strife
Through the torpid marble—fires them, though they all so steadfast stay!
Lo! as ever more and more music with the dawn doth soar,
Breezes whisper, leaflets murmur, waters warble joy for day;
What a thrill—as if of Life stirring with triumphant strife
Through the rigid marble—heaves them, though they all so silent stay!
These are forms that couch and stand, still as marble fountains grand,
Still in meek victorious patience, till the Sea of Life arise;
Till the World-sustaining Sea, Soul of all Eternity,
Once more fill them with Its waters of the Life that never dies.
When the Royal Sun shall leap glorious on yon eastern steep,
Gazing grand athwart this province of his measureless domains;
Straightway at that conquering sign, straightway at that glance divine,
Soul shall fill them, stone encarnate, life-blood gush through all their veins.
And this Nature which doth dream in Titanic sloth supreme,
Hill and river, wood and meadow, heaven of azure, careless sea,
Shall have all its want fulfilled, strength employed and bosom thrilled
By a lordly domination—soul and thought and passion free.
Oh, that these who in this hour shall attain such solemn dower,
Consecrated Lords and Bridegrooms wedding this fair virgin Earth,
Have such holy strength of will, love, faith, truth unquenchable,
Wisdom, justice, making concord of inheritance and worth,
As shall give a nobler being from the blissful marriage birth!

XVI.

As one who in the morning-shine
Reels homeward, shameful, wan, adust,
From orgies wild with fiery wine
And reckless sin and brutish lust:
And sees a doorway open wide,
And then the grand Cathedral space;
And hurries in to crouch and hide
His trembling frame, his branded face.

The organ-thunders surge and roll
   And thrill the heights of branching stone;
They shake his mind, they crush his soul,
   His heart knells to them with a moan:
He hears the voice of holy prayer,
   The chanting of the fervent hymn;
They pierce his depths of sick despair,
   He trembles more, his eyes are dim.

He sees the world-wide morning flame
   Through windows where in glory shine
The saints who fought and overcame,
   The martyrs who made death divine:
He sees pure women bent in prayer,
   Communing low with God above:—
Too pure! what right has *he* to share
   Their silent feast of sacred love?

How can he join the songs of praise?
   His throat is parched, his brain is wild:
How dare he seek the Father's gaze,
   Thus hopeless, loveless, and defiled?
How taint the pureness though he yearn
   To join such fellowship for aye? . . .
He creeps out pale—May he return
   Some time when he shall dare to stay!

As he within that holy fane,
   Was I upon that solemn shore;
One murky cloud, one spoiling stain,
   One jarring note,—all these and more:
A Spectre from the wicked Past,
   Familiar with the buried years;
The joys that fade, the griefs that last,
   The baffled hopes, the constant fears;

The fair, fair dawn of many a day
   That sinks in storm-clouds red and wild;
The souls that in their huts of clay
   Are crushed and buried, all defiled;
The Lusts that rage like savage steeds,
   While Will with reinless hand sleeps on,
And drunken Thought but goads their speeds,—
   Then one mad plunge, and all is gone;

The Moods that strew palm-branches now
  And with Hosannas fill the sky,
Then shortly crown with thorns the brow
  And mock and scourge and crucify;
The error, guile and infamy,
  The waste of foul and bloody strife,
The unforeseen catastrophe,
  That make the doleful drama, Life.

Ah, what had I to do with these
  Young lovely souls serene and clear,
Awaking up by fine degrees
  To life unsullied as its sphere?
The Spectre that has roamed forlorn,
  Sin-restless, through the sombre night,
Must creep to its old grave at morn,
  Nor blot the world of life and light.

XVII.

Where I had left it, on the lonely strand,
  Uninjured lay my boat, and lovely; seeming
  Some fair sea-creature, of the midsea dreaming
To light foam-whispers on the yellow sand.

While yet we skimmed the wavelets of the bay,
  Methought there rose, ev'n as the sun arose,
  A vehement Chorus hurrying to its close—
Fresh as the breath of the awakened day.

With vital fires the morning seemed to glow
  While it rang onward like a trumpet-blast
  Of keen reveillé crying: NIGHT IS PAST!
AROUSE YE DREAMERS, TO THE DAY AND FOE!

The stars for ever sweep through space, surrounding
  Their sun-kings and God's central hidden Throne
With splendour and deep music far-resounding,
  Though heard by pure celestial ears alone:
Their music chants His lofty praise for ever,
  Their splendours burn to Him the Light Divine;
In their grand uneager motions pausing never,
  They live and sing and shine.

Eternally they sweep on their vast courses,
With solemn joy fulfilling His behest;
While the balance of stupendous counter-forces
Buildeth up a stable Infinite of rest.
And the Æther, breathing life through vast pulsations,
Thrills with rapture to their God-supported flight;
And its waves against the rushing constellations
Break in the foam of light.

Each world-sphere groweth grandly through the ages
From its lifeless weltering unsubstantial birth,
Through unnumbered fiery throes and cyclic stages
Till it shines in heaven a life-abounding earth;
Till its vapours are green fields and glorious oceans,
Till with countless living beings it is rife:
By harmony constraining dread commotions
It is crowned and thronged with life.

Until conscious, doubting, worshipping Immortals,
As they journey on their infinite Life-way,
Passing through its Birth and Death mysterious portals
Inform with spirit-fire the clothing clay:
And the dead, spectral, consciousless Material
Is a dwelling-place for essences divine;
Throbs with thought and passion deathlessly ethereal,
A Heaven-honoured shrine.

All spirits from their infancy's bland sleeping
Must struggle to a strong and noble prime
Through sins, dangers, anguish, terrors,—ever reaping
Costly fruits in every season of swift Time:
From their fountain in its deepest dark foundation,
Glory-shrouded in the shadow of God's Throne,
Through all worlds to their highest-soaring station
By unrest all have grown.

Life *is* only by perpetual on-flowing;
Torpid rest is the true life-devouring death;
Through stern struggles all things ever are upgrowing;
Sighs and meanings prove a vital-throbbing breath.
One alone—Eternal, Infinite, All-holy,
Is in changeless rest; the Perfect grows nor grew:
Finite souls and all things live by progress solely,
All *are* but what they *do*.

PART IV.

THE RETURN

I.

Long tranquil days one more than seven
  The beamless sun from out the main
Went burning through the vault of Heaven,
  And circled to the deep again:
While day by day in dreamful ease
We glided o'er the glistening seas.

Long calm autumnal nights just seven
  The moon with all her starry train
Went shining through the vault of Heaven,
  And circled to the deep again:
While night by night in dreamful ease
We glided o'er the glimmering seas.

Long days so rich in rest, so still;
  As warm as love, as calm as truth;
Long nights which did those days fulfil,
  As some sweet girl a fervent youth:
While day and night in dreamful ease
We floated o'er the silent seas.

Time set within his circled sky
  A topaz sun, a diamond moon,
And thick star-pearls, and made thereby
  A marriage-ring of blissful boon;
With which in ever-dreamful ease
We floated o'er the happy seas.

Did Nature sleep, and dream in sleep
  Of all the Spring and Summer toil
Her children were about to reap,—
  The wealth of corn and wine and oil:
As day and night in dreamful ease
We floated o'er the sleeping seas?

Or was it her deep-thoughted mood;
  A little sad, such loss had been;
And grieved, the dear Past seemed so good;
  Yet proud, triumphant and serene:
As day and night in dreamful ease
We floated o'er the solemn seas?

I lay in one long trance of rest
  And contemplation,—free from thought
Of Future issue, worst or best
  To be from Past and Present wrought:
While day and night in dreamful ease
We glided o'er the trancèd seas.

II.

Before me, in the drowsy night outspread,
The City whence in anguish I had fled
    A vast dark Shadow loomed:
    So still, so black, it gloomed,
It seemed the darkness of a great abyss
    Gulfed in a desert bare;
    Around whose precipice
Dim lamps burnt yellow in the vacant air,
Lifted on high portentous. Yet to me
Its dark suggestions were of Life, not Death;
Its awful mass of life oppressed my soul:
The very air appeared no longer free,
But dense and sultry in the close control
Of such a mighty cloud of human breath.
The shapeless houses and the monstrous ships
Were brooding thunderclouds that could eclipse
    The burning sun of day;
Surcharged with storms of such electric life,
Keen as the lightning to its chosen prey,
Curbless and dreadful when aroused to strife . . .
Who once has gazed upon the face of Death
Confounds no more its calm with calmest Sleep;
The terror of that beauty shadoweth
His spirit with an influence too deep.

III.

And while I gazed upon the sleeping City,
And pondered its unnumbered destinies,
A flood of awe and fear and love and pity
Swelled in my heart and overflowed my eyes
    With unexpected tears.
The burden of the message I had brought
From that great City far across the sea
Lay heavy on my soul; as if for years
And years I had been wandering wearily
In travail with it: now the time was spent;
Now, as a cloud with fire and thunder fraught,

I must give birth with throes of agony,
And perish in the bearing. So I leant
Back in the boat, all desolate and distraught,
Pangs shuddering through the faintness of cold fears:
Death passed his hand across my brow; but went
To lay its plenary pressure on some heart
That throbbed true life—"for this poor pulse," thought he,
"Is not worth quelling"—Him I watched depart
Bearing all peace with him; when suddenly
That Spirit which will never be withstood
Came down and shook and seized and lifted me,—
As men uplift a passive instrument
Through which to breathe whatever fits their mood,
Stately triumphal march or war-note dread,
Anthem, gay dance, or requiem for the dead;
And through my lips with irrepressible might
Poured forth its own stern language on the night.

IV.

"Haughty and wealthy and great, mighty, magnificent, free,
Empress in thine own right of the earth-surrounding sea!
Broad and deep flows the river that feedeth thy mighty heart,
Bringing from all the zones to crowd thine imperial mart
Of all their produce the best—their silks, their gems, their gold,
Their fruits and corn and wine, their luxuries thousand-fold:
Thy merchants are palaced princes, thy nobles scorn great kings,
Thy meanest children swell with pride beneath thy shadowing wings;
And thy voice throughout the world, complacently serene,
Proclaims 'Of all my Sisters, I am the rightful Queen!
This one is blind, this deaf, and that other is but a mute;
This one is fair indeed, but drunken and dissolute;
This is a very slave, dishonourèd long ago;
This one is dying of age, that other of want and woe;
This one is proud and great, but a heathen in her soul,
And subject to fatal frenzies, raging beyond control:
But I, I am rich and strong, I am wise and good and free;
Throned above them, Empress sole of the earth-surrounding Sea!'

"Yes, indeed thy power is great, but thy evil is great no less,
And thy wealth is poor to pay the debt of thy guiltiness;
And the world is judged with justice, and thou must pass through that fire
Which hath tested so sternly the glitter of Venice and Carthage and Tyre:
For no wealth can bribe away the doom of the Living God,
No haughtiest strength confront the sway of His chastening rod.
Repent, reform, or perish! the Ages cry unto thee:
Listen, oh listen, ere yet it be late, thou swarthy Queen of the Sea!

"Thy heritage vast and rich is ample to clothe and feed
The whole of thy millions of children beyond all real need;
One of the two main wheels whereon thy Faith doth move
Is that each as he loves himself so shall he his neighbour love:
But thy chief social laws seem strictly framed to secure
That one be corruptingly rich, another bitterly poor,
And another just starving to death: thy fanes and mansions proud
Are beleaguered with filthy hovels wherein poor wretches crowd,
Pining in body and soul; untaught, unfed by those
Who are good if they merely dribble bland alms upon fatal woes—
Resigning scarcely aught of their pleasure and pride and content,
Nor dreaming that all their life is one huge embezzlement.

"The sumptuous web of thy trade encompassing all the globe
Is fretted by gambling greed like a moth-eaten robe,
Is slimed by creeping fraud, is poisoned by falsehood's breath,
Is less a garment of life than a shroud of rotting death.

"The mass of thy rulers live with scarcely one noble aim,
Scarcely one clear desire for a not inglorious fame;
Slaves to a prudence base, idolaters unto Might,
Jailors of lofty zeal, infidels to pure Right,
Deaf to the holy voice of the Conscience of the World,
Blind to the banner of God when it floats in the storm unfurled;
They, and with them the array of thine actual Priesthood, thy proud
And numberless Father-confessors—ineffable crowd
Of scribes who by day and by night, unceasingly blatant, dictate
Thine every move in the contest with Time the Servant of Fate.

"Thy flaring streets each night affront the patient skies
With an holocaust of woes, sins, lusts and blasphemies;
When thy thousands of harlots abroad with the other thousand are met
Of those who made them first and who keep them harlots yet:
So dreadful, that thou thyself must sometimes look for the fire
That rained from heaven on Sodom to make thee one funeral pyre.

"Thy Church has long been becoming the Fossil of a Faith;
The Form of dry bones thou hast, but where are the blood and breath?
Dry bones, that seem a whole, with dead sinews binding the parts,
Inert save when bejuggled to ghastly galvanic starts:
Though thou swearest to thy people, 'The King is but sick, not dead'—
Gaining the time while you choose you another in His stead;
Though thy scribes and thy placemen all, most of whom know the fact,
Vouchsafe in His name to write, pretend by His will to act:
Where are the signs of His life?—While living He never ceased
To thrill with the breath of His being thy realm from the West to the East;
While He lived He fought with sin, with fleshly lust and pride;
While He lived His poor and mean were wealthy and dignified;

While He lived His reign was freedom, faith, chastity, peace and love;
And the symbol borne on his banner was not the raven but dove;
While He lived there yawned a Hell with a Devil for His foes,
And a God-ruled Heaven of triumph before His followers rose;
While He lived the noblest of men were wholly devoted to Him,
The saints, the bards, the heroes, in soul and mind and limb,—
Who now without a Leader, mournful in silence wait,
Girding each one himself to his lonely fight with Fate.

"But thou, O Queen, art false: a liar, if He is dead
And becoming a mammoth fossil whose æon is wholly sped;
A traitor if still He lives and shall for ever reign,
For thou spurnest the laws most sacred of all He doth ordain,
Should Christ come now from Heaven, to reap the harvest sown
When He buried Himself in the earth, watered with blood of His own,
How many Christians indeed could He gather with strictest care
From thy two hundred myriads who claim in Him a share?
He agonised to save thee and thy children all;
And He saveth scarcely enough to delay thy deadly fall.

"For fall thou wilt, thou must—so proud as thy state is now,
Thou and thy sisters all, scarce better or worse than thou,
If ye do not all repent, and cleanse each one her heart
From the foulness circling with its blood to poison every part.
Woe to thy pampered rich in their arrogant selfishness;
Woe to thy brutelike poor who feel but their bread-distress;
Woe to thy people who dare not live without hope of wealth,
Who look but to fruits of the earth for their life and saving health;
Woe to thy rulers who rule for the good of themselves alone,
Fathers who give their children crying for bread a stone;
Woe to thy mighty men whose strength is unused or sold;
Thy sages who shut their eyes when Truth is stern to behold;
Woe to thy prophets who smile Peace, Peace, when it is a sword;
Thy poets who sing their own lusts instead of hymns of the Lord;
Thy preachers who preach the life of what they feel to be death;
Thy sophists who sail wild seas without the compass of faith;
Thy traders trading in lies and in human bodies and souls;
Thy good men cursing those better who strive on to loftier goals:—
The final Doom evolveth, burdened with woe on woe,
Sure as the justice of God while yet by His patience slow;
For the earth is pervaded wholly, through densest stone and clod,
With the burning fire of the law of the Truth of the Living God;
Consuming the falsehood, the evil, the pride, the lust, the shame,
With ever-burning, unrelenting, irresistible flame;
Until all save the purest spirit, eternal, of truth and love,
Be altogether consumed away, beneath as well as above."

1857.

LINES ON HIS TWENTY-THIRD BIRTHDAY

Last evening's huge lax clouds of turbid white
  Grew dark and louring, burthened with the rain
Which that long wind monotonous all night
  Swept clashing loud through Dreamland's still domain,
Until my spirit in fatigue's despite
  Was driven to weary wakefulness again:
With such wild dirge and ceaseless streaming tears
Died out the last of all my ill-used years.

The morn his risen pure and fresh and keen;
  Its perfect vault of bright blue heaven spreads bare
Above the earth's wide laughter twinkling green.
  The sun, long climbing up with lurid glare
Athwart the storm-rack's rent and hurrying screen,
  Leapt forth at dawn to breathe this stainless air;
The strong west wind still streams on full and high,
Inspiring fresher life through earth and sky.

Yon hazeless river flashes silver signs
  Of where it flows; how delicate and clear
The distant hills curve far their grey-blue lines,
  Steadfast amidst the rushing atmosphere:
With every blade distinct the green grass shines,
  Untouched by frost; those old trees dark or sere,
Swaying and soughing in the lifeful dawn,
Have every leaf and twig distinctly drawn.

This day my own particular year has birth;
  The general year is very old to-day:
Yet, with what healthful life o'er heaven and earth
  The death-bound monarch holdeth steadfast sway!
Not too austere for much of hearty mirth
  And energetic pleasure, nor so grey
But that he still can deck himself with flowers;—
Would that like his could be my dying hours!

Still dew-pearled fuchsias shine like pendent gems,
  While some lie purely on the deep-dark mould
Beneath their glossy leaves and ruddy stems;
  The thick chrysanthemums range white and cold;
Of all its wealth of marvellous anadems,
  That gleamed amidst their fruits of orange gold
Glowing red-hearted in the Autumn sun,
The passion-flower has still for me kept one.

I pace the garden in this genial morn,
  And meditate the dirge of my dead year,—
With even less of grief than sharp self-scorn.
  The retrospect in truth brings little cheer;
As if of one long-tired, who stares forlorn
  Across flat marshland, barren, gloomy, drear;
Where fields, nor home, nor church, his vision greet
Which he has toiled through with unsteady feet.

He turns; before him, as behind, all round
  The pathless waste outstretches flat and bare;
From sullen pools amidst the dark heath-ground
  Frogs jar their croakings through the murky air,
Which up that vault of solid sky stone-bound
  Heaves huge dense glooms to shut on his despair.
Let him crawl on as he has crawled all day,
Till Night comes down upon his homeless way.

My golden morning hours, which should have brought
  Strength, wisdom, faith and love, or hope of all,
Have sunk and dribbled while I heeded not
  Into the slush of sloth beyond recall.
O nerveless hands, O brain of aimless thought,
  O slow dim eyes that never marked their fall—
Absorbed in dreams both waking and asleep
Our golden hours for ever lost, now weep.

All lost for ever! and the hours to come,
  Poor refuse! but our sole remaining wealth,
So much the likelier thence to share doom!
  The brain unused to mark insidious stealth,
Short-sighted eyes long filled with mist and gloom,
  Lax hands uncustomed to the grasp of health,
That lost the fight in their best youth,—shall these
Victorious prove in languor and disease?

Oh, for the flushed excitement of keen strife!
  For mountains, gulfs and torrents in my way,
With peril, anguish, fear and strugglings rife!
  For friends and foes, for love and hate in fray,—
And not this lone base flat of torpid life!
  I fret 'neath gnat-stings, an ignoble prey,
While others with a sword-hilt in their grasp
Have warm rich blood to feed their latest gasp.

Wrathful and dangerous, restless, free, profound,
  With fair green islands shining o'er its verge,
The Sea of Life there heaves and roars around.
  To pierce its depths, to throb against its surge,
Breasting to gain the Happy Isles!—if drowned,
  The loser pays; he fought his game; no dirge!
But to be whelmed in torpor at the last,
As one with this dead crag which holds me fast!

Flushed grapes, full-charged with life's delirious wine,
  Brush my wan temples, hanging thick about:
Chained fast I cannot reach them, while I pine
  To press their very inmost rapture out,
Flooding with fire these dust-dry lips of mine;
  Better, wild drunkenness than hectic drought:
And torture breeds new tortures, in the dread
That ere they fall my power to drink be dead.

The prisoner loses other years than yearn
  Within the lifeless dungeon crusht and pent:
Late freedom frees dead ashes from their urn;
  His torture has become his element.
This Bride of Life for whom I waiting burn
  May grow a withered hag ere she relent,
Herself refused then; or our worn-out eld
In bridal chimings have its funeral knelled.

O pure West wind, strong life-breath of the day,
  Inspire my wasted heart with strength and hope!
Sweep thou its grievous doubts and fears away,
  Who swept far-scattering down the eastern slope
The brooding rain-clouds massed in dense array
  Till this green earth shone laughing to the cope
Of this pure heaven, whose naked form austere
Yet genial glows with sunshine warm and clear.

I hope, I feel that I can yet break free
   From this accursèd cage wherein I pine;
There comes a vision of the sounding sea,
   The all-sustaining, all-intombing brine:
Through want and peril, wretchedness and glee,
   Wrestling with lives more coarse and strong than mine,
I yet may woo its love and dare its strife;
By self-dependence earning careless life.

And so attaining strength! The crazy ship,
   Frigate or bumboat, slaver, mission ark,
Shall surely in the first squall heel and dip;
   The strong may hope to sail its voyage: and, mark,—
What of the ends, means, issues of its trip
   Knows holy vessel or Brazilian barque?
Through storm and calm it does its best to float;
For what? He knows who steers and rules the boat.

So much more strength, so much more life, I say;
   So much more love and thought, more soul and sense:
We pare our members bit by bit away,
   Because they're damning us with foul offence:
Cowards! be strong and force them to obey!
   Is virtue but a eunuch's continence?
Napoleon, ev'n, seems nobler than such saint
As eighteen centuries have learned to paint.

Thus Hope is born,—pale birth of grim Despair.
   Whether the Father Shall his child devour,
Or this poor Babe, maturing strong and fair,
   Shall dispossess the parent of his power,
I know not: yet I think that I could dare
   A death-stern struggle with the fiercest hour,
Would foolish Wisdom's whirls of dreary thought
But leave my doubt-vexed spirit undistraught.

Meanwhile, then, let me wait and hope, and learn
   To curb with galling steel and ruthless hand
These strong and passionate impulses that burn
   To sweep me from my post of self-command,
Into the battle raging thick and stern,
   Into the desert's freedom vast and grand:
That horseman proves full strength, firm skill indeed,
Who holdeth statue-calm his savage steed.

1857.

FOUR POINTS IN A LIFE

I.—LOVE'S DAWN

Still thine eyes haunt me; in the darkness now,
The dreamtime, the hushed stillness of the night,
I see them shining, pure and earnest light;
And here, all lonely, may I now avow
The thrill with which I ever meet their glance?
At first they gazed a calm abstracted gaze,
The while thy soul was floating through some maze
Of beautiful divinely-peopled trance;
But now I shrink from them in shame and fear,
For they are gathering all their beams of light
Into an arrow, keen, intense, and bright,
Swerveless and star-like from its deep blue sphere,
Piercing the cavernous darkness of my soul,
Burning its foul recesses into view;
Transfixing with sharp agony through and through
Whatever is not brave, and clean, and whole.
And yet I will not shrink, although thou piercest
Into the inmost depth of all my being:
I will not shrink, although thou now art seeing
My heart's caged lusts the wildest and the fiercest;
The cynic thoughts that fret my homeless mind,
My unbelief, my selfishness, my weakness,
My dismal lack of charity and meekness;
For, amidst all the evil, thou wilt find
Pervading, cleansing, and transmuting me,
A fervent and most holy love for Thee.

1852.

II.—MARRIAGE

Come to me, oh, come to me!
Time is long since we were parted;
I am sad and weary-hearted,
Foiled and almost overthrown,
Fighting with the world alone;
What am I when thou art gone?
Come, darling, soon!

Come to me, oh, come to me!
Let my failing head find rest, Love,
On thy pure and tender breast, Love;
Calm my overwearied brain,
Soothe away my heart's chill pain,
Bring me hope and strength again;
Come, darling, soon!

Come to me, oh, come to me!
Evermore the memory lingers,
How your gentle "flower-soft" fingers,
With a touch, when I lay ill,
Through my fevered frame would thrill
Cool rich life, divinely still:
Come, darling, soon!

Come to me, oh, come to me!
Dearest heart of love and meekness,
Is not this unmanly weakness?
But with thee such pure sweet calm
Heals my wounds with heavenly balm,
I, fighting, feel my spear a palm:
Come, darling, soon!

Come to me, oh, come to me!
Though its perils gloomed more fearful
I could fight undaunted, cheerful,
This stern agony, called Life,
Were the pauses of the strife
Blest by thee, my noble wife:
Come, darling, soon!

Come to me, oh, come to me!
Strength, and hope, and faith are waning
With this fierce and pauseless straining:
Ere my soul be conquered quite,
Ere I fail from Truth and Right,
Come, my Life, my Joy, my Light,
Come, Darling, soon!

1857.

III.—PARTING

Weep not, dearest, weep not so;
Soon again we two shall meet
Who now part in deadly woe:
After pain shall bliss be sweet.

Few more years of numb despair
Must we wander far apart
Through the desert dead and bare;
Love is courage in the heart.

Few more years of bitter moan
O'er the rugged mountain height,
Must we toil on, each alone;
Love can make all burthens light.

Few more years of stricken woe,
Erring on an alien shore,
Lone and friendless each must go:
We will love then more and more.

Few short hours of doubt and dread,
Trembling on the brink of Night,
Spectre-haunted, each must tread:
Love can burn all darkness bright.

All the long lone years must die;
Then shall we together come,
Where beneath a calm bright sky,
Bright waves bear us to our home.

Weep not, Dearest, weep not so;
Soon again we two must meet
Where the calm deep waters flow,
Soothing surely care and woe,
With their mystic murmur sweet.

1854.

IV.—AT DEATH'S DOOR

Is this the second childhood's feeble sadness?
My eyes are dim now and my hair is white;
Yet never did the sunshine give more gladness,
Never young Spring burst forth in green delight
More freshly; never was the earth more fair,
Never more rapture in the common air.

Still, as I near great Death, it seems his portal
Glides gently backward, that I may gaze through
And catch far glories of the realm immortal;
The world becomes transparent to my view,
Diviner Heavens expand beyond the skies;
The stars grow thoughtful with eternal eyes.

How all the grass and every flower seem yearning
To hint more clearly some high loveliness,
Whose mystic soul within their forms is burning;
How strives the sea for ever to express,
With infinite heavings, murmurings manifold,
Some secret grandeur that will not be told.

The life of day is lulled to dreamful musing,
And true life waketh in the world of dream;
While with the Present, strangely interfusing,
The Future and the Past together stream,
As if the long-drawn waves of Time should be
Settling and mingling in Eternity.

With every golden dawn awakened lightly,
It seems I must have slept through Death's calm night;
For lo!—how purely, silently, and brightly,
The Heavens unfold their gates before my sight;
The trancèd sea of crystal spreadeth slowly,
The burning Throne shines out with splendours holy.

Whereon I look to see Thee come, swift greeting,
From where thou waitest for my lingering feet;
Assured beyond impatience for the meeting,
Crowned with triumphant love and faith complete:
I look in vain as yet; but any hour,
So summer-rich, may make the bud a flower.

How well, my Love, the thoughtful Heavens endeavour
To make this world and life and time all bear
Dream-lightly on the soul, ere it for ever
Be parted from them!—Did I once despair
Through years of lonely anguish unassuaged?
This calm can scarce believe that storms have raged.

Here is the blessing: I now muse enchanted
In this sweet dawn-like sunset; night comes then
Of restful sleep by gracious visions haunted;
So with new morning I shall rise again,
Full of young life, and find my Love for aye—
My Love whom I have lost this long sad day.

1858.

LINES

FROM A LETTER TO JAMES POTTERTON

And if now and then a curse (too intense for this light verse)
Should be gathering in one's spirit when he thinks of how he lives,
With a constant tug and strain—knowing well it's all in vain—
Pumping muddy information into unretentive sieves:
Let him stifle back the curse, which but makes the matter worse,
And by tugging on in silence earn his wages if he can;
For the blessed eve and night are his own yet, and he might
Fix sound bottoms in these sieves too, were he not so weak a man.

May 1858.

A WINTER'S NIGHT

I.

O mournful, mournful wind!
Sobbing and moaning over moor and height;
Fleeing the dawn, and plunging anguish-blind
Deeper and deeper into doleful night.

II.

O Moon, so faint and wan!
Sinking away from gloomy cloud to cloud,
Whence sleet and snow are shaken; and the dawn
Shall find the earth laid out in one blank shroud.

III.

The noontide breeze may blow
With lifeful pleasure o'er the throngs of men,
Freed from their darkest lusts and bitterest woe,
Earning the bread of healthful labours then.

IV.

Throned in eternal day
The Sun may smile—all joy when joys the King;
Diffusing light and life and wealth for aye,
How should he dream to pity anything?

V.

But thou—pale Priestess born!
Driven for ever through the shoreless sea
Of spectral night; thy pure heart pierced and torn
With sight of our worst sin and misery:

VI.

And thou—O homeless wind!
Flung forth wild-moaning through night's wilderness,
Burdened with all worst agonies of our kind,
To sink far off beneath the fatal stress:

VII.

Well may you sob and cry,
Breathing this night our voice of guilt and pain!
Well may you gaze down sadly, O wan Eye,
To which our wretched lives this night are plain!

1858.

A HAPPY POET

Driven by mysterious care and restless pain
The World rolls round me full of noise and strife,
Racking what is not loss to dubious gain:
I live apart my self-fulfilling life
Serenely happy, breathing golden air
Unvext by these dark storms of pain and care.

The tumult whirls for ever to and fro:
I see it all in vision; strangely wild
And incoherent, yet by some rich glow
Of vigour, thought and passion reconciled;
Its mystery also, wherein dreams Delight,
Brings dear old friends, tho' dimly, back to sight.

O happy-dowered Soul! whom God doth call
To life's imperial Banquet as a guest
Greeted with gladness in its lofty Hall;
Bathed clean and cool, sprinkled with odours, drest
In fair white folds of free and flowing grace,
The festal raiment of the splendid place;

Who then is couched 'midst wise and valiant friends,
In place of honour near the glorious Throne
Wherefrom the Host such kingly welcome sends
That all may feel His treasures all their own;
And who is further gifted to divine
The subtlest savours of the fruit and wine.

Is it not strange? I could more amply tell
Such woes of men as I discern or dream,
Than this great happiness I know so well,
Which is in truth profounder than they seem;
And which abides for ever pure and deep,
Beneath all dreams of wakefulness or sleep.

For this whole world so vast and complicate,
With every being nourished on its breast,
With all its mighty workings-out of Fate,
With that one Soul in all its life exprest,
Must surely all be mine, and mine alone;
Its power and joy are so indeed my own.

Spring, summer, autumn, winter, float for aye,
  Weaving continually their wondrous robe,
Of purple Night inwrought with golden Day
  About our earth, whose calm and mighty globe
Through all the World-strown æther crystalline
Floats ever circling round the sun divine.

The faint voluptuous trance of summer noon,
  Young spring's blithe tenderness so green and fair,
The golden wealth of quiet autumn boon,
  The star-keen life of winter glittering bare,
Carol harmonious beauty and delight,
And proffer all their treasures as my right.

The birds rejoice in singing for my joy,
  And shaking sunshine thro' the clustered leaves:
A brain that never plotteth them annoy,
  A heart that loves them and their injury grieves
Swift bird and beast and jewelled insect free
Full well can trust; one brotherhood are we.

The flowers all love me, and the trees befriend;
  Lily and rose are eager to impart
By fragrance, colour, or some perfect bend,
  Delicious secrets that surprise my heart;
I muse beneath the forests, and they are
With all their countless tongues oracular.

Snow-vested mountains mighty and austere
  Persuade me: Climb us from thy lowly home,
And we will be thine Altars; offer here
  From our pure silence to yon naked dome
Thy sacrificial thoughts, in breathless awe
And adoration of Eternal Law.

And evermore old Ocean murmurs me:
  Come forth, and love our heritage, my Child;
Safe-cherished on my bosom shalt thou be
  In death-sweet calms, in tempests dark and wild;
Cadence of moonlit waves and mid-sea moan
Shall dower thy Voice with many a mystic tone.

O vaulted sky, O bounteous land and sea,
  O perfect World, the Palace and the Shrine
Of infinite beauty, truth and mystery,
  That flood the soul with yearning bliss divine

Till it dissolves in their exuberant might,
As some frail cloud surcharged with noon's full light.

The banquet-hall is noble, and its wine
  A nectar worthy of Olympian lyres;
Solemn and sacred is the infinite shrine,
  With stars immortal for its altar-fires;
Yet shrine and palace are scarce noticed things
When all the guests and worshippers are kings:

Imperial all; each freer than the sun
  Doth live and move, supreme, self-centred, sole;
And yet they are my people, every one;
  My life of heart and brain is in the whole;
Their hopes, fears, woes, joys, virtues, sins, despairs,
Their full-orbed lives are mine no less than theirs.

The stern exultance of the thoughtful youth
  Enrolled against the tyrants of his land;
The noblest victor's self-contemning ruth
  When fireless eye must gaze on bloody hand;
The greed of power, the sateless lust of pride,
Whence kingly robes in blood are purple-dyed;

The deep complacency of subtle skill
  In ravelled games, though winning wins a loss;
The drear perversity with which one's will
  With wretched consciousness persists to cross
His own best good, his dearest friends' best prayers,
Devouring sullenly their generous cares;

The fogs of fear in which their fellows loom
  Like threatening monsters, and the firm earth yields;
The mists of hope and love-joy which illume
  With golden strangeness their poor homes and fields;
The sophistries of passion-moulded thought
By which they use to make "I would," "I ought:"

Free childhood's life, so rich it need not ask
  Poor thought to justify its flower-fresh grace;
Youth's yearning tumult when the constant mask
  Seems falling first from Nature's glorious face,
The infinite joy and sadness of its strife
To probe the awful secrets of our life;

The firm deliberate strength of manhood's prime,
  Appraising well the World, its smiles and frowns,—

Yet for the spoils and triumphs of this Time
  Ceding the heirship of eternal crowns;
Old age with Heaven's first rays upon its brow,
Yet clinging feebly to the worn-out Now:

His nature who from action will refrain
  In plenitude of spiritual thought,
And his who keepeth every nerve a-strain
  In constant labour, hope and fear distraught;
(In thought's pure æther float all worlds of life;
The cold eye sees, warm being lives through strife):

Those eagle spirits native to the skies
  Who drink the Sun's bare splendour, and contemn
Such painted screens as unanointed eyes
  Must interpose between His shine and them,—
The veils and imageries through which their sense
Alone can bear the formless light intense;

(But Suns shine spheric to the eagle-eye,
  Though formless to the owlet-sight, when bare):
The soul opprest with its humanity,
  Which must have God's most personal love and care;
The self-ruled souls, that need not supplicate,
Feeling themselves divine and peers of Fate:

All, all are mine, are Me. How vast the Stage!
  Imperious Doom, unvanquishable Will,
Throughout the Drama constant battle wage;
  The Plot evolves with tangled good and ill;
The passions overflood the shores of Time;
With God the full Solution waits sublime.

If I so much contemplate all the scene
  As if to pleasure me the whole were wrought,
I gaze upon the actors great and mean
  With reverent love, with unaccusing thought;
Their wails and curses are mine own no less
Than their most tranquil strains of nobleness.

And yet, how ever-gracious is my dower,
  Whose noon-tide bliss consumes its first alloy
Whose midnight woe by some celestial power
  Enkindles purest stars of solemn joy:
My lover glows, the world is all June bowers;
My widower weeps, the tears rain April-showers.

For I must sing of all I feel and know;
Waiting with Memnon passive near the palms,
Until the heavenly light doth dawn and grow
And thrill my silence into mystic psalms;
From unknown realms the wind streams sad or gay,
The trees give voice responsive to its sway.

For I must sing; of mountains, deserts, seas,
Of rivers ever flowing, ever flowing;
Of beasts and birds, of grass and flowers and trees
For ever fading and for ever growing;
Of calm and storm, of night and eve and noon,
Of boundless space, and sun and stars and moon:

And of the secret sympathies that bind
All beings to their wondrous dwelling-place;
And of the perfect Unity enshrined
In omnipresence throughout time and space,
Alike informing with its full control
The dust, the stars, the worm, the human soul:

And most supremely of my human kin;
Their thoughts and deeds, their valours and their fears,
Their griefs and joys, their virtue and their sin,
Their feasts and wars, their cradles and their biers,
Their temples, prisons, homes and ships and marts,
The subtlest windings of their brains and hearts.

In all their faiths and sacraments I see
Celestial features through the earthly veil,
In all their dreams some deep reality,
In all their structures beams that cannot fail,
In all their thoughts some truth which doth inspire,
In all their passions sparks of quenchless fire.

For singing, in all thoughts I glimpse the law
Ineffable, eternal, veiled behind,
And robe it in full verse-folds dark with awe;
And singing, in all passions I must find
New secrets more impassioned, crowning them
With golden words, a fulgent diadem.

So heartless gibes of infidel mistrust,
And quibblings spun by some poor wretch to snare
His conscience into sanction of his lust,
Or bind it into cowardly despair,

Come forth from me the universal Nay
That limits all our life's triumphant Yea.

So softest sighings of a maiden's heart
  When first Love's fingers touch the trembling chords,
Thrill through my soul with their delicious smart,
  And fly abroad from me new-winged with words
So bright and beautiful and swift to soar
That all must love them now and evermore.

I sing, I sing, rejoicing in the singing,
  And men all love me for my songs so sweet,
Even as they love the rapturous lark upspringing
  And singing loud his joy the sun to greet;
O happiest lot, to win all love and blessing
For that whose own delight is past expressing!

Are men in truth not joyous strong and whole,
  But lofty strains thro' broken lyres expressed?
My frame is all attunèd to my soul,
  My limbs are glad to do my mind's behest;
To wander through the wide realm many a day
As free as thoughts that wander every way:

To climb the mountain brow thro' moonlit gloom,
  With vigorous breathing of its lonely air,
And watch the trancèd dawn from out her tomb
  To perfect resurrection waking there:
To revel through the storm when fire and rain
And thunder make a man all heart and brain:

To pierce the inmost heart of solemn woods,
  Where our great Mother coucheth grand and dim,
And baring her full breast in solitudes,
  Suckles each child as if she had but him,
With that same milk magnificent and bold
Whence Gods and Titans drew their strength of old;

To plunge away from earth on lonely shores
  And breast the green sea-surges foaming strong,
Free as an eagle when it sways and soars
  The billows of the tempest-sea among;
To sail alone the deep, past rocks and caves,
From isle to isle upon the heaving waves:

To row adown great rivers from their rills,
  Gliding thro' dawn and eve and noon and night,
Winding between the patient woods and hills,
  The broad green meadows, fields and gardens bright;
Past homesteads each sole-sacred as a star
Gleaming thro' clustered foliage near and far;

Past peaceful hamlets loosely gathered round,
  Their spires still pointing from the graves to God;—
Past rich and mighty cities far-renowned,
  So overcharged with life the soul is awed
To think but of such massed intensity;
And so into the earth-surrounding sea.

How the rich days of life and joy and light,
  The unregretful, unforeboding days,
Usher me softly into solemn night;
  Then sleep her spell divine upon me lays,
And I am tranced and fed with perfect rest,
Or wander far through dreamland, fancy-blest.

Then, when the night's dusk curtains are withdrawn,
  And sleep dissolves her spell of mysteries,
With what eternal freshness each new dawn
  Greets me with fair and golden promises!
While born anew and young with day's new birth
I hear the lark out-trill my infinite mirth.

So rich and sweet is Life. And what is death?
  The tranquil slumbers dear and strange and boon
That feed at whiles our waking being's breath;
  The solemn midnight of this glorious noon,
With countless distant stars, and each a sun,
Revealed harmonious with our daily one.

1857-1859.

A REAL VISION OF SIN *

Like a soaking blanket overhead
Spongy and lax the sky was spread,
Opaque as the eye of a fish long dead.

Like trees in a drawing gummed together
Some trees stood dim in the drizzling weather;
Sweating mere blood-flowers gloomed the heather.

Like a festering gash left gaping wide
That foul canal, long swooned from tide,
The marshy moorland did divide.

In a slushy hollow near its bank,
Where noisome weeds grew thick and dank,
And the very soil like an old corpse stank,

They cowered together, the man and crone,
Two old bags of carious bone;
They and a mangy cur alone:

Ragged, haggard, filthy, both;
Viewing each the other loath;
Growling now and then an oath.

She at length with a spasm raised
Her strong grey eyes, still strong tho' glazed;
And thus her meditations phrased:

"No mite left of all our treasure;
Sin itself has no more pleasure:
Drained out, drained out our full measure!"

He quavered back: "It does seem so:
The sun 'e died out long ago;
The earth and the sky are a-rottin' slow."

She writhed her thick brows, dirty grey:
"Then take at once my easy way
Of swamping misery from our clay.

* [At the head of the original MS. is the following remark, by the author, in pencil:—
"Written in disgust at Tennyson's, which is very pretty and clever and silly and truthless."]

"No trembling, dear red-rat-eyes! Come!
We slip together through that green scum,
And then with the world here rot on dumb."

He sat still, nipping spiteful blows
On the snarling cur's amorphous nose;
Relishing faintly her propose.

"Well you look lovely, so you do,
To call me names: a-drowndin' you
Would go to spoil this pleasant view!

"This 'ere damned life is bad enough;
But, say we smother in that stuff,
Our next life's only worse, you muff!"

The woman thereto coldly sneered:
"Of course, as usual all afeared,
Old slaver-dewy stubble-beard.

"Idiot and coward! hell-flames feed
On certain fuel; but, indeed,
A used-up soul won't sate their greed.

"When Earth once gets us cold and stark
She'll keep us safely in the dark:
No fear of rousing with the lark!

"Full long ago in grim despair,
She growled, *How those two witch-fires flare!*
They'll get no second chance I swear!"

She laught this truth out 'gainst the man;
Who shuffling, ill at ease, began:
"You can be devilish sore, you can.

"Suppose you're right; this life's a one
That's cursèd bad, but better than none.
I wish they'd light another Sun.

"We used to spree and we don't spree now;
A screw is loose in the world allow,
We didn't make it, anyhow.

"Say Life's hard-up, No-life's more glum:
Just think—a lashing lot of rum,
And a night with you and a cool old chum!"

She fingered a toad from its love-work sweet,
And flung to the cur with a "mangy, eat;
They say there's poison in the meat;

"And so the next time you bite this dear
He'll die off mad; for else I fear
He'd fester for ever and ever here."

Its loose fangs squashed the nectarous lump;
Then it went and crouched on a doddered stump,
With an evil eye on the Male Sin's hump.

He blinked and shuffled and swore and groaned:
Rasping the bristly beard she owned,
She thought drear thoughts until she moaned.

"I see the truth," with a scornful laugh,
"I have starved abroad on the swine-fouled draff,
While sleek at home sucked the fatt'ning calf.

"Too late, too late! Yet it's good to see,
If only damnation, thoroughly;
My Life has never met with me.

"And *you,* you never loved me, *you!*
A heart that never once beat true,
How could it love? I loved for two.

"This dirty crumpled rag of a breast
Was globed with milk once; I possest
The means of being grandly blest!

"Did the babe of mine suck luscious sips,
Soothing the nipple with rose-soft lips
While her eyes dropped mild in a dear eclipse?

"A babe!—could I now squeeze out three drops
Between that poor cur's ulcerous chaps,
He'd die as livid as yon tree-tops.

"You know where it rests, that child-dream gone?
Come, grope in this charming water-lawn,
Through ooze and slime and filth and spawn:

"Perhaps we shall find a shudderous feel,
Neither of eft nor toad nor eel;
May hear a long long stifled squeal.

"Touch the rotten bones of a murdered brat
Whose flesh was daint to the water-rat,—
If it *does* gnaw flesh it would relish that!"

He ventured, "Curse all memory!
It's more than thirty years"—but she
Continued fierce unheedingly—

"Come, and this loathsome life out-smother,
No fear that we'll ever have another:
The rain may beat and the wind may wuther,

"But we shall rot with the rotting soil,
Safe in sleep from the whole sad coil;
Sleep's better than corn and wine and oil.

"Here's a kiss; now at once!" effused the witch,
And dragged the wildered male to the ditch,
And plunged there prone by a bladdery bitch.

Drowned dead, stone dead . . . and still her grasp
Clawed *him:* but with a frenzied gasp
He shuddered off the scranny clasp.

Up the soddened bank in a fury of funk
He sprawled: "She's awful! but she's sunk;
I daren't die except dead drunk."

He managed at length the hollow to win;
And was gulping down with a pang-writhed grin
The black bottle's last of vitriol gin,

When his gorge was choked by a sudden blight:
The cur growled mad with venom and fright,
And its blotches of hair all bristled upright.

Its frenzy burst out in a wolfish yell;
It leaped at his throat like an imp of hell;
In a spasm of horror the bottle fell:

It griped up his flaccid throat with a force
That made his terrorment gurgle hoarse,
While he turned as blue as a cholera-corse.

It baled him into the festering dike;
So all sank dead in its clam alike,—
The Man, the Woman, the virtuous Tyke.

And the dense rain crooned in its sullen flow
From the sodden sky-stretch drooping low
To the sodden earth; and to and fro

Crept a maundering wind too weak to blow;
And the dim world murmured dismal woe:
For the earth and the sky *were* a-rotting slow.

Friday, March 4, 1859.

ROBERT BURNS

He felt scant need
Of church or creed,
He took small share
In saintly prayer,
His eyes found food for his love;
He could pity poor devils condemned to hell,
But sadly neglected endeavours to dwell
With the angels in luck above:
To save one's precious peculiar soul
He never could understand is the whole
Of a mortal's business in life,
While all about him his human kin
With loving and hating and virtue and sin
Reel overmatched in the strife.
"The heavens for the heavens, and the earth for the earth!
I am a Man—I'll be true to my birth—
Man in my joys, in my pains."
So fearless, stalwart, erect and free,
He gave to his fellows right royally
His strength, his heart, his brains;
For proud and fiery and swift and bold—
Holy-water-uncontrolled, *
The blood of his heathen manhood rolled
Full-billowed through his veins.

1859.

* [An alternate version of this line runs: "Wine of life from heart of gold."]

AN OLD DREAM

The maiden lay in a perfect trance,
As sweet, as sad as Love;
Embowered deep from the night's expanse,
As a forest-nested dove;
Through the leaves came never a single glance,
For the stars were quenched above.

The world seemed doomstruck, almost dead,
Nor dared to breathe aloud;
A wannish mist of grave-light spread
From the moon within her shroud;
No sky,—but the mute woods overhead
Hung like a thunder-cloud.

In a pure white robe lay the maiden there,
A shroud or a bridal white;
Her pale face set in her long rich hair,
Golden and dimly bright;
Free from joy and woe and care,
Entranced within the night.

At length that night was rolled away
With its buried stars and moon;
Advanced the pomp of a royal day
In a dawn of glorious boon;
But consciousless the maiden lay
Till the crowning hour of noon.

And then she opened her large wild eyes
In the universal glow:
Their late trance blent with their new surprise,
They gazed; and drank in slow
Grand gleams of the solemn azure skies
And the clouds of dazzling snow.

The noontide reigned in perfect power,
Full-sphered with heat and sheen;
The soft blue haze of the secret bower
Was lit with golden green;
Feeling their rich life fruit and flower
Basked languidly serene.

Sumptuous rose-leaves flushing red,
    And lilies white as snow
Made for her limbs an ample bed,
    Lying still and low;
But pansies pillowed her solemn head
    With their deepest purple glow.

And the bower's roof and wall and crown
    Was all one mighty vine,
That linked and clothed the tree-stems brown
    With an endless leafy twine,
Which the sultry clustered grapes weighed down,
    Heavy with wealth of wine.

Thus richly couched she lay alone,
    Without one cry or start,
Although her face was set like stone
    Against some cruel smart;
Until her anguish found a moan,
    Complaining to her heart—

"Oh, this is sad, sad, sad!" it sighed,
    "Oh, this is a cruel doom!
What glorious life fills the whole world wide,
    What fruit and flower and bloom!
Yet none for me—who must abide
    In this ever-lonely tomb.

"The sky is all a-daze with light,
    The air one murmurous chime;
The joyous sea sways blue and bright,
    The earth laughs green with prime;—
For me no love and no delight
    In this fair world of Time!"

She moaned—and raised a sculptured arm
    To where the great grapes hung;
Her cold hand drew them dusk and warm
    To moisten her languid tongue,—
To kindle some life through her wasted form
    With the summer's rich blood young.

The whole green-woven umbrage bent
    And swayed to her light stress;
The sun-steeped grapes to her wan lips leant
    In an unreserved caress;
How could she 'plain of famishment
    Amid such grand excess?

The sunlight's fervent golden wine
    Came streaming through the bower,
The clouds of the firmamental vine
    Burst in a crimson shower;
She loomed in the midst like a maid divine
    Veiled, glorious, by her dower.

Over the roses and lilies white,
    Over the mossy ground,
The rills of the vine blood revelled in light,
    Dancing around and around;
With a multitudinous laughter bright
    And a song of murmurous sound.

But look on her pallid brow and face,
    Look on her white robe fair,—
There riot hath left what a bloody trace,
    What a ghastly vestige there!
What a wild weird purple drowns the grace
    Of her shining golden hair!

The blood of the lusty summer prime
    Could pour no life through her,
The noon of the gorgeous summer time
    No health, no strength confer:
She sank back cold from the boons sublime
    To the trance that could not stir.

And who had seen her when the grey
    Was fading into gloom,
Had thought a sculptured lady lay
    Upon a white stone tomb,
Besprent with blood, to mark for aye
    Some awful tragic doom.

Throughout calm depths of heaven were strewn
    The pure stars throbbing bright,
The golden lustre of the moon
    Was spreading through the night,
When next from out that mystic swoon
    Her spirit rose to light.

She woke—"Ah, once I lived, it seems,
    Through ever mournful years;
But now I wake from heavenly dreams
    That fill my eyes with tears;—
From floating far down Eden-streams
    With a band of glorious feres.

"And all my heart a throbbing gush
    Of life and love and bliss;
And all my face a dawn-bright flush
    From some enraptured kiss;
And all our Heaven the breathless hush
    Of crowning ecstasies!"

While thus she murmured soft and low,
    And still half-trancedly,
What calm bright forms came sinking slow
    Adown the moonlight sea?
What strange sweet music 'gan to grow
    Throughout night's mystery?

In the deep heart of all the wood
    Came down the seraphs bright;
Around the maiden's couch they stood,
    All shining with the light
Of the beauty of pure sanctitude
    Upon her ravished sight.

They clasped her in a dear embrace
    Of high and holy love;
Their voices thrilled the lonely place—
    "Meek sister! stricken dove!
Come soar with us, and see the face
    Of Him who reigns above!"

So sang they sweet; and all around
    The music swelled on high
To an ocean of triumphant sound,
    That mingled gloriously
With the moonlight, filling up the bound
    Of all the night-wide sky.

As if rapt heavenwards by the might
    Of that harmonious wind,
The seraph-wings flashed broad and bright
    And left the earth behind;
And dim within their fulgent flight
    The maiden's form reclined.

And up the music-moonlight sea
    They floated calm and slow—
So that it rather seemed to be
    The earth was sinking low
Than that they soared, so steadfastly
    Ascending they did go.

They bore the maiden, still and dim,
    When first they rose from earth;
But ere the splendour and the hymn
    Left all our sphere a dearth,
A seraph with the seraphim
    She soared in her new birth.

Friday, September 23, 1859.

THE DELIVERER

I was a captive. Massive walls sevenfold
  Encompassed all the prison high and bare;
The stone, the brass, the iron, the triple gold,
  And yet another which we knew not there.

Year after year I wasted there alone;—
  Now quiet, crushed beneath that woe immense;
Now moaning with a weary changeless moan;
  Now frantic with still-baffled impotence:

And heard at times through all that stony gloom
  The idiotic laugh, the piercing cry
Of others; each within his living tomb
  Chained, wretched, helpless, impotent as I.

Until one eve, when I felt sick to death,
  I found a love-prayer cowering in my heart:
And clothed it with strong wings of passionate breath,
  And sent it thro' the heavens to plead our part.

"O dreadful Lord, O gracious God, I know
  That I and all the other captives here
Have wrought, each for himself, this doom of woe:
  Yet Thou, All-merciful, bend down Thine ear!

"Alas, alas! what have we for a plea?
  We are most wretched; wretched most in this,
That, tho' we strive, we cannot burn to Thee
  In love as Thou to us and all that is."

In that same night, when I was fallen asleep
  After such agony of yearning prayer,
A voice came gliding through my slumber deep,
  A voice, a glow, a waft of vital air.

I woke; and, raising gloom-attempered eyes,
  They blinked at lustre, but no form could see.
The Voice rang singing sweet, "Awake, arise!
  And come out hither, and be ever free!"

I stood—the fetters kept no longer hold;
 I walked straight forward through the dungeon-wall,
And through the others—brass and iron and gold;
 And passing thro' them felt them not at all.

And all the while that Voice sang full and sweet,
 "Come forth, come forth, poor captives everyone!
Oh, shut not fast your ears when I entreat!
 Come forth, and breathe the air and see the sun!"

I thought myself quite free, when, lo! I found
 An adamantine barrier foil me there:
I could not see, could scarcely feel its bound,—
 A wall, a curtain woven of pure air.

What poignant anguish pierced my blissful trance,
 Thus baffled at the very verge of Heaven!—
"Dear Angel of divine deliverance,
 Assist me here, for I in vain have striven!"

Louder and sweeter rang the glorious Voice,
 "Has one, then, wakened up to feel my breath?
All holy spirits in your choirs rejoice;
 Another soul is saved from bonds and death."

The Spirit was beside me dazzling bright;
 It burned the way before me through that wall;
And I was free beneath the heaven of night,
 Nor felt the barrier I passed thro' at all:

But looking back could see a wall-veil then,
 As smooth as glass, opaquely black as jet,
Towering on high beyond my farthest ken;
 But know not by what name to call it yet.

As one who almost swooning drinks of wine,
 I drank in deep the universal air
And glorious freedom of the world divine;
 Then fell down worshipping the Splendour there.

It raised me gently as a wounded dove,—
 "Revere, but worship not, a fellow soul:
Adore the Infinite Wisdom, Truth, and Love,
 The life and breath and being of the Whole."

It was compact of such intense pure flame,
  That still mine eyes were shut to It, in sooth;
The ardour from It thrilled through all my frame
  Like new and purer blood, new life, new youth.

It kissed my brow with such a ravishment
  Of burning bliss that half I swooned away,
And felt my spirit soaring forth unpent
  From its dissolving funeral urn of clay.

"Henceforward re-assume thy primal dower!
  I bless thee unto perfect liberty
Of holiest faith and love: 'tis in thy power
  As thou art now, in heart to ever be.

"On earth's most miry ways shall slip thy feet,
  This brow itself may catch the evil stain;
But faith and love can burn thee pure and sweet:
  —Farewell, until we may unite again!"

How did these gracious words beneficent
  Fill me with dread and agony!—I cried,
"Great Spirit, if it be Thy blest intent
  To save me truly, leave not yet my side!

"Stay with me yet awhile, Deliverer, Thou!—
  I am too weak with chains, too blind with gloom,
For unassisted life; left lonely now,
  I must relapse into that hideous tomb.

"Or at the least, disrobe awhile Thy form
  Of its too much effulgence, that my sight
May meet Thy face; and so thro' every storm
  Preserve one Guiding-star, one Beacon-light."

"Because I burn in my pure nakedness,
  Thou canst not meet me with thy mortal gaze . . .
Thy prayer is granted: a material dress,
  A form of shadowing gloom my soul arrays."

Oh bliss! I saw Her thro' the sevenfold veil;—
  A mighty Seraph shining ruby-clear,
Clothed in majestic wings of golden mail;
  A sun within the midnight atmosphere.

But still her countenance I scarce could scan,
For living glories of the golden hair,
And rapture of the eyes cerulean
As solemn summer heavens burning bare.

Around her head a crystal circlet shone,
Fore-crested with a pure white flying dove:
In emeralds and in sapphires writ thereon,
Athwart the brow, one word was flaming,—Love.

And when she spoke her voice was now so sweet
In soft low music, tremulous with sighs,
That one might dreaming hear his Mother greet
With such a voice his soul to Paradise.

"He is so weak, so weak who should be strong,
Weak as a babe, faint-hearted, almost blind;
The curse of previous bondage clingeth long:
He must not lapse into that den behind.

"The sun indeed shines ever in the sky:
But when the realm is turned from him to night,
When moon and stars gleam faint and cold on high
Or else are veiled by stormy clouds from sight;

"The traveller then through field and sombre wood
Finds his own poor dim lamp best guide his feet;
The man at home his household taper good
For useful light, his household fire for heat.

"Celestial flowers are set in earthly clay:
However small the circle of a life,
If it be whole it shall expand for aye;
And all the Heavens are furled in Man and Wife.

"So thou, the man, the circle incomplete,
Shalt find thy other segment and be whole;
Thy manhood with her womanhood shall meet
And form one perfect self-involving soul.

"Thy love shall grow by feeling day by day
Celestial love, thro' human, blessing thee;
Thy faith wax firm by witnessing alway
Triumphant faith for ever glad and free.

"By her obedience thy soul shall learn
  How far humility transcendeth pride;
By her pure intuitions shall discern
  The fatal flaws of reason unallied.

"Thou shalt see strength in weakness conquering,
  The bravest action with the tenderest heart,
Self-sacrifice unconscious hallowing
  The lightest playing of the meanest part.

"Chastity, purity, and holiness
  Shall shame thy virile grossness; and the power
Of beauty in the spirit and its dress
  Reveal all virtue lovely as a flower.

"Till love for her shall teach thee love for all;
  Till perfect reverence for her shall grow
To faith in God which nothing can appal,
  Tho' His green world be dark with sin and woe.

"Children, by all they are to glad and grieve,
  Shall teach thee what a loving Father is,
And how to give is better than receive:—
  I bless thee with all household charities.

"A priceless boon! and, like such boons to men,
  A glorious blessing or a fatal curse:
Thou canst not sink back into yon vile den;
  Sinking at all, thou sinkest to a worse."

When thus her words were ended, it might seem
  That I was lapsing from a heavenly trance
Into some scarce less blissful earthly dream,
  So wonderfully did a change advance.

Her supernatural beauty grew less bright,
  Tho' scarce less beautiful; the fiery name
Died out like fire; the wings of flashing light
  Were slowly back-withdrawn into her frame.

The Spirit of the empyréan Heaven
  Was incarnated into human birth,
The purest Seraph of the loftiest Seven
  Became a maiden of this lower earth.

Yet still she was the same, thus different:
 The pinions there, tho' not put forth in power;
The glory there, tho' in the body pent;—
 Both sheathed thus safely till the fitting hour:

And in her mien, and on her face and brow,
 And in her violet eyes, as clear the sign
Of Love supreme and infinite shone now
 As when it blazed in jewel fires divine.

* * * *

I woke. A tender hand all silently
 Had drawn the curtain and dispersed the gloom;
The whole triumphant morning in a sea
 Of warmth and splendour dazzled thro' the room.

The dearest face, the best-belovèd eyes,
 Were shining down upon me where I lay;—
Aglow with love and rapturous surprise,
 Seeing my fever was all passed away.

November 1859.

THE DEAD YEAR

I.

At midnight, in the heart of that great wood,
Whose trunks towered dark and spectral, crowned with snow,
Alone amidst the chill north wind I stood;
And saw, whenas some fiercer gust would blow,
White fragments plunge upon the white below;
   And from the rigid branches heard the blast
   Wring long wild clamours as its fury passed.

II.

There saw I, at that time, the weak old Year
Descend in silence from his chariot-throne;
A weary wight, whose rest-joy dreamed some fear.
But in the face of Him who climbed thereon
Youth's vigorous hope and self-assurance shone;
   Though stern and clouded with the gloomy thought—
   Must this beginning with that end be fraught?

III.

The thronèd King went proudly on his path:
The other turned, and with mysterious sighs
Fled onward with the tempest's gathering wrath.
Beneath the scornful brilliance of the skies,
Crowded with stars like cold unpitying eyes,
   My soul pursued the thin grey quivering form
   That like a cloud was hurried down the storm.

IV.

'Thwart homeless mountains, dead and shrouded plains,
'Thwart roaring woods and billowy wastes of moor,
'Thwart the Mid-sea and Afric's wild domains
Of desert-fire and haunted realm obscure,
His flight as swerveless as a new colure
   Swept down the savage ocean to its goal—
   The icy heart of death, the Southern Pole.

V.

The broad cold joyless glare thrust into sight
A ghastly nakedness of ice, which lay
In livid bulks with grinning points of light;
Sublime though terrible. But from the day
Winding a strange and labyrinthic way
   Through hollows and ravines of frozen gloom,
   The realmless shadow sought and found his tomb,

VI.

And, still advancing, cried in feeble tone,
I come to join my buried Sires in death.
Whereto I heard a congregated moan,
A quavering sigh and moan of feeble breath,
Respond, "Is yet another born for death?"
He cried, A Youth now sways the pauseless car.
They moaned, "Alas! the End, how far—how far?"

VII.

I saw the secret Spectre-peopled tomb;—
A mighty Cavern vaulted like a sky,
Filled with a dreary mitigated gloom;
For out of its dark-frowning canopy,
And out of all its vague immensity,
Cold sparkles glittering keen as naked blades
Wrought constant twilight of inconstant shades.

VIII.

And while yet died away the piteous moans,
The moaning multitude therein I found:
Dim regal shadows, throned on icy thrones
Ranged pace by pace about the vast wall-round,
And stretching still beyond the utmost bound
To which the disinterring light could pierce,
They sat—the Phantoms of the Buried Years.

IX.

Their crownèd brows were hoar and shrunk with age,
Their sceptred hands with nerveless tremors shook,
Their lightless eyes seemed spell-bound to the page
Spread open of a knee-supported book,
So overcharged with writings that my look
Brought nothing to my mind except a waste
Of blots and reckless scratches interlaced.

X.

And every robe was foul, and fiercely rent,
And stiff and dark with heavy clots of gore;
And every crown and sceptre cloven and shent.
They all with finished age were weak and hoar,
Yet in their ages there was less and more;
By slight degrees ascending to an Eld
Whose contemplation mind and spirit quell'd.

XI.

From off his soul-confusing Chronicle
Each drew at length reluctant eyes away,
And quavered to the Shadow standing still,
"You come but now from that fair realm of day;
We long have pined, to this dark tomb a prey:
Ere yet thou take thy throne of silent pain
Inform us, we desire thee, of thy reign.

XII.

"How tends the bitter fate-deciding war,
Constant between the Evil and the Good?
Mankind—have they grown better than of yore,
Less steeped and brutalised in lust and blood,
Less fatally inconsequent of mood,
More valiant, faithful, loving, and sincere?
Is any hope that now the End draws near?"

XIII.

He said, Could you but see me, O my Sires,
Your eyes had read ere this what you would hear;
For I am stained with blood and scarred with fires,
And rent and wounded and amazed with fear.
And they responded with their plainings drear,
"Ah! blood and fire for ever, as of old!
Yet let thy voice thy story now unfold."

XIV.

He sighed, Ev'n as of old; nor is there hope
That yet it neareth to the final doom:
For broad and deep as ever yawns the scope—
An almost unattempted gulf of gloom
Thronged thick with monsters savage to consume,
Taloned and scaled with force and dread for strife—
Between what is and that which should be Life.

XV.

The old deep-founded Temples far renowned,
The vast and lofty Temples quake and split:
A column here reels prostrate to the ground;
A roof-tree there sinks crumbling after it,
Leaving free vision of the Infinite;
Some sudden storm lays flat blank breadths of wall:
Entire destruction seems to threaten all.

XVI.

Their rich adornment of all gems and gold,
Their marbles pure and massy stones displaced,
Their forms of lofty sculpture manifold,
Are left exposed to incoherent waste;
The splendour soiled, the lineaments defaced:
  No Architect appeareth, to assign
  Them saving service in a nobler Shrine.

XVII.

The worshippers abandon them in fear,
And with them God and God's restraining law;
Or, used so long to love and to revere,
Tread down new reason underneath old awe,
And cling with eyes shut blind to every flaw.
  More loud, more proud, the priests declaim their parts,
  To drown the murmurs swelling in their hearts.

XVIII.

Exiled from God and His paternal love,
Far—far from home, men languish desolate;
A dungeon-roof, instead of Heaven, above;
And constant vision through the iron grate
Of one stern Jailor, blind and stony Fate—
  The stony heart unthrilled by wail or prayer,
  The stony eyes that blench at no despair.

XIX.

The noblest given over to his hand
Have no trust left, but to confront his pride
With such endurance, wisdom, self-command,
That they become his peers—are petrified
Against his shafts—erect, though unallied:
  Their sole religion and their comfort sole,
  To love and help their fellows in this dole.

XX.

There ceased he for a while; and all the throng
Of trembling phantoms, till my heart was sore
With their so piteous moaning, moaned "How long?
So was it in the long, long days of yore;
Must it be so for ever, evermore?
  How long, dread Lord, thus weary and opprest,
  Must we await the End of perfect rest?"

XXI.

They moaned: but One arose, of solemn mien
And lofty stature, on whose features grand
Wisdom and love and sorrow dwelt serene;
And swayed a Cross for sceptre in his hand;
And spoke in tranquil accents of command,
  "The mighty tree's slow life doth tower and spread,
  Although the branch whence this was formed be dead."

XXII.

And then Another, on whose turban-crown
A Crescent keenly flamed with blood-red light,
Arose, and flung the gorgeous jewel down,
And cried, "That infant Splendour shone out bright
Between the clouds one dark and stormy night.
  All things of earth succumb to Time and Fate:
  The moons are fuller now; the month grows late."

XXIII.

When all was still the throneless Shade went on:
Blood has been shed, my robe is foul with gore:
Amidst the heights of sacred Lebanon,
In China, in Morocco, on the shore
From Capua to Palermo, war—war—war:
  And these are but a wound's first drops of blood,
  Ere yet the veins bring up their gushing flood.

XXIV.

The war of classes, which has raged so long,
Still groweth more intense, till it attain
The crisis fatal to the deadlier wrong.
Imperial liars, thronèd Kings insane,
Statesmen and placemen selfish, blind and vain,
  The Peoples' inward rottenness avow;
  And Europe's Cæsars are her Aztecs now.

XXV.

Around her churches of the cross and spire,
Around her palaces so rich and haught,
Around her castles of volcanic fire,
Around her polities so subtly wrought,
Rages a wild waste flood of restless thought,
  Sapping the old foundations: those must be
  Full firmly fixed that long defy the sea.

XXVI.

Long gathering foulness stifled all the air:
The storm began in France; then, desolating,
Swept Europe with its lightnings everywhere;
Through fierce destructions ever re-creating.
One woe is past, another woe is waiting:
  The air is still with sullen foulness rife,
  And men still breathe, not life, but death-in-life.

XXVII.

The mass of traders full of lies and fraud,
The mass of rulers cowardly and blind,
The mass of people without faith or God,
The mass of teachers barren as the wind,
The mass of laws unsuited to mankind:
  What doom do these imperiously require,
  But blood and death, and ordeal as by fire?

XXVIII.

He paused again; and straightway all the throng
Of spectral Struldbrugs* thrilled the icy gloom,
Moaning in chorus drear, "How long, how long,
How long are we within our living tomb
Condemned to hateful consciousness of Doom?
  When will the ocean of eternity
  Engulf us, quenching all our misery?"

XXIX.

But one vast Shade (by whom a couchant form,
Monstrous, loomed dim) rose, threatful, far away,
And cried, "This pigmy Man—this evil swarm
Of restless, lawless, greedy imps, that prey
On Earth our Mother—shall he last for aye?
  He dream to last, who gathereth bone by bone
  All that is left now of the Mastodon?"

XXX.

Then all exclaimed, "Thou, youngest in this hell;
Much of the tale thou tellest, each one here
Of many thousands had before to tell:
One thread of crimson wrath or sombre fear
In Fate's wide loom still runs through many a year.
  Hast thou no star in night, no gleam of good
  To mark thee out amidst our brotherhood?"

* See Swift's "Gulliver's Travels."

XXXI.

O venerable Fathers, he replied:
If summer boasteth of her full-blown flowers,
They yet were fostered to their perfect pride,
Through germ and bud, by many previous hours
Of wintry snows, of vernal suns and showers.
I wear, indeed, upon my brow one star,
By which I may be singled out afar.

XXXII.

A nation long was trodden in the dust
'Neath various and discordant tyrannies,
Until it seemed embruted to the lust
Of its base despots,—mortgaging for these
The priceless fame of olden centuries;
And, like the wretchedness of Circe's swine,
Drugging its all-sick soul with sensual wine.

XXXIII.

This nation is aroused from shore to shore;
The drunken lethargy is past away,
The drunken frenzies vex its brain no more.
The night is gone; the sullen lingering grey
Consumes in fires of the advancing day,
Whose crimson dawn shall have an azure noon:
This people rise, to labour for its boon.

XXXIV.

The dreamer graspeth firmly Action's sword;
The coward plunges smiling down the grave,
To drag down with him tyranny abhorred;
The meanest miser and self-seeking knave
Give all up for their country; the poor slave
Of superstition dares to see the truth;
The long-oppressed is full of gentle ruth.

XXXV.

The Niobe * of nations, petrified,
With all her children prostrate at her feet,
Each with a barbèd arrow in its side,
Hath started into sudden life to greet
With yearning love and wonder rapture-sweet
Her darlings waking from their trance of death;
Though two lie still, ev'n they breathe prescient breath.

* Byron, in "Childe Harold."

XXXVI.

Whence hath been poured this great electric thrill,
Of God-like power to quicken very stone
With life and soul, with hope and strength and will?—
Throughout that air, long filled with hopeless moan,
A living Voice was heard supreme and lone,
  Calm as the heavens and mighty as the sea,
  Arise! arise, Italia! one and free!

XXXVII.

A Shade * stood up with interruption keen—
A woe-worn countenance, sad earnest eyes,
Brow-crowned with bitter bays, exalted mien—
"O slow-come triumph of my prophecies!
For this I never ceased to agonise,
  In banishment, in pain, in want—or fed
  As menials are with strangers' bitter bread."

XXXVIII.

Another Shadow †—surely not of man,
But Seraph beautiful—above whose throne,
For motto, these two words "Cor Cordium" ran
In letters throbbing fire, stood next alone;
And chanted in a clear and solemn tone,
  "Since now hope, truth, and justice, *do* avail,
  O Naples and Italia, hail, all hail!"

XXXIX.

The youngest looked up proud to that dim dome:
Florence and Milan, Naples, Sicily,
Are crying out to Venice and to Rome,
"Ye soon shall rise to join our family,
And make us one inviolate Italy:
  With fear-stung rage the Austrian frets, past bound;
  The Papal thunders are innocuous sound."

XL.

How has such fruit by such a tree been borne?
How has this Italy, in sheer despite
Of foes whose legions laughed her arms to scorn,
Of friends as false in heart as great in might,
Of statesmen plotting wrongs to help the right,
  Of Europe selfish, of herself distract,
  Wrought out her grand idea into fact?

* Dante. See the "Divine Comedy" throughout.

† Shelley. See the "Ode to Naples" (1820). Upon his tomb at Rome are inscribed the words "Cor Cordium."

XLI.

She has two noble sons; by these she *is*.
The Thinker; who, inspired from earliest youth,
In want and pain, in exile's miseries,
'Mid alien scorn, 'mid foes that knew not ruth,
Has ever preached his spirit's inmost truth;
  Though friends waxed cold or turned their love to hate,
  Though even now his country is ingrate.

XLII.

The Doer, whose high fame as purely shines
As His, * who heretofore Sicilia won
With victories flowing free as Homer's lines.
Sublime in action when the strife is on,
Sublime in pity when the strife is done;
  A pure and lofty spirit, blessed from sight
  Of meaner nature's selfishness, and spite.

XLIII.

Therefore, O fathers, my best symbol see,
Noble in meanness, rent, and stained with gore:
To future Romans this Red Shirt shall be,
As was that Leathern Apron † borne of yore
To all the glittering pomp of Persian war.
  If any hope despite the Past may be;
  Italia shall be one, great, glorious, free!

XLIV.

He finished; and deep silence followed. Then
The congregated Shades in doubtful chime
Maundered all querulous;—like senile men,
Who, stranded helpless on the present time,
See nought before them but a waste of slime
  Left by that ebbing flood of life, which rolled
  So strong and deep in *their* young days of old.

XLV.

"Egypt, Assyria, Persia, Greece and Rome—
How many a lofty creed and glorious state!—
Have flourished under Heaven's eternal dome,
With vigour emulous to last *its* date.
Go, seek them now: they moulder desolate,
  Or languish ignominiously effete;
  Thus mortal things with Time and Doom compete!

* Timoleon's. See Plutarch's *Lives*; whence the simile in the following line.

† The famous Direfsh-e-Gavanee, or Apron of Gavah the Smith, which Feridoon adopted for the banner of Iran: adorning it with jewels, to which each successive Monarch added until it blazed like a meteor in the front of battle.

XLVI.

"The pure, the wise, the beautiful, the brave,
The darlings of Earth's golden youth, are—where?
Deep-trampled, rotted in the formless grave;
Though still, wan ghosts, they haunt the upper air.
Are wiser, purer, braver, breathing there?
  Plato's broad brow frowns homilies forlorn;
  Nay, Helen's lips smile all your hopes to scorn.

XLVII.

"Then vex not us, nor vex thyself, we pray,
With hopes whose vanity we proved of yore.
One hope is fixed; when earth has passed away,
And sin has perished, *Time shall be no more;*—
Oh, that the grand catastrophe were o'er! * * *
  Behold, awaiteth thee that penal throne,
  Which while thou reignedst there down here hath grown,

XLVIII.

"As by its side another now doth grow
For him who reigneth now so young and proud."
He shuddered to his seat of wordless woe;
The palsied heads to their old pages bowed.
My spirit was withdrawn, amazed and cowed,
  From those cadaverous servitors of Doom;
  Dim, silent, ghastly, in their living tomb.

1860.

ARCH ARCHERY

You ask me, darling, why I smile,
  And at what pleasant thing?
My thoughts go back a few months' while
  To the fairest day in spring;

The fairest day, in the end of March;
  The sun shone warm and bright;
All blue and bland was the heaven's arch
  With its calm clouds soft and white.

And some one said, "I should like to go,
  And shoot in this pleasant breeze."
And I humbly prayed, "Let me be your bow,
  You can bend me as you please."

And the saucy girl said, "A bow of yew!
  O a bow of yew must be good:
They say it is tough and strong and true,
  Though a grave-devoted wood."

Over the rolling waves of sward
  We lightly skimmed along;
While the larks from the cloud and the azure poured
  Freely their first full song:

Then leaf-like came a-dropping down,
  When their joy thro' heaven was told,
To the short sweet grass, to the gorse half brown,
  Half lit with shining gold.

And I said or thought: Not Dian queen
  With her quiver and her bow,
A statelier form, a purer mien,
  A lighter step could show.

Till we came to a long lone quiet glen,
  Much loved of the thoughtful sheep:
Before the Flood—or, who knows when?—
  It perhaps was a river deep.

There were the targets ready placed,
  Right gorgeous to behold;
With their red rings, blue rings, white rings graced,
  Around the central gold.

And there our mighty match we shot,
  Like eager Volunteers.
Hit we the mark, or hit we not,
  What merry laughs and jeers!

Gaily we tripped along the glen
  Between the targets two,
With riant races now and then
  For arrows in the dew.

O arch was she with her jest and smile,
  And arch was I, I ween;
But the Archer archest all the while
  Was shooting there unseen.

Swift, swift and keen his arrows flew,
  Well aimed at either heart;
And pierced the poor things thro' and thro',
  With a strange delicious smart.

Well—when the match was fairly done,
  Who triumphed, she or I?
We both had lost, we both had won;
  It ended in a tie.

For that third Archer, we agreed,
  Alone should judge the case;
And thus he solemnly decreed,
  With wisdom in his face—

"You—maiden of the witching eyes,
  You—happiest of men;
Must share the honour and the prize,
  Nor ever strive again.

"For thus on either I bestow
  The meed that fitteth well—
She is the mistress of the beau,
  He bears away the belle."

Curragh, 1860.

THE "MELENCOLIA" OF ALBRECHT DÜRER

She sits, a Woman like a Titaness:
  Her clench't left hand, the elbow on its knee,
Supports her cheek with concentrative stress;
  The unremembered right unconsciously
Still holds the sphere-describing compasses;
  And strown about the narrow floor we see
The instruments with which she lately wrought
To carve material symbols of her thought.

But, Oh, the stern, strong, swarthy countenance!
  Oh, the intensely fixt sole-thoughted eyes
Gazing athwart the sullen sea's expanse,
  Wherein the sun is drowning from the skies!
A Sphynx thus gazes in eternal trance
  Athwart the desert's gloomy mysteries,
Thus images a soul beyond the scope
Of all fond frailties of fear and hope.

A bat is floating in the waste of air,
  Its uncouth wings outspread to spread the scroll
Whereon—perchance imprinted by the glare
  Of those fierce eyes instinct with fiery soul—
One word is legible; one word, yet ne'er
  In volume heaped on volume was the whole
Of any nature more completely writ:
This "Melencolia" comprehends all wit.

Lo! she has set herself with fierce intent
  Of never-quailing will and desperate pride,
Alike unloving and unreverent,
  To clutch the inmost mysteries that hide
In Nature's being and God's government;
  And she has found but Fate—God petrified—
And not a single word or sign can wring
From the tremendous, dumb, blind, crushing Thing.

Therefore she sits thus sternly desolate;
  Therefore the fruitless thoughts that vex her brain
Have blossomed outwardly to mock her state
  With such a fragile wreath adust and vain;
Therefore the hopeless consciousness of Fate
  Imprisoning her soul is pictured plain
In the metallic polished rigidness
Of the voluminous indented dress.

Those compasses could measure out no arc
  Concentric with the measureless round sweep
Of Heaven and Earth; that globe was ever dark
  And could not mirror in its crystal sleep
One vision of the secret powers which mark
  (Working mysterious in the central deep)
Time's progress on the world's broad dial-face
With grand unlingering, unhurrying pace.

[1860?]

SONNET

Through foulest fogs of my own sluggish soul,
  Through midnight glooms of all the wide world's guilt,
Through sulphurous cannon-clouds that surge and roll
  Above the steam of blood in anger spilt;
Through all the sombre earth-oppressing piles
  Of old cathedral temples which expand
Sepulchral vaults and monumental aisles,
  Hopeless and freezing in the lifeful land;
I gaze and seek with ever-longing eyes
  For God, the Love-Supreme, all-wise, all-good:
Alas! in vain; for over all the skies
  A dark and awful shadow seems to brood,
A numbing, infinite, eternal gloom:
I tremble in the consciousness of Doom.

[1860?]

SHELLEY

Upon a grassy slope of shore I lay
  Hour after hour, from sunset into night,
Outgazing tranquil o'er the tranquil bay,
  And dreaming in a mood of rare delight.
  Yes, for some hours, sky-pure sea-calm star-bright
My spirit was in tune with heaven and earth,
Nor felt the discords of its mortal birth.

The round moon floated half-way up the sky,
  Beneath an arch of clouds serenely fair
As if upfurled where never breeze could fly:
  So that it seemed a lamp suspended there
  To light the sea-floored theatre of air;
Whose curtain raised, whose hush of expectation
Foretold a solemn drama's celebration.

My dream grew deeper, deeper evermore;
  A sleepless dream, a seeing trance, no swoon.
I floated with the throb of sea and shore,
  And felt the earth swift-wheeling with the moon,
  And saw the worlds as they indeed are,—strewn
Above, below, as fish through ocean roam,
Not gliding round an even-surfaced dome.

Until the Drama which that hush foretold
  Did come indeed as at a monarch's call;
Although its pregnant scenes were not unrolled
  Upon that sea-stage, nor within that wall
  Of circling crystal, nor were lamped at all
By that serenest moon,—they claimed a stage
Of ampler scope and grander equipage.

The stars are speeding in their companies;
  God's chariots in divine array, they roll
Circling the sphere of three infinities,
  Our symbol of His thought-confounding Whole,
  As Plato saw them with his clear-eyed soul: *
He saw, we see; and each one tries to tell
The Vision each one knows ineffable.

* See the *Phædrus*.

And every silver-burning chariot-sphere
  Whose wheels churn Æther to the foam of Light
Is guided by its seraph-charioteer,
  Serenely regnant o'er its fulgent flight,
  Sceptred and crowned and clothed with awful might:
The infinite armies of the Lord, whose pinions
Flash fire throughout His infinite dominions.

And yet, as every dreamer seems to be
  The centre of the action of his dream,
Our speck of this poor earth-sphere was to me
  The single central fountain whence did stream
  The growing river of that drama's theme;
Which rolled so far and broadened out so wide
That all the worlds were floated on its tide.

A voice fell past me like a plummet cast
  To fathom that unfathomable sea,
A voice austerely sad,—"At last, at last
  The measure of the earth's iniquity
  Brims God's great urn; at last it all must be
Poured out upon the earth in blood and tears
And raging fire, for years and years and years.

"The Churches are polluted,—let them fall
  And crush old errors underneath their weight;
The royal purples are a bloody pall
  To stifle Freedom,—rend them ere too late;
  The laws are silken meshes for the great
But iron nets to hold the poor and mean,—
Let them too perish. . . . But what next is seen?

"Because the priests were false, the shrines impure,
  Mankind in God Himself all faith have lost;
Because blood dyed old purples, they endure
  To walk all naked in the sun and frost;
  Because old laws the law of justice crost,
They would live henceforth without any law:
No loyal service, no revering awe!

"Who will go down amidst these desolations
  Of fire and blood and lunacies and woe,
To chant aloud to all the wildered nations
  Those heavenly truths no earth can overthrow,
  The changeless truths Eternal? Who will go
To preach the Gospel of our Lord above,
Chanting perpetually the law of Love?"

Throughout the whole sphere-throbbing vastitude
  Deep silence followed when that great voice ended;
Even the music of the multitude
  Of all their rhythmic revolutions blended,
  The ever-rolling music, seemed suspended:
And I then dared to lift my awe-shut eyes
And search for him who spoke throughout the skies.

Search for the moon of night, the sun of day!—
  In centre of the universal round
A broad and steadfast disc of splendour lay;
  Fit field for him who stood upon its ground,
  The solemn angel with pure glory crowned,—
His right hand raised, his countenance divine
Intently listening through the hyaline.

From far; far, far, far even in that vast,
  A voice came trembling ravishingly sweet—
"O Raphael beloved of God! the last
  And meanest of the spirits who repeat
  Eternal praises round the Judgment-Seat
Implores that he, if none of greater worth,
May sing the self-same praises on that earth."

A pure joy lighted up great Raphael's face
  As then he gestured "Hither!"; and there came
A star-like speck from out the bounds of space
  With swift and swerveless flight to reach its aim,
  Developing into a tongue of flame,
Until it stood upon that field of light
A fervent Seraph beautiful and bright.

Most beautiful in the eternal youth
  Of those who ever breathe the heavenly air
Of perfect holiness and love and truth;
  Most bright in full-flusht fervour, standing there
  With half-spread wings and backward-streaming hair,
As if alit for but a moment's rest
While speeding forward on his single quest.

Then Raphael laid a benedictive hand
  On that pure brow, and spake in gentle tone—
"Thou dear, dear Child of God, than whom doth stand
  No purer humbler spirit near His throne,
  And none more ardent to speed forth alone
On any errand from the bliss above
In single-hearted and unbounded love;

"Thy service is accepted: thou shalt pall
In mortal flesh thy seraphood sublime;
A witness of the one true Lord of all
Amidst a world gone mad with sin and crime,
A prophet of the glorious Future time,
And of Eternity when Time is past
Amidst the Present of a world aghast.

"I see the storm's commencing clouds of gloom,
I see the storm's first lightnings fiercely flash,
I hear the storm's first thunders roll and boom,
I hear the storm's first ruins quake and crash,—
O Man, thy judgment-wrath is wild and rash! . . .
Go down, dear Child; and may God give thee power
To serve Him loyally thro' this stern hour."

Then most elastic Time, as oft in dream,
Stretched out until five lustrums came and went,
Swaying my soul upon their stormy stream,
The earth was shaken, the great deeps were rent;
From all the quarters of the firmament
A desolating deluge seemed to pour
Of fire and blood and tears and frantic war.

Amidst whose terrors one stern human form,
Above the mad crowds throned in haughty state,
Appeared to wield the thunders of the storm
And hurl its dreadful lightnings, and dilate—
The Captain-Executioner of Fate;
Until dragged down, and with a galling chain
Bound to a lonely rock amidst the main.

And then another lustrum came and went,
Of peaceful years compared with those before;
Wherein I heard that Voice whose ravishment
I had not heard amid the crash and roar
And shriekings of the earth-confusing war.
Through all the lustrum till the chained Chief died
That glorious Voice the air beatified.

A voice of right amidst a world's foul wrong,
A voice of hope amidst a world's despair,
A voice instinct with such melodious song
As hardly until then had thrilled the air
Of this gross underworld wherein we fare:
With heavenly inspirations, too divine
For souls besotted with earth's sensual wine.

All powers and virtues that ennoble men—
  The hero's courage and the martyr's truth,
The saint's white purity, the prophet's ken,
  The high unworldliness of ardent youth,
  The poet's rapture, the apostle's ruth,
Informed the Song; whose theme all themes above
Was still the sole supremacy of Love.

The peals of thunder echoing through the sky,
  The moaning and the surging roar of seas,
The rushing of the storm's stern harmony,
  The subtlest whispers of the summer breeze,
  The notes of singing birds, the hum of bees,
All sounds of nature, sweet and wild and strong
Commingled in the flowing of the song;

Which flowing mirrored all the Universe,—
  With sunsets flushing down the golden lines,
And mountains towering in the lofty verse,
  And landscapes with their olives and their vines
  Spread out beneath a sun which ever shines,
With moonlit seas and pure star-spangled skies,
The World a Poem, and Earth Paradise.

But ever and anon in its swift sweetness
  The voice was heard to lisp and hesitate,
Or quiver absently from its completeness,
  As one in foreign realms who must translate
  Old thoughts into new language—Ah, how great
The difference between our rugged tongue
And that in which its hymns before were sung!

A glorious voice of glorious inspiration;
  A voice of rapid rapture so intense
That in its musical intoxication
  The Truth arrayed with such an affluence
  Of Beauty half-escaped the ravished sense,—
A sun scarce visible in its own shine,
A god forgotten in his gorgeous shrine.

A voice divinely sweet, a voice no less
  Divinely sad; for all the maddening jar
Of all the wide world's sin and wretchedness
  Swelled round its music, as when round a star
  Black storm-clouds gather and its white light mar:
Pure music is pure bliss in heaven alone;
Earth's air transmutes it to melodious moan.

The lustrum passed. The vultures of despair
  And fierce ambition ceased not to consume
The heart of him rock-bound, who failed to bear
  With Titan-patience his Promethean doom—
  Lacking the Titan's conscience. When the tomb
Had held him but a little while in peace,
I heard the singing voice for ever cease.

And then once more the Vision filled my soul
  Of universal Æther, and the spheres
Whose marshalled myriads through its silence roll
  With life and light and music; while the years,
  Heavy with anguish, blind with blood and tears,
Pant after them, exhausted one by one
Till the last heir of Time shall sink foredone.

Upon his central field of burning gold
  Great Raphael stood; and there with meek head bowed
And drooping wings and suppliant hands, behold,
  The Seraph knelt, whom still the sullen cloud
  Of mortal life enveloped like a shroud,
Through which his native glorious beauty shone
Star-sad, star-pure, star-tremulous, star-wan.

And Raphael said, "How faint and sad and pale
  You now return to us, Belovèd One,
From that far Earth of stormy guilt and bale
  Wherein thy errand now is wholly done!
  Hath ever God deserted a dear Son?"
While bending down, his princely hand carest
The saintly brow so pallid and deprest.

What voice of quivering anguish made reply!—
  "I am unworthy of thy ruthful love,
Thou pure Archangel! Never more may I
  Rejoin in bliss the stainless quires above,
  Who singing in their circles ever move
Around the footstool of the Throne of Grace;
Ah, never, nevermore behold His face!

"I dared—weak worm unconscious of my weakness!—
  To claim a service to our Lord and King;
And I have failed;—in hope and faith and meekness,
  In wisdom, knowledge, patient suffering,
  In prudence, calmness, power, in everything!
The awful eyes of all Thy stars, O Lord,
Transfix me with rebukes, each glance a sword!

"Breathing for ever Heaven's inviolate calm,
  I knew not how on Earth the wild winds blow;
Singing for ever Heaven's ecstatic psalm,
  I knew not how on earth the wails of woe
  And shrieks of rage to maddening discord grow;
Circling for ever in the Sun's full light,
I knew not Earth's black clouds and sphereless night.

"I could not understand men; all their hearts
  Had secrets which I could not even guess.
Their greed for dross upon the daily marts,
  Their pride and fawning in the palaces,
  Their solemn church-attending worldliness,
Their servile fear of Custom's lawless law,
Filled me with sad perplexity and awe.

"Their gods seemed hideous monsters only great
  In power and malice, or such phantoms vain
As self-bewildered thought might evocate
  To mock the yearning heart and weary brain.
  I strove to teach them the true God, Whose reign
Is infinite love for all things that exist;
And I was branded as an Atheist.

"I pitied both the tyrant and the slave;
  The one so cursed with pride and heartless mood,
The other from the cradle to the grave
  With soul and body famishing for food.
  I charged them by their common brotherhood
To fling their mutual bonds off and be free:
They paused in their old strife to spurn at me.

"I who was sent to charm their souls to love,
  Could only vex them to worse hate and scorn;
And yet I swear, O Raphael, that I strove
  With all my power to mend their state forlorn:
  By every pang *they* felt *my* heart was torn, *
And wounded worse by their unkindly spurning:
I loved them with a love of infinite yearning.

* Me, who am as a nerve o'er which do creep
The else-unfelt oppressions of the earth.—"Julian and Maddalo."

"Lo, I have failed: but God, *He* cannot fail.
He speeds a shaft against Hell's Dragon-King,
And it falls shivered from the iron mail;—
There let it rot, the weak and worthless thing!
I dare to triumph in my perishing:
His quiver lacks not many a nobler dart
Equal to pierce the Monster to the heart!"

But Raphael raised the Seraph from his kneeling,
And prest him heart to heart in long embrace;
Then stood erect, to all the heights revealing
The fulgent beauty of his solemn face;
And flung abroad his voice to swell through space
And thrill on all the ever-rolling spheres
Triumphant music for celestial ears.

"I call to witness all the angel-quires
Sphering the heavens with their eternal hymn,
I call to witness all the orbed fires
Bearing the light of life through Æther dim;
The saints, the Cherubim, the Seraphim,
All armies of the Servants of our Lord,
I call to witness to my just award.

"Thou hast *not* failed; where holy love and truth
Contend with Evil failure cannot be:
Their sorest scars claim reverence not ruth,
Their worst repulse is still a victory.
Thou, well-belovèd, who didst bend the knee
In pure self-sacrifice to meet God's frown,
Kneeling wert circled with the martyr's crown.

"Music is sweet, whatever madmen's ears
Be startled and tormented by the strain;
Sunshine is glorious, whatever spheres
Cloud themselves from it in dark storm and rain:
Your spirit is as pure from worldly stain
As is a moonbeam on a shore of slime;
You sank not your Eternity in Time.

"O wretched Earth! God sends thee age by age,
In pity of thy wild perpetual moan,
The saint, the bard, the hero, and the sage:
But still the lofty life is led alone,
The singer sings as in a tongue unknown,
The sage's wisdom lamps his single urn;
Thou wilt not heed or imitate or learn.

"The blood of prophets thou hast loved to shed
  Still keepeth green thy fields, whose costly soil
Is of the dust of nameless heroes dead; *
  The only music in the vast turmoil
  Of all thy complicated strife and toil
Was breathed from poets whom you starved with scorn: †
O ever-unregenerate world forlorn!"

Lo, while the great Archangel's voice rang on,
  The spirit by that tearful earth-cloud shaded
In ever clear and clearer beauty shone
  To full transfiguration; for it faded
  As mists of night whose meshes are unbraided
By the swift beams of morning, so that they
Evanish wholly in the perfect day.

And there, amidst the wheeling constellations,
  Upon the central disc of burning gold
That throbbed harmonious with their palpitations,
  He stood with Raphael glorious to behold. . . .
  Then all the Vision from my brain was rolled;
For that broad disc of palpitating fire,
Consuming far through heaven the dead night's pyre,

And bridging the deep bay with golden splendour,
  Was our own Sun. . . . The sky was clear and calm,
The morning air most fragrant, fresh and tender,
  The green earth glittered with its dewy balm,
  The flashing waters sang a joyous psalm:
All was as beautiful and pure that morn
As if a sinless world had just been born.

Jersey, 1861.

* Carlyle.

† "Poets are the unacknowledged legislators of the world."—*Shelley,* "Defence of Poetry."

BY THE SEA *

I.

The burning golden Rose of the Day
  Droops down to the Western Sea;
And the amber and purple flush of the sky
  And the crimson glow of the sea
Ebb, ebb away, fade, fade and die;
While the earth, all mantled in shadowy grey,
Washes her brow with a restful sigh
  In the cool sweet dews of the gloaming.

Then the shining silver Lily of the Night
  Opens broad her leaves divine,
  Afloat on the azure hyaline
Of the heavenly sea; and her purest light
Kisses the earth that dreaming lies
  In a still, enchanted sleeping;
While the heavens with their countless starry eyes
  Still watch are keeping.

The Earth loves the golden Rose of the Day,
  From which she distils the fiery wine
Of immortal youth and magnificent might;
But the Sea loves the silver Lily of the Night,
For her beams are as wands of a holier sway,
  Whose spell brings the trance divine:
The Rose for Life's feast and the festal array,
  The Lily for Death's shrine.

* [This suite is a series of extracts from the long poem "Ronald and Helen," presumably made by Thomson's friend and publisher Bertram Dobell, but possibly made by Thomson.]

II.

The moving waters at their priestlike task
Of pure ablution round earth's human shores.
—Keats.

The earth lay breathless in a fever-swoon
Beneath the burning noon,
Sun-stricken, dazed with light and sick with heat:
Then came the waters from the cool mid-sea
Trooping up blithe and free,
And fanned her brow with airs so fresh and sweet
And crept about her gently and caressed
Her broad unheaving breast
With the white cincture of a magic zone;
Bathing and swathing her faint limbs, that were
In the fierce sun-fire bare,
With lucid liquid folds of rich green purple-strown.

Then as the sun went sinking to his rest
Down the enamoured west,
The waves were leaving the calm earth to dreams;
Bearing the smirch of her long day's turmoil,
The sweat of her fierce toil,
The sultry breaths and languid feverous streams;
Bearing all far away, and as they went
Whispering with blithe content,
To drown and cleanse them in the pure mid-sea:
The while the earth all dewy sweet and clean,
And drowsily serene
Beneath the star-dewed heavens might slumber safe and free.

III.

A BATHING SNATCH.

O Sun lay down thy golden bridge
Across the waters clear!
O foam flash round each rock and ridge
That soon shall disappear!
O tide swell up a full spring-tide
Upon the shingly shore!
For, oh, I love thy surge-sweep wide
And long-resounding roar!

IV.

A LAMENT.

Leafless and brown are the trees;
And the wild waste rocks are brown,
Which the wan green sea so stealthily
Comes creeping up to drown;
And the north-west breeze blows chill,
And the sky is cold and pale;
And nevermore from this desolate shore
Shall I watch my true-love's sail.

V.

The stars came gliding out of the sea
To gaze on the sleeping city,
With a tremulous light in their glances bright
Of wonderful love and pity.

The breeze was breathing its olden song
In a drowsy murmurous chanting;
While the noble bay, with its moonlight spray,
Kept time in a slumbrous panting.

The city couched in a deep repose
All toil, all care suspended;
The roar and the strife of its turbid life
In the calm of nature blended.

Alas! I sighed with a weary sigh,
That all the sin and sorrow,
Now dreaming there, so calm and fair,
Must wake afresh to-morrow.

Would that the whole might thus rest on,
Entranced, for ever sleeping;
The sea and the sky, and the stars on high,
And those myriads born for weeping!

Jersey, 1861-1862.

TO JOSEPH AND ALICE BARNES

I.

My dear, dear friends, my heart yearns forth to you
  In very many of its lonely hours;
Not sweetlier comes the balm of evening dew
  To all-day-drooping in fierce sunlight flowers,
Than to this weary withered heart of mine
  The tender memories, the moonlight dreams
Which make your home an ever-sacred shrine,
  And show your features lit with heavenly gleams.
I have with some most noble friends been blest;
  I wage no quarrel with my human kin,—
Knowing my misery comes from my own breast,
  At war with Fate by chance and God by sin:
But of all living friends you claim in me
The love most sanctified by memory.

II.

When too, too conscious of its solitude,
  My heart plains weakly as a widowed dove,
The forms of certain women sweet and good,
  Whom I have known and loved with reverent love,
Rise up before me; then my heart grows great
  With tearful gratitude, and no more pines.
You lovely souls that fitly consecrate
  The whiteness of your alabaster shrines!
You tender lives of purest good, that leaven
  The monstrous evils of our mortal birth!
There are no female angels up in Heaven,
  Because they all are women here on earth:
As once God's sons, God's daughters now come down,
But these to share, not lose, the heavenly crown.

III.

Of all these women fair and wise and good,
  Of all save only her who died so young,
Thou art in this angelic womanhood,
  Whose solemn praises bards have seldom sung,
Supreme to me—most lovely and most pure,
  O second mother of my orphaned youth:
Thou patient heart to suffer and endure,
  Thou placid soul to mirror heavenly truth,
Thou gracious presence wheresoe'er you go
  To gladden pleasure, or to chasten strife,
Thou gentlest friend to sympathise with woe,
  Thou perfect mother and most perfect wife,
Whose priceless goodness shed on worthless me
Makes gratitude itself half agony.

IV.

A man of genial heart and liberal mind,
  A man most rich in that rare common-sense,
Whose common absence in its name we find;
  A man of nature scorning all pretence,
And honest to the core, yet void of pride
  Whose vice upon that virtue most attends;
A man of joyous humour, unallied
  With malice, never making foes but friends;
As such all know you, knowing you at all:
  But I, dear Guide and Teacher of my youth,
When deeply shamed, yet strengthened, I recall
  Your goodness, patience, constant loyal truth
In love for one whose life's a long defeat,
Say—Souls like this keep human nature sweet.

V.

When I trace back from this my death-in-life,
  Through years of sensual sin and nerveless sloth,
And weary thought with Earth and Heaven at strife,
  And dull decay preventing natural growth:—
Trace back until that period I attain
  When still stirred in me living seeds of good—
Some faith in soul, some active power in brain,
  Some love in heart, some hopefulness in mood;
I always reach at last that little room
  Wherein we lived a life so sweet and mild,
When he who now lies sleeping in the tomb
  Was but an infant, and your only child:
The happy child! thus saved, still pure in soul,
From our false world of sin and strife and dole.

VI.

Indeed you set me in a happy place,
  Dear for itself and dearer much for you,
And dearest still for one life-crowning grace—
  Dearest, though infinitely saddest too:
For there my own Good Angel took my hand,
  And filled my soul with glory of her eyes,
And led me through the love-lit Faerie Land
  Which joins our common world to Paradise.
How soon, how soon, God called her from my side,
  Back to her own celestial sphere of day!
And ever since she ceased to be my Guide,
  I reel and stumble on life's solemn way;
Ah, ever since her eyes withdrew their light,
I wander lost in blackest stormy night.

1862.

"FROM THE MIDST OF THE FIRE" *

From the midst of the fire I fling
  These arrows of fire to you:
If they sing, and burn, and sting,
  You feel how I burn too;
But if they reach you there
  Speed-spent, charred black and cold,
The fire burns out in the air,
  The Passion will not be told.

1863.

"ALL MUST MOVE TO LIVE"

All must move to live, and their moving
    Moves on and on to Death;
Wherever they pause in their moving,
    There awaiteth them Death;
Let them move as they will, their moving
    Soon brings them unto Death;
Let them move where they will, their moving
    So surely leads to Death:
All Life's continual moving
    Moveth only for Death.

1863.

* [This and the following fragment are from Thomson's story "A Lady of Sorrow."]

RONALD AND HELEN

PART I.

Most bright and genial noon of Christmas Day!
The pale blue sky is cloudless, and the sun
A white intensity of light whose ray
Is gladness unto all it shines upon:
Blue-green and foamless swells the tide-filled bay;
The remnant morning-mist still hovers dun
  Above St. Aubin's shore, and through its veil
  The white-walled houses gleam now tawny-pale.

High on a brig's foremast a boy is singing
In proud supremacy o'er dread and care,
His arms in time with his free music swinging:
How through the ocean of crystalline air
That young and swift and joyous voice comes ringing,
Like birdnotes through the summer greenwoods fair!
  What is his Christmas Carol?—The refrain
  Is "Gra machree ma cruiskeen;" noble strain!

I lay abed this morning half-asleep
And half-awake, in drowsy warmth and rest;
While tender memories, such as smile and weep
Over Life's faded flowers in every breast,
And visionary thoughts, that sometimes steep
(As sunset-glories steep the greying west)
  Life's mournful hours in lucent heavenly balm,
  Came floating at their pleasure through my calm.

And thus at length, amidst the shadowy train,
A little poem, like a song-bird sweet,
First nestled in my heart, then in my brain,
And now exultant with the genial heat
Lets loose upon the air its simple strain:
Perchance some gentle hearts whose pulses beat
  With Love's full symphonies in tremulous chime
  Will welcome his least minion's rustic rhyme.

It is not cold bleak winter any more;
It is the noon of summer; and the isle
Of Cæsaræan Jersey to its core
Is drunken with the Sun's unclouded smile:
The sea is steadfast as the glittering shore;
We think such water never can beguile
  Fair boats, rich barques, brave men, to wreck and death,
  As now it lies unwririkled by a breath.

She sitteth at the window, lone, alone;
Outgazing far across the lustrous bay,
And through the heavens beneath the sun's high throne;
For all her thoughts are wandering far away
About the regions of some Southern zone,
As they have wandered many and many a day,
  Like poor, forlorn, tired, faithful carrier-doves
  With urgent messages for him she loves.

Alas, they cannot come upon his track,
They know not where he wanders or reclines.
O India, if you hold him send him back,
More precious than all jewels of your mines!
O dreadful Sea, if he has gone to wrack
Amidst thy wrath, vouchsafe a few sad lines
  To give her such assurance of his doom
  That she may go unlingering to the tomb!

Never a single note of him to speak,
Never a single word by any ship!
A hectic fire surmounts her pallid cheek,
A peevish trouble agitates her lip;
Through her impatient fingers wan and weak
The torn-off petals of the white rose slip;
  Lividly set, her eyes burn large and bright,
  But with a painful sleepless desolate light.

She often mutters to her own sick heart;
She often mutters to herself alone,
She often turns her with a sudden start,
To find herself too surely all alone:
Anon for weary sighs her pale lips part,
Anon she singeth in a dreamy moan
  A song whose burden plains throughout the air
  The heavy burden of a life's despair:

"Adieu, adieu, my ain true Love,
We must for ever part:
Though I am not of Douglas sib,
I bear the bleeding heart,
My dear,
I bear the bleeding heart!

"From all the farthest quarters of the world
The level snowdrifts of white letters come;
With all the steam-cars o'er the safe land hurled,
With all the ships athwart the wild sea-foam,
Till every happy wreath at length unfurled
Melts in the warmth of loving hearts at home:
And never one white flake to me addrest,
To cool the burning fever of my breast!

"O Sun, thou large and lidless eye of fire,
My soul is withered in thy steadfast gaze;
O hot and heavy air I must respire,
No secret spring this fever-thirst allays;
O cruel Sea, enmasking thy fierce ire
With rippling smiles carest by golden rays:
I would that I were buried cool and deep
From this world-furnace in unwaking sleep!

"I dreamed a dream of superhuman bliss,
And it has vanished in the day's broad glare;
I breathed my soul forth in one rapturous kiss,
And it has died out in the vacant air;
I stretched unheedful o'er a precipice
To pluck Life's crowning Love-rose,—Oh, how fair!—
And, all its fragrant beauty unenjoyed,
I plunge down shuddering through the gulfy void.

"O Ronald, Ronald, wheresoe'er you be:
Whether lone-sleeping in an alien tomb,
Or overswept by the remorseless sea,
Or languid in the richest Orient's bloom
Breathing delicious life; I summon thee!
In body or in soul, whate'er your doom,
Come hither; but one moment; so that I
With consecration of your love may die!

"Perchance some Indian witch hath snared your heart
With fiery philtres and enwoven wiles;
Some swarthy Cleopatra, with the art
To melt strong manhood in her tears and smiles: *
I see you there, all powerless to depart,
The more her slave the more you learn her guiles;
  Draining the wine of that voluptuous sin
  Which Heaven and Earth seem both well lost to win.

"Break through her spells, my beautiful, my brave!
Shake off thy swoon, stand up, and come away!
Submit no more to be her doting slave,
Embruted while you grovel in her sway!—
Alas, alas, how misery will rave!
Thou art my own true love; thou art the prey
  Of no fierce lusts, thou, pure and strong and free,
  But of the wild waste all-devouring sea.

"The fair white signal-pennon droopeth down
Against its flagstaff on the fortress high;
The solid serpent-smoke is trailing brown
A lazy bulk between the sea and sky:
How many hearts throughout the busy town
Foresee dear friends or friendly greetings nigh!
  The flag of truce stills none of all my pains,
  The serpent's venom burns through all my veins.

"Yet it is hard, O God, to die so soon,
To feel my life decay before its prime;
To perish in May-frosts when sumptuous June
Is bringing Eden-airs to bless the clime;
To have my day eclipsed before its noon;
To sleep a widow ere the wedding-time,
  Down in the cold dark Earth—there truly wed,
  For Death the Skeleton will share my bed."

Then all the memories of her happy hours,
Her girlish hours of hope and health and glee,
And love a-budding like the other flowers
When April whispers of the June to be;
Of moonlit waters and of sunny bowers
Ere one went forth upon the desert sea;
  Swelled in her heart and filled her eyes, and bore
  Out through her lips their passionate *Nevermore!*:—

* The one priceless pearl Cleopatra dissolved and drank in the wine of her love was the noble manhood of Antony.

"O thou happy, happy Island-home,
  So rich and green and fair,
Which I and my true-love used to roam
  Without a thought of care.

"O thou many-peopled busy town
  Upon the broad bay's marge
Into whose full life we went down
  And felt our life as large.

"O the ringing of the hammers on the building ships,
  And the bustle of the pier,
With the gleaming eyes and the trembling lips
  And the last embraces dear.

"O the mile-long sweep of the full tide swell
  Far up the soft white sand;
O the flashing of the foam when it scales so well
  The rocks of the Castle grand.

"O the flutter of the flakes in the broad bay mouth,
  Like myriads of sea-birds white;
O the gliding of the sails in the hazy south,
  Like spirits calm and bright.

"O the wondrous mists that enchant the whole,
  And make it what they please,—
A faërie realm for the dreaming soul,
  Or a wreck beneath dull seas.

"O the banks of the golden gorse and broom,
  And the lanes that wind like a burn,
With the soft snowflakes of the apple-bloom
  Shed thick on their hedgerow fern.

"O the slant-stemmed orchards, ripe and old,
  When the rich fruits everywhere,
Like flames of ruby and globes of gold,
  Burn in the quivering air.

"O the sleek and tethered kine that graze
  The valley-bottoms sweet,
And look up with such long, slow, patient gaze
  As you pass with lingering feet.

"O the singing of the larks in the fields of air
  Above the fields of grain,
When the sky is blue and the clouds are rare,
  And the hedges laugh with rain.

"Can it indeed, then, can it be,
  That I so young in years
Must fade from the land and the air and the sea
  And the heaven of shining spheres?

"Must fade away to a joyless ghost,
  Or moulder in the earth,
While all the world and the starry host
  Live on in their glorious mirth?

"From all the life and the beauty part
  Without one loving tear
Of those eyes that lit the flame in my heart,
  That burns my life out here?

"O Father, Father, I beseech
  Before I go but this,—
To see his face, to hear his speech,
  To feel his fervent kiss!

"When he again has sworn the vow
  Which long ago he swore—
'My Love, I loved you, love you now,
  And must love evermore!':

"Then I can breathe my latest breath,
  And feel Thy will be done!
Assured that in the after-death
  We ever shall be one."

PART II.

The same hushed vault of dim blue marble sky,
All over-wandered with its thin white veins;
The same fixed marble sea whose blue-green dye
Brown sunken rocks enrich with purple stains:
For still the same despotic sun on high
In haughty splendour bare and beamless reigns;
  The earth beneath his too impassioned love
  Is Semele embraced with fire by Jove.

What royal vision issues calm and free,
Making the isle at once her beauty's throne?—
For all the sphere of earth and sky and sea
Pavilions not too grandly her alone.
Can this erect and glorious woman be
The pining girl whose weary heartsick moan
  Fretted the long still hours of yesterday?
  Can that rich life have ever known decay?

With what pure bloom and firm elastic grace
She glides among the flowers, a flower more fair;
With what undazzled eyes and dew-fresh face
She fronts the South in all its quivering glare;
Her arms stretched forth as if to the embrace
Of some Olympian lover burning there;
  Her lips just parted, and her bosom's breath
  Suspended in the bliss as calm as death.

Her mother follows her, a matron mild,
Now panting with astonishment and fear:
"My poor, poor Helen! my unhappy child!
What change is this, what madness brings you here? . . .
She heeds me not . . . her look is fixed and wild . . .
It is your mother speaking to you, dear!
  O God! what terrors hast Thou still in store?—
  She does not know her anguish any more!"

The cry has troubled her serenest trance;
She turns, and with reluctant effort slow
Draws back her spirit from the bright expanse
To comprehend her mother's clamorous woe;
And then with such a strange, calm, pitying glance
As angels on our sufferings may bestow,
  Bends down to kiss her: "Mother, sweet and kind,
  God has at length restored me my right mind.

"Last night I laid a wild, wild burning head
Upon the pillow whence this morn arose
A sweet cool shrine of happy thoughts instead:
If I had slept death's slumber from my woes,
A shroud my sheet, a narrow grave my bed
(How often have I yearned for such repose!),
  And risen to the Heavenly Life, the change
  Could scarcely be more glorious and strange.

"Whether in sleep or not I cannot tell—
Ah, life was all one restless dream insane!—
A casual thought like some wind-seedling fell,
And struck firm root within my infirm brain,
And drew up all my soul as by a spell
To feed its strength (and all my soul was fain),
  And grew up an oracular vast tree
  Whose leaves all murmured, *Oh, the sea! the sea!*

"Till I felt stifled in my little room
And could not rest for irresistible yearning;
But like a ghost that leaves its midnight tomb,
Went forth and hurried forward without turning
Over the hill-paths chequered gleam and gloom,
And down the snow-white sand, to bathe my burning
  Tumultuous forehead deep in the divine,
  Calm cool refreshment of the deep-sea-brine.

"The sands late flooded by the sounding tide
Wore luminous silver spoil of its retreat;
But till I felt the glassy waters slide
With thin spent whispers round my naked feet
(The gathering volume of the next wave wide
Nearing me fast with murmur full and sweet),
  I could not raise my eyes to see indeed
  Being intent alone on my great need.

"I looked, I stood: there never was a night
Of such heart-breaking beauty for despair!
Our world's one darling and supreme delight,
Golden Beatitude! the moon couched there
'Midst golden-tissued cloudlets; and her bright
Serene regard entranced the breathless air,
  And dazzled her old slave, the fawning sea:
  Oh, how the cruel splendour maddened me!

"Why linger here, where tireless ripples run
Enraptured in the glory of her gaze?
All lightsome creatures my dark sorrow shun,
No fiery wine a fiery thirst allays.
But I must reach those low rock-ridges dun,
Where wrinkled shadows bar the silver rays;
  There shall I find some deep dark silent pool,
  Dark as oblivion, deep as death, grave-cool.

"So I walked forth along the pathway paved
With tremulous lustre; and no thought of fear
Or wonder told me of the peril braved:
And though the light transfixed me like a spear,
Yet o'er that sea of crystal, many-waved,
To walk right on into the magic sphere
  Of that low gorgeous moon, was such a dream
  As made the pang a too sharp rapture seem.

"I reached the ridge; and as by instinct went,
Eyeless with dreaming, to the dear old place;—
A pebbled floor with small bright shells besprent,
A pool at lowest ebb when not a trace
Of moisture in hot noons is elsewhere lent
To those black calcined rocks that need the grace
  Of living waters round them, and instead
  Have white sand-powder thick with worm coils spread.

"Here on this sloping ledge we sat alone
That last sad day, and let the long hours swim
Unheeded over us; and like a moan
From far away each voice gasped strange and dim;
His eyes were blank, his face was set like stone.
What now is left me of the place and him?
  A book of lovely, delicate, sanguine weeds,
  A heart of thoughts whose every fibre bleeds.

" 'Here let me lie; the shadow is so deep,
The little water is so cold and pure—
A font baptizing me to blessèd sleep;
To slumber which for ever shall endure,
Being o'ershrouded by the refluent sweep
Of the great tide; or else whose balm will cure
  My soul to fitness for this world of life:
  Mysterious prescience soothes my inward strife!

" 'So first I knelt to dip my weary head,
And then lay down as if the hollow were
My natural resting-place, my nightly bed;
And weedlike on the water streamed my hair.
Then a strange peace was on my spirit shed;
Beyond inert unconsciousness of care:
  I felt the world's smooth, silent, solemn wheeling;
  A mystic, restful, and triumphant feeling.

" 'The burning golden Rose of the Day
  Droops down to the Western Sea;
And the amber and purple flush of the sky,
  And the crimson glow of the sea,
Ebb, ebb away; fade, fade and die;
  While the Earth all mantled in shadowy grey
Washes her brow with a restful sigh
  In the cool sweet dews of the gloaming.

" 'Then the shining silver Lily of the Night
  Opens broad her leaves divine,
  Afloat on the azure hyaline
Of the heavenly sea; and her purest light
Kisses the Earth that dreaming lies
  In a still enchanted sleeping;
While the heavens with their countless starry eyes
  Still watch are keeping.

" 'The Earth loves the golden Rose of the Day
  From which she distils the fiery wine
  Of immortal youth and magnificent might;
But the Sea loves the silver Lily of the Night,
For her beams are as wands of a holier sway
  Whose spell brings the trance divine:
The Rose for Life's feast and the festal array,
  The Lily for Death's shrine.'

"Who was the singer, singing thus alone
Amidst the tidal rocks, beneath the moon?
What gave his voice that mighty murmurous tone?
Where had he learned that preternatural tune?—
Melting all melody into a moan
Of infinite yearning, then from music's swoon
  Striding to marshal armies of proud sound
  Whose trampling shook the earth and filled the air around.

"I rose, but gently, gently, not to spill
A single drop of that enchanted wine
Brimming my soul; and crept to where a sill,
Backed by dark rock from all the gleam and shine,
Served as a window; and there settled still,
And gazed—if one indeed can gaze whose eyne
  Are fixed in blank dilation, while her ears
  Drink in oracular rhythms from all the spheres.

"Yet in my round of vision, very near
He sat, and merged in my unconscious sight
To union with his music in the clear
Tropical splendour of the liquid light:
An old, old man, reverend yet not austere,
Who on a lower rock-ledge sat upright
  Fronting the moon, and chanting for her grace,
  While all his soul shone steadfast in his face.

" 'The Earth lay breathless in a fever-swoon
    Beneath the burning noon,
Sun-stricken, dazed with light and sick with heat;
Then came the waters from the cool mid-sea
    Trooping up blithe and free,
And fanned her brow with airs so fresh and sweet;
And crept about her gently and caressed
    Her broad unheaving breast
With the white cincture of a magic zone;
Bathing and swathing her faint limbs, that were
    In the fierce sunfire bare,
With lucid liquid folds of rich green purple-strown.

" 'Then as the sun went floating to his rest
    Down the enamoured West,
The waves were leaving the calm earth to dreams;
Bearing the smirch of her long day's turmoil,
    The sweat of her fierce toil,
The sultry breaths and feverous steams,—
Bearing all far away, and as they went
    Whispering with blithe content,
To drown and cleanse them in the pure midsea;
The while the Earth all dewy sweet and clean,
    And drowsily serene,
Beneath the star-dewed heavens might slumber safe and free.'

"His foam-white hair and beard fell floating down
In flowing curves like tendril-plants sea-swayed,
Over his sea-like green-blue silken gown,
Ample, of ever-shifting gleam and shade.
Upon his knees the mighty hands dark-brown
Grasped a great chorded shell, whose sleek lips played
  Wild freaks of rainbow lightnings to illume
  The gorgeous thunders of its hollow womb.

"Why speak of hair, harp, hands, when in his eyes
The wonder dwelt? A small intense lone mere,
Which under thick tree-shadows airless lies,
As deep and blackly splendid may appear
As if the whole night gloom beneath the skies
Were concentrated in its narrow sphere:
  Such were those orbs, those well-shafts of black splendour,
  Through which a soul gazed, solemn, powerful, tender.

"Deep wells lead down to all-mysterious death,
Deep eyes lead down to a mysterious soul,
And both thrill fascination; but who saith
What lures us on to plunge for either goal?
I dared not stir or speak, and yet my breath
Hysterically bursting from control
  Cried through his chanting in a plaint forlorn,
  Learnt by the sea-beach one drear winter morn:

" 'Leafless and brown are the trees,
  And the wild waste rocks are brown
Which the wan green sea so stealthily
  Comes creeping up to drown;
And the north-west breeze blows chill,
  And the sky is cold and pale;
And nevermore from this desolate shore
  Shall I watch my true-love's sail.'

"As if indeed, omnisciently aware,
He had been calmly waiting all the while
My own announcement of my presence there,
He turned his glance with an assuring smile,
And said, 'So young, and singing of despair!—
What tyranny of fate, what human guile,
  Or what mere folly of your own weak heart,
  Makes you bewail an ever-cureless smart?

" 'My poor Child! come and tell me all your woe;
And I perchance may find some healing balm:
Howe'er the billows rage and tempests blow,
The sea's deep heart lies brooding ever calm:
Wild waste above may have pure peace below.' . . .
I knelt there at his feet and felt his palm—
  Palm of a mighty hand—caress my hair,
  As erst the harpstrings, with fine tender care.

"And I could tell him all my woe and pain,
As scarcely I could tell you, mother dear;
All the wild dreams that haunted my vexed brain,
All the sharp agonies of doubt and fear,
All the despair of longings ever vain:
And as I poured them forth into his ear
I felt they never could return to me,
But were as torrents drowned in the great sea.

"His hand was a strong blessing on my head;
His eyes drew out the fever from my soul,
And filled it all with cool sweet light instead,
And held me calm in their supreme control
By some high magic free from awe and dread,
A spiritual charm; and when the whole
Of my sad tale was sobbed forth, I felt sure,
Before he named a remedy, of cure.

"Thoughtfully, father-tenderly he smiled,
And held a moonlike jewel out to me:
'This crystal-clear and hollow gem, my Child,
Contains one pure drop from the deep mid-sea;
And all the ocean-volumes calm or wild
In all their depth and power and mystery,
Clothing the round world with a living robe,
Are represented in its little globe.

" 'Take it, and seek in it with trustful care,
Turning it slowly; and if He you mourn,
Lord of your life and death, is anywhere
Within the sea's dominions—whether borne
Upon its bosom breathing happy air,
Or buried in its depth a corpse forlorn—
The blank will stir and breathe until you find
His image in its magic sphere enshrined.'

"I took it, full of faith; but could not see
At first,—my hand so trembled, and my eyes
Were clouded with such rushing mystery
From my heart's fiery throbbing. But his wise
Serene regard, steadfastly holding me,
Soothed and restored; as tender moonlight lies
In beautiful calm upon the ocean's breast,
Enchanting into peace its great unrest.

"Upon my open palm the jewel gleamed,
Faint, semi-lucid, almost colourless:
I gazed, gazed, turning slowly, till it seemed
Expanding by soft pulses in the stress
Of my persistent gaze, whose full light streamed
Triumphant with prophetic consciousness;
Pulse after pulse, wave after wave, poured still
From eyes protending with imperious will.

"A golden star is kindled at its core,
The spherelet fills with the dissolving light;
Gather and shift and vanish shadows hoar:
It is pervaded with miraculous might,
Swelling in musical triumph more and more:
Behold! within and yet beyond our night
Another heaven, another sea unfurled,
Another vast horizon of our world!

"A vault of sky; the wan moon near its crest
Fades from those fiery armies of the dawn,
Whose van is up with golden spears in rest:
A plane of sea as level as a lawn,
But sapphire-blue; upon the far north-west
A low grey land-cloud delicately drawn;
And in the centre of the faërie sphere
A single ship: all steadfast, solemn, clear!

"A lonely ship; through the crystalline air
I see it as beneath a microscope
We see an insect, every scale and hair;
I hear its panting, and the plash aslope
Its prow of languid wavelets green:—and there!—
Oh, heart be firm, or this fierce shock of Hope
Leaping up Bliss, will slay us!—Who is *He*
Yearning across the ocean-leagues to me!

"Hush, hush; he murmurs . . . How dark-bronzed and brown
The face that was so ruddy! Noble face,
With lordly lion-locks for golden crown!—
As pious Moslems in whatever place
Turn always Meccaward when kneeling down
For adoration of the Throne of Grace,
He has turned hither, praying steadfast-eyed,
Leaning impassioned o'er the vessel's side.

"Listen! 'O Helen, this mysterious chain
Which links us heart to heart, gives mine no rest,
Dragging with such persistent cruel strain
As if to tear it bleeding from my breast.
From utmost India, over land and main,
It draws me wild with longing to the West:
  What crushing grief, what bitter worldly strife,
  Or inward agony, exhausts your life?

" 'I come, I come, Belovèd! tender heart
Swooning transfixed! no wonder mine must bleed,
Pierced by our sympathy with the same dart.
I come, I come, to stay you in your need,
And nevermore in life shall we two part! . . .
Lo, with what beautiful and tranquil speed
  The morning drowns the gloom and fires the grey,
  And breathes triumphantly night's fears away!'

"Oh, murmur sweeter than the sweetest psalm
On Sabbath eve in Summer, through the air
Floating with outspread wings that rain pure balm
On who may through some quiet valley fare!—
How picture-motionless, how crystal-calm
And crystal-lucid, sea and sky spread there,
  Ringed by the far horizon's perfect ring;
  That lonely ship the only human thing!

"I could not dare to break the magic peace
By crying ev'n to him, my Love so near;
But gazed and listened: then a milk-white fleece
Fell in vast volumes through the æther clear,
And surged in violent growth and swift decrease;
Whereon the suddenly thus-muffled sphere
  Span round, all ruining in with hollow roar.
  I cannot, though I try, remember more.

"Something there was: that old Sea-god benign,
Glaucus the wonderful, to whom I raise
Within my heart a rich and secret shrine
For floral gratitude and incense-praise;
Glaucus, and Ronald, and dear mother mine
Yourself, seen flitting all before my gaze
  In glimmering dusk; strange music stirs sweet bowers:
  The rest has fled with the swift-flying hours.

"With the swift flying hours that bring to me
My Love, my Own, my Beautiful, my Brave!
Swift may their flight sweep over the broad sea,
Soft fall their shadow on the halcyon wave!
The hours are Seraphs bright with holy glee,
Whom I thought sombre bearers to the grave!
   There is no grave, no death, no gloom of night;
   The World all overflows with God's pure light."

PART III.

Nature had roused herself from that still trance,
Her long siesta in the noon o' the year;
Vast clouds had gathered in the dim expanse,
High gales had swept the brooding atmosphere,
With thunders and broad lightnings, with the dance
Of joyous rain upon the meadows sere,
   And trees tumultuous as a roaring tide,
   And wan green bay and livid offing wide.

And now a morning of delicious breath,
A clear-skied morning full of hope, whose life
Has no remembrance of past gloom and death,
Whose peace abjures its birth in stormy strife,
Welcomes the Wanderer as he entereth
That noble bay-mouth which for him is rife
   With all the golden treasures of rich youth
   And perfect love, safesealed by perfect truth.

The pathos of dear Memory's best delight
Had filled his eyes with tender tears before,
As they came pulsing in the early light,
Sole on the waves, aslant the happy shore;
And all the sister islets full in sight
Unshrouding from their mist-veils thin and hoar
   Gleamed faintly blue: but now his soul was thrilled
   With fearless triumph of life's end fulfilled.

"O fair green Isle, my Love's delightful nest,
Deep in this silver branch of the great sea!
Watched by the royal Lion of the West,
Safe from the Eagle, 'oure sweete enemie':
Look,—as a Lion couched in haughty rest,
Slumbrous but watchful for emergency,
   Guarding a monarch's threshold night and day,
   Thy Castle lies out massive in thy bay.

"Nest of my Love! the cradles of our birth
Were rocked to mightier airs than thou hast known;
Wild winds that raved round hills of gloomy dearth,
And overswept vast heathery moorlands lone,
And swayed deep solemn lochs as if old earth
Were yawning into ruin: every tone
  Of those sublimest anthems swells once more
  Within me, O our stern dear Mother-shore!

"But youth and youth's Love-Eden, rich and fair
As that first Eden which the Lord God planted;
Wherein we wandered sole as the first pair,
And with the same divine new bliss enchanted;
Are linked with thee for ever, everywhere,
Sweet islet of the West, whose cool gleams haunted
  The burning splendours of the oldest East
  Shaming the wine of its voluptuous feast.

"Wine of the East! not wine, but poison, call
That flood of fire which through the parched frame rolls;
'Thou art the wine whose drunkenness is all
We can desire, O Love! and happy souls,
Ere from thy vine the leaves of Autumn fall,
Catch thee and feed from their o'erflowing bowls
  Thousands who thirst for thy ambrosial dew:'
  The thousands thirst; the happy souls how few!

"Thus chants the glorious Seraph?—And this wine
Brimming a golden cup was at my lips;
Yet I could put away the draught divine
After the first short, trembling, rapturous sips,
And leave the great Olympian revel-shine
And downward fare into the earth-eclipse:
  And after long long years when I return,
  Still my wine waits me, still the star-lamps burn!

"Because the Banquet of the Gods doth last
For ever and for ever, day and night!
Because their wine when years on years have passed
Is fresh as at that instant when its light
Streamed like a ruby chainlet holding fast
The golden cup to Hebe's wrist curved white;
  Because his place who once hath sat there blest
  Is never taken by another guest.

"And I did well, and I did well O Love,
To love yet leave; do well to now return!
How should a boy with great gods feast, and prove
The nectar's inmost potency, discern
Its subtlest fragrance, feel its ardours move
Thrilling in slow rich growth until they burn
  Through all the being in a still desire
  And pure white flame of unconsuming fire?

"The boy was all too weak: one full-breathed draught
Had been intoxication; then dull swoon
Had drowned remembrance of the nectar quaffed,
Or left him sated who had dared too soon;
While all the ever-glad Immortals laughed
To see so misapplied their crowning boon:
  But I come back from years of toil and strife
  Strong and mature to claim my Feast of Life."

Whereon he shook himself erect, to feel
The rich blood mantling through his stalwart frame,
A fervent wine of life from brow to heel;
And all his spirit like a pointed flame
Burned out intensely pereceant as the steel
Flashed from its scabbard at a hero's name,—
  Burned glittering from his eyes, and darted keen
  Swift herald fire-thrills to his Love unseen.

He stamped, "But, O my steamer, how you crawl!
I would your horse-power were a horse indeed,
Thin-flanked and spur-able! Good hap befall
This cautious steering, friends; but where's the need
When thick surf escalades the pier-head wall?
High tide—the sun mounts high—Oh speed, speed, speed!"
  Half hummed half sang he mellowly and low,
  A bathing snatch of mornings long ago.

"O sun, lay down thy golden bridge,
  Across the waters clear!
O foam flash round each rock and ridge
  That soon shall disappear!
O tide, swell up a full spring-tide
  Upon the shingly shore!
For, oh, I love thy surge-sweep wide
  And long-resounding roar!"

Early she sat; not restless, but in awe
Trembling at intervals with rhythms of fear;
As from the leafy window-seat she saw
The vessel freighted with life's bliss appear,
And slowly to the hidden harbour draw
Over the joyous waters blue and clear:
  When still the ship was but a shapeless speck
  Her true eye fixed Him lordly on the deck.

The mist dissolving in the morning glow
Still faintly streaked the blue abyss of air,
And left a purple tinge on all below:
The well-loved scene looked strange and still and fair,
As some grand picture painted long-ago,
Now for the first time brought before her there;
  Or some dear dream of childhood now once more
  Come back as wonderful as heretofore.

If ever she relaxed her vision strong
Which thus had drawn him from the unknown climes,
It was to read again with kisses long
A letter she had read a hundred times,
And still found always new,—like some old song,
Some old sweet song of simple passionate rhymes,
  And more than mortal tenderness—a lay
  Fit for a wedding and a dying day.

"Has the old writing startled you, my dear?—
Old schemes expanding, new ones striking root,
Threatened to keep me tending year by year;
Still as I gathered in one crop of fruit
Finding another ripe,—with long arrear
Of fresh plantations blossoming to boot:
  So wealth grew great, and great wealth's care and toil;
  But what became of love in all the coil?

"Stunned, snared, deep-smitten!—so my heart cried out,
With passionate scorn, imperative demands,
And blood-dark proofs convicting murderous doubt.
My lonely hours became as desert lands
When hot simoon glares purple through the rout
Where whirl the columns of the billowy sands:
  I felt that I must leave; yet how arrange
  That work should live and grow despite the change?

"One night the glowing stars and golden moon,
The perfect fruit of heaven, hung down so bright
In their unwasting beauty, that a swoon
Of pure love-longing and divine delight
Melted me wholly—'Thou consummate boon,
Crown of the fruitage of the Tree of Night,
  Fringing cloud-leaves with splendid spray, and through
  The quiet air distilling nectar-dew:

" 'Some swift hours hence my Love's own islet green
Comes floating under the enormous shade;
Oh, when she looks to thee, thou heavenly queen,
Do thou shed blessings down on her!' I prayed;
'Fill her with shining hope and joy serene,
Tell her,—He cometh now, no more delayed!
  This message bear, thou white and golden dove,
  Thou light of lovers whom all lovers love!'

"I heard you then cry, *Ronald, come to me!*
As plainly as I ever heard you speak
When we together sat, and I might see
The glorious eyeglow pale the flushing cheek,
The curved lips falter into utterance free,
And feel the moist hand quiver strongly weak;
  I heard your clear voice ringing through the air,
  I felt you straining at my heart-strings there.

"Whereon I forthwith registered a vow,—
There was such anguish in the bell-sweet tone
To write no single line more, to allow
My throbbing heart no language of its own,
Till I could date from—where I date from now,
Here, on our England's ever-green sea-throne:
  This vow made short sharp work of all that stood
  Between me and departure, bad or good.

"I started, I am here: what voyage was mine,
All my long Odyssey (without the zest
Of lotus, or Calypso more divine),
Until I passed the Pillars of the West,
Spare now from scripture's ink for speech's wine:
When one has reached the Islands of the Blest,
  The perils and the storms he came through seem
  Dim fragments of an interrupted dream.

"Two days for London, or at longest three;
I dare not come to you first, knowing well
That when you once have laid soft hands on me
I shall be impotent to break your spell:
Meanwhile for some few hours more I am free,
And ere they ring my this life's passing-bell
  Would wind up business with the world in peace;
  We make our wills just as our wills must cease.

"But lest you wonder how I dare assume
That my mad silence pregnant with dismay
Has not already scared you to the tomb,
Read this: you tortured me the whole sad way
To Malta, pallid phantoms stern as Doom;
But in the dawning of the perfect day
  That brought us to Valetta, you came forth
  An Angel of glad tidings from the North."

A telegraphic note had followed this,
"I come on by the next Southampton mail:"
Therefore she read and dreamed in solemn bliss,
Watching the slow hours through, from when the veil
Of misty darkness on the deep abyss
Trembled and opened to the dawnlight pale:
  And now and then throughout the vigil long
  She murmured dreamily a little song:—

    "A fuchsia lay on the sodden mould;
      I stooped, and held it up
    To the morning sun, and a wine of gold
      Seethed in its purple cup:
    A lucid, lucid golden wine—
      The dewy bloom of the flower
    By the joyous beams of the morning shine
      Transfused with mystic power.

    "My heart was lying on a grave;
      I dared to hold it up
    To the Sun of Heaven, and a glorious wave
      Swelled in its purple cup:
    A glowing golden wine of love,—
      My heart's best blood in the kiss
    Of the living light of the Sun above
      Burning to perfect bliss."

PART IV.

The quiet evening of that day of days
Held the two lovers walking side by side,
As slowly as a summer cloudlet strays
From noon to eve across the heavens wide,
Or distant barque whereat full long we gaze
Ere sure its snowy pinions really glide:
They paused and loitered in such indolence
Of perfect Joy's eternal present tense.

For perfect Joy would hardly care to baulk
Poor perfect Sadness in her logical fit:
"Better to walk than run, to stand than walk,
To sit than stand, to lie down than to sit;
And better than to lie awake and talk
Or think, to lie in dreamless sleep; and it
Is better to lie dead than lie asleep;
Which better is the best we mortals reap."

Three hours of this world's time—such hours as make
A heavenly life-time each—they lingered through
The valley winding out to Grève de Lecq,
Before the placid waters met their view;
And much they spoke, yet speech would often slake
To let the grander harmonies ensue
Of Silence—great dumb Poet, overfraught
With utterless passion and ineffable thought.

As they turned up the highway, to ascend
A narrow path amidst the golden gorse,
A soldier brought his cane down on his friend
With hearty comradeship's most heavy force,
"Hammer my eyes, Bill! why don't you attend?
There is a chest for the Victorier Crorss!
That pair's the finest pair I ever see
In this 'ere isle of poisoned ho-devee."

The speaker spoke more loudly than he meant
(Enough of drink will make a whisper shout,
As too much makes a shout of bold intent
Huskily whisper); those he pointed out
Thus heard quite well the sudden compliment.
She drew herself up with a pretty pout,
Arching her neck with grace superbly free;
While his strong eyes laughed with a world of glee.

"Your soldier is a judge; he knows a man,
And eke a woman, tho' he loves his beer;
I've fought a little in my time, and can
Be proud to bend thus an old ramrod, dear:
Old ladies, too, with awesome sharpness scan:
And even as I leapt upon the pier,
  A jolly dame with marvellous cap snow-white
  Burst out *Quel homme!* in very frank delight.

"Learn what a peerless prize you come to gain,
Know what a god is prostrate at your feet!"
"You big bad boy, come back to me as vain
As ever! If some giant would but beat
The boasting out of you!—I'll shear this mane
Flung haughtily to every wind we meet,
  All the thick lionlocks of tawny hair
  Wherein your turbulent strength may have its lair!"

"And who, of all men in the whole world wide,
Crowned with the consecration of your kiss,
Would not exult and overflow with pride
Unmeasured as the ocean of his bliss?
What dullest Apis ever deified?
What Bottom in rare metamorphosis,
  Titania's flower-sweet hands like soft white doves
  Hovering round Donkey-head with delicate loves?

"Yes, I am vain, all-happy and all-vain;
As peacock when full noon lights up the eyes
Emerald and amethyst that star his train,
Dazzling the sober splendour of the skies;
As whidah-bird in his new love's first gain,
When he would front an eagle for the prize,
  And all his rapturous vanity unreprest
  Leaps like a fountain in the monstrous crest.

"If I can bring my Love great store of wealth,
Good tho' all gold is dross beside my Love;
If I can bring her beauty, vigour, health,
Good—tho' her worth is all world's grace above:
And shall I bring her these good things by stealth,
As if ashamed my worship thus to prove?
  Not so; my life's best incense shall aspire
  Upon the hilltop in a flaming fire."

They sat them down where they could look abroad
Through the sweet gloaming o'er the dim sea-space;
And long they sat in silence hushed and awed,
The while she nestled close in his embrace.
Surely they felt the very breath of God
Leaning down softly from the Heavenly place,
  Even as a mother leans with yearnings deep
  To watch her infant sink in happy sleep.

At length she whispers in soft little gasps
Of slender tremulous shadowy distant sound;
Fearing to break the silence that enclasps
With infinite love and peace the world around;
Yet fearing more the silence, through which grasps
Too powerfully her soul all tranced and bound
  His conquering soul imperious: and her will
  Spends its last free pulsation in the thrill.

(All silently the lily's globe of dew
Is drunk up by the great sun's hot desire;
The burning cloudlet in the burning blue
Is still as death, and overfraught with fire
Dissolveth ever upward through and through
Successive heavens, and would aspire—expire:
  It has condensed to cold and dark again
  Ere it showers earthward in wide-whispering rain.)

"Are we in Heaven? or are we still on earth?
Is this indeed Eternity or Time? . . .
Oh, Love, the foretaste of another birth,
Another life from blossoming to prime,
That showed our richest foison arid dearth,
Our tropic summer a dark polar clime,
  Was given me in an ecstasy of fear;
  How deep our roots cling to the Now and Here!

"And this *is* Earth; and in the glass run by
The sands that surely then for ages stood,
As all the stars stood steadfast in the sky—
The burning ranks, the golden multitude
Of chariots wherein unweariedly
The Lords of Time have evermore pursued
  The flying Future through the realms of Space:
  Sands run, and stars renew their solemn chase.

"And shall we wish to hurry to the End?
To sleep—to lose the rush, the stress, the glow,
The rapture of the chase, because we bend
At whiles faint bruised and dusty? Ah, no! no!
Let all the seasons in the good fruit blend!
And yet it was but three short months ago
  I sat as now we sit above the sea
  And this was all the thought that dwelt in me:—

"The stars came gliding out of the sea
  To gaze on the sleeping City,
With a tremulous light in their glances bright
  Of wonderful love and pity.

"The breeze was breathing its olden song
  In a drowsy murmurous chanting;
While the noble bay with its moonlight spray,
  Kept time in a slumbrous panting.

"The City couched in a deep repose,
  All toil, all care suspended;
The roar and the strife of its turbid life
  In the calm of Nature blended.

" 'Alas!' I sighed with a weary sigh,
  'That all the sin and sorrow,
Now dreaming there, so calm and fair,
  Must wake afresh to-morrow!

" 'Would that the whole might still rest on,
  Entranced, for ever sleeping;
The sea and the sky, and the stars on high,
  And those myriads born for weeping!' "

"What pansy's most imperial purple dye,
What rapturous flush of redness in the rose,
What lily's perfect moon-white purity,
From that dark rain of weeping gleams or glows!
For as the sun shines ever in the sky,
And ever round our earth the free wind blows,
  So evermore the tears of heaven distil
  Beauty and good with sorrow for our ill.

"But I waste costly hours: for this fair Isle
Is Ithaca; and poor Penelope,
Who has been constant all the dreary while,
Weaving wan hopes of vain embroidery,

Clasps her Ulysses, young, withouten guile,
And famishes to hear his Odyssey.
  When he has told what wonders him befell,
  She has a little tale of home to tell."

"And she shall be cross-questioned to and fro,
Backwards and forwards, sideways, up and down,
Anent the tale of suitors who we know
Were victims to a starry-bright renown,—
Rash moths that plunged into the burning glow,
Lovely, but crueler than tempest's frown.—
  No outward chances gave that voyage a story;
  But from within came all the gloom and glory.

"My soul was like a jewel-amulet, *
Pale, troubled, day by day more dim and wan;
The fatal shadow of a vast regret,
The pallor of an awful fear, were on
And in its lustre, that seemed always wet
As with dull tears of hope for ever gone:
  If fitfully it gleamed again, the light
  Was such as oozes up from graves by night.

"Life wasting out by saddest slow degrees;
Life's heart-blood, love, a thin warm crimson thread,
Trickling so long that scarce the bitter lees
Kept the pale corse half-living and half-dead:
Indian, Arabian, and Egyptian seas
Gave me this vision of too-dreadful dread,
  Blurring their splendour; as the storm took shape
  To Gama in the Phantom of the Cape.

"The City of the Greek, whose uproar jars
The silence of sad Sphinx and pyramid,
Affronts the desert's solitude, and mars
The solemn mystery of millenniums hid
In unknown mountains under other stars,
Scared not the Spectre; pale and cold amid
  The rainbow throngs, the hum, the savage cries,
  It held me with its deep accusing eyes.

* Under favour of Göthe, who (having mentioned talismans) sings
    Amulete sind dergleichen
    Auf *Papier* geschriebne zeichen.
        —*West-östlicher Divan.*
  The term, however, has been commonly used in the wider sense.

"We crept upon the smooth Mid Sea; the air
Was feverous with Sirocco; the red sun
Burned fiercer for the haze that dimmed his glare;
All life drooped sick: yet in that hour begun
A fiery change for me,—the dull despair,
The pallor and the stagnant tarnish dun,
  Fermented with keen flames and flashes bright;
  New battle opened with a burst of light.

"The amulet, that had been dim and pale
As ghostly moon in northern night forlorn,
Dead-still and shrouded in a wan mist-veil,
Grew then blood-crimson as that high sun shorn
Of beams—that red hot cannon-ball; a wail,
A long keen passionate terrible cry was borne
  Rending the lethal dumbness; pierced, I sprang
  As if to grasp a foe who dealt the pang.

"Quivering with agony as blind as doom,
And rage as impotent as nightmare-sleep;
Restless as one who even in the tomb
Finds that malignant Memory will not steep
Her burning heart in the oblivious gloom;
I paced the deck; I glared athwart the deep,
  As if intense volition could enslave
  Your anchored isle to float across the wave.

"The day burned out sublimely in the West,
My soul was burning till the night was gone,—
Until the moon sank withering from heaven's crest
Before the fiery armies of the dawn,
Whose van was up with golden spears in rest;
And my sea calenture became a lawn—
  An English lawn, that loveliest lakelet green
  Guarding an English home of life serene.

"Ruthlessly brilliant as the crowded eyes
Of Roman ladies glittering down intent
On some barbarian's mortal agonies,
The stars thick-gathered in the firmament—
That amphitheatre of solemn skies
Round earth's arena dark with hot blood spent
  In so much barren and ignoble strife—
  Had gazed upon the Passion of my Life.

"The beautiful alien stars were pitiless
As bland white statues of the gods could be
To suppliants leaguered with the direst stress
Of earthquake, fire, or flood, or storm-swelled sea;
Gods unperturbed in their high happiness:
But the pure infant Dawn compassioned me;
  The day-spring bathed my fever in its balm,
  Divinely sweet and cool, divinely calm.

"And even as I felt its first sweet rest,
And knew myself once more alive and sane,
And yearned toward peaceful English homesteads blest
In looking out upon the waveless main;
Even in that instant from the far north-west,
Where like a pearl-grey cloudlet with no stain
  Malta grew visible, a swelling psalm
  Floated you on its rapture through the calm.

"Clad all in white, you Angel; crystal-bare
The feet that did not touch the sapphire sea;
Your head clothed only with its own rich hair,
Flowing dishevelled even to the knee;
God's dove athwart the deluge of despair
Bringing the blessing of the olive-tree:
  For you were radiant, and your brow's moon-splendour
  Shed on your glowing cheeks a veil most tender.

"You rested floating upright, when so near
That my stretched arm had almost reached the place;
Your vision swept the lonely hemisphere
As if with triumph in the ample space,
Then fixed on me, so that I felt you hear
My mute emotion; then, with glorious grace
  Leaning, you whispered: *'It is well, well, well!'*
  And vanished as my bosom's first breath fell.

"And from that moment it was well indeed
With me, and well grows better evermore;
Well on the white waves whitened by our speed,
Well in the gloaming on this lovely shore;
And ever well it must be now decreed,
Whatever yet the Future holds in store;
  Our love is fixed; therefore erect, elate,
  With awe, but with no fear, we welcome Fate."

When thus his tale was done, to him she told
What she had told her Mother on the morrow
Of that same night, whose wonders manifold
Transfigured two sick lives of fear and sorrow
Into twin raptures, rich with all the gold
That Earth could ever from Heaven's pathways borrow;
The nights were one, the solemn dawns were one,
Both triumphs mounted with the selfsame sun.

All she had told before she told to him,
And more that could be told to him alone;
And while the moon ventured its faery rim,
Then floated up the vague, he drank the tone
Of her low voice and marked her pure eyes swim
As on the vast vague sea of the Unknown,
Which floods and ebbs with infinite longing awe;
And kissed them back to earth's most tender law.

"Some night," she whispered, "when the moon shall be
As then a little later than to-night,
And self-withdrawn as then the quiet sea
Has left the sands to glitter in clear light;
And all the rock-strown shore around is free
From human presence and all else that might
The dread charm break, the secret spirit scare,
We two alone, my dearest, will go there.

"And we may hear a music, full of power
As the great sea with all its waves in storm,
Yet lovely as the purest lily-flower,
And mystic as the moonlight soft and warm;
And when the singing has entranced the hour
We may discover an immortal form,—
Glaucus, our sea-god reverend and benign,
Among the rocks that seem his ruined shrine.

"And we will kneel as one before him there;
And you shall utter all the gratitude
And reverence of both our hearts, which were
Too great for me to utter. If he should
But lay his hands with the old tender care
Upon our heads and bless us,—Oh that would
Make holier to us evermore the place
With antique pieties and natural grace!"

"Heathen of heathens! I am all unmanned;
Wicked as is your will, it must be done.
Good hap for me that this old sea-god bland,
And not the radiant Monarch of the Sun,
Met you and charmed you: think! I come to land,
And ask for Helen; they my asking shun;
  What strange sad sunflower haunts the garden's mouth?
  A modern Clytie yearning toward the South!"

These lovers have arisen, and have left,
Together gone into the night away;
And I seem standing on the shore, bereft,
Watching the weaving of the waves and spray,
But cannot weave into my halfspun weft
Another flower, or golden from the day
  Or purple from the night; for, day and night,
  In that moondusk they have evanished quite.

The lots are huddled in the fatal urn;
The fairest souls may draw the darkest doom,
And so long years their innate splendour burn
Struggling disastrously with stormy gloom:
Yet some fair souls find Fate and Chance not stern,
Their light has but to shine and not consume;
  God's vestals feeding the eternal flame
  In beautiful temples hallowed by His name.

The doom of these whom I have ever lost
I know not—whether calm as temple air,
Or wild as mountain-beacon tempest-tost;
Nor need we search it with an anxious care . . .
But one thread more the dusky loom has crossed,
Some lines in her own writing firm and fair;
  No date, no place; these pretty words above:
  "Two petals of our Fadeless Rose of Love."—

I.

"I went of late amid the dancing throng,
  To dance with *Him*—my Love who loveth me;
His whisper caught me up, 'How long, how long,
  Have I been seeking, desolate, for thee!
And now—Oh well a man might seek and trace
  For twenty lives, in hope at last to see
The perfect vision of this fairest face
  Of all fair faces in the world that be!

II.

" 'Such joy as our dark world has when the moon
  Comes floating sole and regnant in her skies;
Such joy to me, such glorifying boon,
  When one sole Presence floateth in my eyes.
More beautiful to-night than ever, Sweet,
  And yet most beautiful at every time:
How do you make perfection more complete?
  How leave like infancy the queenliest prime?

III.

" 'Upon my hopeless night your dawn arose;
  I said, The World can never be more bright:
Yet ever, more and more, the splendour grows,
  And leaves that dawn confused with ancient night.
I cry, This moment must be full-crowned noon!
  The moment brings new bursts of life and light!
No more! no more! my heart and spirit swoon
  In thine infinity of heavenly might!

IV.

" 'A dawn?—Your brow itself is what a dawn!
  Emerging from that Indian dusk of hair,
With all its poor pale pearl-stars backwithdrawn,
  The archèd Promise shines so proudly fair.
I find you out at last: you stir one tress,
  You let some young smile dream, you change a flower;
And straight you are transformed! O Sorceress
  And Queen of Spells, I tremble at your power!'

V.

"I went last night amid the dancing throng,
  To dance with *Him*—my Love who loveth me:
He sprang a-flush, 'How long, how long, how long!
  The twenty lives I waited here for thee!'
My dark-brown hair, the string of pearls, I wore,
  As when his praises flowed so royally:
'I bring the self-same spell that charmed before;
  To prove, indeed, your own inconstancy!'

VI.

"We stood together in the far recess:
  His noble eyes dilated full and bright,
With love triumphant throbbing happiness;
  He bent down o'er me from his stately height—
'How can our Queen, whose spirit sways the sun,
  Deign to enchant so mean a youth as this?
Of all her countless spells the weakest one
  Would trance him evermore in perfect bliss.

VII.

" 'Dear twilight mystery of hair, that now
  Art starred with pearls, I bid all night farewell;
Pure archèd Promise of the dawn-bright brow,
  The full noon neareth, grand as you foretell!'
He placed a kiss upon my brow and hair,
  His kiss of Love enthroned and glorified;
I felt it burning like a ruby there,
  The pallid pearl-gleams in its fulgence died:

VIII.

"I felt it flushing all my neck and face,
  What time we danced among the dancers free;
To all the youths and maidens in the place
  It signalled proudly of my Love and me:
It lights and warms me in my chamber now,
  It lights the world, the years, all things that be
A royal jewel sacred to my brow,
  A Splendour lamping all Eternity."

JERSEY, *Xmas 1861.*
LONDON, *July 1864.*

VERSIFICATION OF THOMAS COOPER'S ARGUMENT

IN A DEBATE ON THE EXISTENCE OF GOD BETWEEN THAT GENTLEMAN AND CHARLES BRADLAUGH

My poor friends, I come to you kindly,
With a brotherly kiss, not a rod;
For I know that sincerely, though blindly,
You look up in vain for a God.
For a very long time I have sought you—
Since we met last the years are now seven—
And here I have found you and brought you
My Ladder for climbing to Heaven.

My wonderful Ladder, that reaches
From Self here to God (be not vext);
Though its rungs are so few, and though each is
A quite simple step from the next.
For five years and eight months precisely
It has borne me to either extreme,
As cleverly, safely, and nicely
As those angels of Jacob's sweet dream.

You have seen a lamp-lighter at work, friends?
Well, just in his fashion I'll stop,
Set my Ladder, mount quick, give a jerk, friends,
And light up a God at the top.
And Bradlaugh, this ignorant fellow,
May pelt at my lamp as he likes
(Young fools often do so when mellow);
I wager no stone of his strikes.

I plant it on *I;* you can never
Persuade me *I* am not, now, here:
But as I have not been for ever,
I must have a Cause—that is clear.
And as *I* am a personal being,
Intelligent, conscious, I claim
That the stupidest cannot help seeing
My Cause must be ditto—the same.

Take another neat step: there is nowhere
Where Nothing at all can be found;
Wherever our thoughts go, they go where
Unlimited Something's around:
And the Cause of this infinite Something
Must be certainly infinite too;
For it would be a monstrous and rum thing
To fancy a finite would do.

So ourselves and the whole world of Matter
Have *one* Cause—for who would explore
(Without he was mad as a hatter)
Still backwards forever for more?
One cause, without cause, thus eternal;
And infinite, therefore the power
Of His will uncontrolled is supernal—
Omnipotence must be His dower.

And this all-wise, all-good, and almighty
Creator of spirit and clod,
At the top of my Ladder of light, He
It is whom we worship as God.
O my friends, is the climbing not easy?
And are not the steps safe and strong?
And how should my Ladder not please ye
When *I*'ve trusted to it so long?

O my luminous, logical Ladder,
My natural musical scale,
Whose notes swell up gladder and gladder
In glory and triumph—all hail!
The Cross, though a very good notion,
And on the whole rather divine,
Inspires no such fervid devotion
As doth this grand Ladder of mine.

P.S. penn'd for such as Truelove there
And Bradlaugh: My God in the sky
Is the little round dot up above there
Perfecting this neat little *i:*
For i wants the dot for completion,
But no dot is wanted by *u:*—
O Plato, much lecturing Grecian,
The Metempsychosis is true!

1864.

SIREN'S SONG

Realm of the sea! Listen to me,
  Rising up softly to sing you to rest;
Your queen and your love, your lily, your dove,
  Soothing with music your broad-heaving breast;
Guarding your isles from bad spirits' wiles,
  When the weary sun closes his lids in the west.
    What shall I sing you to-night?
  Listen and listen, the waters all glisten
    A-gaze on the ever-sweet moon:
      She gives you beauty of light,
    I give you the bountiful boon
  Of slumber-sweet singing so lovely and free,
      Delicious for glee.

All the sun-perfect day I dive and I play
  Adown through the azure and soft-yielding streams,
To the golden-green waves and the coralline caves
  And the pale purple bowers lit with clear crystal gleams;
Or I float swayed in rest, embraced and caressed
  In the mid-sea's entrancement of noon-languid dreams:
    Then in the night I may roam,
  Singing so sweetly, and chasing so featly
    The stars all a-dance in the deep;
      Or, like a beautiful foam,
    Ride up the shore on the sweep
  Of the long-sounding waves, and with wild laughs of glee
      Melt back to the sea.

Realm of the sea! Mighty and free!—
  None else can hear now—list to my sigh;
With a sweet love and dear do I charm you down here,
  As the moon with her love from on high;
And I reign all alone on my pearlèd throne
  As the moon in her star-gemmed sky:
    I ever-sole like the Moon!
  This is the sadness that fretteth my gladness—
    Oh! for a lover so dear!
      Oh! for love's bountiful boon!
    Ah! there is no one to hear:
  How I would love him, how happy were we,
      My realm of the sea!

[1864?]

AQUATICS (KEW)

Tommy Tucker came up to Kew,
And he got in a boat—an outrigger too:
O, but the pity, the pity!
For Tommy had made up his mind to show
His pals and the gals how well he could row.
Would he were safe in the city!

The thing like a cradle it rocked in the tide,
And he like the blessèd babby inside:
O, but the pity, the pity!
To hire out such shells so light and so slim,
Is cruel as murder, for Tommy can't swim.
Would he were safe in the city!

And why should they stick out the rowlocks that way?
He couldn't keep both hands together in play:
O, but the pity, the pity!
He spluttered, missed water, and zig-zag'd the boat,
Each pull made a lurch, brought his heart in his throat.
Would he were safe in the city!

The river was crowded behind and before,
They chaffed, and they laughed, and they splashed, and they swore:
O, but the pity, the pity!
He twisted his neck to attend to some shout,
A four-oared came rushing, *Confound you, look out!*
Would he were safe in the city!

They made him so nervous, those terrible men,
That he caught enough crabs for a supper of ten:
O, but the pity, the pity!
He crept back, a steamer came snorting astern,
With hundreds on deck—it gave him a turn:
Would he were safe in the city!

A mass of strange faces that all stared and laughed,
And the more Tommy flustered the more they all chaffed:
O, but the pity, the pity!
They passed him and roared out, *Head on to the swell!*
But he thought he would rather keep out of it well:
Would he were safe in the city!

So it caught him broadside, and rolled him away,
As a big dog rolls over a puppy in play:
O, but the pity, the pity!
It rolled him right over—*Good Heavens! he'll drown!*
For his arms they went up, and his head it went down.
Would he were safe in the city!

Three men dragged him out with a hook through his coat,
He was blue in the face and he writhed at the throat:
O, but the pity, the pity!
They hung his head down, he was limp as a clout,
But the water once in him refused to turn out:
Would he were safe in the city!

To the house by the bridge then they carried him in;
He was taken upstairs and stripped to the skin:
O, but the pity, the pity!
They wrapt him in blankets, he gave a low moan,
Then lay there as stark and cold as a stone:
Would he were safe in the city.

Then they forced down his throttle neat brandy galore,
He had taken the pledge, too, a fortnight before:
O, but the pity, the pity!
As it mixed with the water he woke in a fog,
For his belly was full of most excellent grog:
Would he were safe in the city!

He got very sick, then felt better, he said,
Though faintish, and nervous, and queer in the head:
O, but the pity, the pity!
He paid a big bill, and when it got dark
Went off with no wish to continue the lark:
Would he were safe in the city!

His coat was stitched up, but had shrunk away half,
And the legs of his trousers just reached to the calf:
O, but the pity, the pity!
No hat; they had stuck an old cap on his head;
And his watch couldn't tell him the time when he said:
Thank God I'm safe in the city!

1865.

LOW LIFE

AS OVERHEARD IN THE TRAIN.

That jolly old gentleman, bless his white hat!
Wouldn't come in to spoil our chat;
We are alone and we can speak,—
What have you done, Miss, all the week?

"Oh, all the day it's been fit and shew,
And all the night it's been trim and sew,
For the ladies are flocking to Exeter Hall
In lovely light dresses fit for a ball."

Under your eye a little dark streak,
And a point of red on the top of your cheek,
And your temples quite dim against your hair;
This sha'n't last very much longer I swear.

And what is the news from the workroom now?
"The week began with a bit of a row;
Emmy Harley married young Earl
Just in the busy time!"—sensible girl!

"That was on Monday; Missis said
It was very ungrateful, very ill-bred,
And very unkind to us when she knew
The work so heavy, the hands so few.

"But this was nothing: the minute we woke
On Wednesday, before it seemed any one spoke,
We knew that poor Mary Challis was dead;
Kate Long had been sleeping in the same bed.

"Mary worked with us till twelve, when tea
Was brought in to keep us awake, but she
Was so ill then, Miss Cooper sent her to bed;
And there in the morning they found her dead;

"With Kate fast asleep by her side: they had come
To see how she was, and the sight struck them dumb:
At last they roused Kate and led her away;
She was sick and shuddering all the day.

"Kate says when she went up at four to their room
She was stupid with sleep; but she marked a faint bloom
On Mary's pale face, and she heard her breathe low—
A light fluttering breath now quick and now slow;

"And feared to disturb her, for *she* had a cough,
But the moment she laid her head down she was off,
And knew nothing more till they stood by the side
Of the bed: p'r'aps Mary slept on till she died.

"They buried her yesterday. Kate was there,
And she was the only one Missis could spare;
Some dresses were bound to be finished by night,
For the ladies to go in to Church all right.

"Poor Mary! she didn't fear dying, she said,
Her father drinks and her mother is dead;
But she hoped that in Heaven the white garments wear
For ever; no fashions and dressmaking There."

My Love, if the ladies most pious of all
Who flock to the Church and to Exeter Hall
Find Heaven has but one dress for rich as for poor,
And no fashions, they'll very soon cut it I'm sure.

I saw you ten minutes on Tuesday night,
Then I took the 'bus home for I had to write;
And I wrote and I wrote like an engine till five,
When my fingers were dead and the letters alive.

A fair bill of costs from a deuce of a draft
In our Cashier's worst scrawl like Chinese ran daft;
With entries between, on the margin, the back,
And figures like short-hand marks put to the rack.

But our Common-law Clerk is going away,
And the Gov'nor had me in yesterday,
And said he would try me, he thought I might do;
And I jumped at the chance, for this child thinks so too.

Just fancy, each morning a jolly good walk,
And instead of the copying, bustle and talk!
And if I do well—and well I will do—
A couple of sovs. a week for my screw!

And then when I'm free of the desk and the stool,
Do you think you will keep to the nunnery rule
Of the shop, till you go off like Mary some night
Smothered in work from the air and the light?

We'll use our professional talents, my dear:
You shall make such a wedding dress, best of the year!
And a wonderful marriage-deed I will draw
With magnificent settlements perfect in law,

Thus doing our duties in those states of life
In which it has pleased God to call us, *my wife!*
"And how much a year will you settle on me?"
My body and soul and—what we shall see.

1865.

ONCE IN A SAINTLY PASSION

Once in a saintly passion
  I cried with desperate grief,
"O Lord, my heart is black with guile,
  Of sinners I am chief."
Then stooped my guardian angel
  And whispered from behind,
"Vanity, my little man,
  You're nothing of the kind."

1865.

ON THE TERRACE AT RICHMOND

Fixed to a tall stem like a mast,
A board with certain rhymes
Here overlooked the vale and stream:
Where is it in these times?

The lines were scarcely of the best;
Not one can I recall;
The board looked like a board of rules
Against a workhouse wall.

Yet they were meant to honour one
Who honour merited;
A gentle heart and free from guile,
A poet long since dead.

My great-great-grandfather he was,
Although no child had he;
Yet as the lineal heir I'm blessed
With all the property:—

The Castle hight of Indolence,
And all the rich domain
Which to that Castle and its Lords
Doth ever appertain;

Thereto a noble royalty
Of rhymes and various verse,—
The quantity is now much less
The quality much worse.

The Castle is so beautiful,
The land so rich and wide;
Such sweet birds sing, such sweet flowers spring,
Such silver streamlets glide!

The Landlord and the Tenants all
Are far too indolent
For that which troubles most estates,
The payment of a rent.

II.

You're not quite sure you ever heard
  This pleasant poet's name?
But you will like him womanlike
  Since someone bears the same?

I'm sure you never read a page
  Of anything he wrote;
I'm sure for all his books of verse
  You would not care a groat.

Were I to read you some, of course
  You'd make a fine pretense,
How pretty! pleased to see me pleased,
  Not caring for the sense.

And you are right: Doth Lycidas
  Leave Milton's tome and urge
Young Adonais to recite
  His supramortal dirge?

Do roses gaze on pictured walls
  Where scentless roses bloom?
Do stars read sonnets where we praise
  Their shining through the gloom?

Sweet living Poem! Why should you
  Read dull dead words that shrine
Dim echoes of your voice, rude hints
  Of your own grace divine?

III.

The Castle hight of Indolence
  Holds many pictures fair;
And many portraits with his own
  The Architect placed there.

But one grand portrait lacked, alack!
  And in his secret Will
He gave his heirs a solemn charge
  This mighty void to fill.

The Portrait of the very Lord
  Of all the Lords who sway
The Castle and its happy realms
  Was wanting to this day!

He ever lives, this Lord supreme,
  In many a quaint disguise;
Full hard to meet, and then when met
  Full hard to recognise.

I met him, knew him, loved him well;
  For me he dropped his mask;
To place his portrait in our Hall
  Has been my pleasant task.

Here is the sketch,—how thin and blurred!
  He dreams, beyond desire,
Clothed with the ninefold robes of verse
  Loved by our Eastern Sire.

1865.

WILLIAM BLAKE

He came to the desert of London town
  Grey miles long;
He wandered up and he wandered down,
  Singing a quiet song.

He came to the desert of London town,
  Mirk miles broad;
He wandered up and he wandered down,
  Ever alone with God.

There were thousands and thousands of human kind
  In this desert of brick and stone:
But some were deaf and some were blind,
  And he was there alone.

At length the good hour came; he died
  As he had lived, alone:
He was not missed from the desert wide,
  Perhaps he was found at the Throne.

1866.

MR. MACCALL AT CLEVELAND HALL

(April 15, 1866)

Mr. Maccall at Cleveland Hall,
Sunday evening—date to fix—
Fifteenth April, sixty-six,
Speech reported and redacted
By a fellow much distracted.

I.

Who lectures? No mere scorner;
Clear-brained, his heart is warm.

She sits at the nearest corner
Of I will not say what form.

II.

The Conflict of Opinions
In the Present Day, saith Chair.

What muff in the British dominions
Could dispute that she is fair?

III.

Mammon-worship is horrid,
Plutocracy is base.

Dark hair from a fine small forehead;
I catch but the still side face.

IV.

We wallow in mere dimension,
The Big to us is Great.

If she stood at her utmost tension
She *might* pass four feet eight.

V.

We lay on colour in splashes,
With a mop, or a broom for brush.

How dark are her long eyelashes!
How pure is her cheek's slight flush!

VI.

But we have no perception
  For form—the divinest—now.

Each curve there is perfection,
  In nostril, chin, and brow.

VII.

Our women are good kind creatures,
  But they cannot dress at all.

Does her bonnet grace her features?—
  Clear blue with a black lace fall.

VIII.

Low Church—very low—in the gutter;
  High Church—as ven'son high.

O'er the flower of her face gleams the flutter
  Of a smile like a butterfly.

IX.

Herder, Wieland, Lessing;
  Bossuet, Montalembert.

Fine names, but the name worth guessing
  Is the name of the sweet girl there.

X.

The individual; true man;
  Individuality.

A man's but one half; some woman
  The other half must be.

XI.

Persistent valour the sternest,
  With love's most gentle grace.

How grand is the eye fixed earnest
  In the half-seen up-turned face!

XII.

"How did you like the lecture?
  Was it not beautiful?"

I should think *she was!* "I conjecture
  That your brains have been gathering wool!"

P.S.

The Chairman was a rare man;
  At every telling point
He smiled at his post like a jolly host
  Carving rich cuts from the joint;
Which the name he bore was Richard Moore
  Whom Heaven with grace anoint!

That conflict of opinion
  It had its counterpart
In conflict for dominion
  Between my head and heart.

April 16, 1866.

DON GIOVANNI AT COVENT GARDEN

Who is this appealing, with archly tender feeling,
  To that sturdy rustic as sullen as a boar?
Sweet Zerlina Patti singing *Batti, batti;*
  Rustical Masetto sulking sulking more and more.

Enviable peasant! sulking must be pleasant
  Feasted with such beauty, such caresses and such art;
Adelina Patti singing *Batti, batti,*
  Soul and body singing with the voice that sings Mozart.

By that sweet love's token, even had she broken
  All the ten commandments and twice as many more,
I would cry, Dear Patti, singing *Batti, batti,*
  Sin and sing, you angel, sin and sing *encore!*

Darling young Zerlina, charming Adelina,
  Long be you the Hebe of this heavenly music-wine;
First, O Patti, Patti, pouring *Batti, batti,*
  Then *Vedrai carino,* the nectar more divine!

June 8, 1866.

VERSICLES

Wherever on this round earth
Your shaft shall enter,
Strike it straight, and never fear
But you'll reach at last the centre.

———

Each doth by his birth belong
To some sphere wherein he's strong;
Nine of ten with passion seek
Alien spheres wherein they're weak;
Whence in almost every man
Such incongruous *Will* and *Can.*

———

Dear Mother Earth, tell us, tell us, tell us!
What is the meaning of all the things we see?—
Oh! what a family of puny little fellows,
Calling me always, *Tellus, Tellus, Tellus!*
Eat your bread, drink your wine, snatch at all you see;
But I am very busy, do not bother me.

November 1866.

ON GEORGE HERBERT'S POEMS

What are these leaves dark-spotted and acerb?
"A very holy *herb:*"
To what good use may I this herb convert?
"Press it on thy soul's *hurt:*"
When *herb* unto the *hurt* I thus apply?
"*Herb-ert* is sanctity."

[1866?]

THE PAN-ANGLICAN SYNOD

Is it prudence? is it courage? is it fear?
  Our bishops have avoided quite
All notice of the things most clear
  To everybody's sight—
The wild waste rocks that rear
  Round the church-ship left and right;
The black storm-clouds that near
  With the fast approaching night;
The desperate privateer,
  Lurking in every bight;
The mutinous growl and jeer,
  The plots in broad daylight
Of the crew, only fit, we hear,
  Among themselves to fight:
The needle so ready to veer
  To any point but the right;
The helm that will not steer,
  And the anchors that will not bite;
The leaks, while the pumping gear,
  Is all in a useless plight;
The guns that would burst up sheer
  If ever the powder would light;
The cry of the engineer,
  That he works in a constant fright;
The water as muddy as beer,
  The provisions all mildew and blight;
Yet they sit in solemn cheer,
  And they plan with sweet delight
Voyages round the sphere,
  Commerce with black and white;
And profits that grow every year,
  Till at length they will reach such a height,
That this whole little world down here
  Shall seem an estate very slight,
And a mansion in Heaven shall appear
  The fit home for each fortunate wight!
You may fleer, you may leer, you may sneer,
  Ishmaelite! they are quite in the right;
A bishop is an overseer;
  Our bishops have immense oversight.

1867.

L'ENVOY *

When the sixties are outrun,
And the seventies nearly done,
Or the eighties just begun;
May some young and happy man,
Wiser, kinder, nobler than
He who tenders this one, bring
You the real Magic Ring.

This one may have pleasant powers;
Charming idle girlish hours
With its tales from færie bowers;
Tinting hopeful maiden dreams
With its soft romantic gleams;
Breathing love of love and truth,
Valour, innocence and ruth.

But may that one bless the life
Of the woman and the wife
Through our dull world's care and strife;
Year by year with rich increase,
Give you love, and joy, and peace;
And at last the good death bring,
Sweet as sleep: your Magic Ring.

December 1868.

"BETTER THE LOVE OF A WOMAN" †

Better the love of a woman you love,
  Better a myriad times,
Than all the fame that ever came
  From grandest prose or rhymes.

1869.

* [Written on the fly-leaf of *La Motte Fouqué's* "Magic Ring," given at Christmas time by Thomson to Mr. Bradlaugh's daughter Hypatia, then ten years old.]

† [This and the following fragment are from Thomson's essay "A National Reformer in the Dog-Days."]

"WHO BUT A FOOL"

Who but a fool of his free will
Would write mere prose, or well or ill,
Of his free will would write mere prose
During the season of the rose?
None but a fool would thus write prose
During the season of the rose.

1869.

SUNDAY { LILAH, * ALICE, HYPATIA } 14/2/69.

Who was Lilah? I am sure
She was young and sweet and pure;
With the forehead wise men love,—
Here a lucid dawn above
Broad curved brows, and twilight there,
Under the deep dusk of hair.

And her eyes? I cannot say
Whether brown, or blue, or grey:
I have seen them brown, and blue,
And a soft green grey—the hue
Shakespeare loved (and he was wise),
"Grey as glass" were Silvia's eyes.

So to Lilah's name above
I will add two names I love,
Linking with the bracket curls
Three sweet names of three sweet girls,
Sunday of Saint Valentine,
Eighteen hundred sixty nine.

* [Thomson bought a second-hand copy of La Motte Fouqué's *Undine*, with the name "Lilah" already inscribed in the middle of the front page. With this he bracketed the two other names, and, adding these lines, gave the book to the little girls, "Alice" and "Hypatia."]

SUPPLEMENT TO THE INFERNO

I.—RELATING TO THE APOTHEOSIS OF A NOBLE UNIVERSAL GENIUS. *

(See especially opening of Canto V., and close of Canto XXI.)

"A Great Soul! A great bladder for dried peas to rattle in."
—GEORGE ELIOT, *Middlemarch.*

Ere we left Minos after parleying
To trace the second circle's storm of gloom,
There came with haughty strides a monstrous Thing

Among the spirits crowding for their doom:
I ween that when it crossed in Charon's boat
No other freightage in that boat found room.

Who, what art thou, roared hard the judge's throat,
More hugeous than my grandson's fierce man-bull?
The thing swelled chanting on a lofty note:

I am a poet of the Beautiful,
Priest of the Good, and Prophet of the True;
Clothed thick with glory as a sheep with wool:

I sole have done what twenty great men do;
Historian, statesman, orator and sage,
Wit, dramatist, and Fiction's master, who

Have pictured every clime and every age,
Have written everything in every style,
And read the Tome of Thought through page by page:

The Pilgrim-Genius, travelling mile by mile,
This orbèd whole of Matter and Idea,
Is comprehensive and not versatile;

And I—Be damned! Great Jove, did e'er one see a
Creature like this 'mong men or beasts or birds?
A dictionary with the diarrhœa

Could hardly spout such feculent flux of words:
Strip, strip; I cannot judge you till I know
What core of life this shaggy bulk engirds.

* [In this poem Thomson satirizes Edward Robert Lytton Bulwer-Lytton, First Earl of Lytton, who published several collections of poetry under the name Owen Meredith.]

The thing screamed: Aï! Aï! ever woe
For the Promethean-souled; uncomprehended
By men on earth, abhorred by fiends below,

Pursued with fear and jealous anger blended
By the monopolising Gods above!
Be firm, O Titan heart, thou unbefriended;

Nor sour the sweetness of thy solemn love
For the Illimitable Fathomless,
Wherein the eagle droops as droops the dove,

With thought of gnats that sting thy nakedness!—
Strip naked first! snarled Minos; and the Shapeless Shape
Must piece by piece cast off its wondrous dress:

Cloak, tunic, surplice, toga, mantle, cape,
Hood, bonnet, hat, boot, slipper, buskin, sock,
Bulged slowly to a heap that well might drape

A college of professors with their flock,
And furnish 'guises for a masquerade,
And still leave six old clo'-men ample stock.

The process went on till we grew dismayed;
The Bulk and Voice together dwindling down:
And when at intervals the sad work stayed

For desperate protests, Minos with his frown
And snarl of Strip, strip! urgent as a whip,
Compelled renewal. Ah me! take a brown

Ripe Spanish onion, and proceed to strip
It very patiently fold after fold;
So small at length you'll find the central pip,

So large the volume of the swathes unrolled;
And even so through piteous tears your eyes
That core when reached but dimly will behold.

But soon my tears were dashed off by surprise:
The Kernel of that Shapeless Shape hopped there
Upon its mount of cloth of many dyes,

A restless bladder-skin distent with air,
And sundry pebbles or baked peas within
That rattled as it danced. Then Minos sware,

The while some humour curled his savage grin:
I sit to judge real living human souls,
Not lively windbags: now you next, begin:

And went on with his calling o'er the coals
As who would make up for lost time. I said,
How gayly, Master dear, it leaps and rolls

Unto its own dry rhythmus, quick or dead:
Where are the Good, the Beautiful, the True?
Whither have Wisdom, Wit and Genius fled?

And he: That heap of clothes must answer you;
I can't think how it ever made them fit on,
For they are of all fashions old and new,

And of all sizes: whensoe'er it lit on
Garments which to its fancy beautiful were
Of Greek, Jew, Roman, German, Gaul or Briton;

And whether they of linen, silk or wool were
It must have begged or filched them for its pile,
Till froggy swelled as large as if it bull were:

Mark well, those peas which frisk in rapid style
From point to point within the orbèd bladder
Are comprehensive and not versatile.

Then I who always in his smile grew gladder
Said: Master, ere in this we touch the ground
Behoves another step down reason's ladder:

Dried peas within, a tumid film around,
Which call you soul, or essence of this wonder?
And He: Its soul is hollowness with sound;

While it exists these two can never sunder;
The selfsame soul in bladder and balloon,
In thin pea-rattle and in far-heard thunder:

When thou revisitest the sun and moon
Remember this, and pay no heed at all
To bulks of noisy emptiness. As soon

As he had spoken an outreaching squall
From the great cyclone of that second cirque
Scattered the robes and bore away the ball,

Which soon was lost to vision in the mirk;
And so I thought Its spurious being ended,
And quite forgot it in our serious work.

But often afterwards as we descended
It flitted past us like a twilight bat,
And seemed to hover wheresoe'er we wended;

As if endowed with more lives than a cat,
Or by its very want of substance safe,
Dancing upon the tempest which laid flat

Substantial human souls; and it would chafe
With its most arid noise our ears intent
On solemn words of sinners. Thus the waif

Annoyed us much throughout our sad descent
Until we stood anear that broken bridge
In Malebolge, where the demon lent

Us demon escort to the farther ridge.
* Just as he blew the signal to set out,
The bladder, flung abruptly as a midge

Against the troop, became a silent clout,
Collapsing pierced by Graffiacave's hook;
Who wheeling his third step faced right about

And held it forth to Malacoda: Look!
If thy sweet lips are moist with trumpeting,
Here is a rag to wipe them! and he took.

We saw no more of that preposterous Thing.

May 1870.

* "Et egli avea del cul fatto trombetta."—A verse too easy to translate. Note that the austere Dante so enjoys this Aristophanic touch that he chuckles over it, not grimly, through twelve lines of grave burlesque opening the following Canto XXII., the only case of such self-indulgence I remember in the *Divine Comedy*.

"I CURSE THE EVIL" *

I curse the evil and disgrace
  Which have my birth defiled,
Who would have been in other case
  A happy Muslim child!

1876.

SONG

"The Nightingale was not yet heard,
    For the Rose was not yet blown." †
His heart was quiet as a bird
    Asleep in the night alone,
And never were its pulses stirred
    To breathe or joy or moan:
The Nightingale was not yet heard
    For the Rose was not yet blown.

Then She bloomed forth before his sight
    In passion and in power,
And filled the very day with light,
    So glorious was her dower;
And made the whole vast moonlit night
    As fragrant as a bower:
The young, the beautiful, the bright,
    The splendid peerless Flower.

Whereon his heart was like a bird
    When Summer mounts his throne,
And all its pulses thrilled and stirred
    To songs of joy and moan,
To every most impassioned word
    And most impassioned tone;
The Nightingale at length was heard
    For the Rose at length was blown.

February 1877.

* [From Thomson's essay "Some Muslim Laws and Beliefs." The verse parodies the hymn by Isaac Watts: "I thank the goodness and the grace / Which on my birth have smiled, / And made me in these Christian days / A happy English child."]

† "Traveller in Persia" (Mr. Binning); cited by Mr. Fitzgerald in the notes to his translation of Omar Khayyam.

"I HAD A LOVE"

I had a Love; it was so long ago,
      So many long sad years:
She died; and then a waste of arid woe,
      Never refreshed by tears:
She died so young, so tender, pure and fair;
I wandered in the Desert of Despair.

What kept me then from following my Love?
      I ask in drear amaze;
What held me wingless from my flying Dove,
      To tread Life's barren ways?
What drugged my keen intent, for bale or bliss,
To sink or soar in Death's most dark abyss?

How have I lived in this tremendous waste,
      So long, so lone, so lorn?
No well-springs for my soul, no food to taste
      For my poor heart forlorn;
No Love, no Faith, no Hope to pass the Sands
And sojourn in the friendly fruitful lands.

My heart hath fed upon itself, reply,
      The bitter, poisoned meat!
My soul hath drunk its own scant sources dry,
      Bitter as blood; my feet
Have trodden their old footsteps year by year,
Circling for ever in the desert drear.

Upon the burning sands and bruising stones
      I plod the pathless ways;
Of all my fellow-creatures dry bleached bones
      Are all that meet my gaze,
Or men and camels dying or just dead
With eager vultures hanging overhead.

Whereon my weary feet and famished heart
      Whereon my wasted brain
Would of that carrion banquet make a part,
      Would perish there full fain;
But we are goaded by some goad unblest
From such long-wished-for everlasting rest.

Songs in the desert! Songs of husky breath,
    And undivine Despair;
Songs that are dirges, but for Life not Death,
    Songs that infect the air
Have sweetened bitterly my food and wine,
The heart corroded and the Dead Sea brine.

How strange! we can confront the direst grief
    Erect, and scarcely quail,
If we can only have the poor relief
    Of uttering our bale,
In music, sculpture, painting, verse or prose,
Who else were crushed beneath the heavy woes.

So potent is the Word, the Lord of Life,
    And so tenacious Art,
Whose instinct urges to perpetual strife
    With Death, Life's counterpart:
The magic of their music, might and light
Can keep one living in his own despite.

Their splendours cleave the deep sepulchral glooms,
    Revive the ancient dead;
They build high palaces of lowly tombs
    Wherein high lives are led;
Funereal black to royal purple glows,
And corpses stand up Kings from long repose.

And yet, my Love, I do not know a night
    Since first you left me here,
I had not welcomed with serene delight
    A Voice authentic, clear:
Go sleep, go sleep, thy long day's travail done;
Thou shalt not wake to see another sun.

Ah Love, my Love, with what perpetual moan,
    While yet I half believed
That you were radiant by the Heavenly Throne,
    From all Earth's pains retrieved,
My weak and selfish desolate heart did pine
To have you back here from the realm divine.

You would have kept me from the Desert sands
Bestrewn with bleaching bones,
And led me through the friendly fertile lands,
And changed my weary moans
To hymns of triumph and enraptured love,
And made our earth as rich as Heaven above.

But now, my only Love, when I must see
You are no more, no more;
As I and every living thing shall be
When pushed off from the shore
Of narrow Life into the Dead Sea waves,
Those never-satiate unsurrendering graves:

Now, when I see that we are all resolved
Into the Universe
Whence so mysteriously we were evolved;
That all our parts disperse
Never to build our very selves again,
Though roses spring from roses, men from men:

Now, when I see that all our little race
Must have its death as birth;
Motes in infinities of Time and Space,
Less lasting than our Earth,
This many-insect-peopled drop of dew
Exhaling in a moment from the view:

Yea, now that I have learnt by grievous thought
Something of Life and Death;
And how the one is like the other, naught,
Except for painful breath;
And now that I have learnt with infinite toil
To know myself, involved in such a coil:

Why, if there were a living God indeed,
And I should hear His Voice:
"Her death shall be abolished for thy need,
That ye may both rejoice;
She shall come back as young as when she died
To thee as young, fit bridegroom for such bride:

"And ye shall live together man and wife
Unto a reverend age;
And love shall be your balm in grief and strife
Whatever wars may rage;
And young ones fill your home with tender cheer
And keep your name green when yourselves are sere."

I would reply: "Lord of the Universe!
Pity and pardon now!
I shudder from this blessing as a curse;
Down to the dust I bow,
And from my inmost spirit supplicate
Thou wilt be pleased to alter not our fate.

"For she has perfect and eternal rest,
She is not evermore,
Save as an image graven in my breast;
And I am near the shore
Of that Dead Sea where we find end of woes
Unconsciousness, oblivion, full repose.

"I would not tear her from her resting-place
For any human bliss;
I would not one of my past years retrace
Who seek the black abyss;
I would not have the burden on my soul
Of bringing babes into this world of dole."

Yes Love, my Love, dissolved so long ago,
Alive but in my heart,
It gives me solace now instead of woe,
Sweet joy instead of smart,
To brood and murmur in my desert bare:
She died so young, so tender, pure and fair.

And I have comfort that its own good time
Must now at length be near:
How Life is piteous, and how Death sublime!
O World of doubt and fear,
Of mystery, grief and yearning that appal,
Why were we ever brought to life at all?

What profit from all life that lives on Earth,
    What good, what use, what aim?
What compensation for the throes of birth
    And death in all its frame?
What conscious life has ever paid its cost?
From Nothingness to Nothingness—all lost! *

1878.

CREEDS AND MEN

Two hosts received me in one day,
And poured their best to greet my stay;
The bottles, labels, seals were twins
Alike as penalties and sins:
Yet one flowed forth the richest wine;
The other acid, gall, and brine.

Two hosts received me the next day,
And poured their best to greet my stay;
The bottles, labels, seals in sooth
Unlike as falsehood unto truth:
Yet both flowed forth a liberal wine
Of festal jubilance divine.

Seals, labels, bottles are but vain;
Regard the spirit they contain.

*   *   *   *

A poor gin-bottle I found one day,
Full of the wine of rich Tokay;
A Tokay-bottle I found, within
Only the vilest vitriol gin:
No more of the outward form I ask,
But, what is the spirit that fills the flask?

1878.

* [Thomson's manuscript contains the following note at the end of the poem:

"Writing the foregoing lines I have felt like a man making his Will at the gates of Death, summing up Life's scores and settling accounts when about to leave its inn. Yet I do not truly feel very near to Death, for with a seeming partial revival of the creative energies, in thought and imagination, it is impossible to realise death, even when absorbed by its sombre fascination. It may be merely the throes of some new birth that give the lethal illusion; for birth is so like death.

"I do not hate a single man alive,
    Some few I must disdain;
I have loved heartily some four or five,
    And of these there remain
Just two, I think, for whom I would outface
Death gladly; for the one, death and disgrace."]

THE PILGRIMAGE TO SAINT NICOTINE

OF THE HOLY HERB

PART I.

THE PILGRIMS.

Behold our Pilgrims how they shine
Upon their Pilgrimage divine
Unto the wonder-working Shrine
Of sacrosanct SAINT NICOTINE.

In every country and in every age
Have men been wont to go on pilgrimage,
As I have read,—each visiting that shrine
Which seems to him most blessed and divine;
Athwart far lands, athwart the wild sea foam:
Some to Jerusalem, and some to Rome;
And some to Lourdes,—*très lourdes, très lourdes* God wot,
Les pauvres âmes which seek *that* sacred spot;
And some to Santiago far in Spain,
Anear the roar of the Atlantic main;
And some unto our Lady of Lorette,—
Full many votaries this Dame doth get:
The very Paynims bring their vows and prayers
To Mecca and to Yeddo and Benares:
While others piously seek out the tombs
Of mighty men who have fulfilled their dooms,
The fields where battles long ago were fought,
The scenes wherever wondrous works were wrought,
The sites of antique cities overthrown,
The fanes of fair gods dead and turned to stone:—
What need write more? when saint and bard and sage
Declare our whole life but one Pilgrimage;
A journey from the cradle to the bier
Of all the restless millions wandering here;
A toilsome travel of all things alive
Unto the Temple where they all arrive,
And bowing down before the Shrine of Death
Find peace at last in breathing their last breath.

But furthermore thus teacheth the wise man;
That age by age our human caravan
Is like unto all those that went before
And all that shall come after evermore:
New names, new robes, new thoughts and words and deeds,
New toys and treasures, sciences and creeds
But ever the same passions and same needs:
The same old Drama on the same old Stage,
The same old tears and laughters, joy and rage;
The selfsame characters upon the Scene,
Wise, foolish, rich and poor, and great and mean
Old actors fall away with weary hearts,
Fresh actors come to take the selfsame parts;
And whosoe'er the destined rôles may fill,
Hamlet is Hamlet—Osric, Osric still;
And ever with the fifth act come the knaves
To vent their clownish jests and dig the graves;
And ever with the last scene entereth
Some princely one demanding—"O proud death,
What feast is toward in thine eternal cell?"
And so the Play is over: very well,
It shall be played again, and have a run,
Coëval with the earth's around the sun.

Lo this is what men call philosophie,
Whereof I know not anything perdie,
But it hath brought us to our proper theme,
Our CARD of beauty and of joy supreme,
Our peerless PILGRIMAGE unto the SHRINE
Of most beneficent SAINT NICOTINE.
Five hundred years agone DAN CHAUCER went
A-riding through the pleasant lanes of Kent,
In April on the eight and twentieth day,
Which were with us I ween a week in May, *

* There has been much learned astronomical discussion, of dubious import, about the exact time of the year, as indicated in the opening of the Prologue to the "Canterbury Tales." If the deep scientific gentlemen engaged had but condescended to look forward to the Man of Law's Prologue they might have read in the beginning thereof—

"And though he [the host] were not depe expert in lore,
He wiste it was the eighte and twenty day
Of April, that is messager to May."

This may suffice to fix the date accurately enough for us who are not astronomers. The Old Style, I suppose, would then be about eight days behind the New, as the difference I believe increases three days in every four centuries (one in each of the three which is not a multiple of four), and was eleven days in 1752, when the New Style was adopted in England (we all know how the populace vociferously demanded the eleven days of which they conceived themselves defrauded): the Russians, who keep to the Old Style, now date twelve days behind us. Thus Chaucer's April 28 would be our May 6. In reading Herrick and his contemporaries on the delights of going a-Maying, we are apt to forget that their May-day the 1st was our 11th; so with many old weather proverbs.

He and his compagnie of twenty-nine,
Both men and women, to the holy shrine
Of Him by hot Knights at the altar slain,
And now by Master Froude killed over again
All in cold blood; alas! a piteous doom,
Sword-pierced in life and pen-pierced in the tomb:
But Master Freeman now hath set to work
To maul this Froude as if he were a Turk;
And he who kicked A'Becket as he lay
Is like to kick the bucket in this fray.
This compagnie it was of all degrees,
The high, the low, the midway; and all these,
Yea, each and all, our POET doth rehearse
And picture lifelike in his cordial verse;
As sweet and rath as his own daisy was
"Upon the smalè, softè, swotè gras,"
As rich and free and cheerful as the gush
Of gratulation from a mid-June thrush:
I rede you read him once and twice and thrice,
And over again; it is my boon advice;
And learn what all these men and women were
In mind and body, state and garb and air;
And feel what full red-blooded life did flow
Thorough their veins five hundred years ago;
And find what Tales they told upon their way
Of noble tragedy and jolly play;
And see that we are now what they were then,
Since fashions change, not women, neither men.

What this first Poet, whom we love so well,
Of merrie England, in his verse did tell
Of these glad Pilgrims, both their mind and make,
That Artist of the Visions clepèd BLAKE,
Who also sang delightful young-world songs,
Soaring aloof from all our old-world wrongs,
Did picture forth with pencil and engrave,
Form after form to match the POET brave:
We touch not him, for he was grand and wild;
We leave this giant who became a child
A graceful limner, STOTHARD was his name,
Did set himself to enterprise the same,
And him we follow in our noble CARD;
But whereas he went backward to the BARD
Through all the centuries, to match his rhyme,
We choose our Pilgrims from our very time:
For why? our SAINT is not the Saint of old,
But hath more votaries a hundredfold;
Lo you shall hear of him anon, but first

Behoves the jolly Pilgrims be rehearsed;
New Saint, New Pilgrims, but the counterparts
Of CHAUCER's rout *en route* in brains and hearts.

Now first of all the many-hued array
We look at him who leadeth them the way;
Though he is of the Highlands and the Greeks
He rides not in the kilts but tartan breeks,
And blows his Gaelic pipes full loud and shrill;
Our Miller [1] who rejoiceth in a mill;
Perfervid and pugnacious, keen and spry;
Wherefore men call him Blackie or Black-eye.
And next to him there rides our jolly Host [2],
Dhudeen in hand; I wis his very ghost
Were fatter than full many a man we see,
So that O'Gormandiser he might be;
He keepeth the great House in right good cheer,
So may he keep it many and many a year;
He makes his Home Rule pleasant, for he glories
In fine old whisky and in fine old stories.
Our Doctor [3] then, who surely is no gull,
And recketh not the eyelids of a skull
When people cry upon his path Bravo!
Whether they mean it for a fleer or no.
Our Merchant [4] who doth sit in Parliament,
And dealeth more and morely in dissent;
The dis. may be the discount for his pains,
The cent. the poor per centum of his gains.
Our Man of Law [5] most eloquent and wise,
And merrie as a lark in April skies:
A hugeous fat man weighed upon him long
Like him on Sinbad; but he was so strong,
He heaved this bulk of bad sin right away
To Dartmoor—would it had been Plymouth Bay.
Our Franklin [6] is transformed into an Earl,
With large face set in triple sausage curl;
No proverb-fed "Poor Richard" Franklin he,
This pious warder of the fair Ladye,
Whose jewels suffering a slight subtraction
By some one in a fit of deep abstraction,
Our thane announced reward to the adept,
No questions asked, the secret safely kept,
The trinkets for an honest thousand pounds;
Thus a *grand seigneur* felonie compounds:
For which the hot *Times* thunder fell on him:
As if a great man should subject his whim
Or private interest to the common law
Made to keep common men, poor serfs, in awe!

And were not free to feed his mordant humours,
Despite all Grub-street grubs that live on rumours!

And now we reach the noblest in our Knight [7],
Grey with great deeds, a hero wise and wight:
For he hath followed Cromwell through the wars
Of middle England, and upon the shores
Of Scotland and of Ireland; sans demur
Foes got a Roland for their Oliver:
And he hath swayed his mighty sword and lance
With Fritz the Only; and again in France
Fought through the whole wild Revolution time:
But where hath he not fought in youth and prime
And strenuous age? What hath he not endured?
And what hath he not conquered? Well-assured
His fame shall live; and he is called Carlyle,
That is, the doughtiest carle in all our isle.
Him followeth his loyal Squire [9]; and he
Hath wrought brave things in Venice of the Sea,
And many another spot; by lakes and fountains,
And wreathed with clouds and snows on Alpine mountains,
In many a wild wood green and windy gorge;
He rideth ramping like a new St. George,
His style embroidered "as it were a mede
Al ful of fresshè flourès white and rede:"
Beneath his horse a scurvy wretch is sprawling,
With vast jaws open for a monstrous bawling;
A lank and long-eared mar-joy, mainly bent
On shuffling through the sloughs of discontent;
Incapable of pleasure even in pelf,
He'd have all others wretched as himself;
A blatant brawler, bilious and bad-blooded,
With heart, mind, soul and sense all muddle-muddied;
An Anti sour 'gainst all things sweet and good,
Who'd make earth ante-hell an if he could,
Whose head is wooden and himself stark wood; *
A puny infidel to our sweet Saint:
There let the horses kick him till he faint;
Why should he come a-lying by the way
In hopes to disarrange our fair array?
And then the Yeoman [15], bearing that long bow
He drew for Harry and for many mo;
And drew against the loveliest Queen of Scots,
Ever intent to try to hit the blots;
Let us ignore what this may have of rude,
The spite is but his femininitude.

---

* *Wood* here means *mad*.—PRINTER'S DEVIL.

The Pilgrimage to Saint Nicotine of the Holy Herb
John Wallace ("George Pipeshank"), 1878
Image reprinted courtesy of David Levy.
For identification of personages, see APPENDIX A.

Our little Manciple [19] comes next in torn,
Breaking the ranks as he were somewhat lorn;
Smoking a sad pipe to allay the qualms
Which he hath gotten snuffling through the Psalms:
Our old nobilitie have lost their pith;
Even Percy is become a Son of Smith;
And Camp-bell turned a Kirk-bell is so crackt,
The doleful jangle drives us all distract.

Our very daynt and gentle Prioress [14],
Who is it but our dear and good Princess?
For hath she not in truth prioritie
Over all others in the land that be?
Her Nun [13] the Lady of all Bountihead;
None can she not deny, as it is said,
Were they brute beasts, in suffering or in need,
But she comes to their help with earnest speed;
Though they have made her Baroness, perdie
No barrenness attaints her charitie.
Her Priest [12] he looketh somedele dour and sullen,
As from the Land of Ire; men call him Cullen.
Next our good Parson [11]; if I do not err,
Though men err well, his town is Manchester;
He "Cristes lore, and his apostles twelve,
Doth teach, but first doth follow it himselve;"
He is no bigot, no fat sluggard he,
A very fisher of men in all his see;
And though he speaketh much, beyond demur,
No phraser but a trusty messenger.
And next beside him rideth here his brother,
For that the one is worthy of the other;
Our Ploughman [10], who though dwelling in a town,
Soweth good seed to stow well harvests brown.
Our Reeve [8] is clepèd Reade, "a colerike man,"
Albeit men read him whensoever they can;
Thus doth he reave, tho' he be somewhat rash,
From the good people, Oh but much hard cash;
Yet he is generous withal, nor brooks
Any injustice should escape his books.

Next look on Whalley [23] our right noble Monk,
Sitting his ass as he were jovial drunk,
Ready despite of beads and cowl and cope
To sing a jolly song and curse the Pope.
And see, by Potiphar! there at his side,
Ogling his rubicundity, doth ride
Our Wife of Bath [20]! and she can be no other
Than who was erewhile Queen and is the mother

Of who is for the moment King of Spain,
This moment that I write—I would be plain—
For when you read he may no longer reign:
Ah, Isabelle she was a belle, I trow,
But sore misdoubt me whether she be now:
Who knows her not? I follow on my path;—
Go read the Prologue of the Wife of Bath,
And learn how she had had her husbands five
And would have more whilever she was alive,
And how that she laid down her moral rules
For womenkind in scorn of all the schools.
And next to her upon the other hand
Our Poet [18] his own self; you understand
He is not the glad Poet whom we follow,
This child of the old age of great Apollo;
Nor can he be a chaw, sir, as you know,
Who 'gan a-versing fifty years ago:
This is the Lotus-eater of old time,
The Dreamer in great Haroun's golden prime,
Who since hath lost no little of his laud
In idle *Idyls* and in maudlin *Maud*,
In doited dramas and in dowie sonnets
As flimsy as our ladies' summer bonnets,
And other stuff of sadly thoughtless thought:
Yet let him pass with honour; for we ought
Measure all men by that which they have wrought
Of good and great; their failures are but naught:
Wherefore we here bestow our gracious benison
Upon the Lotus-eating Alfred Tennyson.
And now, the second or the third in glory
Of all the noble Pilgrims whom we story
(The gentle Squire and he must make accord),
Our learned and subtile Clerk of Oxenforde [17]:
Alas! he left that city and his home,
To pay as tribute to the Pope of Rome
His very reason and his very will;
O priceless good gifts that have come to ill!
Ah Oxenforde, ah Church, ye long shall wait
Ere ye can boast a new man half so great.
And next to him our Shipman [16], who maybe
Knoweth both Chel-sea and eke Batter-sea,
And so is first Lord of the Admiraltie;
And being so well seen in (printers') galleys,
Speaks for our squadrons in Palaver Palace:
His office it should be in Downing Street,
For down, down, down, doth go our ironclad fleet,
And soon we trust, tho' not a ship be seen,
To have a powerful navy submarine.

Next comes our Frere [24] "a wanton and a merry,"
Too much men sayn like him who liked his Sherry,
Both man and wine, deserting perhaps the friend,
But not the bottle even unto the end:
In sooth good Master Friar of Wales we guess
You should keep closer to our Prioress,
Nor ever go a-gambolling * on your path
Divided from her by some wife of Bath.

Our Sompnour [22] or our Summoner comes then;
Ah no, he comes not tho' he came but when
Our Card came forth a little while ago;
Fate dealt so suddenly the fatal blow:
He the great Summoner of all who live,
The inexorable, who never will forgive
For any bribe or prayer or piteous moan,
Hath summoned him from off the Italian throne
He was the first to sit upon, and, more,
From the sweet air and light, unto the shore
Of that Black Sea in which we all go down,
Yea every voyager therein must drown,
And drown all lonesome in his little bark
Tho' myraid others take the waters dark
At the same hour; this is that Sea of Dread
Which yields not up its secrets or its dead:
His people mourn howe'er the Church may ban
That rarity amongst the kingly clan,
Galantuomo or the Honest Man:
The laurel-garland withered from his brow,
This Victor is the vanquished victim now;
Thus with the greatest monarchs it must be,
And thus no less with little you and me.

And now our Pardoner [21]; I need not tell
Who that he is, because you know too well
That bearded front of brass bewigged no more;
Who seeks or feigns to seek with huge uproar
The pardon which he knows he will not get
Of that gross blackguard-butcher-baronet;
Who seeketh rather his own profit thus
From fools whereof we have great overplus;
And who himself shall never pardoned be
His shameless humbug and scurrilitie:
The Irish *Englishman*, the patriot
Of Dr. Johnson, always reeking hot;
The lion with the dew-drops on his mane,

* Aint the right spelling *gambling*?—PRINTER'S DEVIL.

Whose voice reveals the fox, not ass, full plain;
The beggar of a million sixpences
Whereof he got but sixty pounds we guess
(Two dozen hundred dupes we thus may count
Who still believe in him to that amount).

Our Haberdasher [29] is M'Laren hight,
Of Edinboro', and a worthy wight,
Tho' he would dash away from our poor chops
All other cups than tea and suchlike slops.
Our Tapisser [27] he is a Taylor now,
And he hath patched together as we trow
Full many a piece of half-worn-out French stuff,
And sold them as new clothes quite bold and bluff;
And he hath clad our poor old senile *Punch*
In sombre raiment, muffling up his hunch;
Alas! the verve and motley bright and gay
Of Hood, of Jerrold and of Thackeray!
Our Weaver [26] in the Parliament sits he
For that great Weavers' town yclept Dundee;
A modest man, who weaveth evermore
New pamphlets, lectures, tracts and tales galore;
And once when he would play his highest jinks
He went and made a baby for poor Ginx.
Our Carpenter [25] a right whole man is he,
For whom you must go hunt in Galilee
Or otherwhere in sacred Palestine,
Since there to work he chiefly doth incline:
Full three long years he in the workshop wrought
Of good St. Joseph, unto whom was brought,
The Virgin's Babe Divine; and there with awe
The ominous Shadow of the Cross he saw:
And he wrought in the Temple with great joy
When doctors learnt much from the marvellous Boy;
And he pursued into the wilderness
The scape-goat, all amorphous with distress;
Anon on London Bridge he laboured well,
And elsewhere that I have not time to tell:
In sooth a workman of rare skill is he,
Altho' he works at his own phantasie.
Our Dyer [28] of a surety he hath dyed
Full many a stretch of canvas long and wide,
With many shapes, from Pilate and his spouse
Unto the haunters of the gaming-house;
Thereto he hath designed with flying ease
Some myriads of various effigies,
Tennyson's, Milton's, Bible's (ah, me!) Dante's,
But best he followeth Balzac and Cervantes:

Since all these works have brought him muckle gold
He is hight Doré; yet is far from old.
Now last of all this jolly rout there goes,
With bottle in his hand and bottle nose,
Our lusty Cook [30], of whom well runs the tale
"Wel coude he knowe a draught of London ale:"
Look into the Italian lexicon,
If need there be, for *Sala*, and anon
You learn that it doth mean a dining-room,
Whence it may suit our Cook as we presume:
He can cook articles from anything
From anywhere as fortune may it bring;
He can hash up the very stalest meat
So that a-many shall be fain to eat;
He hath concocted for the *Telegraph*
More dishes than all others of its staff,—
This is our London's terrible *D. T.*,
In which it raveth every morn we see,
Possest with legions of blue devilrie,
(There is one *Telegraph*, it hath been said,
And Sala is its prophet: bow the head!);
He knows to season with the herb-of-grace
Or spicy condiments, each in its place;
Can serve you up with equal gust and ease
Réchauffés of St. Paul and Dumas *fils*,
Scarcely less unctuous in those than these;
And if he signeth G. A. S. be sure
That he can cook up to the signature:
Truly a wondrous Cook in all he dresses,
And myriads daily hunger for his messes.

Thus have I told you as it might befall
The full tale of our Pilgrims one and all;
In sooth it tallies not with CHAUCER's list
In number or in order, as I wist,
And wist our artist PIPESHANK none the less:
Thus there are three priests to the Prioress, *

* Tyrwhitt, it appears, condemned as spurious the distich,
Another Nonne also with hire had she,
That was her chapelleine, and Preestes three.
But Stothard admitted the Nun and one Priest: why then not the other two? It must be remarked, however, that in the body of the work (*Nonnes Preestes Prologue*, vv. 14,773-14,826) there is only one Priest.

Tyrwhitt's rejection makes the number of the Pilgrims too small by three; nor can we conceive such a lady as the Prioress travelling unattended. The present number is one too many: but Blake has suggested (see the masterly exposition in the Descriptive Catalogue in the second volume of his Life) that instead of "A webbe, a deyer," Chaucer may have written "A webbe deyer," a cloth-dyer; this seems to me very probable, and would make the number of the Company just the correct twenty-nine in addition to the Poet himself. It may be worth while to add that when the Second Nun's Tale was finished, the "jolly compagnie" was over-

While of the Reeve we read beyond a doubt
"And ever he rode the hinderest of the route."
Then blame not us, good people, if you blame,
Let Stothard whom we follow bear the shame;
We might in sooth have tracked and followed Blake,
But would not with him such a freedom take.—
Now cheer up all! for lo we reach the Shrine
Of most beneficent Saint Nicotine!
The altar of the Holy Herb Divine!

PART II.

THE SAINT AND HIS SHRINE.

Behold the Legend and the Shrine
Of Him of all Saints most benign,
The blessedest SAINT NICOTINE,
The Patron of our HERB DIVINE.

And now behoves me tell you of our Saint,
And try to sketch, since never a pen could paint,
The dreadful persecutions which he bore;
Beyond all parallel, enough and more
To set up common martyrs half a score.
He was a native of that large New World
Which we knew not until Columbus furled
His sails at last after that weary quest
For utmost East which led to utmost West;
Since ever as men sayn extremes will meet,
That so Life's circles may be all complete.
Millenniums beyond the range of story
He lived and died and won supernal glory,
As sent by the Great Spirit in its grace
For solace to the suffering human race;
But at the first, as ever is the case
With poor mankind so stupid or so base,
They did maltreat, then torture, and then kill
Their greatest Benefactor; and as still
Malignant having slain him, sans remorse
Wreaked direst outrages upon his corse:
Go murder myriads of your fellow men,
You shall be hailed a glorious Conqueror then;
Go bear some message of new love and truth,

taken by a Canon and his Yeoman, of whom the former soon "fled away for veray sorwe and shame," but the latter held on and contributed his story (*Chanones Yemannes Prologue and Tale*, vv. 16,022-16,187; 16,188-16,949).

You shall be smitten without any ruth:
So be it; who shall criticise the plan
Whereon the good God hath created man?

They first exposed him in the open air
To stand long days and nights unmoving there;
Then scalped him as their Indian custom was,
And pinced out pieces from his sides, alas!
And still he smiled with more benignitie
Upon these cruel men, ah, woe is me!
They cut his legs from under him the while
He stood regarding them with that sweet smile;
Then he was hanged, immitigable Fates!
Then taken down and crushed with monstrous weights;
And when the body was all mummy-dry
They cut the backbone out, Oh fie! oh fie!
Then shred down all the flesh as we may shred
A salted ox-tongue, poor dear body dead!
And of the morsels some they ground to dust,
And snuffed it with an eager savage lust;
And some they put in censers to consume
To ashes, and inhaled with joy the fume;
And some these horrid cannibals did bite
And chew and savour with a wild delight:
Such were some tortures of this sweetest Saint,
Whose mere recital makes us sick and faint.

Yet ere that he was wholly done to death
He spake unto them, yea, with his last breath:—
"My friends, my brothers, ye poor wretched men
Who know not your own good; never agen
Will ye be troubled with my voice and glance,
Who came in love, but whom your ignorance
Misweeneth for a foe; my words attend,
And ye shall know I was in sooth your friend;
For I must bless you in your own despite,
Since ill with good we ever should requite:
The boon I brought for you I must bequeathe
Who cannot now bestow it while I breathe;
My gift must be a legacy, I fear
Less rich tho' rich than if I still were here:
Lo from my blood, yea from this very place,
Shall spring and spread an Herb of Holy Grace;
Shall spread from North to South, from East to West,
Until the whole land shall by it be blest;
And in the aftertime shall carried be
To other lands beyond the Eastern Sea,
To other lands beyond the Western Main,

Whereof ye wot not, and they shall be fain
Its bountiful beneficence to share,
And tend and cherish it with loving care.
And you must treat it as myself you treat,
That it may still my martyrdom repeat;
Nor this for your reproach, friends, but because
It standeth written in the eternal laws,
That what is good in man and everything
Is proved and fortified by suffering.
Its powder then shall spur the weary brain
And make its heavy dulness bright again;
Its juice shall be instead of drink and food
To famished hunters in the solitude;
Its fumes all pain and sorrow shall allay,
And soothe fatigue and cark and care away:
Yea it shall be to all who peak and pine
A sweet nepenthe and strong anodyne,
And unto all in health and sans annoy
A deep refreshment and a quiet joy:
Sore-wounded men shall yearn for its sweet breath
Beyond all drugs and simples foes to death;
Many diseases shall by it be cured,
And many more prevented ere endured;
A safeguard shall it be against the pest
And all infections that are most unblest;
An incense of devoutest joy and calm,
A nectarous food, a most ambrosial balm,
The Holy Healing Herb, the Plant of Grace,
The Panacea of the Human Race;
Whose epithets in the far future time
Among far peoples shall be the Sublime,
The Sovereign, the Divine, and truly this
Shall best express its universal bliss.
Nor when this comes to pass do ye repent
And over my brief martyrdom lament;
I have sad prescience that your progenie
Remote shall rue and dree it, do not ye;
Ye have but wrought as men are wont to do,
And I have looked for this my whole life through;
Ye only send me earlier to that rest
Where I shall in Eternitie be blest."—
Thus spake our sweet Saint calmly ere he died
Under those savage tortures multiplied.

Because the solemn words of dying men
Are awful, hushed they hearkened to him, then
Began to jeer and torture him agen;
Too good by far was what he prophesied,

They could but disbelieve him and deride:—
"Lo if he speaketh truly, by his death
We gain at once the prize he promiseth;
But if mere falsehoods, then he merits worse
Than we can wreak upon him, with our curse."
And so they carried out their fell intent
As ye have learnt from this true muniment.

But when they found his marvellous prophecy,
Incredible for gloriousness, no lie
But in its every word the solid truth;
Then joy and sorrow, then delight and ruth,
Then love and anguish, triumph and remorse,
Then wailings for the unexistent corse:
For it is verily a law of Fate
Repentance evermore must come too late;
Since what is done can never be undone
Till backward on his pathway rolls the sun;
Since that which hath been as it was must last,
Nor gods themselves have power upon the Past.
Then they adored his Name as one divine,
And eke the Plant his symbol and his sign;
And evermore its fragrant incense rose
In mild propitiation for his woes.
And when the destined periods were past
Columbus and the others came at last;
Lustful for gold and land, in bands and legions;
And then the peoples of those Western regions
Were punished for the murder of our Saint;
For some were conquered into hard constraint
Of cruelest servitude; and others killed
By myriads, yea by millions, all unskilled
To cope with the white Centaurs hurling fire;
Some tortured even to a priest's desire;
While countless others perished in stark dearth,
Or piously improved from off the earth:
Thus was fulfilled what our sweet Saint foresaw,
Divining the austerities of law,
How frequently the sins of men and nations
Are visited on distant generations,
The sinners going scathless to the tomb;
It is a common ordinance of Doom.

But these adventurers so barbarous there
Brought back to us a blessing past compare,
Back to our poor Old World emerged to light
From the long dreary Mediæval Night;
I mean not those poor things they mainly sought,

As jewels, gold and silver; but they brought
The Legend of that martyrdom acerb,
And above all the testimonial Herb;
The Holy Herb, TOBACCO the Divine!
The tale of him we call SAINT NICOTINE!
(For verily we hold that Master Cope
Can canonise as well as ever a Pope;
And our Saint hath more votaries by far
Than all the other blessèd saints that are,
Nor in the whole huge hagiologie
Is Legend more authentical perdie.)
And ever since, this Plant of glorious grace,
For now three centuries, hath blest our race.—
Doth not compassion make you sigh and moan
When ye reflect that it was all unknown
Unto the lofty ones of former ages,
The heroes, prophets, poets, scholars, sages?
That it did never bless with joy and peace
Egypt, Assyria, Persia, Rome or Greece?
But we who have its bounties in full store
Behoves us to be grateful evermore,
To ever love and cherish and adore.

Lo now you know for why our motley train
Set forth upon this Pilgrimage full fain;
And now you are prepared to look above
And love the image of the Saint they love.
Behold Him as they see him in his Shrine
In Nephelococcygia the divine,
The City of the Clouds, where took his ease
Our smoker *manqué* Aristophanes:
The cloud-compeller of the *Clouds* and *Birds*,
The smoker of crass Cleon and the herds
Of fools, knaves, rowdies, all the catalogues
That swell the fortunes of your demagogues;
Your shameless charlatans whose dirty tricks
And frothy gab defile all politics,
Shame honest Liberals, delight old Tories,
Retard sure progress,—damn such vomitories!
Ah, if thou hadst but known our precious Herb,
How had it soothed thy humours most acerb!
How its fine fragrance had dispelled the fogs
On fens of *Brekekekex-coax*-croaking Frogs!—
(Our poor ears know too well what rancous rant is,
O ye aquatic accents of old Antis!
But now the tadpoles of our squashy noddies
Have just no heads, but are all tumid bodies.)
Its Pythian fumes inspiring heart and brains

To yet more glorious phantasies and strains!
Thou jolliest of all antique roistering jokers,
Only less jolly than our Saint of Smokers.

Yea after all his earthly sufferings rude
This is his likeness in beatitude,
As he revealed himself to our PIPESHANK
In lofty vision, for the which we thank
His graciousness right fervently be sure:
Regard his radiant aspect fit to cure
All hypochondriacs without other aid;
The sheaf of censers on his left arm laid
(The more he is incensed the blither he,
For that the incense is so sweet perdie);
The missal in his left hand, or indeed
A pix for *Weeds* or powder of the WEED?
(Like to the silver missal given Rabelais,
A flagon for all wines from Beaune to Chablis;
Because that great one loved to drink his prayers,
And in the honour of the gods upstairs
To pour libations down his proper throat);
And above all things else I pray you note
The glorious halo of the Golden Cloud
Wherein his sanctity shines all avowed.
On either side of Him a Lady stands,
Sisters of Mercy with fair liberal hands,
His almoners, the bountiful dispensers
Unto all Pilgrims of his long-stemmed Censers
(Scorners of censorship, that burn sans doubt
All censors' fingers who would put them out),
The kindlers therein of the Sacred Fire:
And to them throng with ferventest desire
And adoration not to be exprest
All devotees who would be truly blest;
Pell-mell they throng in their ecstatic need,
No matter what their politics or creed,
Or rank or nation; actors, men of state,
Journalists, singers, nobles, small and great:
Would you have thought that Shaftesbury and Manning
Could come together without mutual banning?
Could you conceive that Gladstone and Ben Dizzy
Might meet and yet no wordy warfare busy?
Or could you think the Sultan and the Czar
Would worship at one altar from afar?—
Manning and Shaftesbury are side by side,
Gladstone and Dizzy by one hope allied,
The Czar and Sultan to the same Shrine press,
Grim Bismarck elbows eloquent Grant, U.S.—

Just note our Liberal leader, well I wis
Behind his followers, as he always is!
His mouth and arms stretched yawnful, eyes a-closing
In heavy-headed and oblivious dozing;
From which if he be wakened, in a scare
He'll slope and leave his comrades planted there:
No party-leader he, this placid Hartington,
Who like the nobly-valiant Mrs. Partington,
As if engaged with some mere puddle-slop,
Opposes stolidly a poor house-mop,
Soft-headed with bedraggled worn-out wigs,
As thus-far-and-no-farther to the rigs
Turbulent, wanton, never-pacified
Of the great Liberal Atlantic tide:
He cuts his party, does he? soon, we wish,
They'll cut and smoke him as cut Cavendish.—
Some have already got the censers burning
For which the others unappeased are yearning;
While some in pastils the rich Herb consume,
Enraptured with the perfume of the fume.
This is the glorious scene our Pilgrims see
As they approach the Saint and bow the knee;
And all its very truth I can attest,
I, Sigvat, * who slipt in among the rest,
Wishing like others to be fully blest.

Good people all, your grateful hearts incline,
However wretched Antis may repine
And whet against us pens and tongues malign,
Their goose-quills and sweet voices asinine,
Let none be aughtways backward at the sign
To echo fervently this hymn of mine,
But lustily in unison combine,
Be it with beer or toddy, grog or wine,
Or coffee of aroma rich and fine:—
Glory for ever to the gracious SHRINE!
Glory for ever to the HERB DIVINE!
Glory for ever to our most benign
And blessèd Patron sweet Saint Nicotine!

SIGVAT.

1878.

* [Thomson had used this pseudonym previously in the story "Sayings of Sigvat," collected in *Essays and Phantasies.*]

ON A BROKEN PIPE

Neglected now it lies a cold clay form,
So late with living inspirations warm:
Type of all other creatures formed of clay—
What more than it for Epitaph have they?

1878 [?]

FRAGMENTS FROM "IN PURSUIT OF DIVA NICOTINA"

But what of Him, our Minister of Doom,
Whom spite and envy steep in livid gloom?
He is not Death, as Patron's motto saith,
"The end of these things (yea, of all) is Death;"
And yet he is a sort of Death-in-Life
Or living death, essentially at strife
With all the good that Nature has unfurled,
With all the joyance of the vital World:
He the embodied Puritanic Cant is;
The patron Demon of all dismal Anti's,
Of all those murky soulless souls of DANTE'S
Adust, with verjuice for their only juice;
Scrofulous, atrabilious, lank, uncouth,
Dry-rotted doubtless in their greenest youth;
Blatant and latrant, every-streperous croakers
In loose brown-seedy black and limp white chokers;
Blotched with bad blood, unwholesome to the core,
Wolf-gaunt and grim and hunger-bitten, or
Pallid flat-flabby as a skin of lard,
With rancid unctuous speech, furtive regard,
And prurient pawing benedictive hands
Toad-pleasant in their touch: these are the bands
Of holy ones who would reform the earth
From all its damning sins of harmless mirth
And innocent joy and healthy human love,
And make a lively set of saints above!

* * * * *

The drama is most damnable, but hear
The fluent claptrap gross and insincere,
The grosser mutual flatteries and greetings,
The grossest pious fictions, at their meetings;
Dancing's lascivious and to be abhorred,
But catch them with dear sisters in the Lord.—
Pah! let us leave this howling congregation,
Apostles of the Gospel of Damnation,
Canters and ranters symboled in this feller
Whose only sword's a bloated umbereller;
This Minister of Dooms as false as dire,
This Sulphurous Prophet of the Nether Fire,
This croaking frog of Stygian waters dark,
This ominous raven of the holy ark:
What can our Diva of the glorious mien,
What can the fervent followers of our Queen,
Care for such rancous carrion fowl obscene?
Behold our DIVA beautiful and bright!

* * * * *

(So Quakers flourish in a martial State;
But what would be a Quaker-people's fate?
Affronted, harried, put to fire and sword
Or slavery by the nearest fighting horde:)
Say this, they are most harmless in their place,
Most harmful out of it, when evil case
Sets them in posts of peril or great trust,
Demanding royal minds and wills robust
And hearts full-charged with the imperious flood
Of Nature's passionate dauntless hot red blood:
Say this, they are unto themselves a law,
But not to others; let them learn with awe
That goodness weak is evil very strong
When called to sway in realms where Right and Wrong
Wage their Titanic warfare; [. . .]

1879.

BILL JONES ON PRAYER

Well, I'm not much of a hand at prayer,
It's hardly in my line;
I am pretty fair at a laugh and a swear,
But a duffer at a whine.

And if so be that a God there be
On high above the sun,
Why, who can know so well as he,
What's the best thing to be done?

And since he is no less good than wise,
And has all power thereto,
Why should one pester him with cries
Of what he ought to do?

God helpeth him who helps himself,
They preach to us as a fact,
Which seems to lay up God on the shelf,
And leave the man to act.

Which seems to mean—You do the work,
Have all the trouble and pains,
While God, that Indolent Grand Old Turk,
Gets credit for the gains.

November 1, 1880.

ADDRESS
ON THE OPENING OF THE NEW HALL
OF THE LEICESTER SECULAR SOCIETY,
March 6, 1881.

"So Man created god in His own image, in the image of Man created He him; male and female created He them."

—*The New Book of Genesis.*

Lo, all the lands wherein our wandering race
Have led their flocks, or fixed their dwelling-place
To till with patient toil the fruitful sod,
Abound with altars To THE UNKNOWN GOD
Or GODS, whom MAN created from of old,
In His own image, one yet manifold,
And ignorantly worshipped. We now dare,
Taught by millenniums of barren prayer,
Of mutual scorn and hate and bloody strife
With which these dreams have poisoned our poor life,
To build our temples on another plan,
Devoting them to god's Creator, MAN;
Not to MAN's creature, god. And thus, indeed,
All men and women, of whatever creed,
We welcome gladly if they love their kind;
No other valid test of worth we find.

We gaze into the living world and mark
Infinite mysteries for ever dark:
And if there is a god beyond our thought
(How could he be within its compass brought?);
He will not blame the eyes he made so dim
That they cannot discern a trace of him;
He must approve the pure sincerity
Which, seeing not, declares it cannot see;
He cannot love the blasphemous pretence
Of puny mannikins with purblind sense
To see him thoroughly, to know him well,
His secret purposes, His Heaven and hell,
His inmost nature—formulating this
With calmest chemical analysis,
Or vivisecting it, as if it were
Some compound gas, or dog with brain laid bare.
And if we *have* a life beyond our death,
A life of nobler aims and ampler breath,
What better preparation for such bliss
Than honest work to make the best of this?

He who is faithful in a few things found
Becomes the lord of many; he whose pound
Is well employed may look for many more;
Waste adds to waste as store increaseth store.
Who cannot run a mile will win no place
Among the champions for a ten-mile race;
Who cannot order well a little farm
Shall have no great estate to bring to harm;
Who squanders months and years can never be
Entrusted with an immortality;
Who loveth not the brother at his side,
How can he love a dim dream deified?

We know our lives at best are full of care,
But we may learn to bear and to forbear,
By sympathy and human fellowship,—
Sweet cup of solace to the parching lip,
Doubling all joy, diminishing all grief,
Soothing despair itself with some relief.

Each life is as a little plot of ground,
Whose owner should not blankly wall it round
To shut it in from others, shutting out
Himself from those that neighbour it about:
The plots must differ both in size and soil,
The poorest will reward kind care and toil
With fruits of sustenance and flowers of grace;
All good, though varying in every case.
Down with our dead walls!—let us all enjoy
Our neighbours' industry without alloy;
The bloom and odours of their fruits and flowers
Which are so like and yet so unlike ours;
The singing of the birds among their trees,
Their glancing butterflies and honey-bees:
And sharing thus the pleasures of the whole,
Tend that which is within our own control
More cheerfully, more earnestly, lest weeds
Disgracing ours, taint theirs with wafted seeds;
And let us cherish kindly interchange
Of help and produce in our social range.

This is the spirit in which we have wrought
To build our little Temple of Free Thought
And mere Humanity—to us Divine
Above the deity of any shrine:
This modest Hall for Club and Institute
Which we now open; may it bear good fruit!

No rigid barriers of sex or sect
Or party in these walls do we erect:
*In*clusion not *ex*clusion is our aim:
Whatever freedom for ourselves we claim,
We wish all others to enjoy the same,
In simple womanhood's and manhood's name!
Freedom within one law of sacred might,
Trench not on any other's equal right.

Our creed is simple, All men are one man!
Our sole commandment, Do what good you can.
We gladly welcome truth where'er it shines,
The gold and silver of the ancient mines,
Dug out and smelted by good men of yore,
And mines but newly opened, still in ore;
Submitting old and modern to the test,
Most surely fallible but yet our best,
Of self-experience, knowledge, reason; then
Inviting the assays of other men.
Buddha and Jesus, Zeno, Socrates,
Mohammed, Paine, Voltaire,—alike from these
The precious metals we accept with joy;
But pray, friends, spare us from the proved alloy!

Having no rich endowments from the State,
Our means are small as our good-will is great:—
A platform for Free Thought in courteous speech,
And free discussion of the views of each;
Some books, our true "Communion of the Saints,"
To feed the mind and cheer the heart that faints;
Some classes for instruction and delight;
A club wherein our members may unite
For cordial converse and such innocent pleasure
As makes a blessing, not a curse, of leisure!
Some social gatherings, where we trust to see
Not the Man only but the Family,
Where poetry and music, dance and song,
Shall make the sweet hours blithely dance along.

Thus all our youths and maidens, girls and boys,
Must link this place with all their purest joys,
And growing in their turn husbands and wives,
Fathers and mothers, may devote their lives,
Not as an irksome task, but gracious duty,
Full-fraught with light and sweetness, love and beauty,
To cherish, cultivate, and propagate,
Or here or elsewhere as shall be their fate,
When we ourselves are dead save in our deeds,

This nursling from the ever-precious seeds
Which we have in our time inherited
From the brave culture of our noble Dead;
Our small addition to their great work done,
The present work in our loved town begun
This Sunday, March sixth, Eighteen eighty-one.

TO H. A. B.

ON MY FORTY-SEVENTH BIRTHDAY.

Wednesday, November 23, 1881.

When one is forty years and seven,
  Is seven and forty sad years old,
He looks not onward for his Heaven,
  The future is too blank and cold,
  Its pale flowers smell of graveyard mould;
He looks back to his lifeful past;
  If age is silver, youth is gold:
Could youth but last, could youth but last!

He turns back toward his youthful past
  A-throb with life and love and hope,
Whose long-dead joys in memory last,
  Whose shining days had ample scope;
  He turns and lingers on the slope
Whose dusk leads down to sightless death:—
  The sun once crowned that darkening cope,
And song once thrilled this weary breath.

Ah, he plods wearily to death,
  Adown the gloaming into night,
But other lives breathe joyous breath
  In morning's boundless golden light;
  Their feet are swift, their eyes are bright,
Their hearts beat rhythms of hope and love,
  Their being is a pure delight
In earth below and heaven above.

And you have hope and joy and love,
  And you have youth's abounding life,
Whose crystal currents flow above
  The stones and sands of care and strife.
  May all your years with joys be rife,
May you grow calmly to your prime,
  A maiden sweet, a cherished wife,
A happy mother in due time.

All good you wish me, past my prime,
  I wish with better hope to you,
And richer blessings than old Time
  And Fate or Fortune found my due:
  For you are kind and good and true,
And so when you are forty-seven
  May spouse and children in your view
Make Home the happiest life-long Heaven.

PROEM

O antique fables! beautiful and bright
And joyous with the joyous youth of yore;
O antique fables! for a little light
Of that which shineth in you evermore,
To cleanse the dimness from our weary eyes,
And bathe our old world with a new surprise
Of golden dawn entrancing sea and shore.

We stagger under the enormous weight
Of all the heavy ages piled on us,
With all their grievous wrongs inveterate,
And all their disenchantments dolorous,
And all the monstrous tasks they have bequeathed;
And we are stifled with the airs they breathed;
And read in theirs our dooms calamitous.

Our world is all stript naked of their dreams;
No deities in sky or sun or moon,
No nymphs in woods and hills and seas and streams;
Mere earth and water, air and fire, their boon;
No God in all our universe we trace,
No Heaven in the infinitude of space,
No life beyond death—coming not too soon.

Our souls are stript of their illusions sweet,
Our hopes at best in some far future years
For others, not ourselves; whose bleeding feet
Wander this rocky waste where broken spears
And bleaching bones lie scattered on the sand;
Who know we shall not reach the Promised Land;—
Perhaps a mirage glistening through our tears.

And if there be this Promised Land indeed,
Our children's children's children's heritage,
Oh, what a prodigal waste of precious seed,
Of myriad myriad lives from age to age,
Of woes and agonies and blank despairs,
Through countless cycles, that some fortunate heirs
May enter, and conclude the pilgrimage!

But if it prove a mirage after all!
Our last illusion leaves us wholly bare,
To bruise against Fate's adamantine wall,
Consumed or frozen in the pitiless air;
In all our world, beneath, around, above,
One only refuge, solace, triumph,—Love,
Sole star of light in infinite black despair.

O antique fables! beautiful and bright,
And joyous with the joyous youth of yore;
O antique fables! for a little light
Of that which shineth in you evermore,
To cleanse the dimness from our weary eyes,
And bathe our old world with a new surprise
Of golden dawn entrancing sea and shore.

January 1882.

EPIGRAMS

IPHIGENIA À LA MODE

How many a noble father since Agamemnon sinned,
Has sacrificed his daughter just to raise the wind!

1864.

LOVE'S LOGIC

Love's Logic:
I am and thou art . . . . must be marriage.
(A syllogism who will dare disparage.)

1865.

A TIMELY PRAYER

Thou great Physician, fair play is divine
To "M. D." add "V. S."; for, by the powers,
The cattle on a thousand hills are thine,
The cattle with a thousand ills are ours. *

1866.

WHO KILLED MOSES?

Who killed poor Moses?
Goethe supposes
That the terrible son
Of a masculine Nun,
And Caleb his crony,
Whose sire is Jephone,
Together killed Moses;
So Goethe supposes!

1866.

* This was written at a time when the cattle-plague was very prevalent. ["V. S." refers to *Vesicular stomatitis*, a virus related to Rabies which affects cattle, horses, and pigs.]

SUGGESTED FROM SOUTHAMPTON

Mr. Kingsley's faith is just
What a candidate should swear;
Mr. Kingsley takes on trust
All these trifles light as Eyre. *

September 1866.

POOR INDEED!

The earth is the lords' and the fulness thereof,
The country and also the towns;
Our dear old Queen is our only sov.,
And she's hardly worth three crowns;
And we very much fear when her loss we deplore,
The sovereign or crown we shall never see more.

April 1871.

IN EXITU ISRAEL

The Jew came up from the land of Goschen;
Now Gladstone makes that land the ocean;
A miracle which brings to thought
The plaguey wonders Moses wrought.

March 1871.

THE SUCCESSORS WHO DO NOT SUCCEED

I.

The first Apostles, called to be
Fishers of men in Galilee,
By hook or crook, as all agree,
Did catch their men by shoal;
Now each Successor has his see,
Fine gold and silver fish nets he,
Some jolly place, p'raps two or three,
But never any soul.

* This refers to Mr. Kingsley's professed faith in the necessity of the severe measures taken by Governor Eyre in the suppression of the rebellion in Jamaica.

II.

Could the Twelve see their faith's retrogression,
The Bishops they would not bless,
"These rich rogues claim our succession,
But the Infidels have our success."

April 1871.

BLESS THEE! THOU ART TRANSLATED

Dizzy translated the Bishop *
For his Irish eloquence;
But who can translate his sermons
Into English, and common sense?

April 1871.

CROSS LINES FROM GOETHE

(BEING NO. 67 OF THE EPIGRAMS DATED VENICE, 1790)

Very much can I put up with. Most things that are trials of temper
I in tranquillity bear, as if imposed by a God.
Some few, however, I find as hateful as poison and serpents:
Four: the smoke of tobacco, garlic and bugs, and the +.

April 1871.

WE CROAK

When Stork succeeded Log as King
The poor frogs fared but ill;
We've both at once—the senseless thing,
The damnable long bill.

May 1871.

IN A CHRISTIAN CHURCHYARD

This field of stones, he said,
May well call forth a sigh;
Beneath them lie the dead,
On them the living lie.

May 1871.

* Bishop Magee.

OUR CONGRATULATIONS

ON THE RECOVERY OF HIS ROYAL HIGHNESS

Though we have not a God to thank for this grace,
Though we care not a fig for the man,
We have yet our share in the general joy
At the lengthening of his span.

Yes, because we scorn himself and his race,
And because we love not the crown,
We are truly pleased that this model prince
May add to its bright renown.

If we wished him well we might wish him gone;
As it is, we rejoice in his breath;
For his life is likely to damage the throne
Such a great deal more than his death.

January 1872.

PATHETIC EPITAPH

I.

Gould and Fisk in sacred league
Were full bold:
Gould has lost his precious fisc,
Fisk his gold.

II.

When one leads an Erie life,
He must risk
Even such an eerie death,
Sweet James Fisk. *

1872.

* James Fisk, a great American "financier," famous for his dealings with the Erie Railroad Stock, was shot in 1872 by Gould, one of his victims.

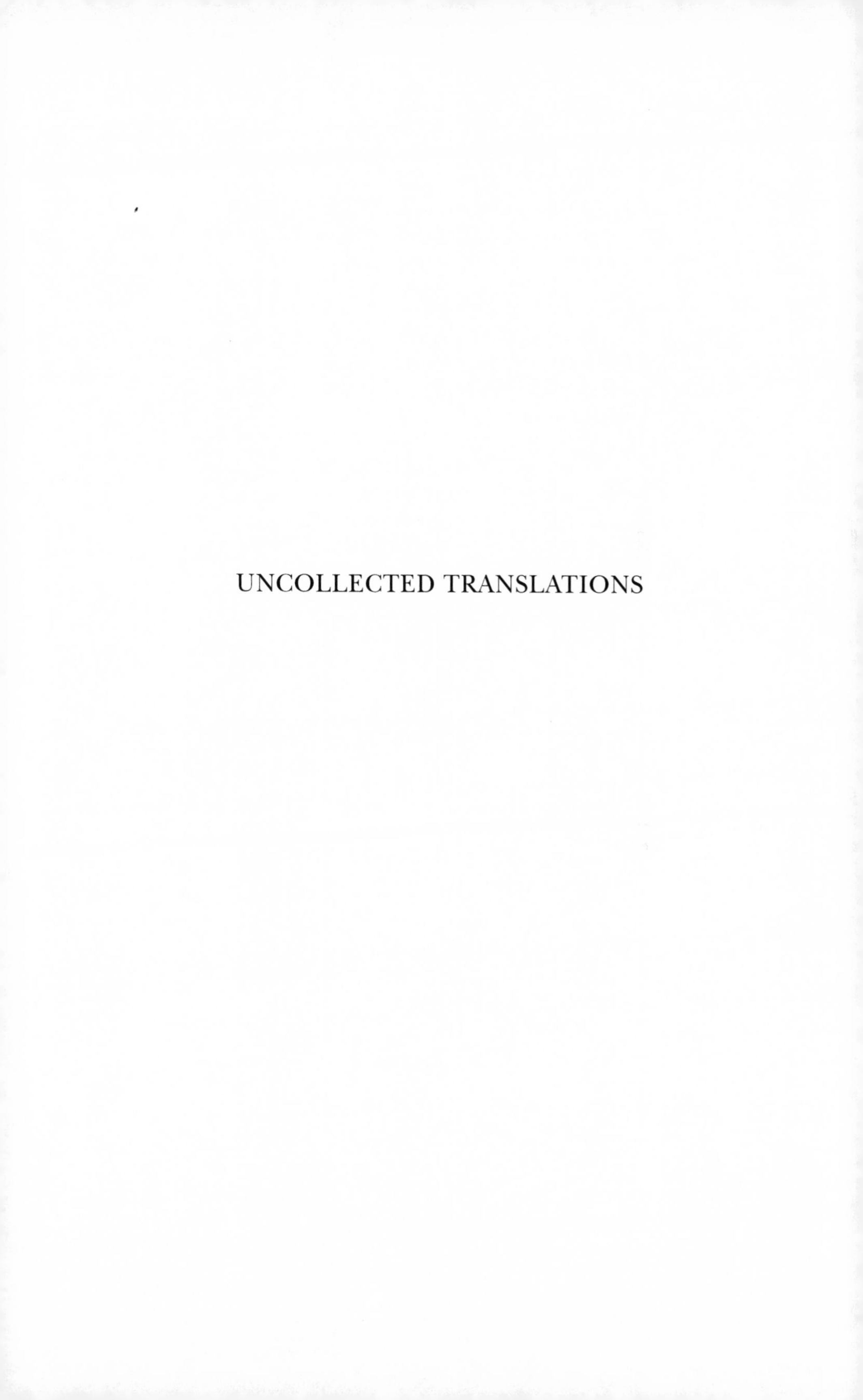

UNCOLLECTED TRANSLATIONS

PIERRE-JEAN DE BÉRANGER

THE GOOD GOD

One day the good God got out of bed
In a very good humour for us 'tis said;
He put his nose to the window light,
"Perhaps their planet has perished quite."
Not yet: in its corner very far
He saw it twining, our little star.
If I can think how they get on there,
Said he, the devil may take me, I swear,
The devil may take me, I swear.

Black or white, frozen or broiled,
(He said, like a father to children spoiled),
Mortals whom I have made so small,
They pretend that I govern you all;
But, God be praised, you shall also see
That I have ministers under me:
If I don't give the sack to one or two pair,
My children, the devil may take me, I swear,
The devil may take me, I swear.

To make you live in peace divine,
Have I not given you women and wine?
Yet in my teeth with prayers and boasts
The pigmies call me the Lord of Hosts?
And even dare to invoke my name
When they light the murderous cannon's flame!
If I ever commanded column or square,
My children, the devil may take me, I swear,
The devil may take me, I swear.

Who are these dwarfs so richly drest,
On gilded thrones in sumptuous rest?
The head anointed, so proud and pert,
These chiefs of your insect-swarms assert,
That I have blessed their rights of place,
That they are kings by my special grace.
If it is by me that they reign thus there,
My children, the devil may take me, I swear,
The devil may take me, I swear.

Then these other dwarfs, all black, of whom
My poor nose hates the incense fume:
They make of life a dismal fast,
And in my name fierce curses cast
In their sermons, very fine, said he,
Only, by gad, they're Hebrew to me:
If I believe anything they declare,
My children, the devil may take me, I swear,
    The devil may take me, I swear.

Children, enough of this: no sect
But the good kind hearts shall be my elect:
Make love to each other and live in joy,
Without any fear that God will annoy;
Laugh down the great and the canting crew—
But suppose the *mouchards* should hear me! adieu.
If into heaven those fellows fare,
My children, the devil may take me, I swear,
    The devil may take me, I swear.

1864.

THE DEATH OF THE DEVIL

For the miracle that I'll retrace
Quickly as the sketcher paints,
Glory be to the Saint Ignace,
Patron of all our little Saints.
By a trick which really would seem most
Infernal if ever Saints misled,
He has made the Devil give up the ghost:
The Devil is dead, the Devil is dead.

Satan found him going to dine:
Drink, or own yourself second-best:
Done!—but he poured in the Devil's wine
A powerful poison potently blest.
Satan drinks, comes the colic quick;
He swears, he writhes, he dashes his head,
At last he bursts like a heretic:
The Devil is dead, the Devil is dead.

He is dead! the monks all cry,
None will purchase another *agnus*:
He is dead! the canons sigh,
Who will pay now for an *oremus!*
The conclave shook in mortal fear,
Power and strong-box, adieu! they said,
We have lost our Father dear:
The Devil is dead, the Devil is dead.

Love won't serve us as Fear of old,
Whose gifts have overfilled our hands;
Intolerance is almost cold,
Who will kindle again its brands!
If Man escapes us, slips our rope,
Truth will begin to lift her head,
God will be greater than the Pope:
The Devil is dead, the Devil is dead.

Ignatius runs to them with the cry,
Give me, give me his place and power;
No one was frightened of him, but I—
I will make even the monarchs cower:
Robberies, massacres, plagues, or wars
Everywhere, O I'll flourish, he said;
God may have what I fling out of doors:
The Devil is dead, the Devil is dead.

Ah! brave homme! cried all the court,
We bless thee in thy malice and hate;
And at once his order, Rome's support,
Saw its robe flutter Heaven's gate.
From the angels tears of pity fell;
Poor Man will have cause to rue, they said,
Saint Ignatius inherits Hell:
The Devil is dead, the Devil is dead.

1865.

JOHANN WOLFGANG VON GOETHE

FROM THE
"WEST-ÖSTLICHER DIVAN." *

BOOK OF THE SINGER, I.

"Hejira"

North and West and South are quaking,
Thrones are falling, empires breaking;
Let us to the pure East fare,
Breathe the patriarchal air;
We will love and drink and sing,
Youth renewed by Chiser's spring.

There in pure and just relations
Will I track the various nations
In that primal period
When they still received from God
Heavenly lore in earthly strains,
When they never racked their brains.

Where the sires were venerated,
Alien service execrated;
Where the youthful mind is treasured,
Narrow thought, belief unmeasured;
Where the Word profoundly stirred
Just because a spoken word.

I will be the herdsmen's guest,
In the green oases rest;
Join the caravans and lade
Coffee, musk and shawls for trade;
Follow every track that fit is
Through the desert to the cities.

* [These translations first appeared in Thomson's essay "The Divan of Goethe." Presumably Thomson drafted his versions around 1864; "Ronald and Helen," finished that year, refers to the work. Goethe's text is arranged in twelve books, corresponding to the titles given here.]

Evil rockpaths rough and weird,
Hafiz, by thy songs are cheered,
When the leader with delight
From the mule's high back at night
Singeth loud the stars to wake,
And to make the robbers quake.

In the baths and taverns free,
Hafiz, I will think of thee;
When my Love her veil redresses,
Shaking perfume from her tresses;
Yea, the poet's soft love song
Maketh even houris long.

Would you envy him this charm,
Or indeed account it harm:
Know the poet's words arise
Hovering round Paradise,
Gently tapping at the portal
And beseeching life immortal.

BOOK OF HAFIZ, V.

The Mufti read through Misri's poems, took
  One with the other, gathered all the quire,
Deliberately cast them in the fire,
  And thus destroyed the finely written book.

Let every one, the high judge said, consume,
  Who speaks and thinks as Misri; he alone
Shall be exempted from the fiery doom:
  Each poet's gift derives from Allah's Throne;
If he abuses it to sin and shame,
With God Himself he reckons for the same.

BOOK OF HAFIZ, IX.

"Open Secret"

They have called you, O holy Hafiz,
  They have called you the Mystic Tongue;
Nor knew, the great word-scholars,
  The sense of the words they sung.

Mystic you call themselves
  Who so foolishly of you think,
And in your great name deal out
  Their muddy wine to drink.

But you are mystic only
  As quite transcending their wit;
That you are not pious and yet are blest
  They cannot at all admit.

BOOK OF LOVE, XV.

SUBMISSION

"You waste, and you are so kindly,
You perish while singing so gay?"
Love treats me cruelly, blindly!
This openly I say;
I sing with a heavy heart, dear,
I act the taper's part, dear;
It shines consuming away.

POET

Love's woe sought out a place apart,
Some desert and quite lonely spot;
And found at length my wasted heart,
And habited its empty grot.

BOOK OF MAXIMS, XI.

My heritage, how rich and great!
Time is my field to cultivate.

BOOK OF MAXIMS, XXXIV.

If you will the country see,
Climb up to the roof with me.

BOOK OF SULEIKA, XLIV.

Lady, say what mean those whispers?
What so softly moves your lips?
Whispering to your own self there,
Sweeter than the sweet wine sips!
Think you to your mouth's twin sisters
Thus to draw another pair!
    I will kiss! will kiss! I murmured.

Look! how in the doubtful darkness
All in bloom the branches glow;
Downward glitters star on star;
Greening through the leafage low
Rubies by the thousand sparkle:
Yet from all thy soul is far.
    I will kiss! will kiss! I murmured.

Even thus, afar, thy lover
Proveth now the bitter-sweet,
Feeleth an unblissful bliss.
Solemnly you vowed to greet
At the full moon, greet each other;
Now the very moment is.
    I will kiss! will kiss! I murmur.

BOOK OF THE TAVERN, IV.

Drunken we all must be, in fine!
Youth is drunkenness without wine;
If age can drink itself back to youth,
Drink is of wonderful virtue, sooth.
Poor life is careworn with much black care,
Which the grape blood melts into golden air.

1864.

— GIACOMO LEOPARDI —

CHORUS OF THE DEAD *

In the world alone eternal, unto whom revolveth
Every thing created,
In thee, Death, reposes
Our naked nature;
Joyous no, but secure
From the ancient suffering. Profound night
In the confused mind
Obscures grave thought;
For hope, for desire, the arid spirit
Feels itself void of strength:
And thus from affliction and fear is free,
And the blank slow ages
Consumes without tedium.
We lived: and as confused remembrance
Of terrible phantom
And sweating dream
Wanders in the soul of the suckling child;
Such memory remains to us
Of our life: but far from fear
Is our remembrance. What were we?
What was that sharp point
Which had the name of life?
A thing mysterious and stupendous
Now is life to our thought, and such
As to the thought of the living
Unknown death appears. As from death
Living it drew back, so now draws back
From the vital flame
Our naked nature;
Joyous no, but secure;
For to be blest
Fate denies to mortals and denies to the dead.

1867.

* The chorus in the Italian is one of the marvels of literature. Unable to translate it into anything like poetry, and feeling that it could not be left out altogether, I have been reduced to give the baldest literal version; a version even less like the original than a mummy of Ruysch is like a living man; for the mummy preserved form with substance, while the version preserves the substance only, and is equally lifeless. [This poem opens Leopardi's "Dialogue of Frederik Ruysch and His Mummies" in the *Operette morali*, which Thomson had translated by 1867.]

HEINRICH HEINE

THE GREEK GODS

Full-orbed Moon! Beneath thy light
Like molten gold far shines the sea;
With noonday clearness twilight-enchanted
It overflows the broad level strand;
And above in the clear blue starless Heaven
I see white clouds,
Like colossal God-forms
Of shining marble.

No, never, they are not clouds!
They are indeed the Gods of Hellas,
Who once so joyously ruled the world;
But now, dethroned and desolate,
Enormous phantoms, wander
Through the midnight Heaven.

Astonished and dazed I watch
The aërial Pantheon,
The solemn, dumb, mysterious procession
Of giant shapes.
He there is Kronion, the King of Heaven;
Snow-white are the locks of his head,
The renowned Olympus-shaking locks.
He holds in his hand the quencht thunderbolts,
In his countenance is misery and grief,
And yet evermore the ancient pride.
Ah, they were better times, O Zeus,
When thou divinely enjoyedst thy lust
With youths and nymphs and hecatombs—
But even the gods reign not for ever,
The young vanquish the old,—
As thou once wert allowed to vanquish
Thy hoary father and thy Titanic kindred,
Jupiter Parricida!

Thee too I recognise, haughty Juno,
In spite of all thy vigilant anxiety
Another has grasped the sceptre,
And thou art no more the Queen of Heaven,
And thy large eyes are beamless,
And thy pure white arms have no strength;

And never more shall thy vengeance smite
The God-embraced damsel,
And the God's irresistible Son.
Thee too I recognise, Pallas Athene!
With thine Ægis and thy wisdom could'st thou not
Avert the destruction of the Gods?
And thee also know I, thee also, Aphrodite,
Once the golden, now the silvern!
Still thou art adorned with the love-charm of thy cestus,
And I yearn with compassion for thy beauty,
And could'st thou give me but one embrace,
Like other heroes, I might pine to death:
As the corpse of a goddess appearest thou to me,
Venus Libitina!
No more with love burns towards thee
The gaze of the terrible Ares.
And, oh, how sad looks Phœbus Apollo,
The ever young! His lyre is silent,
That thrilled such joy thro' ambrosial feasts.
And even sadder looks Hephaistos,
And verily, poor Cripple! nevermore
Shall he stumble above there in his office—
Busily pouring out the divine nectar;
And long, long, has been utterly extinguished
The inextinguishable laughter of the Gods.

I have never loved you, O ye Gods!
For not at all to my mind are the Greeks,
And the Romans I thoroughly hate;
Yet pious compassion and sorrowful sympathy
Possess my heart,
When I see you now above there
Desolate deities,
Dead, night-wandering shadows,
Frail clouds, driven by the wind,—
And when I think how mean and blatant
The Gods are who have overcome you,
The new, dominant, melancholy Gods,
So malignant in their sheep's clothing of humility—
O then seizes me a gloomy rage,
And I could shatter the new temple,
And fight for you, you ancient Gods,
For you and your joyous ambrosial sway,
And before your high altars
Broad-built and steaming with sacrifices,
I could even kneel and pray
And suppliant arms uplift.

Though always aforetime, O ye Gods,
In the battles and dissensions of men,
Ye have fought on the side of the strongest;
Yet man is more magnanimous than you,
And in the battle of the Gods I range myself
With the followers of the vanquished Gods.

December 1862.

PHILOSOPHY

This World and Life are battered and shattered;
I must on the German Professor call:
For he puts together Life's pieces scattered,
And makes a beautiful system of all;
With his worn-out nightgowns and old nightcaps,
He stops up the whole of the poor World's gaps.

February 1866.

HINDOO MYTHOLOGY

The great King Viswamitra
Has no rest for his vow
By fighting and by penance
To win Vasishtha's cow.

O, great King Viswamitra,
O, what a bull art thou
To court such strife and sorrow,
And only for a cow.

February 1866.

THE GODS OF GREECE

(ANOTHER VERSION.)

Full-blossomed Moon! Beneath thy light
Liquidly golden outshines the sea;
Noonday clearness with twilight glamour,
It overflows the broad level strand;
And in the clear blue starless heaven
Float the white clouds,
Like colossal God statues
Of purest marble.

No, never, no, these are not clouds!
They are themselves the very Gods of Hellas,
Who once so joyously ruled the world;
But now disinherited and slain,
Wander, enormous phantoms,
The waste of the midnight heaven.
Astonished and dazed, I behold
The aerial Pantheon,
The solemnly dumb, terribly advancing
Gigantic forms.
He there is Kronion, the King of Heaven,
Snow-white are the locks of his head,
The locks at whose shaking Olympus shook.
His hand still grasps the quenched thunderbolt,
In his countenance woe and sorrow,
And yet evermore the ancient pride.
Those were better times, O Zeus,
When you divinely delighted
In boys and nymphs and hecatombs;
But even the Gods do not rule for ever,
The young supplant the old,
As you yourself supplanted
Hoary sire and Titan-uncles,
Jupiter Parricida!
Thee also I recognise, proud Hêrê!
Maugre all thy jealous anxiety
Another has won the Sceptre,
And thou art no more the Queen of Heaven;
And thy large eyes are quenched,
And thy white arms are powerless,
And nevermore shall thy vengeance smite

The God-caressed damsel,
And the labour-conquering Son of the God.
Thee also I know, Pallas Athênê!
With thy shield and thy wisdom couldst thou not
Avert the catastrophe of the Gods?
Thee also I know, thee also, Aphrodite,
Once the golden, now the silvern!
Still adorns thee the love-compelling girdle,
And in secret I have terror of thy beauty;
And could thy liberal body bless me,
Like other heroes I should die with anguish—
As Goddess of the Dead appearest thou to me
Venus Libitina!
No more with love gazes toward thee
There the terrible Ares.
How mournfully regardeth Phœbus Apollo,
The Youth ever young; silent his lyre
Which so joyously rang at the feast of the Gods.
Yet more miserable looks Hephaistos,
And truly, the Lameter, nevermore
Will he take Hêbê's office,
And pour, busy in the assemblage,
The sweet nectar. And long has been extinguished
The inextinguishable laughter of the Gods.

I have never loved you, O ye Gods!
For not at all to my mind are the Greeks,
And the Romans I thoroughly hate;
Yet holy compassion and shuddering sympathy
Stream through my heart,
When I see you now there above,
Desolate Gods,
Dead, night-wandering Shadows,
Frail clouds driven by the wind;
And when I reflect how dastardly, how windy
Are the Gods who vanquished you,
The new-reigning melancholy Gods,
The malignants in sheep's-clothing of humility,
Oh then I am seized with a sombre rage,
And would tear down the new Temples,
And fight for you, ye older Gods,
For you and your good ambrosial sway;
And at your high altars
The re-erected, smoking with sacrifice,
I could even myself kneel and pray,
And supplicating arms uplift.
I know right well, ye ancient Gods,
That always of old in the strifes of men

Ye have held with the party of the victors;
But Man is more magnanimous than you,
And in the Battle of the Gods I hold
With the party of the conquered Gods.

* * * *

So I spake, and visibly thereover
Blushed the pallid cloudy forms,
And regarded me as regard the Dying,
Pain-transfigured, and suddenly vanished;
Even then hid the Moon
Behind clouds darkly advancing;
High resounded the sea,
And triumphantly came forth into heaven
The eternal Stars.

July 1866.

EPILOGUE

As in the fields grow wheatears,
So grow and wave in the human mind
Thoughts.
But the delicate thoughts of Love
Are the joyous therein-between-blooming
Red and blue Flowers.

Red and blue Flowers!
The sulky reaper casts you away as useless,
Wooden flails thresh you in scorn,
Even the penniless wanderer
Whom sight of you pleases and refreshes,
Shakes his head
And calls you useless weeds.
But the country maiden,
The garland-wreather,
Honours you and plucks you,
And adorns with you her beautiful locks,
And thus adorned speeds to the dance-place,
Or to the silent beech-tree,
Where the voice of the dearest yet sweeter sounds
Than pipes and rebecks.

August 1866.

IN HARBOUR

Happy the Man who has reached his haven,
And left behind him the sea and its tempests,
And now warm and tranquil sits
In the good Wine-cellar at Bremen.

How all the world familiarly and sweetly
In the wine-glass is perfectly mirrored,
And how the mantling Microcosmos *
Sunnily flows down through the thirsty heart!
All things I see in the glass,—
Ancient and modern people's stories,
The Turks and the Greeks, Hegel and Gans, †
Citron-forests and esplanades,
Berlin and Schilda and Tunis and Hamburg;
But above all the image of my Darling,
The little angel-head on the Rhine-wine-gold-ground
O how fair, how fair art thou, Beloved!
Thou art like the rose!
Not like the rose of Shiraz,
The rose sung by Hafiz, the nightingale's bride;
Not like the rose of Sharon,
The Holy, the prophet-consecrated:
Thou art like the Rose in the Wine-cellar at Bremen;
That is the Rose of roses!
The older it grows the lovelier it blooms;
And its heavenly fragrance, it has me enraptured,
It has me inspired, it has me intoxicated:
And held me not fast, to his apron fast,
The Wine-cellar Master of Bremen,
I must topple over!

The dear fellow! we sat together
And drank like brothers,
We spoke of high mysterious things,
We sighed and sank in each other's arms,
And he has restored me to faith in love;
I drank to the health of my bitterest enemy,
And all poetasters I freely forgave,
As once myself I shall be forgiven;

* The Microcosmos, the glass of wine wherein the Macrocosmos is mirrored.
† Gans, Edward, a distinguished pupil of Hegel—but Gans also means *goose*.

I wept with devotion, and at last
Opened before me the Portals of Prosperity,
Where the Twelve Apostles, the holy great barrels
Silently preach and yet so intelligibly
For all peoples.

These are the fellows!
Uncomely without, in wooden jerkins,
They are within more beautiful and brilliant
Than all the haughty Levites of the Temple,
And Herod's sycophants and courtiers
The gold-bespangled, the purple-arrayed:—
Have I not always affirmed,
Not among your commonplace people,
No, but in the very best society
Lives constantly the King of Heaven.

Hallelujah! How lovely wave around me
The palms of Beth-el!
How fragrant are the myrrhs of Hebron!
How rushes the Jordan and whirls with joy!
Also my immortal soul whirls,
And I whirl with it, and whirling
Brings me up the steps into the daylight,
The brave Wine-cellar Master of Bremen.

Thou brave Wine-cellar Master of Bremen!
See'st thou on the roofs of the houses sit
The Angels, and are fuddled, and they sing.
The glowing Sun above there
Is only a ruddy drunken Nose,
The Nose of the World-Spirit;
And round the World-Spirit's ruddy Nose
Reeleth the whole intoxicate World.

1866.

FROM

"WIND AND WEATHER"

The air is always airy,
Be it storm, be it zephyr mild;
The doubt is, which is airier,
The air, or you, my child?

1868; 1871.

REMINISCENCE OF HAMMONIA *

Orphan children pair by pair
March along with joyous air;
All are in blue dresses cosy,
All with cheeks so plump and rosy:
    Oh, the pretty foundling children!

None unmoved can see the sight,
Money box rings left and right;
From the hands of secret fathers
Many a goodly gift it gathers:
    Oh, the pretty foundling children!

Bashful this poor fellow goes
And a thaler in he throws,
For he has a heart; then budges,
Gaily with his wallet trudges:
    Oh, the pretty foundling children!

Then a golden louis d'or
Gives a pious Sir; before
Just a glance at Heaven crooking
To make sure that God was looking:
    Oh, the pretty foundling children!

Porters, coopers, servants gay,
Working-men keep holiday;
Many a flask will drink such groundlings
To the health of these poor foundlings:
    Oh, the pretty foundling children!

Patroness Hammonia
Follows them incognita,
Waggling proudly the stupendous
Masses of her rear tremendous:
    Oh, the pretty orphan children!

On the green before the gate
Music fills the tent of state,
Pennons streaming, spangles shining:
There comes off the happy dining
    Of these pretty orphan children.

* Hamburg.

There they sit in long drawn file
Eating in most hearty style;
Tarts, too, cakes, and dainties munching,
Mouselike all the teeth are crunching
Of these pretty orphan children.

But, alas, the thought occurs
Of an orphanage much worse,
Where is no such glad regaling;
Wholly wretched dwell bewailing
Millions there of orphan children.

Not alike the clothes they wear,
Many have no dinner-fare;
None goes with the others yonder;
Lonely in their anguish wander
Many million orphan children.

July 1870.

FROM "DER TANNHÄUSER"

I passed through Weimar, where I heard
A noise of desperate grieving;
A cry of, Goethe the great is dead,
And Eckermann is living!

Undated.

FROM "THE HOMECOMING"

Ever the eunuchs whimpered
When I sang out with force;
They whimpered, and they simpered:
My singing was much too coarse.

Undated.

FRIEDRICH SCHILLER

A DISTICH OF SCHILLER'S

Privileged rank obtains in the moral world; commonplace natures
Pay us with that which they do, noble with that which they are.

1867.

GOTTHOLD EPHRAIM LESSING

PRAISE OF INDOLENCE

Indolence, I will to thee
  Some small song of praise now bring;
Oh—it—sorely—troubles me—
  Thy—great—worth—to fitly sing!
Yet I'll try to do my best;
  After labour comes sweet rest.

Highest Good! who has but thee,
  Who untroubled life doth live—
Ah!—I—yawn—tired out—you see—
  So—you—really—must forgive—
For how can I sing your lay
  While you kiss my breath away!

1867.

— CHARLES DE VION D'ALIBRAY —

TWO FRAGMENTS

I.

Thou who, like Bacchus, has drunk through all the world,
Teach me, Saint-Amant.

II.

I will make myself famous, at least in the cabaret;
They shall speak of me as they speak of Faret.
What matters it, friend, whence our glory may swell?
  I can acquire it with trouble scant,
For, thanks to God, I already drink well,
And I have been on the spree with Saint-Amant.

[1880?]

— ANTOINE GIRARD DE SAINT-AMANT —

FROM
"LE PASSAGE DE GIBRALTAR"

Already aloft on the poop,
To pledge me he takes his cup,
Where sparkles and laughs the nectar;
And crying Masse! to the troop,
His voice alarms Gibraltar.

FROM THE SONNET
"LE VOL NOCTURNE"

Gods, who look on while they rob me asleep,
In which of you now can men have any faith,
Now that Bacchus has betrayed Saint-Amant?

FROM THE "EPISTRE DIVERSIFIÉE A MONSIEUR DESNOYERS"

Whatever's the custom in any nation
Is always sure of approbation.

FROM "LE SOLEIL LEVANT"

The pretty butterfly comes then,
    Its tremulous pinions rise,
And seeing the sun shines again,
    From flower to flower it flies,
To tell the good news of the time
That day returns to bless our clime.

There in our gardens rich and bright,
    Where many a rare thing grows,
It carries from the lily white
    A kiss unto the rose;
And seems, a messenger discreet,
To tell her some love-message sweet.

FROM "LA PLUYE"

Falling on the foliage green,
What a pleasant sound rain stirs!
How should I charm every ear,
If the sweetness whispering here
Could be breathed into my verse!

* * *

The heavens are black from base to top,
  And their influence benign
  Pours so much water on the vine,
That we need never drink a drop.

FROM
"LA NUIT"

Peaceful and lonely night,
  Without or moon or stars,
With thy most sombre veils
  Enshroud the day that jars;
Come quickly, goddess, grant this boon to me;
  I love one dark like thee.

* * *

The winds no longer blow,
  The rain has ceased to dash,
The thunder sleeps; I hear
  Only the fountain's plash,
And some delicious lutes, whose notes arise,
  Languid with lovers' sighs.

FROM
"LA JOUYSSANCE"

But dare I hope, O wonder of the skies!
  To be as surely in your soul
As I can see myself within your eyes?

FROM
"LA DÉBAUCHE"

By this pipe from which I wave
All the incense thou dost crave.

FROM
"LE FROMAGE"

O of Bacchus thou sweet lure!
Cheese, thou art a treasure sure!
So may but of thee to think
Spur me evermore to drink!
    FILL LACKEYS!

FROM
"ORGYE"

Bring wine! bring wine! the freshest, sparkling red!
   Pour, waiter, pour, till to the brim it fills,
   For I would drink a toast in mighty swills—
Here's to the health of all alive and dead!

      Pour me yet of this rich red wine,
      For it alone makes my red blood run;
      It is my fire, my blood, and my sun.

Oh, but it's sweet! it ravishes my soul;
No such pleasure in life as the bowl,
No such pleasure in life as to drink;
      Keep pace with me, my dear friend Faret,
      Or you shall be, ere you can wink,
      Stripped of the name that rhymes with cabaret!

FROM
"LE ENAMOURÉ"

Since to good ham I prefer
The visage of a damsel fair,

*   *   *

I can smoke not as of yore,
And in wine exceed no more:
Now ten pints a day suffice;
   Even this, you lovely droll,
Who enslave me with your eyes,
   Is to drink your health, my soul!

FROM
"IMPRECATION"

If to Evreux I e'er go,
May I burn with fever slow!
May I turn into a dog!
May I turn into a frog!
Let me be cut off from wine,
Nor get trust when I would dine;

* * *

May for ever civil brawls
Trouble those accursed walls;
May the sweet sun, glad and bright,
Never bless it with its light;
May it rain there swords and spears;
May all ills which in old years
Bards have prophesied, all those
Horrors, outrages, and woes,
Poison, murder, streams of blood,
Pest and famine, fire and flood,
Be right soon accomplished there,
Filling it with black despair.

This is what just anger heated
Him to cry, at table seated,
Furiously excited thus
'Gainst that city infamous,
Him of all men most benign,
Who in these days drink good wine.

O good tipplers! Dear Faret!
  With just cause you scorn that lair
  More than thirty churches there,
And not one poor cabaret.

SONNET

Of careless souls this is the meeting-place,
  Which sometimes I frequent for my delight,
  The master calls himself La Plante with right,
For to a plant his fortune he can trace.
You see there Bilot pale as in sad case,
  From both whose nostrils vapour takes its flight,
  While Sallard tickles at the servant light,
Who laughs with nose up and foreshortened face.
How much this one-eyed * better friends must be
With Fortune than those alchemists we see
  From wise bcoming mad, from rich quite poor!
They find at length their health and strength decay,
Their money all in smoke consumed away;
  But he from smoke gets money more and more.

[1880?]

* La Plante was "*un cabaretier borgne qui tenait un cabaret borgne,*" the one-eyed host of a low wine-shop, or, as we should say, pot-house.

DANTE ALIGHIERI

FROM
PURGATORIO

(CANTO VI, 58-66)

But look and mark that spirit posted there
  Apart, alone, who gazes as we go;
He will instruct us how we best may fare.

We came to him: O Lombard spirit, lo,
  What pride and scorn thy bearing then expressed,
The movement of thine eyes how firm and slow!

No word at all he unto us addressed,
  But let us pass, only regarding still
In manner of a lion when at rest.

Undated.

APPENDIX A:

KEY TO THE ILLUSTRATION OF "THE PILGRIMAGE TO SAINT NICOTINE"

Lower Tier

1. John Stuart Blackie
2. James Patrick Mahon (the "O'Gorman Mahon")
3. Sir William Gull
4. Samuel Morley
5. Henry Cockburn, Lord Cockburn
6. William Ward, 1st Earl of Dudley
7. Thomas Carlyle
8. Bishop James Fraser
9. John Ruskin
10. Hugh Stowell Brown
11. Charles Reade
12. Cardinal Paul Cullen, Archbishop of Dublin
13. Angela Burdett-Coutts, 1st Baroness Burdett-Coutts
14. Princess Victoria
15. James Anthony Froude
16. William Henry Smith
17. Cardinal John Henry Newman, the "Clerk of Oxenforde"
18. Alfred, Lord Tennyson
19. John Campbell, the "Marquis of Lorne"
20. Queen Isabella II of Spain
21. Edward Vaughan Hyde Kenealy
22. Vittorio Emanuele II (the late King of Italy)
23. George Hammond Whalley
24. Prince Albert Edward (later Edward VII)
25. William Holman Hunt
26. Edward Jenkins
27. Tom Taylor
28. Gustave Doré
29. Duncan M'Laren
30. George Augustus Sala
31. John O'Connor Power
32. Joseph Biggar
33. Charles Stewart Parnell

Upper Tier

34. John Philip Nolan (in bottle, above)
35. Edmund Dwyer Gray (in bottle, below)
36. Alexander Martin Sullivan, "O'Sullivan" (identification uncertain)
37. Sir Wilfrid Lawson
38. Sir Edward Sullivan
39. Czar Alexander II of Russia
40. Otto von Bismarck
41. Ulysses Grant
42. Robert Lowe
43. Spencer Cavendish, 8th Duke of Devonshire ("the Marquis")
44. John Bright
45. William Gladstone
46. Joseph Chamberlain
47. Anthony Ashley-Cooper, 7th Earl of Shaftesbury
48. Cardinal Henry Edward Manning, Archbishop of Westminster
49. Mary Elizabeth Braddon

— Saint Nicotine (unnumbered, center)

50. Ouida (Maria Louise Ramé)
51. Sir Henry Irving
52. P. T. Barnum
53. Edmund Yates
54. Edward Stanley, 15th Earl of Derby
55. Benjamin Disraeli, 1st Earl of Beaconsfield
56. Sir Stafford Northcote, 1st Earl of Iddlesleigh
57. Sultan Murad V
58. Richard Assheton Cross
59. "Elcho," Francis Charteris, 10th Earl of Wemyss
60. George Sutherland-Leveson-Gower, 3rd Duke of Sutherland
61. Robert Gascoyne-Cecil, 3rd Marquess of Salisbury
62. Charles Santley
63. Lord Ronald Gower
64. Henry Labouchère
65. Albert Grant

1
2
3
4
5
6
7
8
9
10
11
12
13
14
15
16
17
18
19
20
21
22
23
24
25
26
27
28
29
30
31
32
33
34
35
36
37
38
39
40
41
42
43
44
45
46
47
48
49
50
51
52
53
54
55
56
57
58
59
60
61
62
63
64
65

APPENDIX B:

PROSE INTRODUCTION FROM "COPE'S CORRECT CARD" (1878) ENTITLED "SAINT NICOTINUS: HIS SHRINE AND THE PILGRIMS THERETO"

SAINT NICOTINUS:

HIS SHRINE AND THE PILGRIMS THERETO *

IT IS lawful to question whether this world—or, for that matter, any world that is or has been—ever knew a queerer set of characters than have gone to make up the company of the Saints. The forces that rule the universe are quick with the spirit of paradox; for which mysterious ordinance it behoves us to be humbly thankful, when we reflect how stale this human life would be, were it not for its impossible realities and its staggering surprises. How much of wisdom's purest treasure is crusted over with the dross of cynicism! The man who coined the scoffing phrase, "The unexpected always happens"—and that man was not Benjamin Disraeli, Earl of Beaconsfield, as too confiding youth would fain believe—had suffered and grown wise. When Saul also is found among the prophets,—when Milbank and Portland take tithe of Exeter Hall, when some good thing comes out of Nazareth, and "Full many a gem of purest ray serene" is fished up from the slimy depths of ocean,—when the passions of the Middle Ages burst anew through the thin skin of 19th-century-civilisation, and the death struggle of the Turk laughs to scorn the milk-sop philosophers who preach "Eternal Peace" on the strength of a spurious veneer of sentimental socialism and æsthetic Christianity,—when London roughs rub out with the nails of their shoe-soles the hieroglyphics on Cleopatra's Needle, and half-fledged students dictate to Vivian Grey the solution of the Asian Mystery from the pedestal of Nelson's Column in Trafalgar-square, while Britannia's ironclad fleet steams to and fro' the Golden Horn in fluttering sympathy with the fevered heats and chills of that prince of paradoxes, a cautious, timid son of "Rupert,"—what wonder is there that "Hope springs eternal in the human breast"? Why need any man despair—be he knave or fool, honest or wise, upon the crest of the wave or down in the depths—while Justice is blind, and Fortune fickle, and rogues fall out, and doctors disagree? Time has been when a hopeless hypochondriac has been bidden, for cure, to go and see himself play the clown. Robert Burns thought it fine physic for conceit "To see oursels as ithers see us!" But if a man would have a talisman against despondency, and potently bid the foul fiend "Begone!" let him sit down aud write afresh (with honest resolve to "nothing extenuate, nor set down aught in malice") the Lives of the Saints. There's more truth than fiction in the Ingoldsby Legend of Saint Gengulphus; and boisterous souls have warrant when they swear "by Jingo!" Stranger mortals have figured in the Calendar as patrons of red-letter days than the canonised Jackdaw of Rheims. It is good to turn from the historic memory of proud King Henry's pen-

* Although it is signed "J. D.," Thomson may have authored or collaborated on this prose version of the "Pilgrimage." The text identifies the personages numbered 34-65 in the preceding illustration (APPENDIX A), and all numbers match those in Thomson's verse.

ance at the shrine of A'Becket, and from Chaucer's story of the Canterbury Pilgrims, and from Stothard's pictorial rendering of that ancient scene, to Froude's "unvarnished tale" of great Saint Thomas's unsaintly life. Falstaff's men in buckram were a mighty force compared with the good men and true amongst the canonised; and their habiliments superb, in comparison with the garments of righteousness that decked many saintly in the days of their fleshly pilgrimage. Be it confessed that the roll of the Saints is in need of recruits; that the Canterbury Pilgrims are out of date; that Mr. Stothard's panorama has seen its best days;—and if "Saint Nicotinus" be proclaimed, who will play the part of *Advocatus Diaboli?* It may be that the age of chivalry is past, as Mr. Burke opined and a thousand penny-trumpets have echoed in later days; but the age of pilgrimages and of hero-worship is perennial and unending. "To the Shrine of Saint Nicotinus" wend we then our way, along with the goodly company whom that incorrigible limner of paradox who veils his modest identity behind the pseudonym of "Pipeshank" has portrayed on Cope's latest "Card."

Saint Nicotinus—whose worldly and unchristianised forename was Tobacco, and whose patronymic, despite the researches of the curious learned, is involved in much obscurity—was of heathen parentage, and is with much show of reason believed to have been an aborigine of the North American continent. Of his early years the record has been lost, except so far as it can be traced in vague and most imperfect outline amongst the relics that have survived the once powerful tribes or nations over which he would seem to have exercised an almost miraculous (or, possibly, magical) sway. There are indications, scattered here and there upon the face of that Older World which the ignorance or arrogance of the Modern Eastern World calls "New," that the influence of this remarkable being partook, at a very early and remote epoch in pre-historic time, of a religious character. From the mounds which strew the romantic valleys of the Ohio and the Mississippi—graves of warriors, tombs of cities, cemeteries in which the altars of the devout and the fortresses of the brave, the trinkets of the fair, the symbols of the pastoral, the Lares and Penates of the homely, have lain in silence through unnumbered centuries—there has come to light a mass of mute but eloquent testimony to the truth that Nicotinus was a Chief of Chiefs in the heyday of a civilisation as far anterior to our own as sunlight is to coal. From amidst the ashes of generations that perchance had left the prairies and forests of that Western World and betaken themselves to the Happy Hunting Grounds beyond the Silent Land ages before the Aryan Race was evolved, or the foundations of modern speech were laid amongst the nomad races of Asia, have been brought the carved stone pipes with which the devout initiated offered incense at the Shrine of Nicotinus in the depths of pagan darkness, ere saints began to be. The simple, natural, kindly faith he taught or fostered is impressed in artistic emblems upon these relics, bringing down to a superficial and a sceptic age the evidence of a grand and sympathetic unity of Man and Nature in an era whose antiquity mocks our intelligence to recall.

The mission in which he spent himself was a mission of Peace. In all the smoke of strife and battle since the world began, there has been no breath of Tobacco. When the warriors of the Far West gather from the wigwams around the Council Fire, the perfumed incense rising to the clouds betokens that the end of war and enmity is reached for a time, and the smoking-tube that passes from brave to brave is called "The Pipe of Peace." For, to all who have sought him and known him, Saint Nicotinus has been Soother and Consolator; his influence has ever been known as the spirit of quietness; and wheresoever two human creatures unite to observe the rites he taught, strife is forgotten and harmony of soul prevails. His shrine, in sacred miniature, has been erected on ten thousand hearthstones; and day and night his gentle intercession is invoked by millions upon millions of humankind; who, but for him and his potently benevolent spell, would beat out their spiritual strength against the ills of destiny, as doth the imprisoned lark his wings against the bars of his narrow cage at break of day. Unlike some other saints that one may wot of, Saint Nicotinus is the very genius of domestic comfort; and the fumes of his worship bring assurance of rest to multitudes of weary hearts.

But there is higher warrant for the nimbus round the beatified head of our Saint than either his legendary origin or his supernal goodness. Not saintly only, but martyred, was the good Tobacco, before his memory was elevated to the rank that befits the presiding spirit of a Shrine. And if there be truth in tradition,—verity in legend,—if the testimony of the countless faithful be worthy of regard,—never was martyrdom so perpetuated and renewed and constant as the martyrdom of St. Nicotinus. For it is related, and this upon excellent authority, that he was torn from his native land, carried far across the sea to foreign shores, and sold to traders of the East; by whom be was subjected to torture and disfigurement, and degraded to that lowest slavery which ministers to the pleasures of the white man. It is recorded that he was severed limb from limb, his tender form crushed out of recognition in ponderous machines, and his vitals dissected with knives, or ground to powder between millstones driven by steam. And, finally, as a thousand witnesses have testified, he was burnt, that the fragrance of his cremated substance might gratify the nostrils of his tormentors. Yet, in all his agony, and even in the very article of dissolution, the Saint breathed blessings on the men who thus abused his goodness, diffusing happiness and peace on humankind. Hence his elevation to the saintly order; hence the consecration of his shrine; and hence the pilgrimage that "Pipeshank" has depicted.

Behold the Pilgrims! First, there comes ambling, with his pipes and plaid, that classic Celt, the Stuart Blackie (1), foreshadowed in Chaucer's prologue as the miller—

> "a thikke gnarre,
> Ther n'as no dore, that he n'olde heve of barre,
> Or breke it at a renning with his hede."

And next mine Host The O'Gorman (2), mounted upon an appropriate steed, and jovial after Hibernian fashion—

> "a mery man,
> And after souper plaien he began,
> And spake of mirthe amonges other thinges."

The six in line behind and two that follow close betoken the subjugation of learning, art, and taste to "good Tobacco." Sir William Gull (3), the "doctour of phisike"—"a veray parfite practisour"—who loves the Prince's Mixture; Sam Morley (4), who keeps his Bristol Bird's-eye fixed on politics, smokes quick returns in Cheapside, cultivates Cavendish at the Devonshire Club, and takes the best roll at Exeter Hall,—

> "His resons spake he ful solempnely,
> Souning alway the encrese of his winning,"—
>
> "Forsothe he was a worthy man withalle,
> But soth to sayn, I n'ot how men him calle;"

the Lord Chief Justice Cockburn (5)—"ful riche of excellence, discrete he was, and of gret reverence"—

> "Nowher so besy a man as he ther n' as,
> And yet he semed besier than he was,"
>
> "and for his high renoun,
> Of fees and robes had he many on;"—

the artistic Dudley (6), Earl and picture-buyer, who gives his thousands for a vase, his ten thousands for a painting—

> "To liven in delit was ever his wone,
> For he was Epicures owen sone;"—

Thomas Carlyle (7), the modern knight, who—

> "fro the time that he firste began
> To riden out, he loved chevalrie,
> Trouthe and honour,"
>
> "He never yet no vilanie ne sayde
> In alle his lif, unto no manere wight;"—

and Ruskin (9), the ever youthful squire, so "wonderly deliver"—

> "Singing he was, or floyting alle the day,
> He was as freshe as in the moneth of May;"

Charles Reade (8), the reve, "a slendre colerike man," who yearns for the millennium when every human being will have two hands, and meets conspirators with Scriptural phrases, believing that he lives in "Naboth's Vineyard" close by Tattersall's at Knightsbridge; and Froude (15), a yeoman of renown, who would cleave paths of truth through the tangled forests of history, and bring down flaunting lies with shafts of daylight—

> "His arwes drouped not with fetheres lowe.
> And in his hond he bare a mighty bowe.
> A not-hed hadde he, with a broune visage.
> Of wood-craft coude he wel alle the usage."

And now come churches, principalities, and powers, commingled in a crowd of eager devotees. Our honoured Princess (14)—

"That of hire smiling was ful simple and coy;"—

"And sikerly she was of grete disport,
And ful plesant, and amiable of port"—

is accompanied by that most worthy ornament of the peerage, the Baroness Burdett-Coutts (13), of whom, like the Nun in Chaucer who prefigured her, as the best one could say would fail to do full justice to her merit, one may be content to let her good deeds tell. That proven lover of royal ladies, the Marquis of Lorne (19), attends, his locks all breezy with the air of Highlands, with a cutty to remind him of the pipes that re-echo in his Argyll glens. On the other side three priests—Cardinal Cullen (12), who lives to watch for the return of the Dark Ages; Bishop Fraser (11) of Manchester—translator of creeds into words of common-sense, and of faith into actions—of whom the poet says—

"A good man ther was of religioun,
That was a poure persone of a toun:
But riche he was of holy thought and werk.
He was also a lerned man, a clerk,
That Cristes gospel trewely wolde preche
His parishens devoutly wolde he teche;"—

and Stowell Brown (10), most protestant of dissenters, rough and honest plowman of men's hearts—

"A trewe swinker, and a good was he,
Living in pees, and parfite charitee."

"He wolde thresh, and thereto dike, and delve,
For Christes sake, for every poure wight,
Withouten hire, if it lay in his might."

The "shipman" comes next, in the guise of the First Lord of the Admiralty, Mr. W. H. Smith (16), who has been put in charge of fleets because he managed well a business on the Strand; and of whom it may be said, as of his prototype at the Tabard in Southwark—

"If that he faught, and hadde the higher hand,
By water he sent hem home to every land."

And then that Clerk of Oxenforde, Dr. Newman (17), "that unto logike hadde long ygo," and to whom the Protestant Church has said, as Festus to Paul—"Thou art beside thyself; much learning doth make thee mad." The Lauteate Tennyson (18) close by, whose verse owes more to good Tobacco than Tobacco owes to his verse; but who is a faithful pilgrim nevertheless. The ex-Queen of Spain (20) and Kenealy (21) "Arcades ambo:" and who should say but Chaucer looked forward to the 19th Century when he painted the Wif of Bathe—

"Of remedies of love she knew parchance,
For of that arte she coude the olde dance;"

and the "gentil Pardonere"—

> "whanne that he fond
> A poure persone dwelling up on lond,
> Upon a day he gat him more moneie
> Than that the persone gat in monethes tweie.
> And thus with fained flattering and japes,
> He made the persone, and the peple, his apes"?

That Mr. Whalley (23) should ride in the habit of a monk will not surprise his foes; and that the late King of Italy (22) should personate the "sompnour," whom Chaucer does not flatter, would not astound that merry monarch's friends; but that His Royal Highness Albert Edward (24) should represent the "worthy limitour" of a "Frere" will shock some proper souls. Be it confessed, whate'er his garb, he is a Prince among smokers. With Holman Hunt (25), the carpenter, who can find poetry in a rusty nail; and Edward Jenkins (26), the weaver of literary shoddy; and Tom Taylor (27), tapiser, who has vulgarised and emasculated *Punch;* and Gustave Doré (28), dyer of canvas, who drowns his genius in seas of paint; and Duncan M'Laren (29), haberdasher, who preserves the pure Scotch accent in the halls of St. Stephen's; and George Augustus Sala (30), the best of literary cooks,—this motley cavalcade is closed; and the rest of the pilgrims come a-foot, or on their bended knees—save those who creep, or are preserved in spirits.

That insects who believe their country is well served when she is made contemptible should drop by the way and be transformed, as Parnell (33), Biggar (32), and O'Connor Power (31)—the Colorado Beetles who devour the metaphorical potato; or bottled for exhibition—as Nolan (34) and Gray (35), over whom the compatriot O'Sullivan (36) keeps watch—is not wonderful. The congratulation arises on the happy circumstance that no orisons of theirs can reach the shrine of Nicotinus.

The Pilgrims thus far noted we have passed upon the way. The rest, dismounted, crowd the approaches of the saintly *sanctum.* Enter we therein, and gaze upon the emblematic presentment of the Saint himself, with smile ineffable, and full of blandest benison; with comfortable toes combined at ease; with pipes galore, and snuff-box near his heart; with fragrant circlet of the golden cloud around his kindly brows. Lo! ministering nymphs attend, and light with jets of sacred fire the offerings of the bending worshippers: Miss Braddon (49), whose thirty story-books have taught men how to value at a higher price the weed that soothes sensation-tortured nerves; and Ouida (50), from whose tales the wise find refuge in the herb divine, remembering late that they "should never let their (burning) passions rise." So Manning (48), missing the tiara, leaves awhile the red hat of the Cardinal, and is consoled with fumes of good Tobacco; and Shaftesbury (47) finds fellowship with Papists in the smoke that smacks of no theology; and Chamberlain (46) learns a fourth franchise—"a free Pipe"—in the Nicotian Republic; and Gladstone (45) seeks refuge from the toil of axe and pen and sounding Senate in the peaceful fumes of the Indian plant; John Bright (44), always a man of peace—save when Ottoman barbarism calls for a new Crusade—is happy in a smoker's reverie of "auld lang syne"; the noble Marquis (43), whose sheep (like the Irish drover's pig) "won't stand still to be counted," comes yawning and weary for refreshment and repose; and

Robert Lowe (42) would fain discover in the pleasant oblivion of a smoke some palliative of the agony in store for cultivated minds when Hodge shall have a vote. The warriors follow—that Ulysses Grant (41) who stamped-out state-rights in James River swamps, and watered liberty with the blood of thousands on Virginian fields; Bismarck (40), Prince and Chancellor, who sowed the wind, that Europe might reap whirlwinds; and Alexander (39), Emperor of All the Russias, who would atone with plenteous blood of Turk and Infidel for blood of Pole and Uniate slain, and for Siberian horrors. Sir Wilfrid Lawson (37) sits him down to wait for company more jocular; and Sullivan (38) squats patient, till a better theme for Dublin oratory may be found.

Turn we to gentle Ouida's side. First, Henry lrving (51), to whom the Bard of Avon is so much obliged; good Barnum (52), that "Prince of Humbugs," whom cabbage-leaves should amply serve for smoking; Edmund Yates (53), the man of the *World;* Lord Derby (54), who forgets that "fine words butter no parsnips"; the Earl of Beaconsfield (55), redolent of Turkish; Sir Stafford Northcote (56), soft-spoken spender of the millions; that luckless Sultan (57) who bids fair to see the end of Ottoman glory; Mr. Cross (58), a Home-ly Minister whose wits have lately gone too much abroad; Elcho (59), the valiant Volunteer of England's blood and treasure for dubious strife; the Duke of Sutherland (60), who thinks the Geneva Cross has no mercy for dying Muscovites; Lord Salisbury (61), who would gladly forget how men are apt to spell Constantinople; Santley (62), deep-voiced songster who believes that while "The Lord is a man of war," peace is conducive to harmony everywhere outside an oratorio; Lord Ronald Cower (63), who was born to correct our tastes, and means to do it; the great Labouchere (64), who would have all men believe in *Truth;* and the "Baron" Grant (65), who pines and fades away, for that none believe in him.

Come out of the crowd, good friends! Let us smoke in solitude, and leave these all-too-eager pilgrims to pursue their public penance and their ostentatious rites, since thus it pleaseth them. Would that the gentle and benignant spirit of Saint Nicotinus might descend upon them, one and all! But for us, who stand aside, and note how many strifes are typified in the figures that make up the composition of this pageant, it is well that the Saint can be honoured in privacy and apart. "Pipeshank" does well to remind us for how many fevered ills of life there is soothing in the leaf that has won its way across the seas and continents, till its shrine is in the hearts of millions of men, who have grown less way-worn since they sought virtue in the rites that Nicotinus taught. If the springs of life are eased,—if the wheels run less joltingly on the roads of labour,—if there is less creaking in the working of men's brains, and less straining of their heart-strings,—because of "our dear Tobacco," what matter, though it end in smoke?

J. D.

APPENDIX C:
THOMSON'S LETTER TO W. M. ROSSETTI FROM CENTRAL CITY, COLORADO, DATED 5 AUGUST 1872

TO W. M. ROSSETTI

Central City, Colorado, U.S.A.,
August 5, 1872.

Dear Sir,—Your letter of the 28th April reached me here about a fortnight since, having been forwarded by a friend. I cannot say anything about the Shelley notes now, as the only books I could find room for in my portmanteau were the Globe Shakespeare and Pickering's diamond Dante (with Gary's version squeezed in for the notes and general assistance). But I hope on my return to resume the attentive reading of your Shelley, and to send you any remarks upon it which may occur to me and seem worth sending. Your liberal reception of the few already sent would encourage me to proceed even were I not impelled by so strong an interest in the subject.

Mr. Bradlaugh promised to forward you a copy of the *National Reformer* containing a piece of verse called "In the Room," which I left behind me. I learn that it appeared in the issue for May 19th, but don't know whether you received a copy or not.

From the close of your letter I gather that you somewhat misapprehended what I said about my business trip. When I wrote to the effect that I was going in search of the heathen Chinee in the Rocky Mountains, I did not mean to convey that I was about to start for China. I believed that John Chinaman had already swarmed thus far east from California, and was alluding to the popular poem by Bret Harte, a writer who seems to me capable of doing really excellent work, and some of whose poems and sketches I am very fond of. As to the Chinese, they have not got here yet, with the exception of four or five who are male laundresses (the proper masculine for this feminine noun I am quite ignorant of), and whom I never see.

I have been out here since the 12th May, having left London on the 27th April, but have seen very little of the country as yet, business confining me to this place. I am hoping to have some trips around shortly. Every village out here is termed a city; this Central with Blackhawk and Nevada, the three virtually forming one straggling town, numbers between four and five thousand people. Of these the great majority are miners, perhaps a thousand being Cornishmen, who earn from $3 to $4 a day wages, and much more when they take leases or work by contract. The stores are well stocked, but nearly everything is very dear. The working miner can get most of the mere necessaries of life almost as cheap as at home; the comforts and little luxuries are so priced that I find living here twice or three times as expensive. A small glass of English beer costs twenty-five cents, or say a shilling currency. To get your boots blacked (I always clean my own) you pay twenty-five cents; but then they get a "Dolly Varden shine," and are wrought upon by a "Boot Artist." A "tonsorialist" very naturally charges seventy-five cents, or three shillings, for cutting your hair; etc., etc., etc. We have churches, chapels, schools, and a new large hotel, in which a very polite dancing party assembled the other evening. This week we are to have a concert, and also a lecture on the Darwinian Theory, admission one dollar. We have a theatre, in which we now and then have actors. The old rough days, with their perils and excitement, are quite over; the "City" is civilized enough to be dull and commonplace, while not yet civilized enough to be sociable and pleasant. There are no beggars, and petty larceny is almost unknown; storekeepers extort your money blandly and quietly, and the large larceny of selling mines at preposterous prices makes the people despise all larceny that is petty. You might as well carry a revolver between Euston Square and Somerset House as here. I brought one, under persuasion, and have never taken it out of the bag.

This Central City is the headquarters of gold-mining in Colorado Territory; but it has been very dull for some time past, the working of most of the large mines having been suspended, in some cases through want of capital, in others through litigation (mines are wonderful breeders of lawsuits), and in others because the ores are not rich enough to pay the enormous charges for haulage and reduction and smelting out here, though they would be of immense value in an old country. However, a railroad connecting with the whole east is now within ten miles of us, and is being pushed on rapidly, so things are likely to improve ere long.

The houses, chiefly of wood, and some of them pretty enough in themselves, though spoiled by their surroundings, are huddled and scattered along the bottom and slopes of a winding ravine, intermingled with prospect-holes, primitive log-huts, mill-sheds, of which many are idle, fragments of machinery that proved useless from the first, heaps of stones and poor ores, and all sorts of rubbish. No one has ever cleared up anything here; the streets and roads are usually many inches deep in dust, which the rare heavy rains and the more frequent turning on of some foul sluice make mud which is very abominable unto one who cleaneth his own boots. Men dig a shaft shallow or deep, and leave it gaping for any one to tumble into. Trees are cut down, and the stumps all left to make night-wandering safe and agreeable. The hills surrounding us have been flayed of their grass and scalped of their timber; and they are scarred and gashed and ulcerated all over from past mining operations; so ferociously does little man scratch at the breasts of his great calm mother when he thinks that jewels are there hidden. The streams running down the ravines, or, as they say here, the creeks running down the gulches, are thick with pollution from the washing of dirt and ores.

We are 8,300 feet above the level of the sea, and 3,000 feet above Denver, which lies about forty miles eastward. The highest peaks of the Rocky Mountains hereabout are 14,000 feet; we are among the foothills. To get out of the city in any direction one must climb for a considerable distance. These foothills are distributed remarkably amongst the snowy ranges of the mountains, curtain beyond curtain, fold within fold, twisting and heaving inextricably. Those immediately around the city are of flat, tame curves, as if crouching to their abject mercenary doom; but beyond there are keen crests and daring serrated contours, green with firs and cottonwood-aspens or nobly dark with pines; and one massy range ends in a promontory whose scarped, precipitous upper flank gleams grand and savage in its stony nakedness, like the gleaming of set white teeth in some swart Titanic barbarian. Some of the loftier hillsides are as smooth meadows; but their grass at this season can scarcely be distinguished through the multitudinous flames and broad blaze of countless species of wild flowers, nearly all of the most positive intense colours—scarlet, crimson, purple, azure, yellow, white. Few of them remind me of English flowers, and the people here (if I may judge by the few I have asked) don't seem to know their names. From these higher hills one gets magnificent views—vast billowy land-seas, with dense woods and deep ravines and exquisite emerald dells, whereon and whereover sleep and sweep immense shadows, and of all shades, even at noonday, from bright green to solid black; beyond, a crescent of the mountains, some with broad fields or deep furrows of snow, some sheathed wholly with this white splendour; eastwards towards the plains, what the keenest eye cannot distinguish from a distant sea-line, faint or dark-blue, level to the horizon, with pale streaks like the shadows of clouds and long shoals and the haze of evaporation. The sky is wonderfully pure—azure, or deep, burning blue; the clouds are large and white; however hot the sun, there are cool, fresh breezes on these hills. There are few birds, and they scarcely sing. Butterflies abound, some of them almost as brilliant as the flowers. Crickets keep up a continual song like the whistling of the wind through reeds; and one species take long jumps and short, rapid flights, making such a rattle with some bodily machinery that one can scarcely believe it comes from so small a creature.

The nights are always cool, and mosquitoes there are none. Snakes or any other vermin I have not heard of. One would have to go some distance now to find any wild animals such as bears and cougars.

I don't think that I have been out a single night, however cool and clear, with moon and stars, without seeing frequent lightnings play up from behind the surrounding hills. Almost every day we have a slight shower. On the day of my arrival we had a hailstorm with thunder as we drove up the cañon, the largest stones being quite as big as good-sized walnuts. Our horses were so nervous that we had to unhitch and hold them. A few days after they had snow, thunder, and lightning all together among the same hills. Occasional waterspouts sweep away bridges and destroy roads for miles. I have seen from here a terrible storm raging over the plains, dead-silent through remoteness; white lightnings momentarily surging up, veiling the stars, making the lower clouds ghostly, striking pale reflections from clouds at the zenith; and these broad sheets of white light were seamed and riven by intense darting lines of forked lightning, zigzag, vertical, transverse, oblique.

We have no dew here at night; one can lie out in a blanket between earth and sky with perfect safety and comfort.

Six miles from us is Idaho, the pleasantest place I have yet seen in the mountains. Going to it you ascend about a thousand feet in three miles to the Divide (and climbing on foot tests your wind in this thin, pure air), and then descend about 1,800 feet in three miles, winding down Virginia Cañon, whose hill-walls range from six to twelve hundred feet in height, and are still well-wooded with firs and pines. The roadway is good, wild-flowers abound, and a clear rill runs down with you all the way.

Idaho, which its boldly prophetic inhabitants call the Saratoga of the West, and which is just now full of visitors, lies comfortably at large on the level floor of a broad and long valley. The houses are of wood, shingle-roofed, most of them neat, many of them pretty. The hills around rise to the height of a thousand feet, and, as little mining has been attempted on them, they are delightfully green, and their timber has not been felled. Between them, southwards, you see the scalped heads of two mountains (until lately covered with snow) reckoned about 11,000 feet high, with a lower rounded height between; these are the Old Chief, the Squaw, and the Pappoose. Westwards also you glimpse snowy mountains. A stream, rapid and broad in summer after the rains and melting of the snows, runs from west to east through the midst of the village the whole length of the valley. Excellent trout have been caught in it. Two creeks join it from the south in this valley. There is a hot-water spring impregnated with soda and sulphur, which feeds private and swimming baths. There is a cold spring chemically allied to it, which people drink with faith or hope, and which to me tastes like seltzer-water bewitched. There are beautiful walks and rides in all directions. I reckon that this village of Idaho or Idaho Springs will indeed ere long be one of the fashionable holiday resorts of America. Gray's Peak, over 14,000 feet, is within twenty-four miles of it. A good horse-trail goes right up to the scalped crest of Old Chief, a distance of about eight miles.

I have chatted with the man who first struck Virginia Cañon and found the Idaho Creek (South Clear Creek) through the dense woods which filled the valley, and caught fine trout for himself and fellow-prospectors. This was in '59. Men used to make marvellous sums by mining and gold-washing then, and pay marvellous prices for the necessaries of life. For some years existence was pretty rough, though never perhaps half so wild as in California during the early days of its gold-fever.

I was told in Idaho (by a Justice of the Peace, too) of a couple of men who were on terms of shoot at sight, of whom one tried to avoid and the other sought a meeting. At length the latter attained his desire, and in the "difficulty" which ensued was shot by the other; who was tried, but got off clear, as the evidence was not considered perfect. The dead man had $64 odd in his pockets; so it was resolved to give him a decent burial. They stopped the funeral procession at a store, drank to his salvation out of his own money, and also took a bottle of whisky with them to the burial-place, that they might be not altogether without comfort when they had finally deposited him in the earth. Both deserved shooting, said the Justice of the Peace, philosophically; and himself was one of the funeral party.

In a tobacconist's here, among specimens of ore, is an object labelled "Burr from the pine-tree on which Pennsyltuck was hanged." Pennsyltuck was so called because Pennsylvania and Kentucky somehow shared the honour of raising him. He was a bad lot, so bad that the citizens at length determined to promptly relieve him and themselves of his noxious existence. Accordingly, without any tedious legal preliminaries, they took him forth and hanged him on a pine-tree, and there left him. As the night was very cold, someone suggested that it was doubtful whether Pennsyltuck met his death by strangulation or freezing. As the citizens, on cool reflection, thought it wise to discourage Lynch-law, they generally agreed to consider that he had been frozen to death.

As to the drinking, one anecdote (true or not) will suffice. An officer sent out to cater for some division of the army in the West returned with six waggon-loads of whisky and one of provisions. The commanding officer, having overhauled the stock, cried out: "What the hell shall we do with all these provisions?"

I did not intend to inflict all this nonsense upon you; but, having begun to write, it seemed queer to send a mere note five or six thousand miles and not say something about this country; so, having leisure, I let my pen run away with me. Fortunately, you are not in any way called upon to read what I was not called upon to write.

I may be here for two or three months yet, for all I know.—I am, dear Sir, yours truly, JAMES THOMSON.

INDEX OF TITLES AND FIRST LINES

PUBLISHED BY

CHARLES AND WONDER

CHARLESANDWONDER.COM